The impact of social policy

Radical Social Policy

GENERAL EDITOR:

Vic George

Professor of Social Policy and Administration and Social Work University of Kent

The impact of
social policy

Vic George and Paul Wilding

Routledge & Kegan Paul
London, Boston, Melbourne and Henley

First published in 1984
by Routledge & Kegan Paul plc
39 Store Street, London WC1E 7DD, England
9 Park Street, Boston, Mass. 02108, USA
464 St Kilda Road, Melbourne,
Victoria 3004, Australia
Broadway House, Newtown Road,
Henley-on-Thames, Oxon RG9 1EN, England
Set in Press Roman 10/11 pt by Columns of Reading
and printed in Great Britain by
T.J. Press (Padstow) Ltd, Padstow, Cornwall

Library of Congress Cataloging in Publication Data

George, Victor.
    The impact of social policy.
    (Radical social policy)
    Bibliography: p.
    Includes index.
    1. Great Britain–Social policy. I. Wilding, Paul.
II. Title. III. Series.
HN385.5.G46 1984   361.6'1'0941   83-21166

British Library CIP available

ISBN 0-7100-9670-4 (p)

Contents

Contents

Introduction

The 1960s and 1970s witnessed a growth of speculative thinking about the diverse effects of British social policy. It ranged from the hopes that the social services were contributing to the development of a more humane altruistic society to the fears that social services were restricting individual freedom and choice and were not providing value for money. There were also those who saw social policy playing a positive role in the creation of a technologically dynamic and prosperous society, only to be opposed by those who saw nothing but economic gloom for a society that spent a high proportion of its wealth on social services; and so on. These hopes and fears were not unique to British scholars but they found a more fertile climate here partly because Britain was one of the earliest 'welfare states', partly because it never achieved the rates of economic growth which made the financing of social welfare expenditure as painless as in some other countries in Europe and it was also one of the first countries to feel the chilling winds of economic recession.

We have felt for some time that there was a need for a book that would look at these claims and counter-claims in some organised form and with the use of as much empirical evidence as possible. The first step in our work was to differentiate between the aims of social policy and its achievements. What governments or individuals claim that social policy does and what it achieves in practice are not always one and the same thing. We felt that this distinction had often been blurred. Chapter 1 elaborates on this theme. Our second step was to categorise the effects of social policy in some coherent and logical way. Clearly there are several ways this could have been done but we chose to group them under social, economic and political. Chapters 2 and 3 look at the social effects and, no doubt, there will be legitimate objections about all the possible 'social effects' that we have not included in our discussion. There is no discussion, for example, on the effects of social policy on marriage, the family, child-rearing practices, and so on. Under economic effects — Chapters 4 and 5 — we have examined the claims that social policy contributes to economic growth as well as the counter-claims that it undermines economic development. Though there may still be objections on the issues not covered in these two chapters, we feel that they are not as substantial as those on social development. Economic issues have been better conceptualised and debated than social issues and we have benefited from this. The political arguments and counter-arguments are discussed in Chapters 6 and 7. Here the degree of conceptualisation is of variable quality but what is missing most is the empirical evidence.

The provision of empirical evidence was the third part in our plan. We were anxious to separate rhetoric from reality as far as possible. After three years of work, we feel we have only partially succeeded in this, partly because there is no empirical evidence on some issues and partly because the range of topics is so wide that we found ourselves at times fishing in unfamiliar waters. Even where there is evidence it is often contradictory or vague or both, with the result that no firm conclusions can be drawn. The fact that we attempted to cover the post-war period down to 1980 exacerbated these difficulties.

Like our previous two publications this has been a truly collaborative effort. We are grateful to several of our colleagues for comments on individual sections of the book, though we do not, of course, hold them responsible for any inadequacies. We owe a particular debt to the Nuffield Foundation for a generous grant which enabled us to meet regularly. Without this, the book may well have been impossible to complete. Our thanks, too, to Margaret Joyce, who typed several drafts of the book over the last two years.

Finally a book that attempts to cover the impact of social policy on a whole country over a period of three decades is bound to be wanting in several respects. We hope, however, that others will take up the challenge of both conceptualising and providing a solid base for the exploration of the effects of social policy on society. The need for such a debate is greater than ever now that social policy is under threat by government monetarist policies in this and other countries.

Vic George
University of Kent at Canterbury
Paul Wilding
University of Manchester

1

The aims and consequences of social policy

Our concern in this book is with the impact of social policy mainly on contemporary British society, though many of the issues we discuss and the conclusions we reach are of relevance to other advanced welfare capitalist societies. A great deal of time and space in the literature of social policy has been given to the impact of economic, political and social factors on the development of social policy.[1] We reverse the coin to look at the impact of social policy on the main sub-systems of society. We examine the impact of social policy on economic development, social development and political development.

It is important to state clearly that we are not concerned with the aims of social policy but with its consequences. Aims and consequences have often been confused in social policy literature and it is helpful to discuss them briefly here. The aims of social policy are what social policies intend or hope to achieve. Inevitably there is disagreement among different groups in society about the aims of social policy. Thus the view of the Conservative government on the Industrial Relations Act, 1971, was that its aim was to restore industrial peace and hence improve the economic position of all groups in society. The view of the trade unions was that the aim of the legislation was to curb their activities, reduce their power and hence lower the economic position of their members vis-à-vis that of the employers. It was, therefore, understandable that the trade unions opposed the legislation. Even where there is agreement, however, on the desirability of a specific piece of legislation, there may be disagreement about its aims among the groups supporting the particular piece of legislation. Industrialists, for example, may have supported the extension of primary education in

1

England in 1870 because they saw it as aiming at creating a literate labour force that would be more efficient and productive to the obvious benefit of private profit. Some politicians may have seen it as a means of educating the masses and strengthening their allegiance to the existing socio-economic order. Some working class groups may have seen the legislation as a means of educating and hence improving the economic and social status of their children.[2]

As far as governments are concerned, aims can be stated and unstated. The stated aims are those given by ministers responsible for a particular piece of legislation or by other official government spokesmen and documents. The aims which other members of Parliament attribute to a particular policy, whether they are members of the government party or the opposition, are not necessarily government aims. Stated aims are not, of course, always or necessarily the real or most important aims which governments have in putting forward a particular measure. There is a tendency for governments to glorify the aims of social policy and to make little or no reference to less popular aims. All the government White Papers on social policy during the last war were thus inclined. The White Papers on health, for example, proclaimed that the government 'want to ensure that in future every man and woman and child can rely on getting all the advice and treatment and care which they need in matters of personal health'.[3]

Unstated aims are basically of two kinds. There are those aims which are not stated publicly in the sense that they are confined to the smaller inner circle of government and the civil service, even though they may have been explicitly stated and agreed in the upper echelons of a ministry or around the Cabinet table. Such unstated aims eventually become stated − or at least apparent. There are also, however, those aims which were not stated explicitly but which, it can be claimed, were implied in the pronouncements of government ministers. Clearly, the identification of such aims is not only difficult but problematic, because it is subject to the interpretation of the individual investigator. Sometimes, the unstated aims may be trivial, at other times they may, in fact, be the most important aims. The aims may be furthered by their public statement or by their complete concealment and denial − and this affects whether or not they are publicly proclaimed.

Conclusions about what are the real aims of policy and about the likely consequences depend on value judgments and ideological stances and are related to ideas about the development and functions of social policy. Those Marxist writers who see the causes of social policy development primarily, though not exclusively, in terms of class conflict in society will see the real aims of social policy as containing conflicting strands − the improvement of the conditions of working-class groups as well as the maintenance of the existing socio-economic order. The resolution of conflict situations usually results in varying compromises in the area of social policy. Functionalists, who see the causes of social policy development as lying in the natural, inherent tendency of the social system to return from states of temporary disequilibrium to order and stability, will see social policy as aimed at benefiting the whole of society, at restoring the orderly and smooth functioning of the social system to the benefit of everyone. The idealists, who see social policy as the result of the increasing level of enlightenment, rationality and humanitarianism, will maintain that social policy aims at improving the conditions of either the disadvantaged groups or the whole of society depending on the particular piece of legislation. Any verdict on the real aims of social policy is essentially a matter of inter-pretation and value judgment.[4]

The consequences of social policy are those changes which social policies have actually achieved in relation to their aims or any other impact general or particular, expected or unexpected, which they may have had in society. Consequences can be anticipated or unanticipated: they sometimes coincide with aims and sometimes they do not. The relationship between aims and consequences can be shown diagramma-tically, as in Table 1.1. It can be seen that both stated and unstated

TABLE 1.1
Aims and consequences of social policy

Aims		Consequences
Stated	Anticipated	
	Unanticipated	By government or by other groups
Unstated	Anticipated	
	Unanticipated	By government or by other groups

aims can have anticipated as well as unanticipated consequences. The anticipated consequences obviously correspond to some of the stated aims, but a government may also have clear expectations of the antici-pated consequences of a policy which it deliberately leaves unstated. The unanticipated consequences of a policy may be related to the stated or unstated aims, or they may be totally unrelated. The conse-quences of a policy can be more far-reaching than the stated/unstated aims — or they may be negligble when aims are not achieved and there is little other impact.[5]

The government's view of the anticipated consequences of a policy may be endorsed or challenged by other groups and, similarly, conse-quences not anticipated by government may be in line with the expec-tations of other groups. Thus the government's stated aim, in the 1944 Education Act, was to ensure that every child was educated according to its age, aptitude and ability. One of the major unanticipated consequences of the Act, as far as the government was concerned, was that it led to the early segregation of children in different types of secondary schools possessing different status and bestowing different career prospects on their pupils — something that was in conflict with the basic aim of the Act. Critics of the Act, however, felt vindicated — for them this was an anticipated consequence of the legislation.[6]

Our definition of social policy embraces more than the traditional five main social services — health, housing, education, social security and personal social services — but narrower than the field of study of social administration — the study of welfare in society. No study of social policy can today ignore the operation of the tax system. It redistributes income, subsidises dependency, creates poverty and furthers certain supposedly desirable social ends. Equally, occupational welfare is an instrument of government social policy because it is substantially financed from public funds by virtue of certain decisions by government. Legislation which seeks to secure basic social rights to social minorities and to women is equally clearly a new and important instrument of social policy. At a time of rising unemployment, employment services and programmes take on a new significance as do regional policies. All these are included in our definition of social policy. We also acknowledge that economic policies, such as the way in which the economy is tuned, the rate of inflation which is permitted, the interest rates which are established, the incomes policies which are pursued — and not pursued — have important social policy implications. All have aims, stated and unstated, all have consequences for the distribution of goods and services, rights and opportunities in society. An examination of such economic policies, however, is beyond our competence and it is not, therefore, part of this book.

Our concern is with those consequences of social policy which transcend individual services. To do this, one has to look at the consequences of particular individual policies, but only as a means to a broader end. Thus our concern with such policy issues as, say, staff/ pupil ratios, positive discrimination policies, is to assess their contribution to one or more of the general consequences that we intend to examine. Any choice of general consequences is, to some extent, an arbitrary affair reflecting the investigator's views of what is possible and what is important.[7] In the chapters that follow, we will examine the extent to which social policy encourages or undermines economic growth, how far it succeeds in achieving minimum standards of living in society, the degree to which it increases or reduces inequalities and the ways in which it makes for political stability and instability. Though these consequences are examined separately, they are obviously inter-related. They affect one another positively and negatively, reinforcing and undermining one another in a variety of explicit and implicit ways. For example, the payment of cash benefits to various population groups has implications for the achievement of a minimum standard of living; the methods used to finance such benefits have distinct implications for the reduction of inequalities; the injection of such vast amounts of money into the economy has positive and negative consequences for economic growth; and, lastly, such payments have political implications though they have long been in dispute, with claims that they strengthen the political system and claims that they undermine it.

Any attempt to assess the impact of social policies faces at least three difficult problems: the problems of the adequacy of available data; the cause and effect issue; and the potential bias of the investigators. The problem of data adequacy takes several forms:[8] there are situations where data are simply not available; instances where what is available is not sufficient or reliable; comparisons over the years may not be possible, not only because data are non-existent, but also because they may be based on different definitions. These difficulties are obvious enough. What is perhaps less well appreciated, particularly in social policy, is that all types of statistical evidence, including official statistics which assume the mantle of objectivity and impartiality, represent a specific way of looking at issues and problems. Official statistics are as much a social product as statistics collected by other organisations: they quantify reality as seen and defined by a particular organisation operating within existing dominant ideologies. Crime, illness, poverty, wealth, etc., are defined in specific ways which reflect dominant ideologies and hence affect the outcome of the survey process. Poverty defined in relative terms has different implications from poverty defined in subsistence terms as regards the size of the problem, the policies needed to deal with the problem and the possibility of such policies being implemented. Similarly, crime defined in such institutional terms as the pollution of the environment by private industry, resulting in illness, disability and death among the population, has different policy implications from crime defined in terms of individual misconduct. Since our study is based on existing data, we inevitably reflect the assumptions of those who collected the data, however much we try to be aware of that fact in our discussions.

The cause and effect issue consists of three related aspects. First, it is necessary to disentangle the effects of social policies from the effects of independent economic, social and other changes in society, as well as from the effects of other government policies.[9] For example, a larger proportion of young people staying at school beyond minimum leaving age and taking public examinations may be a consequence of a particular education policy. It may, equally, be the result of fashion, the decline in job opportunities for younger leavers, the increase in job opportunities for older, better qualified leavers, or of an economic recession judged by young people and their parents to be temporary and best endured by staying in school. Clearly, the broader the consequences to be assessed, the greater the difficulty of establishing a cause and effect relationship. Thus it is less problematic to examine the relationship between the size of class and reading ability than it is to assess the impact of educational priority areas on the reduction of social class inequalities in education. There will be many instances in the chapters that follow which will highlight this particular problem. Second, the establishment of statistically significant correlations does not necessarily imply causal links between the variables involved. They may be both the effects of another factor. Third, even when a causal link is statistically inferred between two factors, it is not always clear which is the cause and which is the effect. The fact that affluent societies spend a greater proportion of their national wealth on education than poorer societies, for example, may be an indication that education promotes economic growth or it may simply reflect the fact that they can afford to spend their resources on such non-essential services as education. Indeed, in many of the complex issues we discuss it is doubtful whether causal proof can be really established. As Popper insisted,

> no conclusive disproof of a theory can ever be produced; for it is always possible to say that the experimental results are not reliable or that the discrepancies which are asserted to exist between the experimental results and the theory are only apparent and that they will disappear with the advance of our understanding.[10]

The issue of personal bias or value freedom has had its fair share of space in the social science literature and needs no extensive review here.[11] The values and beliefs of the social scientist affect the outcome of his or her studies in at least two ways. First, values and beliefs are important in defining the questions that a research project investigates. However ingenious, complicated and competent statistical calculations may be, they cannot escape the fact that the data they try to evaluate are based on certain value assumptions. Second, in broad and complex policy issues, research evidence rarely points unambiguously in one direction. The author's values play a special role in the ways he or she draws conclusions and makes recommendations from such research evidence.

There are three possible ways in which we could have approached the mass of evidence that is reviewed in this book. We could, first, have adopted a specific theoretical framework within which to examine the data. Such an approach encourages and displays two of the essential ingredients of a good study – clarity and commitment. The main disadvantage – and it is a crucial one – is that such an approach in a field as complicated and uncertain as the study of the impact of social policy can lead both to the exclusion of important data from consideration and to excessive emphasis on some data rather than other. It could make good reading but could easily lack the solid under-girding which in our view a study such as this must at least attempt to provide. Second, we could have presented data from various perspectives and allowed the data 'to speak for themselves'. The difficulty is that data rarely do speak for themselves. They often need to be evaluated and interpreted for their 'true' meaning to emerge. Unless the attempt at evaluation and interpretation is made by the author, the reader is not pressed or challenged to take account of all the data and arguments before coming to his own conclusions. He can be allowed to be as selective as his own prejudices and preconceptions allow. We have adopted the third approach: we have tried, as far as possible, to collect and present data and arguments from different sources which stem from different value assumptions but we have interpreted this data from our own explicit set of value assumptions – the democratic socialist perspective that we put forward in our previous book.[12] We have tried, however, to be cautious in our conclusions; and whenever data could have been interpreted in different ways, we have indicated the alternatives and our own preferences. Like Rein, we are 'very aware of the dilemmas that arise when one is morally committed to a point of view, but also of the difficulties caused by a lack of commitment to any value perspective'.[13] We have tried to avoid both a totally 'open-minded' textbook that simply summarises the literature and a totally committed book which is highly selective of the evidence and its interpretation.

The period that we have covered begins in the late 1940s and ends in the late 1970s – a period of thirty years. To assess the consequences of social policy for the economic, social and political development of the country over a thirty-year period is obviously no easy task. The result is bound to be inadequate and inaccurate in several ways. Similarly, the analytical framework we have adopted for this assessment will be found wanting in several respects. Nevertheless, it is important to attempt it, particularly in the light of the view that social policy is today at some kind of crossroads. We trust that, if nothing else, we have asked questions that are important in social policy and which others will be stimulated to explore further.

2

Achievement of minimum standards

The achievement of socially acceptable minimum standards in the various aspects of life affected by social service provision has been the most generally agreed aim of social policy since the last World War. Other aims have also been mentioned but without the same degree of emphasis or agreement that is found in the case of minimum standards. This basic aim has united people of very different political persuasions and it has, in Peter Self's words, 'provided a strong ideological platform for the development of social services and the creation of the welfare state'.[1]

Writers of such different political persuasions as Crosland, Beveridge and Hayek are agreed on the primacy of minimum standards in social policy. Crosland was most emphatic that social policy is not so much about equality but about the creation of a social minimum of civilised life. 'Social equality', he wrote, in 1956, 'cannot be held to be the ultimate purpose of the social services. This must surely be the relief of social distress and hardship, and the correction of social need.'[2] Fourteen years later he reiterated the same point when he set out his first objective for Labour policy 'an exceptionally high priority when considering the claims on our resources for the relief of poverty, distress and social squalor — Labour's traditional "social welfare objective" '.[3]

A similar theme runs clearly and consistently through Beveridge's writings. The underlying aim of his plan for social security, he wrote, was 'to establish a national minimum above which prosperity can grow, with want abolished'.[4] He wrote of the five evils that governments should eradicate from post-war British Society — Want, Disease,

Ignorance, Squalor and Idleness, i.e. mass unemployment — and perceptively commented that the abolition of the first was the easiest 'because we're all agreed in principle and we're very nearly agreed on the methods'.[5] Just how central the idea of a national minimum income was for Beveridge is neatly illustrated by his suggestion to delegates from the Co-operative Congress that if a family man was so badly paid that he got less from wages than from benefits, then it was his moral duty, given his responsibilities to his family, to apply for benefit.[6]

If we look at the other end of the political spectrum the concern with minimum standards is a continuing thread in Hayek's work. In 1944, he distinguished between two kinds of security: 'security against severe physical privation, the certainty of a given minimum of sustenance for all', which is limited and legitimate, and 'the security of a given standard of life, or of the relative position which one person or group enjoys compared with others', which Hayek regards as impossible to guarantee in a free society. The first kind of security can be provided for all 'outside of and supplementary to the market system', while the second kind 'can be provided only for some and only by controlling or abolishing the market'.[7] As far as Hayek is concerned, 'There is no reason why in a society that has reached the general level of wealth which ours has attained [in 1944 note], the first kind of security should not be guaranteed to all without endangering general freedom.'[8] Sixteen years later, Hayek argued in the same vein that it had become a necessary and 'recognised duty of the public to provide for the extreme needs of old age, unemployment, sickness, etc., irrespective of whether the individuals could and ought to have made provision themselves'.[9] While such state responsibilities were acceptable to Hayek, he was keen to emphasise again the sharp line which separates acceptable from unacceptable social policy.

> It is essential [he emphasised] that we become clearly aware of the line that separates a state of affairs in which the community accepts the duty of preventing destitution and of providing a minimum level of welfare from that in which it assumes the power to determine the 'just' position of everybody and allocate to each what it thinks he deserves.[10]

In a free society, Hayek argued, it is possible to provide a minimum level of welfare for all but it is not possible in such a society to share out 'income according to some preconceived notion of justice'.[11]

This general consensus on the desirability of minimum standards achieved through social policy may have its roots in diverse ideologies but fundamentally it stems from the basic fact that minimum standards pose no real threat to the values or the practices of the capitalist system.

Indeed, many see the achievement of minimum standards as reinforcing the capitalist system because they provide a floor below which no-one should live and above which people should compete with one another as hard as they can. Moreover, by abolishing or reducing the worst excesses of capitalism, they undermine those political forces that pose a threat to the system. Minimum standards, in brief, act as economic incentives and as political stabilisers.

Agreement in principle, however, does not mean agreement on the actual service provision of minimum standards. Two main and related differences emerge between the anti-collectivists and their supporters on one hand, and the socialists and others on the other. The first see the provision of minimum standards as the beginning and end of social policy; they also consider the appropriate level of such standards to be at subsistence level. The second group see minimum standards as the creation of a floor on which further welfare systems with more egalitarian aims and optimum standards can be established; as no more than the foundations of a building yet to be gradually designed and erected. This double difference has emerged time and again over the years not only between political scientists but between central political figures. Thus Crosland not only considered the Beveridge Report as 'the most complete and explicit statement of the philosophy of the national minimum,'[12] but also saw it as the beginning of more government intervention in economic and social affairs for the creation of a more egalitarian society. Churchill, on the other hand, found the recommendations of the Beveridge Report extravagant and warned his war-time Cabinet colleagues against the 'false hopes and visions of Utopia and Eldorado' engendered by the report.[13] In principle he was, of course, strongly in favour of the report.

In spite of these differences in the operationalisation of minimum standards, the whole edifice of the social services erected during and immediately after the last World War was based on the ideal of a national minimum. This had two strands to it: universality and minimum standards. Social services should be made available to everyone and they should be of uniform standard at least at the minimum. The series of White Papers which ushered in the new social services reflected this dual ideal of service provision. Thus education services would be free and compulsory for all children aged 5-14 years and they would strive to educate every child according to its age, aptitude and ability.[14] Health services, too, would be universal and free of any charge for every man and woman and child.[15] Social security benefits, too, would be provided in such a way that no one would have to live on an income that was lower than the government's stipulated minimum standard.[16] Even in housing, 'The Government's first objective is to afford a separate dwelling for every family which desires to have one.'[17] Finally, and perhaps most important of all, the government committed itself to maintaining full employment when the war ended.[18]

In brief, the political consensus on minimum standards was reflected in the White Papers and was enacted in the legislation of that period. Before examining the extent to which the relevant aims of that legislation have been achieved, it is necessary to clarify the notion of minimum standards. The idea has three elements — inputs, throughputs and outputs. Inputs refers to the resources expended on the provision of a service — expenditure, personnel, buildings, materials, etc., in absolute or relative terms. In the education service, for example, it refers to local authority expenditure per pupil, the number of such specialised equipment as computers for secondary schools, and so on. Throughputs refers to the degree of activity, the amount of work carried out in a service or a section or institution of a service. In the health service it refers to the number of patients seen by doctors and surgeons, the number of operations performed, the number of teeth treated, filled or extracted, the number of children vaccinated, and so on. Outputs refers to the outcomes of a service in broad or in specific terms. The outputs of the education service can be measured by such broad criteria as the creation of an educated society or the eradication of illiteracy; or it can be measured by such specific criteria as the number of children passing examinations at different levels, the number of students graduating in different subjects, and so on. Henderson expresses this distinction between broad and specific aims well by referring to the broad aims as goals and to the specific as objectives. He explains the distinction between them as follows:

> Goals are considered to be broad statements with regard to general aspirations upon which a large degree of consensus can often be achieved such as better health or more equitable justice. However, they are not sufficiently specific to be operationally relevant, which is partly why consensus on them is relatively easy to achieve. Objectives, on the other hand, are statements of intent that are sufficiently precise to provide decision-makers with guidelines for policy action, such as the reduction of infant mortality rates . . . or a more equitable availability of good quality legal aid to persons accused of crimes.[19]

In this chapter we are concerned with minimum standards of inputs and outputs only. The notion of throughputs does not appear useful and will be omitted from the discussion. The relationship between inputs and outputs is very tenuous indeed. Obviously if there are no inputs at all, outputs will suffer, but, beyond this, the relationship between the two is difficult to establish partly because of methodological research problems and partly because outputs can be affected by factors other than service inputs. Indeed, one commentator in the area of health has gone as far as to claim that increased provision of professional medical services has had detrimental effects on the health of the general public, 'The medical profession has become a major threat to health', claims Illich, and then adds, 'only a political programme aimed at the limitation of professional medicine enables people to recover their powers for health care.'[20]

In a more restrained way, the Royal Commission on the National Health Service points out that 'in 1977 Scotland, with 50% more hospital doctors and about 40% more nurses and midwives per 10,000 population than England, nonetheless had a comparatively lower life expectancy and a higher infant mortality rate.'[21] It also points out that comparisons between advanced industrial countries do not show any consistent relationship between high levels of inputs and such specific outputs as life expectancy or infant mortality rates. As if to lend support to Illich's claims, it points to the puzzling comparative statistic which shows that 'a high ratio of doctors to patients is associated with a relatively high perinatal mortality rate.'[22] Obviously what the Report had in mind was that economic, social, geographical and other factors can be so important as to override the impact of the health services. Similar comments apply to education and the personal social services, as we shall see later in this chapter.

It is commonplace to state that minimum standards are relative. Referring to socially acceptable minimum income standards, for example, Nicholson reluctantly concluded: 'That the concept of a minimum standard involves a certain degree of relativism cannot . . . be denied.'[23] In other words, deciding the amount of income necessary for social security purposes is relative to the standards of income of a particular society at a particular time. Deciding which level is appropriate may be difficult but money is at least an easy yardstick to use. It becomes even more difficult to make judgments about the minimum standards of inputs which should be laid down for schools, hospitals, old people's homes, and so on. If minimum standards are relative they must change as standards in society change. Social security benefits can be linked to increases in earnings or prices. Raising standards in other fields is much more difficult, partly because there are no such yardsticks and partly because, in the case of buildings, changes take physically longer to make, by which time standards may change again.

Given the problems of setting minimum standards, what are the factors which affect the minima which are established in the different services? It is an unexplored area of social policy and the few commentators who showed an interest in this area have tended to attribute it all to some form or other of incrementalism. Discussing the government circular to local authorities in 1972, which for the first time provided guidelines on the standards of personal social services, Webb and Falk capture the flavour of the *ad hoc* incrementalism that has been so characteristic of social policy standard setting. They argue that these guidelines were developed

> from existing trends and examples of 'good practice'; from research studies which have examined the extent of need as well as the present social services; from admittedly arbitrary guesswork in areas of service where our knowledge is poor; and from judgments of what is administratively, economically and politically feasible to expect local authorities to achieve in the future.

At the end of rhe day, the authors conclude, the new guidelines 'primarily reflect a Departmental assumption about the future availability of resources, rather than an estimate of presently unmet need or future levels and types of need'.[24] Lansley makes a very similar point in relation to housing policy. 'In general', he writes, 'minimum standards have been determined by a mixture of social convention and economic well being, representing a balance between what is socially desirable and what is economically feasible.'[25]

While not disputing the seemingly incremental and haphazard nature of the process of setting minimum standards, it is nevertheless possible to isolate certain factors which influence the pace and direction of government's incremental shuffling and definitions of what is socially desirable and economically feasible. These factors can be divided into two groups: first, the more immediate and observable factors that influence government decisions, and second, the broader economic and political factors that provide the framework within which the more immediate factors operate. Among the first group we include pressure groups, research, scandals, innovation and individuals.

The literature on pressure groups in general as well as in social policy is vast and no attempt will be made to review or evaluate it.[26] Clearly pressure-group activity can give new salience to an issue, so that the way it is dealt with and the current standards of provision are re-examined. Equally evident is the fact that the power and the influence of pressure groups — and hence their effectiveness — vary. Professional groups are more likely to be more convincing than groups of ignorant, if opiniated, laity. Rich groups are more able to publicise effectively their causes than poor groups. Stigmatised groups, or groups concerned with the stigmatised, are less likely to be influential than the more acceptable and prestigious groups. All these are obvious acceptable comments to all those who see power in society as unequally distributed and who view governments not as impartial arbiters of conflicting interests but as agents whose actions and inactions are influenced by those who pressurise it. As for social science research, much of it is unsuitable for policy-making because of its theoretical abstraction, its very localised small-scale nature, its ambivalent findings, etc.[27] Even where research findings are based on satisfactory research projects, there is a tendency for many such findings to fall by the wayside or at best on stony ground; research can, at times, be an influence on standards. It is research that arrives on the scene at the right time and which is either in line with the government's thinking or which is incremental and 'realistic' in its recommendations that can be effective. The more radical the research proposals are, the less likely it is that they will have any impact on social service standards. Thus Townsend's and Wederburn's study of the elderly in the early 1960s which showed, among other things, that the home help service fell short of meeting reasonable requirements[28] was quoted approvingly by the government's White Paper in 1966 in its arguments for extending the home help service.[29] On the other hand, Townsend's recent study on poverty with its radical definition of poverty, and hence radical policy implications, published at a time of economic recession, will be read and discussed by generations of teachers and students in social policy but it is most unlikely to have any impact on government policy in the foreseeable future.[30]

Innovations in the sense of new possibilities or approaches to problems can be another influence on the nature and level of standards in the social services. As medical science finds new ways of dealing with disease, standards in the National Health Service are modified accordingly. New minima become established. As new teaching methods and techniques become accepted, standards in schools can be improved. New ideas or experimental projects in the personal social services that prove successful in one local authority may be copied by other authorities, thus changing and raising the standard of service for specific client groups. Clearly, there is no certainty that innovations will lead to improvements in standards — only a possibility.

These and other immediate factors — scandals, individuals, etc. — can have an influence on minimum standards but this depends on the prevailing economic and political climate in the country. This is clearly illustrated by government plans for the personal social services in the last twenty years. In the 1960s, government pressed local authorities to develop substantially their personal social services and warned any laggard local authority that the minister 'proposes to arrange for his officers to discuss the position with the authority concerned with a view to action to remedy any deficiency'.[31] By the late 1970s, however, social welfare expenditure became the scapegoat for the sluggish performance of the British economy and the government's attitude to improving standards in the same areas sharply changed. 'When resources are limited', announced the DHSS, 'it is clear that growth in any particular service can only be afforded if counterbalancing economies are made elsewhere.'[32] By the 1980s, local authorities which seek to maintain, let alone improve, the standard of their social services are castigated as 'spendthrift' and punished financially by central government. The influence of immediate factors in social policy changed dramatically during such a short period of time.

It is often said, and with a great deal of justification, that in government concerns and interests social policy has always come second to economic policy. At times of economic prosperity, social policy developed as, in Klein's words, 'the residual beneficiary of the growth state'.[33] On the other hand, at times of economic difficulty and recession, social services grow very slowly, remain static, or even contract. This explanation is correct as far as it goes but it does not go far enough. It is also wrong when it argues that at times of economic difficulties, the country cannot afford to maintain, let alone improve, standards in social services. In all societies, except those surviving at the very margins of existence, the level of resources devoted to social welfare is a matter of choice. The economic situation dictates nothing. What is crucial is how the economic situation is interpreted and the priority given to particular policies. In 1979-80, on grounds of the 'needs of the economy', the Conservative government made significant cuts in present and planned expenditure on social welfare. Cuts were necessary, it was insisted, for economic reasons. At the same time as cuts were being made on expenditure in state schools, the government launched a scheme to provide support for children at private schools. One type of expenditure was clearly regarded as more legitimate than another. Equally, many of the cuts in the standards of services could have been avoided had the Chancellor of the Exchequer not felt an overpowering obligation to remit £3,500 million of taxation — largely to the better-off members of society — in his budget of June 1979. The justification for the cuts in standards was argued to be economic. It was accepted as a legitimate priority by most commentators, whether or not they understood the finer points of monetarist philosophy, because they accepted the underlying premise — standards of social welfare are less important than the presumed needs of the economy. It was not so much the abstract needs of the economy that had to be protected but the profits of private capital as well as the high salaries both in the private and public sector and the dominant ideology of inequality and economic incentives. The subordination of improvements in social service standards to the needs of the economy is nothing else but an attempt to maintain a particular kind of economic system at a particular moment in time. In such a system, those public and social services which are thought to serve its stability and development are maintained and expanded; those services which have no obvious and significant functions are cut back. Such an economic system is organised for the maximising of private profit, rather than for promoting individual and social well-being. These are the wider economic and political forces that provide the framework within which the narrow and specific factors for the improvement of minimum standards in the social services operate.

Standards set by the central government have been of two different types during the period covered by this study. First, there have been statutory minimum levels of provision — the physical conditions of houses, hospitals, old people's homes, etc. — which have to be observed by government departments or by local authorities. Failure to observe such standards can result in legal action against the defaulting authority. Second, there have been government guidelines of various kinds which government departments or local authorities ought to take into account when planning their services. Such guidelines have normally been targets which should be reached by a certain year in the future. Failure to achieve such targets cannot result in legal intervention but it can, depending on the government's priorities, mean government pressure on local authorities. The discussion that follows provides numerous instances of these two types of government standards. It also shows that the difference between minimum standards and guidelines is more important in theory than in practice. Governments have persistently failed to enforce minimum standards, even in services provided directly by government departments, let alone by local authorities or other bodies.

Minimum standards in income

Expenditure on social security increased from 5.5 per cent of GNP in 1951 to 10.4 per cent in 1980. To what extent has this fairly costly and very elaborate system managed to guarantee a minimum income to all in the country? To what extent has it succeeded in eradicating income poverty as such in this country? Though we are not concerned with the issue of poverty as such in this section, it is, nevertheless, necessary to discuss its different meanings briefly in order to locate the government's minimum standard, i.e. the level of supplementary benefit, in some sort of context.

Six different definitions of the income poverty line appear in the literature. First, the subjective definition which is based on the opinions expressed by a representative sample of the general public. The comparative study of poverty by the EEC in 1976 found that British respondents felt that 'the absolute minimum income for a family of two adults and two children to make ends meet' was about 75 per cent higher than the amount they would have received in supplementary benefit, inclusive of rent.[34] Interestingly enough, the public had in mind an austere poverty line. This is indirectly borne out by Townsend's study where 62 per cent of the respondents felt there was real poverty in the country despite social security benefits and where also a large proportion (but difficult to estimate precisely) saw poverty in subsistence terms.[35] Thus, public opinion studies tend to see poverty in subsistence terms but, even so, in more generous terms than what is possible under the government's minimum standard.

Second, various commentators have used as their poverty line a certain point on the income distribution scale – usually the lowest decile. The usefulness of this approach is that it sees the poor in relation to other income groups and it also makes it fairly easy to identify the categories of people who are poor. The main weakness of the approach is that it is not useful for policy purposes for as long as income is unequally distributed, there will be poverty.

Third, the subsistence definition of poverty associated with the work of Rowntree which influenced the standard recommended by the Beveridge Report.[36] In his first study of poverty in York, Rowntree considered that a person was in poverty if his income was insufficient to buy those necessities of life without which his physical health would suffer. The poverty lines for his studies of 1936 and 1950 were not only more generous than for his first, but they were also higher than the level of benefit introduced by the National Assistance Act of 1948. It is now generally agreed that a subsistence definition of poverty is both inappropriate and impossible to maintain over long periods of time when the living conditions of a country change so much.

The fourth definition of the poverty line is the level of supplementary benefit – the official poverty line. As already mentioned, when it was first introduced on a national scale in 1948, this level of poverty was below Rowntree's level of 1936. This is vitally important because no post-war government has made clear what levels of income are necessary for subsistence. Governments have merely increased what were, from the start, inadequate benefit rates. Berthoud et al. rightly conclude that: 'The most serious weakness of the 1945-48 legislation was the inadequacy of the benefit rates.'[37] Some improvements in the benefit rates have, however, taken place during the period covered by this study but this does not change the basic fact that they are improvements on what were inadequate rates to begin with. As the table below shows, the level of benefit during the period 1948-78 increased faster than the retail prices index as well as the rise in the net average earnings of male manual workers in full-time employment. In relation to gross earnings, however, the level of benefit has retained a more or less constant relationship. In brief, the poor of today are better off than the poor of 1948, both in absolute terms and in relation to the living standards of the rest of the community. It is also important to point out that there is no one national level of supplementary benefit: the long-term rates are today 27 per cent higher than the short-term rates; moreover, many claimants receive additional payments to their basic rates; and so on. It was this state of affairs that led Donnison (ex-chairman of the Supplementary Benefits Commission) to declare that the idea of a 'national minimum is a myth'.[38] Similarly, Berthoud and his associates refer to the creation of a hierarchy of social security beneficiaries over the years with the elderly and the widows receiving the most generous treatment and the homeless and unmarried mothers lying at the bottom'.[39]

Fifth, most commentators today support a relative definition of poverty. People are in poverty if their incomes are insufficient to buy not only the basic necessities covered by the subsistence definition, but also a list of other items which are culturally necessary in their particular society. But it is not only the length of the list of items that distinguishes the subsistence from the relative definition of poverty — the quality and quantity of these items are also more generous under the relative definition. This approach acknowledges that the poor are an integral part of society and their living conditions must therefore be constantly adapted with the changing standards of the rest of society. It is clearly a matter of value judgment how much higher the relative poverty line should be in relation to the subsistence line.

Sixth, there is the recent deprivation or 'style of living' standard of poverty advanced by Townsend. In each country there are certain 'types of consumption and customs which are expressive of social form'.[40] He used sixty such indicators of 'styles of living' ranging from the type of food, holidays, housing conditions, education, family and friendship networks, etc. in order to paint a picture of the general style of living that was considered socially necessary in the country. He then correlated these to incomes or rather to the total financial resources, and found that, on the whole, the higher one's income, the greater the likelihood of participating or enjoying these styles of living; and, vice versa, the lower one's income, the less the likelihood. His important observation, however, was that below a certain level of income, participation in these styles of living tended to fall off sharply. He called this cut-off point the deprivation threshold, below which people are deprived. It was 38 per cent higher than the basic level of supplementary benefit. Townsend's approach has been criticised on two main counts: first, many of his indicators refer to ways in which people spend their money rather than to whether they have adequate amounts of money. Thus, whether a person has a cooked breakfast or whether he eats out in restaurants, for example, are no indications of deprivation but rather indications of how a person wishes to live. Townsend acknowledges this partially, since he does not claim that any one of his sixty-two indicators is, by itself, sufficient as a measure of deprivation, and by calling for more research to identify those national styles of living that are more pertinent to deprivation. The second criticism has been that such an approach is counter-productive in social policy terms. MacGregor, for example, concludes her discussion on Townsend's work: 'Townsend's insistence on seeing poverty as relative deprivation had the effect of draining the term of its concrete, objective content and inadvertently contributed to the view that poverty no longer exists in our society.'[41] In other words, this approach to poverty has been a disservice to the poor themselves. It is impossible to prove or disprove such a charge but what can be repeated is that whatever the conceptual and theoretical merits of this approach, it is most unlikely to have any effect on social policy in the immediate future. It sees poverty not only as part of inequality and as multi-dimensional, but also as a set of mutually reinforcing forms of deprivation based on low incomes. 'In principle', he writes, 'there could be extreme divergencies in the experience of different kinds of deprivation. In practice, there is a systematic relationship between deprivation and levels of income.'[42] Clearly, this is a view of poverty which necessitates substantially egalitarian government policies for its reduction, let alone abolition.

A similar approach to Townsend's was adopted in a recent study by London Weekend Television. Using a national random sample, the study attempted to establish which everyday items were considered essential and which should be afforded by everyone. Twenty-two such items were considered as essentials, out of a list of thirty-three, by more than fifty per cent of the sample. Applying this finding to the general population in the country, the survey reached the following conclusions: 'Seven and a half million people lack three or more items. Five and a half million cannot afford five or more necessities. Three quarters of a million people cannot afford the majority of the items.' Using a subjective definition of poverty and applying the findings to the whole country, the survey found that: 'More than five million said they consider themselves to be poor all the time; a further 11.8 million answered that they are sometimes poor.'[43]

Our concern in this section is primarily with poverty as officially defined, even though we recognise the inadequacies of such a definition. The living standards and the life chances of those whose incomes are above the supplementary benefit by small amounts are no different from those whose incomes are equivalent to or just below the supplementary benefit level. Leaving these considerations aside, however, how adequate is the supplementary benefit level as a measure of minimum standards in income? The Supplementary Benefits Commission frequently expressed the view that benefit levels were too low. In 1978, the Commission outlined the kind of lifestyle which it felt should be available to claimants to enable them to participate in the life of the community and reviewed the level of benefits in the light of whether or not they made this measure of participation possible. 'For most people', it concluded, 'the current rates of benefit do not achieve that.'[44] The Commission's view is not simply a matter of opinion. There are certain yardsticks by which the standard of living of those dependent on supplementary benefit can be assessed — for example, the guidelines that the Commission uses when deciding to make discretionary payments for the purchase of clothing. Those guidelines specify the kind of stocks of clothing which the Commission regards as a necessary minimum and it is a basic minimum. Evidence shows that rather less than half of sick and disabled claimants and rather more than half of unemployed claimants had stocks of clothing below this rigorous minimum level.[45] The scales were, in other words, generally inadequate, but particularly so for the unemployed who have to rely on the short-term rates, irrespective of how long they have been employed.

Moreover, there is evidence from nutritionists and others that the amount of supplementary benefits for children is inadequate. Walker and Church found that the cost of an adequate nutritional diet for children alone was higher than their total supplementary benefit rates. When the cost of clothing and other necessities was taken into account, the benefit rates were grossly inadequate.[46] Similarly, Piachaud, using a conventional list of necessities for children and costing them fairly modestly, arrived at a very similar conclusion — the supplementary benefit scales for children up to the age of 11 needed to be increased by 50 per cent to meet their minimum requirements in 1979.[47] In brief, then, supplementary benefit rates were inadequate in 1948 and, in spite of some improvement over the years, they remain inadequate today. How inadequate the scales are is impossible to say without a thorough study by the government to identify and cost those needs that must be adequately covered by the supplementary benefit rates today.

What proportion of the population are, then, below the supplementary benefit level? All national estimates, barring Townsend's study, are based on data provided by the government's family expenditure surveys. Table 2.2 provides the most recent position for the whole of the UK. It shows that in 1979 5.5 per cent of all families and 4.1 per cent of all persons representing over 2 million people in Great Britain had incomes below the supplementary benefit level. The table does not cover Northern Ireland where the proportion of the population in poverty has always been higher than that of the rest of the United Kingdom. These figures are also higher today since unemployment has more than

TABLE 2.1

Supplementary benefit scale rates ^{a} as a percentage of gross and net average earnings $^{b\ c}$ uprating dates (%)

	Ordinary scale rates				Long-term scale rates			
	Single householder		Married couple		Single householder		Married couple	
	Gross	Net	Gross	Net	Gross	Net	Gross	Net
July 1948	17.6	22.9	29.4	36.1				
June 1950	17.6	22.3	29.5	35.9				
July 1955	17.6	22.5	29.6	35.7				
April 1961	17.8	24.9	29.9	39.3				
Nov. 1966	20.0	30.0	32.9	47.1	22.1	33.3	34.8	50.3
Nov. 1970	18.2	28.7	29.8	45.3	20.0	31.5	31.6	47.9
Nov. 1975	17.3	29.8	28.2	47.5	21.7	37.5	34.2	57.7
Nov. 1979	16.2	25.6	26.3	39.4	21.0	33.1	33.3	50.0

a   Supplementary benefit scale rates exclude rent additions

b   From July 1948 to November 1969 the average earnings relate to full-time male manual workers. From 1970 onwards they relate to all male workers

c   Net earnings are taken as gross earnings less income tax, national insurance contributions, and average rent and rates

Source: *Supplementary Benefits Commission Annual Reports* for 1975, Cmnd 6615, Table 7 and for 1979, Cmnd 8033, Table 9.4

doubled since 1979 and benefits for the unemployed have been deliberately left behind other benefits. Government estimates also tend to under-estimate the extent of poverty because of the nature of the family expenditure survey data on which they are based. Minority groups with very low incomes are under-represented in both the family expenditure survey sample and in the response rate of the sample chosen. It is therefore to be expected that the only private national study of Townsend found that 6.4 per cent of the population representing 3.48 million individuals had incomes below the supplementary benefit level in the UK in 1968.[48] Both Townsend's and the government's figures refer to people living in the community — they do not cover those of the poor living in residential establishments.

There are two main ways in which trends in the extent of poverty, as here defined, can be examined. First, one can use the supplementary benefit level in any one year, update it according to the rise in the retail prices index over a certain period of years and then estimate the

TABLE 2.2
Number (in thousands) and percentage of families and persons with incomes below supplementary benefit level during 1981, Great Britain

	Families		Persons	
	Number	%	Number	%
All families	1,760	6.5	2,810	5.3
Total families over pension age	880	13.6	1,120	12.7
a Married couples	240	10.4	480	10.3
b Single persons	640	15.4	640	15.4
Total families under pension age by family type:	880	4.3	1,690	3.8
a Married couples with children	200	3.3	850	3.6
b Single persons " "	60	6.4	170	6.6
c Married couples without children	60	1.3	120	1.3
d Single persons " "	560	6.4	560	6.4
e Of which large families (3 or more children)	80	6.3	410	6.3
By employment status:				
a Full time work or self-employed	240	1.5	680	1.9
b Sick or disabled for more than 3 months	50	6.3	100	6.3
c Unemployed for more than 3 months	280	14.8	480	13.8
d Others	310	16.1	440	11.9

Source: DHSS unpublished tables, *Low Income Families*, 1981, House of Commons Library, October 1983

proportion of people below these two levels of benefit. Using this approach – the absolute poverty standard – Fiegehen and his associates estimated that the proportion of individuals with incomes below the supplementary benefit level declined from 4.8 per cent in 1953 to 0.2 per cent in 1973.[49] This approach is not very useful because it sees the incomes of the poor as distinct and separate from the living standards of the rest of society. Second, one can look at simply the number of people at different years with incomes below the prevailing supplementary benefit rates. There are the inevitable problems of data reliability over the years and hence the picture shown in Table 2.3 should be treated with caution. Being a relative standard of poverty based on data provided by the family expenditure surveys, it shows a more stable picture over the years than that painted by the absolute standard. So long as no new policy measures are introduced or new socio-economic processes take place to reduce or increase the number

TABLE 2.3
Number of individuals with incomes below the supplementary benefit level, Great Britain (thousands)

| Year | Individuals | |
	Number	%
1960[a]	1,990	3.8
1972[b]	1,780	3.4
1977[c]	2,020	4.0
1981[d]	2,810	5.3

Sources:
[a] B. Abel-Smith and P. Townsend, *The Poor and the Poorest*, Bell, 1965, p. 58
[b] CSO, *Social Trends*, no. 5, 1974, HMSO, 1974, Table 80, p. 123
[c] CSO, *Social Trends*, no. 10, 1980, HMSO, 1979
[d] As for Table 2.2

of persons not receiving supplementary benefit or its equivalent, it is to be expected that the proportion of the population in official poverty will remain pretty constant over the years. Thus one would have expected the proportion to have dropped between 1960 and 1981 because of the introduction of the family income supplement and the abolition of the wages stop. On the other hand, unemployment increased substantially and the number of one-parent families also rose — both socio-economic processes that could lead to a higher proportion of the population in official poverty. Also, some of the policies of the Thatcher government on social security had the same effect.

The demographic characteristics of the poor are obvious enough. Table 2.2 shows that one-half of the individuals in official poverty, i.e. below supplementary benefit level, were above retirement age — a proportion far higher than expected from general demographic trends. The incidence of poverty among the elderly is particularly high among the very elderly who are predominantly women on their own — single or widowed. Thus poverty during old age is predominantly a problem for women. One-parent families are also more likely to be in poverty than two-parent families — a not unexpected result, bearing in mind the inadequacy of benefits for this group and the low wages for part-time employment of women. Again, it is women that are most likely to suffer. There is, finally, the expected evidence that families with children are more likely to be in poverty than families without. A government study in 1979 showed that the incidence of poverty increases with the size of the family, even though most of those in poverty live in small families. Analysing the data from this study,

Burghes showed that though large families with three or more children made up 19.5 per cent of all families, they accounted for 35.0 per cent of all low-income families. Almost two-thirds of two-parent, low-income families, however, had only one or two children. The corresponding proportion for one-parent families was even higher — almost three-quarters. One-parent families, however, made up 12 per cent of all families but 38 per cent of all low income families. It is worth noting, however, that low income was defined as the supplementary benefit rate, plus 40 per cent.[50] Finally, Table 2.2 shows that the incidence of poverty among the unemployed is far higher than among those at work.

Table 2.2, does not say very much about the socio-economic background of the poor. There is a dearth of official and other statistics linking poverty among the elderly, the one-parent families, the disabled, and so on, to their socio-economic background. There are the occasional brief references but nothing more. Thus Berthoud and his associates, using data from the General Household Survey for 1975, concluded: 'only 3 per cent of professional and managerial workers (without a working spouse) are poor; 19 per cent of the unskilled workers are poor, not so much because they risk poverty while in work, but because two-thirds of them were not full-time, full-year employees.'[51] There is also a great deal of circumstantial evidence which shows that the low wage-earner of one generation is likely to be the retirement pensioner of the future in poverty but the evidence is not detailed enough to take account of the influence of such factors as skill, sex, race, etc.

Leaving aside the question of the exact number of people whose incomes are below the supplementary benefit level, how is it that almost 3 million people have incomes below that level? The first most obvious reason is that large numbers of people entitled to supplementary benefit do not claim it for a variety of reasons — pride, stigma, or ignorance. The Supplementary Benefits Commission reckoned that in 1978 1 million people with a prima facie entitlement to benefit were not claiming — 600,000 pensioners and 400,000 heads of families under pension age.[52] Second, people in full-time employment cannot claim supplementary benefit but can claim family income supplement. Apart from the fact that about one-quarter of those entitled do not claim it, the level of the family income supplement is not always the same as the supplementary benefit level. It is thus possible for people to receive family income supplement and still to have incomes below the official poverty line — the supplementary benefit level. Third, both the supplementary benefit and the family income supplement scheme contain regulations which are designed to protect work incentives and enforce labour discipline with the result that many people can only receive part of their benefit entitlement. Thus people can only receive half their entitlement of family income supplement and even that should not exceed certain specified amounts varying with the size of the family. People who lose their jobs through misconduct, who leave their jobs 'voluntarily' and the unemployed who 'unreasonably' refuse jobs or training can lose their unemployment benefit for up to six weeks and if they qualify for supplementary benefit it will be for a reduced amount.

In conclusion, the social security system, despite its mounting cost, is no nearer today to ensuring that no-one has an income below the supplementary benefit level than it was thirty years ago. This, however, should not conceal the fact that the system has had considerable success. The Royal Commission on the Distribution of Income and Wealth adopted the novel approach of making estimates of the number of individuals and families living below supplementary benefit level before and after the receipt of the social security benefits to which they were entitled. Before receiving social security benefits, 30.4 per cent of families and 22.7 per cent of individuals in the population were below the poverty line. After the receipt of benefits, 4.4 per cent of families and 3.3 per cent of individuals remained in poverty. The social security system was, to look at in one way, 85 per cent successful in raising people to a minimum level of income. The system was more successful with pensioners than with families with dependent children. More pensioners were rescued from poverty by the system and those who were left stranded below the minimum had weekly incomes only, on average, £1.40 per adult below their needs. A larger proportion of families with children were not helped by the social security system and their 'poverty gap' — the amount required to raise their incomes to supplementary benefit level was three or four times greater than that for pensioners.[53] This considerable success of the system, however, must be seen in the light of the criticism made earlier of the inadequacy of the supplementary benefit rates that are being used as the official poverty line.

The amount of the benefit and whether all who are entitled to it receive it are, of course, important issues. But just as important is the way the system and its officers are seen by its customers. A recent government study of callers at a local social security office shows a less than rosy picture of consumer satisfaction with the social security service. Over half the supplementary pensioners and more of the claimants for supplementary allowances criticised some aspect of the system.[54] Very few claimants had seen any publicity for the benefits they were receiving and about two thirds said they did not understand how their benefit was assessed. By far the most frequently criticised aspect of the system — as might have been expected — was the level of social security benefits — criticised by some 40 per cent of claimants.

Overall, 31 per cent of non-pensioners who received supplementary benefit were dissatisfied or very dissatisfied with the service, but only 9 per cent of pensioner claimants took a similar view.[55] Many claimants also saw the system as arbitrary and discriminatory in the way it took decisions on benefits, additional payments, prosecutions, etc. There must be a level of customer dissatisfaction which governments should find unacceptable -- the supplementary benefit scheme has always been hovering on the brink of this level. Progress has been made over the years but obviously not enough and the government's present policies are likely to increase public dissatisfaction with the social security system.

Minimum standards in housing

Minimum standards in housing are obviously more difficult to define, to measure and to compare over the years than they are in social security. Nevertheless, they, too, are clearly relative and their definition has changed over the years. For the purposes of this section, the statement of intent expressed in a recent government consultative document on housing will be used as the broad basis for the discussion: 'The government believe that all families should be able to obtain a decent home at a price within their means. This has been the dominant theme of post-war housing policy.'[56] The minimum aims of government housing policies have been the provision of enough dwellings of an acceptable physical standard and density for all households and at a price within the financial means of each household.

TABLE 2.4
Dwellings and households, Great Britain (millions)

Year	Dwellings	Households
1951	14	15
1961	16	16
1971	19	18.5
1980	21	20

Source: CSO, *Social Trends*, no. 12, 1982, HMSO, 1981, Chart 8.1, p. 145

Table 2.4 shows that the number of dwellings has been increasing faster than the number of households with the result that since 1961 the number of dwellings has exceeded the number of households, so that by 1980 there was a surplus of dwellings over households of about one million. In other words, if dwellings were equally shared among households, there would be a dwelling for each household and a few to spare. Many dwellings, however, are empty, others are second houses for those who can afford them and others are situated in areas where there is no demand for them. Figures for England only show that in 1981 there were at least 600,000 empty houses, representing 3.3 per cent of the housing stock, and most of these — four out of five — were in the private sector, many of them awaiting a buyer.[57] The growth of second homes in rural areas used for holiday retreats by wealthy urban dwellers has grown and it has been a source of grievance recently, particularly in Wales where it has been hotly opposed by Welsh nationalists. Thus, in spite of the substantial excess of dwellings over households, there are still many people who are homeless or who have to share dwellings with their relatives.

A great deal has been written about homelessness and only the briefest of accounts can be presented here.[58] The National Assistance Act, 1948, required local authority welfare departments to provide temporary accommodation for persons who were involuntarily homeless. In practice, local authorities provided such accommodation only for families with children and even then they often excluded husbands. Single homeless persons were made the responsibility of the National Assistance Board and of voluntary organisations. All through the 1950s and the early 1960s local authorities used old workhouses and substandard housing to accommodate the homeless. It was believed that the need for such accommodation would disappear as more housing was built and that homelessness, which was a serious problem because of the war devastation, would eventually disappear in Britain.

In fact, the opposite seems to have occurred. The slum clearance and road building programmes of the 1950s, the Rent Act of 1957, the decline of the private landlord, the rise in rents and other economic and social changes resulted in an increase in the numbers housed under the 1948 Act. 'In 1966', writes Burke, 'there were 2,558 households in temporary accommodation, by 1970 there were 4,296, and by 1976 there were 10,270 — some 50,000 people.'[59] These figures do not include the single homeless who are housed by statutory and voluntary bodies. Rigby's survey for the government in 1972 found almost 27,000 single people in the hostels and lodging houses run by statutory and voluntary bodies.[60] Nor can any statistics for the homeless reflect the true extent of homelessness. As Greve et al. observed in their survey of homelessness in London: 'Nobody knows, or has ever known, how many homeless people there are, and there is no agreement about what in fact homelessness is.'[61] Moreover, homelessness has been concentrated in the urban areas and particularly the inner areas of London with the inevitable strain on the housing stock of these areas.

By the 1970s it was quite apparent that the National Assistance Act was inadequate in its provisions for the homeless. It

27

provided the wrong powers (imposing a weak obligation to provide temporary shelter for small numbers, when the problem of homelessness called for strong obligations to provide permanent housing for large numbers) and these powers were in the wrong hands (resting ineffectively with the DHSS and county social services departments instead of the Department of Environment and the district housing authorities).[62]

The pressure for reform resulted in the Housing (Homeless Persons) Act, 1977 which requires the housing departments of the local authorities to provide accommodation for homeless families, but again the Act excluded those who 'voluntarily' made themselves homeless. Experience has since shown that many local authorities evade their responsibilities by resorting to the 'intentional homelessness' clause of the Act which absolves them from responsibility. Many people who are homeless as a result of family disputes, rent arrears, and other such social and economic reasons are treated by many councils as intentionally homeless and are refused housing.[63] Thus after thirty years, the spirit of the National Assistance Act lives on under a new guise in the Housing Act, 1977. In the meantime, the number of people offered housing under the Act has been increasing, as Table 2.5 shows. It must be stressed again that these figures do not reflect adequately the extent of homelessness among families. They reflect more the extent of provision for such families.

TABLE 2.5
Homeless families housed by local authorities

Year	London	Rest of England	Total
1975	12,600	21,000[a]	33,600
1976	12,400	21,300[a]	33,700
1978	14,000	38,000	52,000
1979	16,000	40,000	56,000
1980	16,000	42,000	58,000

[a] These figures refer to England and Wales
Source: CSO, *Social Trends*, nos 9 and 12, 1977 and 1980, Tables 9.17 and 8.17, pp. 154 and 154 respectively, HMSO, 1978 and 1981

Those offered accommodation are only a fraction of those who apply and though figures are not always available, the evidence for some years shows that only two-thirds of the applications are accepted with wide variations among local authorities. There is substantial evidence that many councils still see homelessness as a problem due to personality inadequacies,[64] and justify their hard line towards the homeless accordingly. What is equally interesting and worrying is that the central government has not so far attempted to enforce the legislation on defaulting local authorities and it is most unlikely to do so in the present economic climate. Some progress may have been made during the period covered by this study but the overwhelming conclusion must be that homelessness is as serious a problem today as it was in the 1950s.

The basic aim of housing policy has then been to provide every family with a decent home. This means not only that families should not be homeless but also that they should not have to share a dwelling against their wishes. It is worth recording the fact that the idea of each family having a right to a separate dwelling is new. Block cites several letters to *The Times* in 1933 which were very critical of such a wild assumption and 'the exaggerated use of the ideal of a separate house for each family'.[65] So progress has been made in the conceptualisation of housing need. But has this been matched by policy practice? It is extremely difficult to identify the exact number of families and of single people sharing dwellings and it is almost impossible to know what proportion does so against their wishes. Government and other data show that the extent of sharing has declined substantially since 1951. Table 2.6 shows that the total number sharing has been more than halved between 1951 and 1976.

TABLE 2.6
Households sharing dwellings, England and Wales (thousands)

Type of household		1951	1971	1976[a]
Multi-person households		1,442	380	275
One-person	"	430	440	375
Concealed	"	935	426	360
Total		2,807	1,246	1,010

a Estimated

Source: *Housing Policy: A Consultative Document*, Cmnd 6851, HMSO, 1977, Annexe B, Table 4, p. 142

Particularly impressive is the decline in families living in the same dwelling with others and having to share with others such facilities as bathroom, kitchen, etc. The concealed households referred to in the table are individuals who have not formed separate households and have had to live as part of another household — it is single people who live with others but not necessarily out of choice. The reduction in housebuilding, particularly in the public sector, in recent years is likely to slow down and perhaps even halt this improvement.

The promise of a 'decent home' to all families implies at least two things: people should not live in overcrowded conditions or in housing which is physically unfit for human habitation. These are relative terms and their legal, let alone social, meaning has changed over the years. Overcrowding was first legally defined and made a potential offence in 1935. As one would expect, the definition reflected the unsatisfactory housing conditions of the period and the standard of overcrowding was therefore low. As Berry observes, on that standard

> a one-room house could be occupied by two people and a five-room house could have ten. On this basis, too, the little terraced house in which the author was born and brought up could have been occupied by ten people instead of the four who in fact lived in it; he recalls that it seemed quite cramped enough with four, never mind ten.[66]

This standard was used not only for legal but for statistical purposes as well, and it is still the law of the land despite some minor changes made by the Housing Act, 1957. The term 'room' includes bedrooms, sitting-rooms and kitchen/dining rooms. Children under the age of 1 are not taken into account; those aged 1-10 count as half a person; and those above that must sleep in separate rooms if they are not of the same sex. Thus a family of husband, wife and two children aged under 10 living in one bedroom and a kitchen/diner is not overcrowded. The standard also takes into account the floor area of rooms and it is thus both complicated and easy to evade. Very few prosecutions have taken place, not only because of the problems of detection and definition, but also because if they lead to eviction, local authorities will have to rehouse the families concerned. A revision of the legal definition of overcrowding has been long overdue. As the Cullingworth Report stated many years ago: 'Certainly the statutory overcrowding standard cannot be considered relevant today.'[67] It reflected the realities of the 1930s and the post-war situation but it is obsolete today.

It was therefore not unexpected when the Housing Survey, 1964, found that only 1 per cent of all households in England and Wales were legally overcrowded. Equally expected was the decline in the number of households statutorily overcrowded – from 341,000 in 1936, to 76,000 in 1964.[68] The survey also used two other overcrowding standards: the number of persons per 'habitable' room; and the 'bedroom standard'. Both of these were more generous definitions and they showed that 2.1 per cent families lived at a density of 1.5 persons per habitable room; and 9.4 per cent of families were below the bedroom standard. The definition of both these standards is important because they have since been adopted for research and statistical purposes. The first made no radical departure from the previous definition because it still used all habitable rooms for sleeping purposes. The second approach, however, was more generous for it uses bedrooms only:

'a bedroom is required for each married couple, and for each person aged 21 and over; each two members of the household aged less than 21 share a bedroom with the proviso that those aged 10 to 21 should share with someone of the same sex. The actual number of bedrooms available for the sole use of the household is compared with this standard.'[69]

It still falls short of the ideal — i.e. a bedroom for at least each member of the household aged over 10 years but it is clearly a vast improvement. Using the 1.5 persons per room standard, the degree of over-

TABLE 2.7
Overcrowding standard, Housing Act, 1957

Number of rooms	Number of persons allowed
1	2
2	3
3	5
4	7.5
5 or more	2 per room

Source: D.Ormandy, 'Overcrowding', *Roof*, March-April 1981

crowding is very small today and the reduction over the years has been very substantial, as Table 2.8 shows. If, however, one uses the more realistic 'bedroom standard' of overcrowding, then the extent of overcrowding is high and the decline over the years is not so substantial.

TABLE 2.8
Extent of overcrowding* in England and Wales

Year	Total number of households	Number of over-crowded households	% of households overcrowded
1951	13,300,000	650,000	4.89
1976	17,600,000	150,000	0.85

* More than 1.5 persons per room
Source: *Housing Policy*, Cmnd 6851, HMSO, 1977, Fig. 1, p. 10 and Table 1, p. 11

TABLE 2.9
Extent of overcrowding*, by tenure, Great Britain (%)

Tenure	1971	1980
Owned outright	3	2
Owned with mortgage or loan	4	3
All owner-occupiers	4	3
Rented from local authority/new town	10	7
Rented privately unfurnished	8	6
Rented privately furnished	19	12
All tenures	7	7

* Refers to 'bedroom standard'
Source: CSO, *Social Trends*, no. 12, HMSO, 1981, Table 8.13, p. 151

Table 2.9 also shows that those living in privately rented furnished accomodation are far more likely to be overcrowded than those in owner-occupied housing.

As one would expect, overcrowding is far more of a problem in the large urban conurbations, particularly London and Glasgow, and it is far more of a problem to the low paid and some of the ethnic minorities. These and other divisions are examined in the next chapter.

It is generally agreed, and with a great deal of justification, that the physical standards of housing have improved a great deal over the years. What is not often made explicit is that this progress is less spectacular if it is seen in relative rather than absolute terms. What are physical standards in housing? The Housing Repairs and Rents Act, 1954, for the first time defined what constituted the minimum physical standards of housing that have to be met to prevent a dwelling from being legally found as unfit for human habitation. These standards related to the purely physical aspects of housing — the state of repair, the extent of dampness, how much natural lighting and ventilation is possible, the state of the water supply and the condition of drainage and sanitary facilities. Moreover, it is often a matter of opinion as to whether these physical standards are met. These minimum standards fall far short of the standards put forward by many individuals and professional bodies over the years. Thus the American Public Health Association published in the 1930s what it considered the 'basic principles of healthful housing' and these included minimum standards for the psychological needs of the family, physiological needs, protection against contagion and protection against accidents.[70] The Parker Morris standards for new council housing after 1968, now abandoned, were far higher and included provisions for heating and storage. There is, in other words, general recognition that the statutory physical standards are too low but there is government reluctance to update them to cover all existing housing because of the costs involved in modernising a large number of dwellings. Government data have, however, begun to distinguish between housing which is statutorily unfit and sub-standard housing, i.e. housing which is not unfit but which lacks one or more of the five basic amenities: a fixed bath, an inside WC, a wash basin, a sink, and a hot and cold water supply. It is in these relative terms that the large improvement in the physical standard of housing should be seen. While in 1951 there were 7.5 million households in unfit or sub-standard housing, the corresponding number for 1976 was 1.65 million. It is a very substantial decline but it still represents 9.4 per cent of all households in England and Wales in physically unsatisfactory housing. A further 1.5 million dwellings, nearly 9 per cent of the housing stock, were assessed as requiring repairs costing over £500 at 1978 prices.[71] Thus, despite the substantial improvement in the minimum physical standards of housing, the government consultative document acknowledged that 'the traditional aim of a decent home for all families at a price within their means must remain our primary objective.'[72] As Lansley, too, points out, much remains to be done to meet even this basic objective.[73] The situation is obviously different in various parts of the country: 'Most of England's unfit homes', concludes Shelter from the evidence of government data, 'are in the three Northern planning regions. Nearly three quarters of those in Scotland are in Central Clydeside. In London, one home in ten is unfit — twice the national proportion. In the older, inner London area, one in seven is unfit.'[74] The situation is also worse in Northern Ireland where in 1979 14 per cent of dwellings as against 5 per cent in England were unfit and where 20 per cent of dwellings as against 9 per cent in England lacked one of the five basic amenities.[75]

The more the minimum standards are upgraded to take account of the country's rising living standards, the more dwellings are found wanting. Table 2.10 shows that, while only 4 per cent of households lacked a bath or shower, the proportion without central heating rose to 43 per cent. Since old people tend to live in old housing, it is more than likely that the proportion living in housing without central heating is even higher. It should surely be statutorily acknowledged that adequate heating for the elderly in the climate of this country is a necessity.

There are also population groups with special housing needs where national data on minimum physical standards are of little relevance. The government's consultative document on housing accepted this when it stated that figures on minimum standards 'take no account of families living in housing of good standard, but unsuited to their needs — for example, families with small children in flats above ground level,

TABLE 2.10
Housing physical standards by tenure, Great Britain (%)

Tenure	Lacking sole use of				Without central heating	
	Bath/Shower		WC inside building			
	1971	1980	1971	1980	1971	1980
Owned outright	12	4	13	5	61	42
Owned with mortgage loan	4	1	5	1	43	25
All owner-occupiers	7	2	9	3	51	32
Rented from local authority/new town	3	1	5	2	76	52
Rented privately unfurnished	33	15	37	15	85	65
" " furnished	58	54	57	54	83	67
All tenures	12	4	13	5	66	43

Source: CSO, *Social Trends*, no. 12, HMSO, 1981, Table 8.13, p. 151

and elderly or disabled people struggling with houses ill-adapted to their special problems'.[76] Hunt's and Heyes's survey of housing for the disabled in the borough of Torfaen in 1977 found that 74 per cent of the disabled lived in housing with stairs – this applied to even 62 per cent of the chair-bound; 68 per cent of the chair-bound disabled felt that they did not have sufficient room for manoeuvring a wheelchair in at least one room; 58 per cent of all the disabled lived in housing which required some form of adaptation or was in need of aids; one-third of the disabled wanted to move to accommodation that was adapted to their needs, and so on. The authors discuss the financial and other problems involved in providing satisfactory accommodation for all the disabled and conclude their study as follows: 'We believe that one measure of a civilised society is the extent to which it cares for those members least able to support themselves, and that there is a pressing need for our society to reconsider the priority it accords to housing for the disabled.'[77] A similar picture can be drawn for the housing of the elderly and a similar plea can be made for them, too. In England and Wales, only 8 per cent of elderly households in 1980 lived in specially designed accommodation in the community – a very low figure and with wide variations among local authorities.[78] The proportion of families with inadequate play facilities for young children is another example where national statistics on minimum standards do not make much sense. Townsend asked his sample who had children under 10, whether the children had enough good play space indoors without troubling the neighbours: 17 per cent of such families said they had not – representing around 1 million families in the UK.[79]

The establishment of statutory minimum standards in terms of density and physical conditions of housing has the dual advantage of enabling easy quantification of the housing problem and of making it easier for local authorities to direct their attention towards remedying the situation. The main disadvantage of statutory minimum standards is that once established they are accepted as the norm and they persist far beyond their usefulness. There is at present an urgent need to redefine these minimum standards to cover safety, recreation, heating, insulation and other socially accepted housing norms.

In spite of the fact that in 1976 2.7 million households lived in physically unsatisfactory houses, in overcrowded conditions or shared dwellings (the figure rises to 5.5 million if overlapping between the various categories is not eliminated),[80] there is a very high tolerance level of unsatisfactory housing. The Government Social Survey in 1976 found that less than half of the households in unfit properties expressed dissatisfaction with the property's state of repair. Over a fifth of households in properties thought by the surveyor to require essential repairs thought that no repairs were needed. Less than half of the households which had no bathroom spontaneously volunteered to the interviewer that they wished to have these fitted.[81] The costs involved in house improvements may be one of the reasons for this apparent satisfaction but the authors of the study conclude that, in addition, 'as householders grow older and become settled in their homes, they become less willing to recognise their defects or to tolerate the disturbance caused by repairs or improvements.'[82] One is reminded of Orwell's miner who said that he and his colleagues only became aware of their housing problem when they were told about it.

Minimum standards in the health services

The notion of statutory minimum standards does not fit easily with such universal social services as health and education. As Shonfield and Shaw observe, 'in advanced industrial societies, notions of what may be said to constitute health or education are no longer concerned with "subsistence" level of performance – the ability to read and write and to live beyond three decades.'[83] They are referring to outputs but the same can be said of inputs in these two social services. It is optimum rather than minimum standards that social policy in health and education has been concerned with over the years. For this reason there are no set statutory minimum outputs and only a few relating to inputs.

Long-term guidelines and professional targets are used but these do not have the backing of legal sanctions as the statutory minimum standards have in housing or social security.

We referred earlier on in this chapter to the weak link between inputs and outputs in the health services and attributed it largely to the fact that the outputs of the health services are affected by many other factors — social, economic and environmental — apart from the quantity and quality of medical inputs. This is not to denigrate the importance of medical inputs for they are indeed important even if their effects are difficult to identify and quantify in a satisfactorily scientific way. In this section we are concerned primarily with medical inputs in terms of professional personnel: are there enough general practitioners, hospital consultants, nurses, and so on, employed in the National Health Service to cope with the need and demand for medical services?

Table 2.11 shows that there has been a substantial growth in the numbers of professional personnel employed in the National Health Service since 1949. The list of professional groups in Table 2.11 is not exhaustive but it shows that the number of professional personnel in the National Health Service doubled during 1949/50-1979/80 with variations ranging from 26 per cent for general practitioners, to 218 per cent for hospital consultants. Similar trends apply to the other parts of the UK.

Before deciding whether there are enough professionals in any group, it is important to recognise the difficulties involved in estimating

TABLE 2.11
Numbers of professional staff in the NHS (as whole-time equivalents), England

Professional group	1949/1950	1979/1980	% Change
Hospital doctors	8,251	20,341	+ 146.0
Hospital consultants	3,484	11,080	+ 218.0
Hospital nurses	137,636	297,684	+ 116.0
Hospital midwives	9,043	17,039	+ 88.0
General practitioners	18,000	22,674	+ 26.0
Community nurses and health visitors	9,529	32,162	+ 238.0
Community midwives	4,820[a]	3,000	− 38.0
Dentists	10,068[b]	11,784	+ 17.0

[a] Refers to 1959
[b] Refers to 1963 but it is estimated that the number for 1949 was similar
Sources: Organisation of Health Economics, 'Doctors, Nurses and Midwives in the National Health Service', *Briefing No. 18*, November 1981, Figs 1, 2 and 3, pp. 1-2

this in the absence of generally recognised staff/patient ratios. The
necessary number of personnel in any of the above professional groups
depends largely on three main factors: how their role is defined, how
effective they are in carrying out their duties and the influence of socio-
economic or demographic changes. If, for example, the role of health
visitors is defined in broad and universal terms, then the necessary
number will be greater than if their role is defined in narrow and
residual terms. It is inherent in the nature of professions to strive to
broaden the role of their members with the result that there are always
demands from professional bodies for an expansion of their services.
It is therefore not unexpected that professional bodies in the National
Health Service have always argued that there is a need for more professionals to meet public need or demand for their services. This tendency
of the professions is not always altruistic but it can, as the Royal
Commission on the National Health Service cautiously observed, reflect
'in part perhaps a wish for extended career opportunities'.[84] The issue
of effectiveness is just as difficult to define and measure as the role
content of a profession. Is the effectiveness of a general practitioner
affected by the length of consultations with his patients? What is the
most cost-effective combination of drugs and personal therapy in the
treatment of the mentally ill? How effective are visits by health visitors
to families with multiple problems in reducing child neglect and ill-
treatment? The list of questions is endless and they all demonstrate in
varying ways and degrees the difficulties of measuring effectiveness.
Clearly, however, the more effective professionals are in their work,
the fewer of them are necessary; and vice versa. The influence of socio-
economic and demographic factors on the number of professionals
needed is so obvious that it needs hardly mentioning: a rise in unemployment can lead to more mental disorder in society; a rise in the
proportion of the elderly can mean more work for many professional
groups; an increase in separation and divorce rates can increase demand
for the services of general practitioners and others; greater consumption
of confectionery can make more work for dentists, and so on. In view
of all this, it is not surprising that estimating how many professionals
are needed is both a hazardous and a contested operation. As the Royal
College of Surgeons, in its evidence to the Royal Commission, pessi-
mistically concluded: 'Previous attempts to forecast the staffing needs
of the National Health Service have not met with conspicuous success
and the most important lesson to be learnt from the past is that the
future is unpredictable.'[85]

In spite of the increase in the number of general practitioners, the
position is still not totally satisfactory. The British Medical Association,
in its evidence to the Royal Commission, argued that the average list
size for a general practitioner should be reduced from its present 2,300

to 1,700 patients. While not unsympathetic to this, the Royal
Commission, however, felt that 'before a maximum or minimum list
size is adopted, considerable research on this important question should
be undertaken.'[86] It should be remembered that the maximum list size
that is legally allowed in the National Health Service is 3,500 patients
today, and this has been so since 1952. As Table 2.12 shows, however,

TABLE 2.12
*General medical practitioners (unrestricted principals) by list size,
England (%)*

Year	Under 1,600	1,600-1,899	1,900-2,499	2,500-2,999	3,000 and over
1963	15	12	31	23	19
1967	10	9	30	27	24
1977	9	12	40	27	12
1981	9[a]	25[b]	38[c]	21	7

Source: DHSS, *Health and Personal Social Services Statistics for England, 1978*,
HMSO, 1980, Table 3.29, p. 63

DHSS, *Health and Personal Social Services Statistics for England, 1982*,
HMSO, 1982, Table 3.27, p. 52

[a] Under 1,500
[b] 1,500-1,999
[c] 2,000-2,499

in spite of the reduction in the proportion of the largest lists over the
years, there are still 42 per cent of practices with more than the generally acceptable standard of 2,500 patients per doctor. The situation is
not as serious in Wales or in Scotland, or even in Northern Ireland,
which normally suffers most from social and economic deprivation. It
should also be born in mind that the proportion of the population
attending doctors' practices with large lists is greater than the figure
for such lists. Thus Ritchie et al. in a large representative sample in the
UK, found that in 1977, the proportion of the public attending practices with large lists — 3,000 and over — was 19 per cent for England,
5 per cent for Scotland, 5 per cent for Wales, 13 per cent for Northern
Ireland and 17 per cent for the whole of the UK.[87]
    The available research evidence on what is an 'appropriate' or
'correct' size of a doctor's list of patients is sketchy and non-decisive.
Butler's excellent review of the research evidence which centred on the
following seven crucial and related questions, is worth summarising in
full. He found no relationship between the hours of work of doctors
and the size of their lists of patients; or between the length of time per

consultation and the size of the list; and a similar finding was established in relation to who initiates consultations — patient or doctor. On the other hand there was a negative association between the number of consultations and the proportion of patients consulting their doctor on one hand and list size on the other. In other words, the longer the list, the fewer the consultations and the smaller the proportion of patients whom the doctor sees during the year. It is a safety valve, a method of coping with long lists of patients even though when they see their patients doctors do not shorten the length of their consultation. The content of care was not related to list size and, finally, it was not possible to draw any firm conclusions concerning the association between the quality of care and list size. At the end of the day, the decision on the size of the list of patients cannot, therefore, be taken simply on research criteria. 'The choice inevitably involves the exercise of value judgements,' comments Butler, 'but it can be informed, and perhaps made more rational by the availability of good information about the likely costs and consequences of variations in doctor/patient ratios.'[88]

Apart from the number of general practitioners and the list size, there is the issue of the quality of care provided by general practitioners. It is, admittedly, difficult both to define and to measure quality of care. Nevertheless, it is equally difficult to ignore completely the views of such an august body as the Royal College of General Practitioners. In its evidence to the Royal Commission it listed 'Our main liability: poor care.' The College accepted that 'care by some doctors is mediocre, and by a minority is of an unacceptably low standard.' Some GPs sitting the examination for membership of the College 'have a level of knowledge and skill', the College confessed, 'which we regard as unsafe'. The College then set out an honest, if depressing, account of the other key elements in poor care — bad communication, neglect, bad record-keeping, poor deputising arrangements and 'work habits which can lead to quite unnecessary mistakes'.[89] The question of the quality of care provided by general practitioners is highlighted in the Acheson Report on London. It quotes evidence from two local surveys in inner London which show that a large proportion of children under the age of 5 — 14 per cent and 30 per cent — are not registered with a general practitioner; a large proportion of people — 20 per cent in one study — have to approach several doctors before they are accepted on a list; and many people find it difficult to contact their own doctors in an emergency.[90] Its own telephone survey confirmed several of these findings. Interestingly enough, all these problems existed in spite of the fact that the average list size of GPs in inner London, as well as the proportion of GPs with small lists of patients, were more favourable than in the rest of the country. Some of the problems encountered by the public in inner London were due to the fact that GPs tend to work individually rather than as members of a group practice, while other problems were the result of the high proportion of GPs in part-time private practice — often a more profitable proposition than full-time private practice.

The problems of inner London were exacerbated by the inadequacies of the other related professions — health visitors and district nurses. Even though the population ratios recommended for these professions may be numerically met, the nature of the population and the working conditions in inner London reduce the usefulness of such statistics. 'The higher numbers of elderly people living alone, single parent families, members of semi-skilled and unskilled socio-economic groups, and immigrants . . . mean that heavy demands are made on the community nursing services.'[91] Moreover, turnover of staff was very high and the services relied too much on young and often inexperienced staff.

To complete the depressing picture, the Acheson Report refers to the high proportion of premises for GPs — 15 per cent to 30 per cent — 'which fall below a standard which could be considered acceptable for the provision of general medical services'.[92] The same applied to the premises of the other related professional groups. It was problems of this severity that prompted the Royal Commission to state: 'Improving the quality of care in inner city areas is the most urgent problem which the National Health Service services in the community must tackle.'[93]

The provision of dentists has always been inadequate to meet dental needs in the community. As Table 2.11 showed, there has been only a very slight increase in the numbers of general dental practitioners since 1949. A recent government study by Todd and Walker indicated that only 46 per cent of the population in the UK in 1978 had regular check-ups with dentists; 14 per cent occasional check-ups; and 40 per cent went to a dentist only when they had trouble. These figures were only a slight improvement over attendances in 1968.[94] It was this state of affairs that prompted the Royal Commission on the National Health Service to declare that 'regular dental care can be given to considerably less than half the population' and the service would have collapsed had the demand been greater — which it would have probably been had dental treatment been completely free of charge to everyone.[95]

Without doubt hospital services are the most expensive part of the National Health Service — they account for 70 per cent of total expenditure in any one year. Table 2.11 showed that the number of professionals employed in hospitals exceeds the number employed in the community by five times and though this is not a completely accurate figure, it does reflect the dominance of hospital care over community care in the health services. Despite this, waiting lists for hospital admission are long – in fact too long even by government standards. In an attempt to reduce waiting lists, the DHSS made a list of recommendations which, in retrospect, proved of little use. The DHSS's concern was based on a study 'which showed that in six major surgical specialities, 37% of patients had been waiting longer than a year, nearly 20% for more than two years, and some for four years or more'.[96] Moreover, waiting lists vary substantially from one health district to another, part of the complex net of health inequalities that are discussed in the next chapter. Clearly, shortages of trained staff and theatre facilities are the reasons for such long waiting lists.

Though all hospital professional groups have claimed that their numbers are inadequate to meet work demands, it is generally accepted that staff shortages are particularly acute in the professions supplementary to medicine – chiropodists, dieticians, occupational therapists, physiotherapists, etc. The Halsbury Committee of Enquiry into these professional groups in 1975 found shortages of 55 per cent for occupational therapists, 25 per cent for radiographers, and so on.[97] The Committee rightly pointed out that these estimates of need were to some extent impressionistic partly because there are no government or other recognised standards of staffing.

The National Health Service inherited a stock of old and unsatisfactory hospitals in 1948. A great deal of piecemeal modernisation has since taken place and some new hospitals have also been built. On the whole, however, the present state of hospital buildings leaves a lot to be desired. In 1971 a government survey showed that in England over one-third of hospitals had been built originally during the last century and the average age of all hospitals was 61 years. Improvements since 1948 have been mainly for acute and maternity hospital provision. Thus in England 'only 12% of hospital accommodation for mental illness (measured in floor space) has been provided since 1948, 23% of geriatric accommodation and 27% of mental handicap, against 35% for acute units over 200 beds and 44% for maternity.'[98] It is for these reasons that the Royal Commission called for a hospital building programme for both acute and long-stay patients as a matter of 'top priority'.

The low standards of care in hospitals for long-stay patients has long been known and it has surfaced several times recently as a result of several 'scandals' in long-stay hospitals. Thus the recent Report of Enquiry in the Normansfield Hospital concluded that 'no reasonably observant and caring person could have been satisfied with conditions there.'[99] Though Normansfield is not typical of standards in all long-stay hospitals, it is not an isolated example either. Standards in many long-stay hospitals are below any generally acceptable minimum. It has been calculated that the average consultant psychiatrist has, assuming he is conscientious, just five minutes per week to spare for each long-stay patient for whom he is responsible.[100] Levels of other kinds of staffing are also far below those in more favoured parts of the health care system. The latest available information still shows patients in long-stay hospitals without personal clothing, without anywhere to keep personal possessions, living at standards of space and amenity significantly below the guidelines set down by the DHSS.[101] It is evidence of this kind that led Bosanquet to conclude his survey of the health services recently: 'It is in the long-stay wards of hospitals for the mentally ill and the mentally handicapped and the elderly that life too often is without hope and without dignity.'[102] In making these criticisms of prevailing standards in long-stay hospitals, one is not denying the fact that progress has been made over the years. Rather, the argument is that progress has been slow and not as fast as in other types of hospitals. This is particularly regrettable because the provisions made for these groups by the personal social services are not, as we shall see later, all that better.

In spite of the fact that it is not possible to attribute changes in health standards completely to the prevailing standards in the health services, a brief summary of the improvements in health standards is provided here. Ideally one should be comparing health standards over a period of time or even between countries. The notion of health, however, is too broad and vague to be of any practical use for such comparisons. One is, therefore, forced to retreat to morbidity data for comparison purposes. But even these are defined differently over the years and are not always available to make comparisons possible. Thus one has no real option but to use only some morbidity rates and to rely more on mortality rates. Table 2.13 shows that the number of infectious diseases notified to the authorities has fallen very sharply

TABLE 2.13
Notifications of infectious diseases, UK

	1951	1980
Tuberculosis	58,600	10,500
Whooping cough	192,300	22,800
Measles	628,600	148,000
Diphtheria	826	5
Acute poliomyelitis	2,609	3
Tetanus	24a	18

a   Refers to 1971
Source: CSO, *Social Trends*, no. 12, HMSO, 1981, Table 7.7, p. 123

over the last thirty years. The use of vaccinations and the improvement in the general living conditions in the country are the main reasons for this dramatic fall.

The Royal Commission on the National Health Service used three mortality rates as 'indicators of health' — perinatal mortality, maternal mortality and life expectancy. As expected, all these and other similar indicators show a marked improvement over the years, as Table 2.14 shows. These overall improvements mask substantial variations along

TABLE 2.14
Mortality trends in UK

	1951	1979/80
Expectation of life — from birth (years):		
Males	66.2	70.2 (1979)
Females	71.2	76.2 (1979)
Infant mortality (a)	32	11.2 (1980)
Perinatal mortality (b)	39	12.8 (1980)
Maternal mortality (c)	80	14 (1979)

(a) Still births and deaths of infants under 1 week of age per 1,000 live and still births
(b) Deaths of infants under 1 year of age per 1,000 live births
(c) Rate per 100,000 live and still births
Source: CSO, Social Trends, no. 13, HMSO, 1982, Table 7.1, p. 91 and Table 7.2, p. 92

socio-economic group lines which are discussed in the next chapter. Using such criteria as morbidity and mortality rates, it can be claimed that the National Health Service has been modestly successful. If, however, one judges the National Health Service by broader standards — the extent to which it went out of its way to uncover and prevent as well as treat illness — then its shortfalls would be greater and more apparent.

How satisfied are consumers with the standard of care provided by the National Health Service? All the studies so far have concentrated on general practitioners and on acute or maternity hospitals — the views of patients in long-stay hospitals have been ignored. What evidence there is, however, shows a high degree of satisfaction. Thus a national survey of patients' attitudes to hospital services conducted for the Royal Commission on the National Health Service 'indicated that over 80% of patients thought that the service they received was good or very good, but 7% said that if they had to go back into hospital, they would definitely not want to go into the same hospital again.'[103] A similar picture emerges of high regard in relation to the services of general practitioners from another study conducted for the Royal Commission on the National Health Service. This study concluded that: 'On the whole, while always capable of improvement, the National Health Service did provide an accessible primary care service which was generally appreciated by its users.'[104] It is a view supported by a more recent government study which also showed that such factors as the condition of premises for GPs, the list size or geographical location made very little difference to the degree of satisfaction with GPs by patients.[105] Interestingly enough, health service workers have proved more critical of the National Health Service than the consumers. The Royal Commission wryly observes that 'if patients give too rosy a picture of the state of the National Health Service, health workers paint one that is too gloomy.'[106]

Minimum standards in education

Minimum standards in education are as free of government regulation as they are in the health services. The Department of Education and Science lays down few guidelines against which Local Education Authority inputs and outputs could be assessed. There are no statutory minimum standards for such inputs as class sizes, staffing costs per child or expenditure on books and educational materials. Only for school buildings are there DES standards. Neither the DES nor Local Education Authorities have accepted the staffing levels proposed by the National Union of Teachers — twenty children in nursery classes and twenty-seven in primary and secondary schools. The position is inevitably even more unregulated in relation to outputs but, as Wright claims, 'there does seem to be an overwhelming consensus about one thing: that all children should acquire the basic skills of reading, writing and numeracy.'[107] Beyond these basic outputs, there is nothing but controversy.

Minimum standards for school buildings were first laid down in statutory regulations for England and Wales in 1945. They relate only to pupils and not to staff and they cover only areas directly used by pupils. The Inter-Departmental Group which examined these regulations recently concluded that there was 'a need to review our current statutory standards for school building generally'.[108] The report of the Group provides the most up to date and comprehensive picture of the standard of school buildings in England and Wales. As Table 2.15 shows, only 51 per cent of primary schools, 72 per cent of secondary schools and 60 per cent of all schools were built since 1945 and of these almost one-tenth are temporary buildings. Clearly a great deal has

TABLE 2.15
Age of primary and secondary school buildings by number of pupil places, England and Wales, 1976 (%)

Period	Primary		Secondary		Primary and secondary	
	All types of places	SSN^a places	All types of places	SSN^a places	All types of places	SSN^a places
Pre-1903	20	26	4	7	14	17
1903-1918	7	11	4	5	6	8
1919-1945	10	16	13	13	11	15
Post-1945	51	42	72	71	60	55
Temporary	11	6	6	4	9	5
Total	100	100	100	100	100	100

aSSN = Special Social Need

Source: DES, *A Study of School Building*, HMSO, 1977, Table 1, p. 7 and Table 2, p. 9

been done since 1945 but equally obvious is the fact that much remains to be done. Modernisation of old buildings for educational purposes is only feasible up to a certain point and it is, of course, costly. There are also the inevitable regional variations – the Inner London Education Authority has the highest proportion, 40 per cent of primary schools built before 1919. These are, of course, the areas of special social need – the areas that the Plowden Committee referred to as areas of educational disadvantage, as we shall see in the next chapter. For obvious reasons, the problem of old buildings is more acute for primary than for secondary schools, with the result that 80 per cent of pre-1946 primary schools had inadequate staff accommodation, 15 per cent had inadequate kitchen facilities and 49 per cent had outdoor lavatories.

Regardless of age, many school buildings were overcrowded, i.e. they did not have sufficient space for pupils according to the statutory regulations. The problem was more acute for primary than for secondary schools at the time of the survey but the position may have since changed. In secondary schools, however, there was a serious lack of space for lessons requiring specialised accommodation – laboratories and workshops for science, craft, home economics, music, geography, etc. More than half of the secondary schools, 52 per cent were deficient in such accommodation. Many primary and secondary schools were also situated in heavily congested areas and many others did not meet the best standards of fire escape and other safety measures.

The recent examination of primary and secondary schools in England by HM Inspectors provided further evidence about the adequacy of classroom standards and teaching facilities. In primary schools about 'four out of five of the classes selected for the survey were in accommodation which was considered reasonably adequate for the normal work undertaken by the class.' In other words, 20 per cent of classes were physically inadequate for normal school work. As far as equipment was concerned, the survey concluded: 'The available material resources — general equipment and apparatus — audio-visual and other teaching materials — were considered to be adequate for four out of five classes.'[109] Again in 20 per cent of classes, teaching equipment was deemed inadequate. The survey found science teaching wanting: 'Few primary schools visited . . . had effective programmes for the teaching of science. There was a lack of appropriate equipment; insufficient attention was given to ensuring proper coverage of key scientific notions.'[110] The survey of secondary schools concentrated more on equipment than on the physical conditions of schools. It found that in 'almost half of the schools visited, the library provision was considered "satisfactory" or better.'[111] For mathematics teaching, the survey found first that in '66% of the schools there was no specially equipped room, and in a further 16% there was only one'; and, second, that 'many schools seemed to be insufficiently supplied with suitable books.'[112] As far as science teaching was concerned, the survey found, first, that about '40% of the schools of all types did not have enough laboratories';[113] second, that '40% of the schools visited were understaffed' with laboratory technicians;[114] and, third, that in 'about half of the full range comprehensive schools and grammar schools, and in about one-third of the schools of other types, the provision of science books was considered to be adequate'.[115]

TABLE 2.16
Proportion of primary and secondary schools which were overcrowded,[a] England and Wales, 1976 (%)

Adequacy of space	Primary	Secondary	All
Schools with adequate area	65.0	51.0	63.0
Up to 10% overcrowding	17.5	24.0	18.0
Over 10% overcrowding	17.5	25.0	19.0
Total	100.0	100.0	100.0

a Overcrowding: less than 40 sq. ft per pupil in primary schools and 70 sq. ft per pupil in secondary schools

Source: DES, *A Study of School Building*, HMSO, 1977, Fig. 1, p. 8 and Fig. 3, p. 10

The evidence on school buildings and teaching facilities must be seen within the context of a vastly expanded pupil population. Not only was the school-leaving age raised first to 15 and then to 16 years, but the proportion of pupils staying on beyond the school leaving age has also increased considerably. As Table 2.17 shows, the primary school

TABLE 2.17
Expansion of maintained primary and secondary schools in England

Year	Primary schools			Secondary schools		
	Pupils	Teachers	Pupil/ teacher ratio	Pupils	Teachers	Pupil/ teacher ratio
1950	3,667,000	118,680	31.0	1,587,000	74,901	21.2
1960	3,925,000	133,534	29.4	2,557,000	123,357	20.7
1970	4,617,000	168,233	27.5	2,860,000	161,154	17.7
1979	4,371,000	192,462	23.1	3,872,000	231,404	16.7

Source: DES, *Statistics of Education, 1979, vol. 1*, HMSO, 1981, Table A, p. 2

population in England increased by 19 per cent while the secondary school population rose 144 per cent between 1950 and 1979. The number of teachers increased even faster with the result that pupil/ teacher ratios fell from 31.0 to 23.1 in primary schools and from 21.2 to 16.7 in secondary schools. It is a substantial achievement, even though it conceals a great many geographical variations. Similar trends have taken place in the other parts of the United Kingdom.

A more refined index of pupil/teacher interaction than the pupil/ teacher ratio is the class size. It relates to smaller units – classes – rather than to national averages of teacher provision. For primary schools in England in 1950, 33 per cent of classes had thirty pupils or less; 38.2 per cent had thirty to forty pupils; and 28.8 per cent had more than forty pupils. The corresponding proportions for 1979 were 71.5 per cent, 27.6 per cent and 0.9 per cent respectively. If one considers thirty primary pupils per class is the accepted standard, then the proportion of classes that can be deemed large declined from 67 per cent in 1950 to 28.5 per cent in 1979.[116] For secondary schools in England in 1950 the figures were 47% of classes up to thirty pupils; 46% thirty-one to forty pupils; and 7% more than forty pupils; for 1979 the corresponding figures were 88.3 per cent, 10.4 per cent and 1.3 per cent respectively.

The decline in class sizes and the improvement in pupil/teacher ratios are seen as a welcome trend by everyone, apart from those that fear quality has been sacrificed for quantity. We will look at this in relation to outputs in pupils' learning later in this section but here we need to assess the validity of this charge in relation to teachers as inputs. 'It is the quality of teachers which matters,' argue Cox and Boyson, 'rather than their numbers or their equipment. We have sacrificed quality for numbers, and the result has been a lowering of standards.'[117] How does one, however, judge the quality of teachers? There are those who believe that teachers are born, not made. For these there is no way one can produce any convincing evidence that the quality of teachers has risen, fallen or remained static over the years. It can be argued, however, that one can use such indicators as academic and professional qualifications as proxies for teacher quality. Using such criteria, the evidence shows that the quality of teachers has risen over the years. Taking academic qualifications first: 10 per cent of primary school teachers today are graduates compared with 3 per cent in 1950. Moreover, as the report by HM Inspectors noted, being a graduate 'was more usual among more recently qualified teachers; of the teachers with more than 15 years' service slightly over one in 20 held a graduate qualification, while one in five of the teachers in their first year of service was a graduate.'[118] For secondary schools, about one-third were graduates in 1950, compared to almost one-half today. It is, however, true that graduate teachers are very unequally distributed among the different types of secondary schools: 'Almost 80% of all teachers in grammar schools were graduates; nearly 50% in full range comprehensive schools, about 40% in restricted range and transitional comprehensive schools, and 30% in modern schools.'[119]

As far as professional qualifications are concerned, it was not until 1968 that the Department of Education and Science decided not to employ unqualified teachers in primary and secondary schools. The result has been that today all new teachers are professionally qualified. The duration of training courses is also longer today than it was in 1950. Questions, however, have often been raised about the quality of teacher training: training is divorced from the real world of teaching; teaching methods are either too 'progressive' or too abstract; the trainers lack up-to-date teaching experience; and so on. As Wright, however, correctly observes: 'It is one thing to admit that teachers are not being taught *how to teach*, but quite another to know what to do about it, given the competing claims on the student's time.'[120] Complaints about teacher training often reflect differing views of the role of the teacher in society. It is often an ideological and political rather than a scientific and technical type of debate.

To conclude the discussion on inputs: in spite of the absence of statutory standards, apart from school buildings, there is abundant evidence that provision made by the most niggardly Local Education Authorities is so far below the provision of the more generous – or even the average authority — that what is provided must be of a disturbingly low standard. More will be said on this in the next chapter when discussing the reduction of inequalities in education. But what of educational outcomes? The economic recession seems to have encouraged a greater acceptance of the view that sees the function of schools in narrow rather than in broad terms. It is certainly a view that lends itself more easily to some degree of assessment but it must, nevertheless be stressed that it is not the only view and, in fact, it was not a fashionable view a decade or so ago. The Plowden Report in 1967, for instance, enthused about primary schools as educational as well as social and cultural communities.

> A school is not merely a teaching shop, it must transmit values and attitudes. It is a community in which children learn to live first and foremost as children and not as future adults. The school sets out deliberately to devise the right environment for children, to allow them to be themselves and to develop in the way and at the pace appropriate to them.[121]

Before looking at the evidence on outputs, it is worth referring briefly to the debate concerning the relationship between inputs and outputs in education. Most of the research, so far, has concentrated on the relationship between class size and a narrow band of easily measurable educational attainments. Very few studies varied the class size experimentally. Most studies concentrated on existing classes with the result that they used a narrow range of class size. All the studies also left out many variables which can affect school performance — motivation and ability of pupils and teachers, school facilities and services, family background, and so on. It is not, therefore, unexpected that they reached conflicting conclusions. Burstall's review of the literature concluded that there was no point in carrying out any more studies of the traditional type. Instead, he called for specific 'enquiries on the quality of classroom life, the effectiveness or otherwise of particular styles of teaching, considered in context and evaluated in relation to the educational goals being sought'.[122] Whether such a research approach will prove any more successful is a moot question but it indicates the problems involved in isolating the impact of any one factor on school performance — a problem similar to that of list sizes of doctors' practices discussed earlier.

The ability to read is one of the basic outputs of schooling and rumours that standards are falling understandably cause public concern. As Hopkins points out, however, the controversy about falling standards is partly political in nature. 'Reformists, generally Labour-inclined, are under some obligation to think standards are improving;

counter-reformists, more often than not Conservative, believe the opposite.'[123] The Bullock Committee, which was set up in response to fears of falling standards, concluded in a way that left the issue unsettled: 'The statistical results . . . are not greatly disturbing but neither do they leave room for complacency.'[124] The Committee found evidence which showed that average reading scores of 11-year and 15-year-olds increased between 1948 and 1970 but this increase was arrested during the 1960s. The HMI survey of primary schools was more positive: 'The results from these tests are consistent with a rising trend in reading standards between 1955 and 1976-77.'[125] Table 2.18 covers the period 1955 to 1976 and it is based on the results of national surveys using a sentence completion type of reading test. The figure for

TABLE 2.18
Reading test results from national surveys of pupils in primary schools aged 11 years 2 months, England (%)

Year	Mean score
1955	28.71
1960	29.48
1970	29.38
1976-7	31.13

Source: DES, *Primary Education in England*, HMSO, 1978, Table 17, p. 161

1970 is not in line with the upward trend and may be due to the low response rate, 73 per cent, which, in turn, was due largely to a postal strike. The survey also found regional differences in test scores: inner city mean score was 27.9 per cent, other urban 32.0 per cent and rural 30.6 per cent.[126]

As one would expect, the reading ability of children of immigrants is lower than that of children of English parents. A recent survey of children in London schools showed this clearly: at all ages tested, the mean score of English children was higher than that of all ethnic groups and, what is more, the gap did not narrow as the children got older. The author of the survey attributed these differences not to length of education in this country but to social deprivation and other unidentified factors. She recommended that any remedial action should take place at 'the early years of primary schooling' rather than later.[127]

These figures refer to average reading standards. What of the trends in below average standards? The available evidence is both scanty and unreliable. Definitions of 'illiterate' and 'semi-literate' vary from one commentator to the next with the result that comparisons over the years are not strictly possible. The Bullock Report reluctantly accepted that the proportion of 15-year-olds in schools who were semi-literate was 4.3 per cent in 1948 and 3.2 per cent in 1971. A semi-literate 15-year-old was someone whose reading age was 7-9 years. The proportion for 'illiterate' school-leavers was not given but it was considered to be much smaller.[128] Adult illiteracy did not fall within the terms of reference of the Bullock Committee but its recommendations led to the establishment of a national adult literacy campaign with 40,000 adult learners enrolled by March 1976, and by 1977 a total of 125,000 adults undertook such courses. A survey of the effectiveness of adult literacy schemes concluded that 'the majority of learners . . . were evidently making progress in their acquisition of skills relating to reading and writing.'[129]

Minimum standards in writing is a relatively unexplored area and the Bullock Report could only comment that 'it is extremely difficult to say whether or not standards of written and spoken English have fallen. There is no convincing evidence available, and most opinions depend very largely upon subjective impressions.'[130] This applied to both handwriting and spelling. As far as the position today is concerned, the two recent reports on primary and secondary education found no cause for concern.

Equally difficult is the assessment of numeracy standards over the years. As far as teaching of arithmetic today in primary schools is concerned, the HMIs concluded that the findings of their survey 'do not support the view that primary schools neglect the practice of the basic skills in arithmetic'.[131] In fact, the survey found that schools paid considerable attention to the subject. The report on secondary schools came to a similar conclusion: mathematics occupied a central part in the school curriculum and 'the number of fifth year pupils studying no mathematics, nationally, is certainly not rising, and may indeed be falling.' It was three per 1,000 boys and nine per 1,000 girls in 1975-8, compared with eight per 1,000 and fourteen per 1,000, respectively, in 1973-4.[132] Another source of evidence is the National Child Development Study of 17,000 children born in March 1958 and followed up later in different stages of their life. In 1974, they were assessed as 16-year-olds and, in relation to mathematics, their teachers reported that 2.6 per cent 'could not do all the calculations normally required by an everyday shopper' with another 0.2 per cent about whom the teachers were uncertain.[133]

The general conclusions on minimum standards in educational outputs must be that not only is there no cause for concern but that there have been some improvements over the years. The only area in which cause for concern does exist is the education of children of the various minority groups. This is an issue not only in the case of minimum standards, but also in other levels of education, as we shall see in the next chapter. If, however, one considers the outputs of the school system not only in the restricted minimum standards way but in terms of relative and optimum standards, then the picture is different. Indeed, the criticisms of classroom standards and teaching facilities reviewed earlier in this section made sense only if one saw outputs in terms of relative and optimum standards. Schools were achieving minimum standards but failing to educate children according to their age, aptitude and ability, as the Education Act, 1944, envisaged. This in no way belittles the considerable progress achieved over the years. 'Rather', as the report on secondary schools observed, 'it bears witness to enlarged ideas of secondary education, and is a reassuring acknowledgment that the commitment remains valid, though the implications require constantly renewed examination.'[134] This was written before the present government cuts in education expenditure which threaten the maintenance, let alone the improvement, of present standards in both primary and secondary schools. The age group, however, which is most clearly failed by the contemporary education system is the 16-year-old school-leaver. Provision for 16-19-year-olds to pursue their education is exiguous in the extreme. Their contemporaries who stay on in the sixth form have a range of facilities, opportunities and amenities to which the 16-year-old leaver has no access. If he seeks to re-enter the education world once he has left at 16 he faces all kinds of difficulties. Our system offers a very poor second chance to the older student.

Minimum standards in the personal social services

The notion of minimum standards has received its most extensive airing in the personal social services, i.e. the local authority services for the elderly, the physically handicapped, the mentally ill, the mentally handicapped and children in need of care. This is not, perhaps, accidental for these services were, until the early 1960s, the most neglected area of the post-war welfare state. There was so much to be done to bring the standard of these services in line with that of the other universal social services that some form of central government initiative to prod local authorities was necessary. It was also a period when the idea of community care was gaining ground and the new Hospital Plan could only hope to achieve its outward-looking policy by an expansion of the health and welfare services of the local authorities.[135] If hospitals were to release large numbers of long-stay patients, particularly mental patients, into the community, the existing personal social services of local authorities had to be expanded, co-ordinated, and improved.

At the request of the Ministry of Health, local authorites submitted information on the range of their personal social services and on the plans they had for expanding these services during the following ten years. Inevitably, the grossest of disparities in local authority provision were unearthed. But what is more important, the range of provison was found to be in general well below what was necessary by the ministry's newly found yardsticks. Yet despite the minister's apparent enthusiasm, the local authority plans for 1962-72 envisaged only modest expansion, bearing in mind the level of unmet need. The number of staff, in whole-time equivalents, were to be increased by 39 per cent in nine years, compared to an estimated increase of 20 per cent during the preceding five years. Similarly, revenue expenditure on these services was to increase by 47 per cent over nine years which was approximately the same as during the preceding five years.[136] The increase in services envisaged by individual authorities were averaged into national figures which the report considered 'as an indication of the scope and nature of the provision at which different authorities with areas of roughly similar population and character are aiming. Each authority will thus be enabled to look afresh at its own plans in the light of others.'[137]

It was difficult to see how this modest gradual expansion could hope to achieve the ministry's new objective — the satisfaction of individual needs.

In the past the emphasis was on the provison of a range of services [declared the report]; now it is on ascertaining and meeting particular needs. In the future, the services will be increasingly sensitive to the specific needs and individual characteristics of the people they are designed to service.[138]

There was a distinct gap between rhetoric and reality. It was this that prompted the criticism of many including those who, on the whole, welcomed the new initiatives. Townsend referred to the temerity of the report and concluded: 'The cynic might be forgiven for noting that the smaller the size of the cost of the service being discussed, the more daring the Minister's phraseology.'[139]

It was, nevertheless, a beginning and during the following year the ministry required local authorities to draw up revised plans 'on a some-what more extended scale' — an exercise repeated in the following year which formed the basis of the new report that covered the period 1966-76.[140] Again, substantial gross geographical disparities in provision were found and though some progress had generally been made, some local authorities had proved unenthusiastic about the whole exercise. The minister was anxious that the level of particular services provided by a small minority of them (local authorities) falls below what is acceptable, and that some of these authorities do not appear to be planning to improve unsatisfactory services to an acceptable standard over the next ten years.

It was a state of affairs that the minister was not prepared to accept and he, therefore, 'proposes to arrange for his officers to discuss the position with the authority concerned with a view to action to remedy any deficiency'.[141] It was an important step forward because what the previous report saw as national indicators of future development now assumed a firmer character — they became targets to be achieved by the end of the plan's ten-year period. It was clearly a more determined attempt to improve services than that displayed in the first report. This is also shown by the rate of increases in staff and revenue expenditure envisaged for the period 1965-75: staff in whole-time equivalents would increase by 50 per cent while net revenue expenditure on the services would rise by 58 per cent.[142] There was also a stronger intellectual commitment to the idea of forward planning. Thus the report justified forward planning by local authorities on three counts. First, it enables local authorities to take stock of their past performance, to review their present needs and to plan their future services; second, local authorities can compare their performance and their plans with those of other local authorities; and third, it enables the central government to view plans for the expansion of the personal social services within the context of its wider plans.[143] In brief, the idea of future planning with specific targets in mind had by now become accepted government practice.

The next logical step in the process was the government circular to local authorities in 1972 which laid down specific guidelines and requested local authorities to submit plans for the decade up to 1982. The guidelines were mostly in quantified terms and though they were not binding on the local authorities, the minister hoped that they would provide a starting point for local authority thinking and planning. Local authorities that planned for expansion below the guidelines were expected to inform the minister of the special circumstances that justified such planning. There is substantial evidence now that these guidelines were variously interpreted and implemented. Webb and Falk show that of the ten local authorities they examined, some adhered to the guidelines, others ignored them, either because they had more faith in the work of their own planning departments, or because 'the guidelines were felt to be largely irrelevant because they were considerably out of line with existing levels of provision in the local authority.'[144] Similarly, Hambleton and Scerri's analysis of the plans submitted by three local authorities showed that expenditure on personal social services varied considerably even between two authorities which were similar in their demographic and socio-economic structures.[145]

What was more imminent, however, for the future development of guidelines in social services provision was the deteriorating economic situation. Judge's review of the progress of the implementation of these guidelines ends with the note that they lost their meaning as a result of the public expenditure cuts introduced by the Conservative government in 1973 and sustained by the Labour government the following year.[146] The government's consultative document on the health and personal social services was based on the premise that during a period of economic recession, expenditure on these services has to be curtailed, with the result that priorities for the limited resources have to be explicitly stated. The document listed the government's priorities in the following order: the elderly, the mentally handicapped, the mentally ill, children and families with children, acute and general hospital services, and, finally, hospital maternity services. No updating or upgrading of standards this time – in fact an implicit admission that standards would have to fall in some areas.[147]

Though this was a consultative document meant to raise issues for discussion and consultation among all concerned, all its main ideas were incorporated in the government's directive document in the following year – with the bold title 'The Way Forward'. The same list of priorities was put forward and the same warnings for the need for constraints were sounded. 'A more rapid rate of growth, both of revenue and capital', the minister warned, 'must depend on an improvement in the general economic situation. I hope we shall not have to wait too long.'[148] In spite of the fact that priorities were set and previously established guidelines were accepted, the new document gave local authorities more freedom than before to proceed at their own pace and direction. Priorities 'simply provide illustrative indications of the *national* long-term direction of strategic development within resource constraints; they do not represent specific targets to be achieved by declared dates in any locality.'[149]

The worsening economic situation and the election of the Conservative government that was determined to reduce expenditure in the social services has meant the abandonment of national guidelines as regards both level of provision and priorities in the personal social services. The evidence given by the DHSS to the House of Commons Committee on the Social Services makes this abundantly clear. Asked by the Committee what were the criteria for minimum acceptable standards of personal social service provision, the DHSS replied as follows: 'The Department has no formalised or precisely quantified criteria of what represents minimum acceptable standards of personal social services provision by a local authority.'[150] The minister for the social services forthrightly endorsed this position and linked it to the economic situation. He felt that 'it is better to leave it to local authorities for themselves to decide rather than to try to set down national standards, certainly at a time when local authorities can turn round and say that they simply do not have the resources to do it in the first place.'[151] Moreover, very rarely indeed does the DHSS pull up local authorities because their services are below standard. Apart from the economic situation, two other reasons were given for this new approach: local conditions vary so much that national standards can be meaningless at the local level; and local authorities are not only in a better position to assess the standard of their services but they should also have the right to do so, so long as it is within the government's policy of financial constraints. We will return to these arguments in the concluding section of this chapter for they are relevant to the other social services.

The debate over standards has been mainly about resource inputs: annual expenditure, number of staff per 1,000 population, number of places in homes and hostels, the physical and crowding conditions of establishments, etc. Very rarely has there been any discussion of standards or guidelines in relation to service outputs, largely because there is no agreement about these — what they are and how they can be operationally defined for easy evaluation. On the few occasions that brief statements in relation to outputs can be found in the literature, they refer to broad goals, rather than to specific objectives — to use Henderson's phraseology mentioned earlier in the chapter. Thus the Seebohm Report, which led to the creation of the personal social services departments, felt that the new departments should embody 'a wider conception of social service, directed to the well-being of the community and not only of social casualties'. Moreover, they should be concerned not only with the 'treatment and relief' but also with the 'prevention' of social problems.[152] Admirable and necessary though the declaration of such broad goals is, they defy meaningful evaluation. Moreover, excessive emphasis on such goals can divert attention from the real task — the setting of specific objectives. There are, of course, other reasons why so little real debate has taken place on specific objectives — the imprecise nature of the aims of some of the personal social services and the near impossibility of establishing causal links between resource inputs and service outputs.

The purpose of the remainder of this section is not to assess the adequacy of the personal social services but to examine the extent to which minimum standards in inputs for two client groups have been achieved. The elderly and the mentally handicapped have been chosen because the elderly are the largest single group among those vying for the attention of the personal social services, while the mentally handicapped have been the most neglected group. Moreover, the DHSS Consultative Document in 1976, referred to several times so far, placed the elderly and the mentally handicapped as first and second respectively in terms of priorities for government action. Many of the issues raised and discussed for these two groups will be of relevance to the physically handicapped and the mentally ill − two of the other three client groups of the personal social services. Table 2.19 provides a rough estimate of the growth of those social services that are used mainly or

TABLE 2.19
Services for the elderly provided by local authorities

Year and service	Number in whole-time equivalent	In proportion to the population	Government guideline
Home helps:			
1953	15,397	2.9[a]	
1961	25,161	4.5[a]	
1974	41,000	6[a]	12[a]
1981	46,600	6.5[a]	12[a]
Home nurses:			
1953	6,829	0.15[b]	
1961	7,658	0.17[b]	
1974	11,000	0.25[b]	0.4[b]
1979	13,900	0.31[b]	0.4[b]
Day centre places:			
1974	11,500	2[a]	3-4[a]
1981	27,200	4.5[a]	3-4[a]
Meals (per week):			
1974	600,000	92[a]	200[a]
1981	796,000	122[a]	200[a]

[a] Per 1,000 elderly
[b] Per 1,000 population

Sources: *Health and Welfare*, Cmnd 1973, HMSO, 1963, pp. 16-20
   Priorities for Health and Personal Social Services, HMSO, 1976, p. 39
   Second Report from the Social Services Committee, vol. II, HMSO,
   1982, p. 25

exclusively by the elderly living in their own homes. Government policy during the 1960s and 1970s has been to encourage the vast majority of old people to live at home supported mainly by their relatives, friends and neighbours and, to a far lesser extent, by the statutory and voluntary services. Thus the burden of responsibility has always been laid on the family and the community with the statutory and voluntary services acting in a subsidiary − but important − role.

It is evident from Table 2.19 that none of the government guidelines, with the exception of day centres, has been fully achieved. The number of home helps has trebled but the proportion per 1,000 elderly is still about half the required figure. Moreover, the government guideline has not been on the over-generous side. Townsend and Wedderburn, for example, estimated the need for home helps at 20 per 1,000 elderly.[153] There is a great deal of evidence which shows that large numbers of elderly in need of home help do not receive it. Hunt's government-sponsored study showed that only 8.9 per cent of the elderly received visits from a home help during a six-month period, as Table 2.20 shows. Even among the most needy groups of the elderly,

TABLE 2.20
Visits received by old people during six months

Visits received from	%
Doctor	33.3
Health visitor	4.4
District nurse	7.8
Home help	8.9
Council welfare officer	4.9
Social security officer	6.0
Meals-on-wheels	2.6
Mobile library	2.8
Other official person	3.6
Voluntary organisation	2.7
Minister of religion	16.2
Insurance man	48.7
None of these	25.0
Insurance man is the only visitor	23.4

Source: A. Hunt, *The Elderly at Home*, HMSO, 1978, Table 11.2.1, p. 87

the proportions were modest − 27 per cent of those aged 85 and over received home help; 31 per cent of the bedfast and house-bound; and 19 per cent of those living alone. She concluded that 'Although those groups who appear on the face of it to be in greatest need of home help are most likely to receive it, in all these groups the majority do not do so.'[154] The rise in the numbers and proportion of home nurses is even lower than that of home help, in spite of the contribution home nursing can make to easing the pressure on hospital and residential accommodation. The number of meals served has also increased but again it has only just reached about half the guideline number. When assessing the rate of progress, it is important to bear in mind changes in the circumstances of the elderly over the years which make for increased need for such services. Bebington's review of social service provision during the period 1966-80 shows that improvements have taken place but these must be seen in the light of 'the rising tide of social isolation, as well as increasing incapacity which has chiefly affected the very elderly living in the community'.[155] Finally, it is a sad commentary on the adequacy of the personal and other social services that an unknown, but substantial number of old people still die of hypothermia. The number of deaths of people aged 65 and over during the period October to March exceeds the corresponding number for the period April to September quite substantially — 39,000 in 1972 — and though it is not possible to be certain about how many of these extra deaths are due to hypothermia, it is, nevertheless, a sharp reminder of the inadequacies of all the services for the elderly.[156] The vast majority of old people have no visitor from any of the statutory or voluntary services, as Table 2.20 shows. The insurance man still remains the most familiar face to most old people.

Ninety-five per cent of the elderly live at home and the other 5 per cent, mainly the very old, the infirm and the isolated, are in geriatric hospitals or local authority and voluntary residential homes. During the 1950s, residential establishments were more positively accepted by official policy circles than they have been since the 1960s when community care became the preferred method of care.[157] However strong the emphasis is on keeping the old in the community, there will always be those for whom residential care is the only possible form of care. As a government report put it, the decision on the type of care must depend on the 'individual's frailty, the person's own wishes or the burdens on informal carers.'[158]

In spite of the emphasis on community care, the total number of people living away from home has not declined very much over the last two decades. This, however, must be seen in the context of an increase in the numbers of the very elderly who are more likely to be in residential care. In 1960, there were 66,000 in geriatric hospitals and 74,000 in local authority residential establishments, representing 9.4 and 14 per 1,000 elderly respectively. In 1974, the number in hospitals was about 55,000 and in residential establishments 120,000; the corresponding proportions per 1,000 elderly were 8.6 and 18.5 respectively. In 1981, the corresponding numbers were about 51,500 and 117,500, while the proportions were 7.9 and 18 respectively. The official guideline for places in geriatric hospitals has been 10 per 1,000 elderly, while for residential establishments it has been 25 per 1,000 elderly. Indeed, the need for places in residential establishments is still so strong with the result that decisions on whom to admit and whom not to tend to be arbitrary. A number of local studies have shown that those who are admitted are not very different from those who are refused admission in terms of need and that applicants may be offered a place in one week when they were refused admission the week before. Excessive scarcity always leads to arbitrary forms of rationing.[159]

The physical standards of care in residential establishments have improved over the years but the social standards of care still leave a great deal to be desired. A recent DHSS study of 124 local authority, voluntary and private homes in London found that 'the standards of physical care in the vast majority of the homes visited was good, but in many the quality of life fell far short of what might be expected.' The criteria used for the quality of life were privacy for the residents, contacts with the local community, visits to the local shops, resident participation in the running of the home, social activities, staff encouragement to residents to maintain any interests they may have, etc. Using such criteria, homes were classified as follows:

> 35% of the homes were described as being relaxed and informal in their organisation and a little more than half of these were described as providing a home, in the true sense, for their residents. 23% were thought to be fairly relaxed places without being described as homely. 18% of the homes were said to be organised on a hospital or nursing home model but two-thirds of these were said to be run in a fairly relaxed way. The third model described was the hotel or guest house and 9% of the homes were grouped under this heading. The remaining 15% were categorised as institutional and the words 'rigid', 'unrelaxed', or 'tense' were used most often to describe them.[160]

In brief, the stated aims of government policy for helping 'the elderly maintain independent lives in their own homes for as long as possible' and for providing residential care to those 'who can no longer continue to live independently in the community',[161] remain unfulfilled. Most of the official guidelines for the various service inputs remain unachieved. It is this gap between rhetoric and reality that led Walker to conclude that 'there is no evidence to suggest that the policy of community care for the elderly (even in the restricted sense of preventive support provided by welfare workers) is any less precarious or ambiguous than it was in the early 1960s.'[162]

The mentally handicapped have always been the most stigmatised and segregated client group in the personal social services. Until the creation of the National Health Service, mentally handicapped adults were segregated in large asylums while community care services were almost non-existent. It is important to bear this in mind when reviewing the progress made recently towards achieving the minimum standards of service inputs recommended by various government and other reports. A complicating factor in discussions and plans for the mentally handicapped is that the exact number of even the severely mentally handicapped is not known. Estimates from local studies put the approximate number of severely mentally handicapped persons in Britain at 160,000, i.e. four to five out of 1,000 children and two out of 1,000 adults. Another complicating factor is that a varying proportion of the severely mentally handicapped suffer from other disabilities — 4 per cent being blind, 3 per cent are deaf, 13 per cent non-ambulant, 20 per cent severely incontinent, and so on.

The White Paper on the Mentally Handicapped in 1971 was the first real attempt to set guidelines for service inputs. These guidelines were, of course, based on a new philosophy concerning the mentally handicapped as persons and as members of society at large. This was that the mentally handicapped had every right to live independent lives and that society had a duty to enable them to do so.[163] The generous guidelines and the broad-minded general principles of the White Paper have become, in theory at least, part of government policies and they have been admirably reiterated by a more recent government committee, the Jay Committee, which was also honest enough to recognise the serious problems involved in translating theory to practice.

> The goals of our model are unashamedly idealistic, and such goals will not be achieved without professional staff, the community, and society as a whole accepting and committing themselves to a very different pattern of services and a very different role in society for the handicapped person.[164]

Table 2.21 shows that a varying degree of progress has been made towards the achievement of the targets set by the White Paper for 1991. Whether the pace of such progress is to continue or whether it will be slowed down by present government reductions in public expenditure remains to be seen. Training centres were to play a pivotal role in rehabilitating as many mentally handicapped adults as possible to .sheltered employment and in the open labour market. The number of places in these centres has quadrupled since 1961 but they have to increase by two-thirds in the next decade before they can reach the 1991 target. Various surveys of the work of such centres have come up with similar findings: their physical standards are adequate but they are far less successful in integrating their trainees with the rest of the labour market. The study by Whelan and Speake showed that very few people left the training centres — 12 per cent in the year prior to the study — and even fewer join the open labour market or sheltered workshops —

TABLE 2.21
Personal social services and hospital provision for the mentally
handicapped – adults

Year and service	Number	In proportion to population (per 1,000)	Guideline (per 1,000 population by 1991)
Places in training centres:			
1961	10,605	0.22	
1974	32,000	0.68	1.50
1981	43,407	0.92	
Residents in hostels and homes:			
1965	1,446	0.03	
1974	7,800	0.17	0.60
1981	13,395	0.28	
Residents in hospitals:			
1961	61,164	1.3	
1974	50,000	1.1	0.55
1981	44,100	0.9	

Sources: Health and Welfare, Cmnd 1973, HMSO, 1963, pp. 16-20
Priorities for Health and Personal Social Services, HMSO, 1976, p. 39
Second Report from the Social Services Committee, Vol. II, HMSO,
1982, p. 25
DHSS, Better Services for the Mentally Handicapped, Cmnd 4683,
HMSO, 1971

4 per cent and 0.4 per cent respectively.[165] Carter's study confirmed
these findings and also commented on the lack of specialised training
for handicapped trainees with different degrees of disability. Centres
tended to be too generalised with the result that they could not possibly devise a programme that could meet the abilities and needs of
different groups of handicapped persons. If changes towards specialisation were not made, declared Carter, 'day services for mental handicap
may become little more than big buildings in which the mentally handicapped are protected from the outside world – an outcome which is a
long way from their intention.'[166]

Table 2.21 also shows that progress towards emptying the large
hospitals for the mentally handicapped has been extremely slow and at
that rate the guideline for 1991 is unlikely to be reached. The main
reason for this is the absence of any real housing policy for the
mentally handicapped. It is assumed that community care means care
by the family and that admission to hospital or to a home will take
place when the family cannot cope. Once admitted to hospital, handi-

capped people will remain there for a long time. Mittler refers to figures which show that '42% of residents living in mental hospitals have lived in the same hospitals for over twenty years; some 80% for more than five years, and a further 15% for periods of one to five years.'[167] The longer this situation continues, the more difficult becomes the rehabilitation of such long-stay patients to the community as ordinary people.

Various surveys have shown that a large proportion of the mentally handicapped in hospitals and residential establishments could cope with living in the community if there was adequate housing and staff backing. The government-established team for overseeing the work of hospitals and residential establishments for the mentally handicapped assessed the ability of 15,000 adult inmates and reached the following conclusions. First, 27 per cent of those in hospital and 71 per cent of those in residential care could be 'discharged home or to hostel immediately without any special facilities necessary for management, apart from those normally provided in a local authority hostel'. Second, 15 per cent should 'be suitable for discharge home or to a hostel after a period of pre-discharge training'. Third, 16 per cent of those in hospital and 9 per cent of those in local authority residential care were considered 'suitable for care in the community after intensive training and with greater supervision than is usually required'. Fourth, only 42 per cent of those in hospital and 2 per cent of those in residential care were so heavily handicapped as to require long-term residential care.[168] Clearly there are thousands of mentally handicapped people who should not be kept in residential accommodation.

Conditions in residential establishments are far from satisfactory in spite of the progress made over the years. The staff/patient ratios in 1976 were as follows: 7.3:1 for all hospital wards; 3.8:1 for children's wards; 4.7:1 for all hostels; and 1.8:1 for children's hostels. These figures were an improvement over the situation in 1965 when the staff/patient ratio for all wards was 16.8:1 and for children's wards 11.1:1.[169] Nevertheless, the Jay Committee recommended 'an approximate doubling in the numbers of the mental handicap residential care staff' for the model of care that it considered necessary.[170] Moreover, the educational qualifications of the staff were not very high: two-thirds of the nursing and hostel staff had no O levels or equivalent qualifications.[171] Finally, many wards in hospitals and hostels are overcrowded even by the modest government standards of 1969: 17 per cent of all adult wards in 1976 had over forty residents and 18 per cent had 31.40 residents; for children's wards, the corresponding figures were nil and 3 per cent respectively.[172]

The overwhelming body of evidence shows that while some progress has been made, the long-term aims set by the White Paper for the residential and day care services remain largely unfulfilled in both quantitative and qualitative terms. What also needs changing is the non-accepting attitude of the general public towards the mentally handicapped. Both resources and attitudes need to be improved substantially before the modest aims of the White Paper, let alone the idealism of the Jay Committee, can be fulfilled.

Most of the comments for the elderly and the mentally handicapped apply to a greater or lesser extent to the mentally ill and the physically handicapped. Government targets were established, expectations raised but only to be partially fulfilled. Of particular relevance is the employment quota scheme for the physically handicapped establishment in 1944 because it is the sole responsibility of the central government. Under the scheme, employers with twenty or more workers have to employ a quota of disabled workers – 3 per cent. Experience has shown that the fortunes of the scheme have waxed and waned in line with the ups and downs of the level of unemployment. The central government has done very little to enforce the scheme and it has prosecuted only ten employers in thirty-six years for non-compliance – a very disappointing record by any standards.

Conclusion

The achievement of minimum standards on a national scale has been the central aim of social policy during the years covered by this study. A great deal has been achieved particularly in the area of universal social services – social security, health and education. A great deal, however, remains to be done particularly in relation to residual services – housing and personal social services. Moreover, all service provision for ethnic groups leaves much to be desired.

The discussion in this chapter has, of necessity, concentrated more on inputs than on outputs. It has, moreover, used rather broad, and at times, crude criteria of minimum standards in inputs. It has not taken enough into account either the quality of inputs or the nature of the social environment in which inputs operate. Yet research evidence has shown that the ethos and the organisational structure of an institution can have a bearing on its outputs. Rutter's work has shown that schools which provide a sub-standard educational experience for their pupils in terms of early leaving, truancy, delinquency, and the like are not necessarily deficient in quantitative inputs such as number of teachers, buildings and equipment but in such qualitative inputs as tradition, commitment and administrative efficiency.[173] Various studies of residential institutions for the elderly, the mentally handicapped, the mentally ill and children have highlighted the importance of such organisational processes as participation, communication, specialisation, etc., in their quality of caring.[174] A full-scale study of the achievement of minimum standards will have to take these into account as well as the problematic nature of the relationship between central and local government which is so characteristic in the area of social services. 'One of the biggest challenges to effective democratic government', wrote Barbara Castle as Secretary of State for Social Services in 1976, 'is how to reconcile two potentially conflicting aims: central government must be able to establish and promote certain essential national priorities, while the local agencies of government should have the maximum scope for making their own local choices in the light of their local needs.'[175] Social administrators have traditionally taken the view that it is the duty of the central government to ensure that all local authorities provide services which meet at least the nationally established minimum standards. The central government has rightly been seen as the facilitator and at times the protector of social services against unenthusiastic local authorities. Today, however, the position is rather different: it is the central government which is unenthusiastic about social service expenditure and it is local authorities, some at least, which are pressing for improvements. The issue of what is the right balance of power between central and local government is, therefore, more problematic today than it was in the past for those who support the improvement of social services.

Minimum standards, as defined in this chapter, cannot possibly be achieved under a government as hostile to the very idea of a welfare state as is the Conservative government of 1983. Even under a pro-welfare state government there will be difficult problems, though not as severe as those in relation to the reduction of inequalities discussed in the Conclusion of the next chapter. As mentioned earlier, the achievement of minimum standards is not, theoretically speaking, incompatible with welfare capitalism. A reforming government anxious to enforce such standards must be prepared, as a first step, to improve its monitoring, inspecting and enforcing services; it must, of course, be prepared to increase expenditure in some services, and it must certainly be prepared to face up to vested interests.

3

Social policy and inequality

Inequality has always been a politically contested issue for it is related to the distribution of power and resources in society. What is theoretically and politically interesting and puzzling is not that it has been defended by the powerful and the better-off sections of the community but that it has been so widely accepted by those who suffer as a result of its continuance. The concern here is not about inequalities which are natural but about inequalities which are socially determined. In the past, most inequalities were seen as natural and were defended as such. Today many inequalities are increasingly seen as socially determined and their defence has become both more difficult and more sophisticated. The defence of wealth inheritance and of income inequalities, for example, is no longer based on some natural or divine right but on social science theories which explain inequality as the result of a trade-off with efficiency, economic growth and prosperity. It is this retreat from natural to social justifications of inequality that provides some hope for egalitarians in the future.

As it was pointed out in the previous chapter, the reconstruction and expansion of the social services during the last war were dominated by one central principle: universality. It was generally believed that if services were made available free to all, then they would be used by everyone who needed them. Universality became identified with equality. Indeed, the various government White Papers that preceded the reorganisation of individual social services gave implicit support to this feeling of vague egalitarianism stemming out of universalism. Thus the impression was created that social services would gradually reduce inequalities in British society. It was never made clear, however, how this was to happen or indeed what kind of equality would result from universal social service provision.

Even though both the Labour and the Conservative Parties supported universal social service provision all through the 1950s and 1960s, they were divided on the issue of equality. Brittan correctly observed in the late 1960s that there were no differences between left and right in British politics on most important domestic issues, except 'around the concept of "equality"'.[1] But even on this issue, party political differences were not absolute, as Beckerman pointed out. 'Even with respect to the equality issue there will still only be a difference of degree; the Conservatives might not want the income distribution to become far less equal than it is, and the Labour Party might not want complete equality of income distribution.'[2] In brief, then, the two main parties have adopted rather different philosophical stands in relation to equality though this does not mean that they have translated these into practical policies when in government. It is a political scenario that has not proved at all helpful to the cause of equality. The practice of consensus politics has meant no determined action against inequalities by any Labour government. In one sense, social services inevitably reduce inequalities. In an influential paper, Marshall argued that social services have brought about

> a general enrichment of the concrete substance of civilized life, a general reduction of risk and insecurity, an equalization between the more and the less fortunate at all levels — between the healthy and the sick, the employed and the unemployed, the old and the active, the bachelor and the father of the large family. Equalization is not so much between classes as between individuals within a population which is now treated for this purpose as though it were one class.[3]

Marshall is referring to the reduction of horizontal rather than vertical inequalities. There is a great deal of truth in this general argument; inequalities of this kind have been reduced.

The concern of this chapter, however, is with vertical inequalities — between social classes, ethnic groups and the sexes. More emphasis will be given to social class inequalities, partly because they are more adequately documented and partly because they partially account for ethnic and sex inequalities. In order to give some structure to the discussion, each of the major social services will be examined under three headings: access, i.e. geographical distribution of social services; use, i.e. the extent to which different groups make use of services; and outcome, i.e. the benefit derived from the use of services. An attempt will also be made to look at changes in the years since the last war in order to establish long-term trends, if any. The difficulties are obvious: lack of adequate data over the period and, more importantly, the thorny issue of cause and effect. An improvement or deterioration in the health conditions of a group in society may be due to factors other than access to or use of medical services. Similar problems apply to education and, to a lesser extent, to the other social services.

Education

The degree of access to any social service can be measured in terms of either equality or equity. An equal distribution takes into account only the size of the population groups that are being compared, while an equitable distribution takes into account the varying needs for the service of the groups as well. Webster and Stewart had this in mind, even though the terms they used were evenness and fairness, when they pointed out that an 'uneven distribution . . . may be regarded as "fair" if the variation is related to need. Conversely a distribution which is identified as even . . . may be extremely unfair.'[4] The same comments apply to the issue of use of the social services, too.

Most of the discussion on variations in access to schooling has concentrated on provision in the inner city areas. The adverse position of children living in these areas in the 1960s was abundantly documented by major government reports. Thus the Newsom Report, which examined secondary schooling for children of average or less than average ability, concluded that the proportion of schools in slum areas which were seriously inadequate was twice as high as the proportion of all schools in the sample.[5] Similarly, the Plowden Report for primary schools concluded that schools in deprived urban areas 'are quite untypical of schools in the rest of the country'. They were older, more overcrowded, less well furnished, more depressing, and so on.[6] In brief, both the quantity and quality of schooling in inner city areas in the 1960s was inferior to that in the rest of the country. These are, of course, areas of high working class and minority group concentration. Successive governments have, as expected, deplored this state of affairs but have not done anywhere near enough to remedy it.

The relationship between the socio-economic character of a local authority (L.A.) and its expenditure on education is a crucial issue but it has not received adequate research attention. Midwinter's examination of government data concluded that the pupil-teacher ratio of rich L.A.s was no better than that of poor L.A.s.[7] Boaden's examination of L.A. expenditure on education reached the conclusion that 'it is the poor authorities who spend most, despite their relative poverty,' because they are run by Labour councils which are more favourably disposed towards high expenditure on education than Conservative councils.[8] Byrne and Williamson, however, in their study of eleven L.A.s in the North-East, concluded slightly differently:

> Those authorities with a high proportion in low social classes resident within their area both devote a higher proportion of their income to education than do authorities with higher social class constituencies, and spend their money on primary education rather than secondary education; the reverse being true of 'high social class' authorities.[9]

Support for this comes from a more recent analysis of local education authority expenditure by Howick and Hassani. In relation to primary education, they found considerable variation, with the most generous authority spending 70 per cent more than the lowest authority. London boroughs spent more than other metropolitan boroughs, which in turn spent more than county authorities. Moreover, they found 'that spending does tend to be higher in areas suffering from adverse conditions; and that such high spending is associated with inner city deprivation (immigrants, overcowding, and one-parent families) rather than with traditional working class areas (unskilled workers and large families)'.[10] For secondary education, similar variations were found, with the highest spending authority surpassing the expenditure of the lowest by 60 per cent. They found the same general correlation between socio-economic variables and level of expenditure as in primary education. There were, however, a number of variables other than positive discrimination policies, which accounted for this relationship. The result was that 'only in London is there convincing evidence that educationally disadvantaged pupils are likely to receive slightly higher expenditure.'[11] They also found a tendency for Labour-controlled councils to spend more on education than Conservative councils but with a number of exceptions to this tendency.

There is no evidence to show what the position was at the end of the last war but in all probability there has been an improvement over the years. Equalising educational provision for children of different socio-economic backgrounds does not do away with the educational disabilities of working class children vis-à-vis middle class children. What is required is a policy of allocating resources in such quantity and quality in favour of working class or ethnic minority groups as will enable them to have the same effective equality of opportunity in schools as middle-class children. In other words, what is needed is not only an equal but an equitable geographical distribution of educational resources.

What then of the use made of schools by the various socio-economic groups? The most striking feature of the post-war period has been the increase of use of educational establishments by all socio-economic groups. This remarkable growth in the use of schools masks some equally remarkable differences between the social classes. The raising of the compulsory school-leaving age, first to 15 and then to 16, and the expansion of further education account for the growth in education. This, however, should not be confused with increased equality. Inequalities of use in the crucial aspects of schooling have changed very little over the years. Even within the compulsory school age, inequalities have remained. Thus the proportion of secondary school children going to grammar schools has always been positively related to social class. The recent introduction of comprehensive schools appears to have made little difference to the kind of schooling that children from different socio-economic backgrounds receive. Streaming within comprehensive schools is common practice and the evidence available shows that children from professional backgrounds are far more likely to be in the top streams than working class children. Streaming seems to operate as much on class lines as the old division between grammar schools on one hand and the rest of secondary schools on the other.[12]

Table 3.1 gives a picture of the situation today in relation to social class and school attendance. It shows that the children of the higher socio-economic groups are more likely than their working-class counterparts to attend nursery schools, as well as independent schools, at both the primary and the secondary school stage. The vast majority of children, however, are educated in state schools — at least 93 per cent of primary children and 92 per cent of secondary children. The proportion of young people staying on at school between the crucial ages of 16 and 19 has always been heavily weighted towards the upper classes. The government reports of the 1950s amply documented the wastage of ability among working-class children. The first report in 1954 showed how the advantageous position of children from professional family backgrounds increased with age,[13] while the second report in 1959 demonstrated not only that 'the available resources of men (and presumably also of women) of high ability are not fully used by the system,' but that this wastage was highest among men of the lower socio-economic groups.[14] As late as 1975, the proportion of young people in grammar schools between the ages of 16 and 19 was 14 per cent for the professional group and only 1 per cent for the unskilled manual group.[15] The same picture emerges from the study by Halsey et al., as Table 3.2 shows. The proportion of young people from classes I and II staying on at school until the age of 18 or later increased by 2.4 times between the first and the last cohort, while the corresponding proportions for the other two groups of classes are 2.3 and 2.1 times.

TABLE 3.1
Socio-economic groups and type of school, Great Britain, 1976 and 1977 (%)

Type of school and age	Professional	Employers & managers	Intermediate non-manual	Junior non-manual	Skilled manual	Semi-skilled manual	Unskilled manual	Total
Under 5 years:								
Day nursery/playgroup								
Nursery school or class	41	39	38	35	31	29	28	34
5-10 years:								
Primary school	85	88	92	96	97	98	95	93
Independent school	15	11	7	3	2	0	0	5
Other (including special schools)	1	1	1	2	1	2	4	1
11-15 years:								
All local authority schools	73	86	90	93	96	94	91	92
Independent schools	26	12	10	4	1	1	1	5
Other (including special schools)	1	2	0	3	3	5	7	3

Source: OPCS, General Household Survey, 1977, HMSO, 1979, Table 5.1, p. 73

TABLE 3.2
Socio-economic group and school leaving age by birth cohort, England and Wales

Father's social class	Percentage staying on at school until 18 or later			
	1913-22	*1923-32*	*1933-42*	*1943-52*
I and II	15.7	20.0	32.2	38.8
III, IV and V	6.1	6.2	5.9	14.4
VI, VII and VIII	3.1	2.3	3.8	6.4

Source: A.H. Halsey, A.F. Heath and J.M. Judge, *Origins and Destinations*, Clarendon Press, 1980, Table 8.11, p. 140

Classes I and II have taken greater advantage of educational expansion than have Halsey's other social groupings.

These socio-economic differences in school-leaving age are not due entirely to IQ differences. Thus Douglas found in the early 1960s that even among the most able, working-class pupils were more likely to leave school early than middle-class pupils with the same IQ scores. Interestingly enough, he found that the wastage of ability was lower in regions like Wales, where the provision of grammar school places was relatively high. It seems as if the lower the competition for places, the greater the likelihood of working-class children staying on or perhaps not being pushed out.[16]

As mentioned, socio-economic inequalities in the use of private schools are very marked. What is more unexpected is that such inequalities have increased over the years. Halsey and his associates show that while about 50 per cent of the pupils in private primary schools were from the professional class in the age cohorts 50-59 and 30-39 years, the corresponding proportion for the youngest age cohort, 20-29 years, was almost 70 per cent.[17] A similar trend applies to private secondary schools, since 70 per cent of children in HMC secondary schools are recruited from private primary schools. Looking at all selective schools together — grammar, direct grant and private — little change in inequalities has taken place over the years spanned by Halsey's study. As Halsey concludes 'the likelihood of a working class boy receiving a selective education in the mid-fifties and mid-sixties was very little different from that of his parents' generation thirty years earlier.'[18]

Inequality of use naturally continues and sharpens at the university stage. Over the years, the picture is one of both remarkable growth and of entrenched class inequalities. During the forty-year period covered by Halsey's study, the proportion of university students from classes I and II increased 3.7 times, from classes III, IV and V 4.2 times, and for

TABLE 3.3
Social class and attendance at university by birth cohort, England and Wales (%)

Father's social class	1913-22	1923-32	1933-42	1943-52
I and II	7.2	15.9	23.7	26.4
III, IV and V	1.9	4.0	4.1	8.0
VI, VII and VIII	0.9	1.2	2.3	3.1
All	1.8	3.4	5.4	8.5

Source: A. Halsey et al., *Origins and Destinations*, op. cit., Table 10.8, p. 188

classes VI, VII and VIII only 3.4 times (see Table 3.3).

Though Halsey's figures reach only up to the mid-1960s, other data show that the expansion of universities from the late 1960s onwards has not benefited the working class as much as the professional classes. The reasons for this are difficult to establish but it may well be that the university expansion coincided with an even greater expansion of candidates with A levels, with the result that competition for university places did not ease. The annual returns of the Universities Central Council for Admissions show that, if anything, a greater proportion of students was recruited from professional backgrounds in 1979 than in 1969, even after taking into account demographic changes, as Table 3.4 shows. The reductions in university places introduced by the Conservative government in the early 1980s are likely to widen even further the gap between the higher and the lower socio-economic groups among the student population.

We now turn to examine briefly the influence of sex on the use of schools. The first report on the wastage of ability in the early 1950s provided abundant evidence that girls, particularly those from lower socio-economic backgrounds, left school earlier than boys of similar class position.[19] The situation has improved substantially since then and girls have achieved parity with boys as far as staying on at school. The changes in relation to women's use of higher education, however, are less straightforward and perhaps less encouraging for women and egalitarians. The ratio of girls to boys going to university fluctuated from 70 per cent in 1925; 50 per cent in 1937; 47 per cent in 1950; 50 per cent in 1960; 66 per cent in 1973; and it has remained at that level since. The position of the two sexes has been the exact opposite in relation to further education, and to teacher training. In both these areas of higher education women have always outnumbered men. The ratio of boys to girls going on to further education was 50 per cent in 1925, and 63 per cent in 1978. The figures for teacher training were

TABLE 3.4
Parental occupation and university admissions, UK (%)

Occupation of parent	Accepted students		Economically active males aged 40-54 yrs	
	1968-9	1978-9	1968-9	1971
Manual workers	27	23	64	62
Clerical, sales and service workers and armed forces	27	23	22	20
Administrators and managers	15	17	6	8
Professional and technical	31	37	8	10
Total	100	100	100	100

Source: Universities Central Council for Admissions, 'Statistical Supplements' to the annual reports for 1968-9 and 1978-9, Tables E.2, p. 19 and K.4, p. 16 respectively

32 per cent and 26 per cent respectively. In brief, sex inequalities in relation to university education have narrowed far more than socio-economic inequalities. There are, however, still substantial differences between the subjects followed in universities and polytechnics, with men far outnumbering women in the science subjects.

The position of ethnic minorities with regard to the use of education services is predictable. Their concentration in the inner city areas where educational provision is generally inferior, as well as the fact that a higher proportion than the British-born is to be found in unskilled and semi-skilled occupations, inevitably mean that their children do less well at schools at all levels. Thus the government enquiry into the educational achievements of West Indian and Asian children in 1978/9 in six local education authorities with high concentration of ethnic minorities showed that West Indian children were under-achieving in relation to other children. As Table 3.5 shows, the proportion of West Indian children that passed one or more A levels was at least six times lower than that of other children, while the proportion that went on to university was three times lower. Asian children performed just as well as other children in the six local education authorities but their admission rate to university was almost half of the corresponding figure for school leavers in all the state schools in England.

How does one measure the outcomes of education? One can refer, of

TABLE 3.5
*Educational achievements of children of ethnic minority groups in 6
local education authorities, 1978/9 (%)*

Ethnic group	A level pass		Destination of school-leavers			
	None	One or more	University	Other further education	Employment	Not known
Asians	87	13	3	18	54	25
West Indians	98	2	1	16	65	18
All other leavers	88	12	3	9	77	11
All maintained school leavers in England	87	13	5	14	74	8

Source: Interim Report of the Committee of Inquiry into the Education of
Children from Ethnic Minority Groups, *West Indian Children in our
Schools*, Cmnd 8273, HMSO, 1981, Tables D and E, pp. 8 and 9
respectively

course, to the intellectual enrichment of individuals and of society but
such a criterion is not amenable to quantification. One is therefore, of
necessity, confined to such outcomes as income, type of occupation,
reading and writing achievements, and the passing of examinations, all
of which are quantifiable to a lesser or greater extent.

Where children attend different types of schools, it is to be expected
that their school attainments will differ. But even where children attend
the same type of school, the available evidence shows that school
attainments vary by socio-economic group from a very early age. The
National Child Development Study, which looked at the progress of
every child born in Great Britain in one week of 1958, found 'a strong
association between social class and reading and arithmetic attainment
at seven years of age. The chances of an unskilled manual worker's
child being a poor reader are six times greater than those of a professional worker's child.'[20] There is no evidence to show whether such
differences have changed over the years. There is evidence, however, to
show that these differences in school attainment at age 7 do not
decrease, but rather increase as children get older.

As far as passing examinations is concerned, the obvious applies. The
proportion of children passing Ordinary and Advanced level examinations is positively correlated with social class. Halsey and his associates
provide abundant evidence in support of this over the years. They attribute it to the class differences in staying on at school and they point to
the similarity in performance of working-class candidates who do take
public examinations with other candidates. 'The relatively few working

class survivors to O and A level competed on equal terms with their classmates from professional and white collar families.'[21] But they do not provide detailed evidence about the number and grades of O and A level passes by children of different socio-economic groups. This is very important for it can decide acceptance or rejection by universities and other higher education establishments. Byrne makes this same point in relation to the apparent equalisation of examination results between the sexes. She notes that a more detailed look at the results above shows that boys are more likely to obtain three A level passes than girls, even though the gap between them has narrowed over the years.[22]

The social class bias in university entrance is not matched by a corresponding bias in university performance. The study by Kelsall, Poole and Kuhn suggests that working-class students perform almost as well as other students. The main difference is that working-class students are more likely to obtain an ordinary degree than other students,[23] but ordinary degrees are, of couse, awarded very rarely.

The human capital theory maintains that increased education raises the earning capacity of the individual and that this is reflected in the higher earnings of people with higher and further education. The available statistical evidence bears out this crude relationship between years of education and earnings. Thus government data for men in full-time employment in 1977 shows that men with university education have earnings which are 55 per cent higher than those with basic schooling. Further analysis of data shows that this is not due to either age or hours worked.[24] A similar picture emerges in the case of women except that women's earnings at all levels are only two-thirds of men's. For both men and women, of course, the differences in real income between the university and the school group are greater than those shown by money income alone because of the better fringe benefits provided in professional and middle-class occupations. The differences widen even further when account is taken of the more satisfying nature of professional occupations.

The relationship between education and earnings, however, is complicated by the influence of such other factors as intelligence and social class, and such personal qualities as motivation and perseverance. Most of the evidence in this area is American and it is contradictory. Becker's review of American data concluded that further education was significantly correlated with high earnings after taking into account both measured ability and social class background.[25] Bowles, however, concluded slightly differently from his review of American data: social class background was more important than years of schooling in deciding a person's earnings.[26] The study by Taubman and Wales of males in the top half of the IQ distribution in the United States concluded that for high school graduates 'ability is a more important determinant of the range of income distribution than is education.'[27] The same study also corroborated the finding of other studies that the status of the college attended, apart from the years of attendance, was closely related to future earnings. Jencks, referring to income from all sources including work, concluded that when social class background and measured ability were taken into account, schooling had only a small effect on income. He estimated that 'an extra year of elementary or secondary schooling really boosts future income less than 4%; an extra year of college boosts it about 7% and a year of graduate school boosts it about 4%.'[28] There can be legitimate disagreement whether these figures indicate only a small effect of schooling on income. Equally disputed is Jencks's other main conclusion that chance factors are crucial to income. It is tempting to attribute an unwarranted significance to these factors because statistical correlations with the more measurable factors leave a certain proportion of income differences unexplained. In a subsequent study, Jencks acknowledged that he may have under-estimated the contribution of education to earnings and anyway his conclusions were 'premature'.[29] This brings him more in line with the findings of a British study by Psacharopoulos. Using data from the General Household Survey for 1972 on 6,873 male employees and using a method of analysis similar, but not identical, to that of Jencks, Psacharopoulos found 'that personal characteristics explain a higher fraction of earnings variance in the U.K. than in the U.S. and that education has a sizeable direct effect on income as well as an indirect effect through occupation'.[30]

The general conclusions that can be drawn from these and other studies are, first, that it is not possible to separate fully the effects of education on earnings from those of other factors, particularly those of such abstract personal qualities as motivation, perseverance, ability to make decisions, etc. Second, in so far as modern complex statistical studies can separate the influence of some of these factors, education is important, though not dominating. Whether, of course, the association between education and earnings is due to the improved productivity of individuals or whether education acts simply as a form of credentialism, is an important debate but beyond the scope of this chapter. Third, the effect of extra education on earnings decreases substantially beyond a certain advanced point. In other words, after a certain point, education becomes more a form of consumption for the individual than a form of investment for increasing his earnings further.

Finally, has the substantial expansion of educational provision increased the chances of working-class youth, relative to those of other young people, of obtaining positions at the top end of the occupational ladder? In other words, has it affected favourably their relative chances of upward social mobility? Goldthorpe's recent study that covers the social mobility records of the same age cohorts as those covered by Halsey reached conclusions that are strongly discouraging to egalitarians. The overall rate of social mobility increased during the period but the chances of working-class youths reaching the top positions have not only been always lower than those of young people of higher socio-economic family backgrounds, but these differences have not changed over the years. The second part of Table 3.6, moreover, shows that the chances of youth of working class backgrounds being found in working-class occupations, relative to those of young people from higher socio-economic backgrounds, have increased over the years. Goldthorpe's crisp conclusion is that 'relative mobility rates . . . have remained generally unaltered; and the only trends that may arguably be discerned . . . are indeed ones that would point to a widening of differences in class chances.'[31]

To summarise this section on education: substantial progress has been made in the last twenty years in relation to the reduction of sex inequalities in education. Social class inequalities, however, remain as strong as ever despite the enormous growth in education provision and expenditure. Children from working-class backgrounds have a greater need of education than other children if they are to compete on more equal terms in the labour market. Yet the schools they attend are, on the whole, not as good in terms of status, teacher input and, sometimes, physical surroundings; they make less use of the educational system beyond the compulsory school stage; they are less likely to pass government examinations and go on to university; and they are far more likely to end up in manual occupations, just like their fathers and mothers. All the available evidence also shows that these social class inequalities have declined very little or not at all, and, in some instances, they have increased over the years. This is not unique to this country but it applies also to other advanced industrial societies. It is for this reason that various commentators from different countries have argued that the path towards a more egalitarian distribution of income lies 'outside rather than inside schools, in social and economic change, rather than in educational change'.[32] This is an issue to which we shall return in the final section of this chapter.

Health

The distinction between equity and equality in the distribution and use of social services is crucial to the debate on health inequalities. The need that different socio-economic groups, age-groups, ethnic groups, males and females have for medical services differs because of their differing susceptibility and experience of morbidity and accidents. An

TABLE 3.6
Relative social mobility rates by social class (by birth cohort)

Class of father	Relative chances of being found in classes I and II in 1972				Relative chances of being found in classes VI and VII in 1972			
	1908-17	1918-27	1928-37	1938-47	1908-17	1918-27	1928-37	1938-47
I and II	3.90	3.73	3.89	3.38	1.00	1.00	1.00	1.00
III – V	1.75	1.89	1.98	1.61	2.18	2.19	2.50	2.84
VI and VII	1.00	1.00	1.00	1.00	3.29	3.71	4.47	4.60

Source: J.H. Goldthorpe, *Social Mobility and Class Structure in Modern Britain*, Clarendon Press, 1980, Table 3.2, p. 75

equal distribution of medical services does not provide equitable opportunities for medical care to these different groups. Only an unequal distribution that takes need into account can achieve the goal of effective equality of access to medical care.

The issue is further complicated by the lack of agreement on what constitutes illness and by the inadequacy of data. The extent of illness has been measured in different ways, each of which has its strengths and weaknesses as an index of morbidity. First, it has been measured by the extent of use made of the health services. This approach has the advantage of providing detailed data about the nature and severity of illness in society, but it suffers from the obvious drawback that not everyone who is ill seeks or receives medical treatment and not everyone who seeks medical treatment is necessarily ill. Second, mortality rates have sometimes been used as a proxy for morbidity rates. Because this approach highlights the link between morbidity and mortality, it can direct attention to the improvement of the most crucial areas of the health services more than other approaches. But it is clearly unsatisfactory because illnesses do not always lead to mortality, particularly during childhood and adult life. Third, work absenteeism on account of illness has been used as an index of morbidity. The weaknesses of this approach are that work absenteeism is under-reported in professional occupations, different jobs can be performed with different degrees of ill-health, attitudes to work can sometimes override states of ill-health, particularly of the minor type, and above all, a large proportion of the population is not in the labour force, so their illness goes totally unrecorded. Fourth, the extent of illness in the wider society has sometimes been measured by intensive medical examination of small communities and invariably this approach highlights the iceberg of disease and uncovers far higher rates of illness than the other approaches. Issues inevitably arise too over the representativeness of the relatively small samples which it is possible to involve in such studies. Finally, morbidity rates can be calculated on the basis of data provided by national surveys of self-reported illness. This approach has the advantage of taking into account the individual's perception of health but it suffers from a variety of weaknesses: certain stigmatising illnesses may be under-reported, the threshold of pain can vary between groups as well as between individuals, and the phrasing of questions can affect the outcome of such estimates. Thus when the General Household Survey changed the wording of its questions in 1977 it uncovered far more self-reported 'illness', particularly among the higher socio-economic groups.

Since 1972, the General Household Survey has provided data on self-reported morbidity every year and the discussion here is largely based on the evidence resulting from this survey. The general conclusion that

emerges from the data over the years, apart from 1977-9 when the
questions were altered, is that there is a strong correlation between
social class and self-reported morbidity — a finding which is supported
by the estimates made by studies using other methods. A more detailed
analysis of the General Household Survey data by Le Grand, taking
into account age, sex and socio-economic group, found the correlation
between socio-economic group and illness still valid, though weakened
as Table 3.7 shows. Thus the proportion of unskilled manual workers
reporting longstanding illness or acute sickness was almost three times
as great as that of the professional group. When, however, age and sex
are taken into account, the gap is narrowed to 170 per cent, as Table
3.7 shows.

This correlation between low social class (or poverty) and illness is

TABLE 3.7
Socio-economic group and illness, England and Wales, 1972

Socio-economic group	% of socio-economic group reporting limiting long-standing illness		% of socio-economic group reporting acute sickness		% of socio-economic group reporting either limiting long-standing illness or acute sickness	
	Actual	Age/sex-standardised	Actual	Age/sex-standardised	Actual	Age/sex-standardised
I Professional	6.5	9.5	6.5	6.7	9.5	14.4
II Employers and managers	9.0	9.6	7.1	7.2	14.2	14.6
III Intermediate and junior non manual	10.4	10.3	7.8	7.6	16.0	15.8
IV Skilled manual and own account non professional	11.3	12.5	7.8	8.1	16.6	17.8
V Semi-skilled manual and personal service	16.2	14.5	9.2	9.0	21.9	20.4
VI Unskilled manual	20.8	17.1	11.3	10.9	27.3	24.1

Source: J. Le Grand, 'The Distribution of Public Expenditure, The Case of
Health Care', Economica, vol. 45, May 1978

neither unexpected nor new. The causal relationship between the two, however, 'is not undirectional', as Rein points out.[33] In other words, poverty can cause illness directly and indirectly, and vice-versa. Nevertheless, in this two-way causal relationship, poverty is primarily a cause of illness and only secondarily its effect. The way in which poverty causes illness is not merely through the lack of adequate material resources but also through the associated forms of employment and the culture that develops out of the material situation.

The distribution of medical services has always been both unequal and inequitable. Beginning with the distribution of medical practitioners, a PEP report in 1944 found that it was 'determined primarily by the income level or the rateable capacity of the locality', and perceptively concluded that this disparity 'is even more serious than it appears . . . because "under-doctored" districts are usually also poor districts with high rates of sickness and mortality'.[34] The policy adopted by successive governments has been to encourage general practitioners to practise in under-doctored areas through a series of positive and negative measures. Four types of areas were created for general practice: designated areas where the size of G. P. lists were the highest through to intermediate and restricted areas where G.P. list sizes were the lowest. Doctors were encouraged through financial incentives to practise in designated areas and they were normally refused permission to start practices in restricted areas. Butler's examination of this policy from 1952 to the 1970s shows that the differences between the average list size of the four different areas have declined, but only slightly over the years and with a number of upward and downward fluctuations. He attributes these changes, however, not so much to the positive or negative measures of successive governments, but rather to changes in the total supply of doctors. 'It would be consistent with the data', he writes, 'and defensible on logical grounds to argue that the growth and decline in the designated areas merely reflects, after an appropriate time lapse, the gains or losses to the total stock of G.P.s in the country.'[35] Moreover, doctors tend to practise in their home area or in the area of the medical school where they trained.

A number of studies have looked at the geographical distribution of doctors both in regions and in smaller districts. Cartwright's study in the early 1960s showed that doctors practising in middle-class areas not only had smaller lists of patients than their colleagues in working-class areas but they were also better trained and they had better contacts with hospitals.[36] West and Lowe concluded from their analysis of data in the fourteen hospital board regions in England and Wales that the provision of GPs and health visitors in the region was negatively correlated with such indicators of need as infant mortality rate, still-birth rate and birth rate to mothers aged 15-19 years.[37] Hart's

TABLE 3.8
Average size of GP lists by type of area, England and Wales

Year	Designated	Open/intermediate	Restricted	Total
1952	2,851	2,184	1,581	2,436
1958	2,627	2,247	1,594	2,267
1966	2,845	2,407	1,807	2,453
1974	2,743	2,353	1,939	2,372
1979	2,713	2,304	1,994	2,277
1981[a]	2,697	2,231	1,943	2,201

[a] Figures for 1981 refer to England only

Source: J. Butler, Family Doctors and Public Policy, Routledge & Kegan Paul, 1973, Table A.1, p. 157 (kindly updated by J. Butler)

comparison of medical care provision in poor industrial areas and in affluent areas led him to conclude that there was an 'inverse care law' in the matching of medical resources with medical needs, i.e. 'the availability of good medical care tends to vary inversely with the need of the population served.'[38]

What is more important is the distribution of general practitioners within geographical units that are smaller than regional areas. A study by Skrimshire of three council housing estates of different socio-economic structures concluded that there were differences in medical care provision not only between middle-class and working-class areas but also between solidly working-class and socially mixed areas:

> The provision of health care and the subjective experience of seeking that care are all partly determined by the socio-economic structure of society on an area basis, so that a working class person is at a greater disadvantage if he lives in a predominantly working class area than if he lives in a socially mixed area.[39]

Inner city areas and particularly those in London, according to the Acheson Report, have inferior medical care services in terms of both numbers of general practitioners and surgery facilities, despite the fact that these are the areas with the greatest need — higher morbidity, accident and suicide rates.[40]

The picture in relation to class inequalities in the geographical distribution of hospitals is even less encouraging than it is in the case of general practitioners. Before 1948, the provision of hospitals was the responsibility of various statutory and voluntary bodies, with the result that their geographical distribution reflected a variety of factors other than need. As the Minister of Health stated in the House of Commons, when introducing the National Health Services Bill, this maldistribution was one of the main reasons for reform.

> Our hospital organisation has grown up with no plan, with no system; it is unevenly distributed over the country and indeed it is one of the tragedies of the situation that very often the best hospital facilities are available where they are least needed.[41]

The formula adopted for financing hospitals after the reorganisation of the health services in 1948, however, was such that existing geographical inequalities inevitably continued. It was, therefore, not unexpected when Cooper and Culyer found in 1970 that regional hospital inequalities had persisted over the years and in some instances were in fact increasing.[42]

Further studies in the mid-1970s have shown that the situation has not changed. Thus Noyce et al. found a negative, though not highly significant, correlation between infant mortality on one hand and spending on community health services and hospital services on the other; more important, they found a strong positive correlation between social class and both kinds of spending. In their words, 'if one knew no other facts, it would be possible to explain two-thirds of the variation in community health expenditure by a knowledge of what proportion of the population in each region were managers, employers, or professional workers.' Moreover, 'hospital expenditure was positively correlated both with the expenditure of executive councils and with that of health authorities.'[43] In other words, inequalities in hospital provision compounded inequalities in the provision of doctors. As with the provision of doctors, so with the provision of hospital resources, inequalities increase at the local as compared to the regional level. Buxton and Klein's study found that in the early 1970s local variations within a region were greater than between regions. Indeed, in some local areas, hospital provision was so low that 'it is doubtful whether some . . . can be considered to be offering a comprehensive service,'[44] and for most people, most of the time, it is provision at the local rather than the regional level which really matters.

During the 1970s, governments have made several attempts to rectify the geographical inequalities of hospital provision. The report of the Resource Allocation Working Party in 1976 is the latest and boldest attempt so far.[45] Maynard's and Ludbrook's analysis of hospital revenues during the three years 1977-80 suggest that the most deprived regions 'have made substantial gains' at the expense of other regions.[46] This trend, moreover, has not been halted by the recent government cuts in public expenditure. Thus the fund allocations for 1982-3 to the four regions with the best hospital provisions -- South-West Thames region, South-East Thames, North-East Thames and North-West Thames -- were the lowest among the fourteen hospital regions in the country, while the fund allocations to the regions with the worst hospital provisions -- Northern, North-Western, Trent -- were among the highest.[47]

Turning now to the use of medical services and beginning with general practitioners, the picture is, as might be expected, fairly complicated. A crude analysis of the use of doctors by the various socio-economic groups shows, for both males and females, either a similar or a lower use by the semi-skilled and unskilled groups than other groups. If, however, estimates are made which take into account need for medical care, then the association between use of doctors' services and socio-economic group becomes stronger. Need is defined as self-reported illness and the data are derived from the General Household Survey. Table 3.9 is indicative of the findings of many other studies.[48]

TABLE 3.9
'Use/need ratios' by socio-economic group, Great Britain, 1974-6

Socio-economic group	Males	Females
I Professional	0.23	0.23
II Employers and managers	0.21	0.24
III Intermediate junior non-manual	0.20	0.22
IV Skilled manual	0.18	0.22
V Semi-skilled manual	0.20	0.20
VI Unskilled manual	0.17	0.19
Total	0.19	0.22

Source: DHSS, Report of a Research Working Group (referred to as the Black Report), *Inequalities in Health*, HMSO, 1980, Table 4.2, p. 97

Two main conclusions can be drawn: the lower socio-economic groups, both males and females, make less use of the general practitioners than the higher socio-economic groups, bearing in mind the need for such services. Second, women of all socio-economic groups make greater use of general practitioners than men, again relative to need.

Taking into account need for doctors' services does not get round the problem that 'many of those with restricted activity may not visit a G.P. whereas others may visit a G.P. for reasons other than restricted activity.'[49] A special analysis of the General Household Survey data for 1973-5, relating to those who reported restricted activity or long-standing illness who went to a GP specifically for that illness, showed greater socio-economic inequalities among men. As one would expect, people who consider themselves ill are more likely to visit their doctor than the population in general and hence the consultation rates of Table 3.10 are higher than those of Table 3.9. In contrast to Table 3.9, Table 3.10 shows higher consultation rates by the lower socio-economic groups, but the Black Report points out that this can only be a tentative conclusion because of the problematic nature of the data on which the table is based.

TABLE 3.10
People seeing a GP for their restricted activity or longstanding illness, Great Britain, 1973-75 (%)

Socio-economic group	Males	Females
I Professional	41	36
II Employers and managers		
III Intermediate junior non-manual	45	41
IV Skilled manual	46	41
V Semi-skilled manual	51	42
VI Unskilled manual		

Source: DHSS, Report of a Research Working Group, *Inequalities in Health*, op. cit., Figs 4.1 and 4.2, p. 99

The complicated nature of this debate is also shown by the fact that analysis of General Household Survey data for 1974 by Klein and Collins reached results which disagree somewhat with the findings reported so far.[50] They found that of those males who reported acute sickness or chronic sickness without any limiting effect on activity, a larger proportion of the lower than the higher socio-economic groups consulted their doctors; there was no consistent trend in the case of the females. This finding, however, conceals the fact that working-class males in these two categories of illness are likely to visit their doctor to obtain sickness certificates – a procedure which is not so necessary for professional employees who receive sick pay from their employers. Thus what appears to be a contradictory finding does not, in fact, negate the consistent findings of other studies.

It is difficult to provide any comparable data over the last thirty years and though the general impression is one of slight reduction in socio-economic inequalities in GP consultation, this should not be taken for granted. Thus Walters's analysis of government data for 1949 and 1951 concluded that different conclusions could be reached depending on the measure of morbidity adopted.

> When consultation rates are matched against incapacity rates, there is evidence that lower income patients under-utilise G.P. services . . . If, on the other hand, we take prevalence rates as the most valid index of morbidity . . . then consultation rates for both years suggest equality of access, or even an under-utilisation of physicians by middle class patients.[51]

Data on consultation rates conceal as much as they uncover. They raise questions about the reasons as well as about the quality of such consultations. For a variety of reasons, working-class employees are more likely to call on their doctors to sign certificates for absence from work than middle-class employees. In her analysis of such data, Blaxter observed that 'middle class consultations have a higher clinical content and working class a higher administrative one.'[52] Cartwright and O'Brien found that doctors spent more time and discussed more problems with middle-class than with working-class patients. They also tended to know their middle-class patients better and communicated with them better than with their working-class patients.[53] Backett noted that doctors were more likely to refer upper-class patients than working-class patients to hospital for treatment both for non-terminal and terminal nursing cases.[54] Cartwright found that G.P.s were more likely to visit their middle-class patients than working-class patients in hospital.[55] In brief, several studies have shown that, in a variety of ways, the upper socio-economic groups receive a better service than the lower socio-economic groups when they visit their general practitioner. This is not an unexpected finding: it is merely a reflection of the fact that the higher socio-economic groups have material and cultural circumstances similar to GPs, a fact which makes interaction between them easier and more meaningful.

Before examining the use made of hospitals, it is important to look at the use made of preventive services in the community. There is abundant evidence from a number of studies which shows that, apart from health visitors, these services are used more by the higher socio-economic groups. Cartwright found that the lower socio-economic groups made less use of such local health services as ante-natal clinics or family planning clinics. Inevitably, unintended pregnancies were more prevalent among the same groups.[56]

Brotherston's data for Scotland showed that working-class mothers were not only less likely to attend ante-natal clinics than middle-class mothers, but that when they did they were also less likely to make

early bookings – a fact which he considers relevant to infant mortality.[57] Equally important are the findings that attendance at post-natal
clinics is also associated with social class. Of particular significance is
the implication that vaccinations and immunisations for young children
must be affected. Thus the National Child Development Study which
covered all children born during a week in 1958 found that at the age
of 7 years there was a far higher proportion of children from the lower
socio-economic groups who had not been immunised against smallpox,
polio and diphtheria. Only health visitors appear to visit mothers from
different socio-economic groups alike. The study by Butler and his associates is the most important in this area because they found not only that
health visiting favoured no one class but also when a more sensitive analysis
of the data was made that took account of over-crowding, house amenities,
parental education, as well as father's occupation, they found that the
lower socio-economic groups received more health visiting.[58]

As far as the use of hospitals is concerned, a distinction must be
made between out-patients and in-patients. The General Household
Survey has been collecting data on out-patient use, though not
publishing them. Analysis of these data for the period 1974-7 'suggests
that there are no systematic class gradients in outpatient attendance for
either males or females.'[59] Local studies, too, seem to confirm this
finding. Thus Morgan et al. found no association between social class
and people attending the accident and emergency department of three
hospitals in the Newcastle area.[60] Data on admission to hospital is not
comprehensive but they suggest that admission rates rise with declining
social class. The Scottish data are the most recent and most reliable and
they show that the lower socio-economic groups are more likely to be
both admitted to hospital and to stay longer than the higher socio-
economic groups. These findings are in line with those of an earlier
study for England and Wales which showed that the mean number of days
professionals stayed in hospital was about two-thirds that of unskilled
workers who also had higher admission rates (see Table 3.11).[61] There
is, on the other hand, evidence which shows that middle-class patients
are more likely than working-class patients to be treated in teaching
hospitals, where the standards of service are higher than in ordinary
hospitals. More information is needed about the composition of the
hospital population in terms of socio-economic background, sex, length
of stay, age, quality of care received, and so on.

To sum up the position so far: expenditure on the health services has
increased substantially since the last war and with it the volume, range
and quality of the health services. The geographical distribution of both
doctors and hospitals has remained in favour of the upper socio-
economic groups with only very slight modifications. The position in
relation to the use of medical services by the various socio-economic

TABLE 3.11
Social class and hospitalisation, Scotland, 1971 (%)

Class	Admission rates		Length of stay	
	Males	Females	Males	Females
I	79.5	95.9	63.7	92.5
II	80.9	98.0	73.3	93.6
III	94.0	90.4	93.9	91.0
IV	115.1	107.4	116.4	106.7
V	141.4	161.1	151.7	153.9

Source: DHSS, Report of a Research Working Group, Inequalities in Health, op. cit., Table 4.5, p. 104

groups is as follows: the higher socio-economic groups make more use of most of the preventive local services; the same, also, applies for the use of doctors; the reverse, however, is the case in relation to the use of hospitals. In brief, social class inequalities in access and use of the health services have remained either unaltered or slightly reduced but they have not increased over the years since the last war.

What, then, is the situation in relation to our third dimension of inequality, i.e. outcome? The outcomes resulting from the use of health services are many and they include the following: reduction of pain, improvement of health, reduction of illness and reduction of mortality rates. Pain is difficult to define and measure and the thresholds of pain tolerance have been lowered over the years. Health is as hazy a concept as pain and, as the Royal Commission on the National Health Service pointed out, 'the state of health of individuals ranges from the ideal through different degrees of illness and disability to the brink of death.'[62] Illness is, as already pointed out in this section, more amenable to definition and measurement than either pain or health. There are, however, no reliable statistics relating to social class and illness over the years. We are, therefore, left with mortality rates: there are obviously no definitional problems and there are no major problems in relation to data. Mortality rates, however, are a very weak proxy of the benefit people received from the use of medical services.

Before looking at the relationship between mortality rates and social class over the years, it is worth referring to some evidence which suggest that similar medical care benefits upper-class patients more than their lower-class counterparts. The study of hospital patients by Ferguson and MacPheal concluded as follows: 'The ex-patients who showed the heaviest mortality at early ages, the strongest tendency to relapse and the poorest record in point of early return to work were the

TABLE 3.12
Socio-economic group of men aged 20-64 and standardised mortality
ratios, England and Wales

Socio-economic group	1921-3	1930-2	1949-53	1959-63	1970-2
Professional	82	90	86	76	77
Managerial & lower prof.	94	94	92	81	81
Skilled manual	95	97	101	100	104
Semi skilled manual	101	102	104	103	113
Unskilled manual	125	111	118	143	137

Source: J. Brotherston, 'Inequality – Is it inevitable?', in C.O. Carter and J. Peel
(eds), Equalities and Inequalities in Health, Academic Press, 1976,
Table 8.17

TABLE 3.13
Perinatal mortality rates (per thousand live births) and social class
(legitimate single births only), England and Wales

Social class	1950	1973	Decrease 1950-73 (%)
I Professional	25.4	13.9	45
II Managerial	30.4	15.6	49
III Skilled	33.6	19.2	43
IV Semi skilled	36.9	21.8	41
V Unskilled	40.4	26.8	34
All social classes	34.9	18.9	46

Source: Report of the Committee on Child Health Services, Fit for the Future,
Cmnd 6684-I, HMSO, 1976, vol. 2, Table E, p. 71

group of unskilled labourers.'[63] The relationship between social class
and mortality rates is clearly brought out in Tables 3.12 and 3.13. For
both adult and infant mortality rates, two trends are clearly discernible:
there has been a substantial reduction in mortality rates for all socio-
economic groups; the reduction, however, has been more substantial
for the upper socio-economic groups with the result that socio-economic
inequalities have widened over the years. Sex has also been an important
variable because mortality rates for women have declined faster than
those for men. The impact of social class has, however, been the same on
the mortality rates of both sexes. Whatever the reasons for this trend
may be, it cannot be anything else but discouraging to egalitarians.

Why, then, have differences in socio-economic mortality rates

widened over the years? It is helpful to look at this question separately
for infants, for children and for adults. The Black Report produced
evidence which showed that during the first year of life, illness, rather
than accidents, is the main cause of death. We need, therefore, to
answer two questions for infant mortality rates: why do working-class
infants suffer more from ill-health than middle-class infants (assuming
that this is correct) and why do more die when ill? Babies of working-
class mothers are more likely to suffer from illness than middle-class
babies for a variety of reasons: the mother's health and style of living,
particularly whether she smokes heavily; the mother's diet; the
mother's type of employment during the late stages of pregnancy;
housing conditions, particularly heating; the use of ante-natal clinics
by the mother during pregnancy. All these conditions make for a higher
incidence of illness among working-class than middle-class babies. Baby
illness does not, of course, always lead to death. But the likelihood of
this happening is higher among the lower socio-economic groups
because of their worse housing conditions, their lower use of post-natal
clinics, their heavier family responsibilities, and so on.

During early childhood (1-4 years) accidents and illness are about
equally important as causes of death. The Black Report summed up the
position as follows: 'Among 1-4 year olds . . . *almost all* the differences
in mortality rate between social class I and V are due to: accidents,
poisoning and violence; respiratory disease; and congenital abnormal-
ities. . .'[64] During late childhood (5-14 years) accidents rather than
illness are the major cause of death. Children of working-class parents
are more prone to accidents than other children for a variety of
reasons: inadequate housing conditions; tendency to play in the street
because of lack of space at home; less parental supervision; and so on.
In adulthood (15-64 years) accidents and illness are equally important
as causes of death. Some types of accidents – industrial – and some
types of illness – diseases related to smoking – affect working-class
people more than others.

In brief, there is enough evidence to show that the ways in which ill-
health and accidents arise are such that the lower socio-economic
groups suffer more than the higher socio-economic groups. In addition,
the access and use of the medical services reinforce rather than counteract this tendency. It is, therefore, not unexpected that mortality rates
are higher among the lower socio-economic groups. What is puzzling is
why these inequalities have widened over the years. Whatever the
answer to this may be, the general policy conclusion that can be drawn
is that making access and use of medical services more equitable will
reduce certain aspects of class inequalities in morbidity and mortality
but will not do away with them or reduce them substantially.

Housing

Government policies since the last war have never been concerned directly with reducing social class inequalities in housing. Even during the immediate post-war days, the White Paper on housing made no references to any kind of equality in the way that the White Papers on education and health did. It simply declared that the government's two aims were, first, 'to afford a separate dwelling for every family which desires to have one', and, second, 'to provide for the rapid completion of the slum clearance and overcrowding programmes'.[65] The government intended to achieve the first aim primarily through council housing, relegating privately-built housing to a secondary position.

Thus, during the late 1940s, five of every six newly-built dwellings were council houses or flats and they were allocated according to need rather than according to income. This is not the place to review housing policy since the war, except to note that market criteria asserted themselves again during the 1950s under the Conservative governments and were accepted by the Labour government in the mid-1960s. Increasingly, privately-built housing for owner-occupation was seen as the norm while council housing was seen as necessary for the low-paid only.

The Labour government's White Paper in 1965 echoed the views of its Conservative predecessor:

> The expansion of the public programmes now proposed is to meet exceptional needs; it is born partly of a short-term necessity, partly of the conditions inherent in modern urban life. The expansion of building for owner-occupation on the other hand is normal; it reflects a long-term social advance which should gradually pervade every region.[66]

The contrast with the Labour government's housing policy in the late 1940s could not have been more striking. It is not surprising, therefore, that by the 1970s, more of the newly built dwellings were privately built. The drive by the 1979 Conservative government to sell council houses to sitting tenants at preferential prices was a logical outcome of the assumption that council housing is really for the low-paid only. Equally predictable is the fact that the vast majority of council tenants who have bought their houses are among the better-paid and live in the better housing estates. Housing today is a commodity bought and sold primarily on profit considerations. It differs from the other consumer goods in the private market in four ways. First, a certain proportion of housing is built, allocated and administered by local authorities. Even this type of housing, however, is not always allocated solely according to need and council tenants are expected to pay economic rents, i.e. rents that would be charged in the private market. Second, governments play a more active role in influencing the volume of new housing as well as the quality and quantity of housing than they do in the case of other consumer goods. Third, unlike most other consumer goods, government has accepted the responsibility of providing financial assistance to house-buyers and tenants through tax concessions, rent and rate rebates, and rent allowances. Fourth, though the concept of a legal right to decent housing has not been fully accepted by government, local authorities are legally required to provide some type of shelter for most of the homeless.

In these four ways, housing differs from other consumer goods though it remains fundamentally a private market commodity. Social class inequalities in housing will therefore be greater than they are in health or education. Moreover, governments will be largely unconcerned with attempts at equalising housing distribution even though their policies will inevitably affect socio-economic and other inequalities in housing.

Social class inequalities in housing take many forms: tenure of housing, density of housing and housing amenities. As expected, the association between social class and housing tenure is very strong. While the majority of working-class people live in council or privately rented housing, the overwhelming proportion of the upper classes own or are buying their houses. House ownership not only confers higher social esteem than council accommodation but it is also a more profitable form of investment, particularly during periods of high inflation. Social class inequalities of tenure have widened over the years if the comparison is made between the unskilled and the professional groups. They have remained stable, however, if a more general comparison is made between manual and non-manual groups, as Table 3.14 shows.

Privately-owned housing varies from the detached to the terraced and, for a variety of reasons, detached housing is the most expensive. Market considerations would, therefore, dictate that among the owner-occupiers, the upper socio-economic groups would not only be more likely to occupy detached housing than the lower socio-economic groups but that this disparity would be even wider than the one existing on simple tenure criteria. Thus, while the professional group was almost four times as likely to own or be buying a house as the unskilled group, it was almost nine times as likely to own or be buying a detached house as the unskilled group in 1971.[67] Clearly, while an increasing proportion of the population have been buying their houses, working-class people have been buying the cheapest housing on the market.

As one would expect, a higher proportion of non-manual than manual workers buy their houses outright but the difference is small presumably because of the tax advantages involved in buying a house

TABLE 3.14
Socio-economic group and tenure of housing, 1961-76, England and Wales (%)

	Professional	Intermediate non-manual	Junior non-manual	Skilled manual	Semi-skilled manual	Unskilled manual
1961						
Owner-occupiers	67	60	51	40	29	22
Local authority	7	11	17	29	32	39
Private landlords, etc.	26	28	32	31	39	39
1976						
Owner-occupiers	80	70	55	50	34	23
Local authority	7	12	25	37	47	61
Private landlords, etc.	12	18	20	13	19	16
Net change 1961-76						
Owner-occupiers	+ 11	+ 9	+ 3	+ 10	+ 8	+ 5
Local authority	+ 1	+ 2	+ 9	+ 9	+ 12	+ 19
Private landlords, etc.	- 12	- 11	- 12	- 18	- 20	- 24

Source: CSO, *Social Trends*, no. 9, HMSO, 1979, Table A.12, p. 17

through loans of various types. Non-manual groups are more likely than manual groups to have loans from insurance societies and banks which involve greater tax concessions or lower interest rates than loans from building societies. Local authority loans for house purchase are more likely to be made to manual groups and they tend to concentrate on the purchase of older dwellings.[68]

Discussions which treat the working class as an undifferentiated group inevitably oversimplify what is a complex situation. Not only are lower-paid workers likely to occupy housing that is different in tenure from that of skilled workers but a certain proportion of the latter may occupy housing that is similar to that of the non-manual group adjacent to them. Lansley's analysis of the housing tenure of the poorest 10 per cent of households shows that the proportion who are owner-occupiers remained the same, i.e. 25 per cent during the period 1953-73; the proportion living in local authority accommodation increased from 13 per cent to 45 per cent, and the proportion living in privately rented and other accommodation was halved from 62 per cent to 31 per cent.[69] This decline in the proportion living in privately rented accommodation also resulted in an improvement in the living conditions of the poorest section of the community — though it made the housing situation of some groups even more difficult as the pool of the cheapest and poorest accommodation shrank. The risks of homelessness increased.

As was pointed out in the previous chapter, substantial progress has been made in reducing overcrowding, as officially defined. It follows that working-class people have benefited from this, but they are still more

TABLE 3.15
Socio-economic group and overcrowding, Great Britain, 1977 (%)

Socio-economic group of head of household	1 room or more below official standard	Equal to official standard	1 room above official standard	2 rooms or more above official standard
Professional	1	18	38	43
Employers and managers	1	23	43	33
Intermediate and junior non-manual	3	32	39	26
Skilled manual	5	33	42	20
Semi-skilled manual	6	36	38	20
Unskilled manual	7	41	32	20
Total	4	32	40	26

Source: OPCS, *General Household Survey, 1977*, op. cit., Table 3.25, p. 34

likely to be overcrowded than non-manual groups. As Table 3.15 shows, the proportion of unskilled workers living in overcrowded conditions is seven times greater than that of the professional group. Vice versa, the proportion of the professional group living in grossly under-occupied housing is twice as great. These are, however, general criteria and a more detailed analysis shows that overcrowding is much more common among privately rented, furnished accommodation, particularly in the city centres where lower working-class and ethnic groups congregate.[70]

Official standards of overcrowding have been raised over the years with the result that comparisons become difficult. Nevertheless, it is more than likely that socio-economic differences in crowding have been reduced since 1948 with the expansion of council housing. It is clearly one area where government housing policies have had an equalising effect. Nevertheless, this decline took place during the late 1940s and 1950s when council housing was increasing. The position seems to have remained unaltered since the mid-1960s. Thus Donnison provides figures which show that in 1962, 1 per cent of the professional households were living in overcrowded conditions, i.e. 1.50 persons per room, while the corresponding proportion for the unskilled was 7 per cent.[71] Contemporary official standards of crowding, however, still lag behind what is desirable for satisfactory child-rearing practices. Children need space to play in the house and in the garden and rooms in which to study. These housing criteria are far more closely associated with social class than the official housing density standards. Thus Townsend's study showed that the percentages of households with insufficient internal play space for children was 1 per cent for the professional and managerial groups, 13 per cent for the other non-manual groups, 24 per cent for the skilled workers and 31 per cent for the semi-skilled and unskilled workers.[72]

A similar picture emerges when the housing amenities of the various socio-economic groups are examined. Judged by the official criteria of availability of bath and W.C., the differences between the various socio-economic groups are small. It is also evident from the available data that these differences have narrowed over the years. Thus, while the proportion of professional households who had sole use of bath increased from 92 per cent in 1962 to 96 per cent in 1977, the corresponding proportions for the unskilled were 60 per cent and 89 per cent. This has been due largely to the growth of council housing and perhaps to the improvement grants policy of successive governments particularly since 1969. The latter, however, may also have had an adverse effect as many housing writers have pointed out. Balchin's study of this policy in West London in the 1970s draws attention to the fact that though improvement grants raised the housing standard of low socio-economic neighbourhoods generally speaking, they did not only benefit residents of the lower socio-economic groups.

The conversion of low income dwellings into owner occupied
properties or high rent luxury accommodation has forced the poor
to consume less housing space, often within the same borough and
homelessness and council waiting lists are increasing — in part a
consequence of rehabilitation.[73]

This is part of the well-known process of gentrification of inner city
working-class areas that improves the quality of housing but leads to
the displacement of working-class residents by professional and other
high-paid groups. Differences between socio-economic groups, however,
increase substantially when such modern housing amenities as central
heating, telephone, freezer and the like are taken into account, as
Table 3.16 shows.

TABLE 3.16
Socio-economic group and housing amenities, Great Britain, 1981 (%)

Socio-economic group	Sole use bath/ shower and WC	No bath/ shower sole use WC	Other bath/ shower/WC combination	With central heating
Professional	98	0	2	90
Employers and managers	99	0	1	81
Intermediate and non-manual	97	0	2	76
Junior non-manual	96	1	3	62
Skilled manual	98	1	1	60
Semi-skilled manual	96	2	3	46
Unskilled manual	94	4	2	41
Total	96	2	2	59

Source: OPCS, *General Household Survey, 1981*, HMSO, 1983, Table 3.21, p. 64

The overall relative improvement of working-class housing standards
masks the fact that a small proportion of inner city areas inhabited by
working-class and immigrant residents contain a high proportion of
inadequate housing. Holtermann's analysis of data from the 1971
census using six indicators of inadequate housing showed that urban
conurbations, particularly Clydeside and London, contained a disproportionate amount of inadequate housing. Moreover, a small proportion
of census enumeration districts, mainly in the inner parts of the large
cities, contained an even greater proportion of inadequate housing, as

TABLE 3.17
Census enumeration districts and inadequate housing, Great Britain, 1971 (%)

Type of housing inadequacy	Proportion in worst 5% of enumeration districts	Proportion in worst 15% of enumeration districts
Sharing or lacking hot water	23	53
Lacking bath	30	64
Lacking inside WC	28	61
Overcrowded	31	61
Shared dwelling	51	83
Lacking exclusive use of all basic amenities	18	47

Source: S. Holtermann, 'Areas of Urban Deprivation in Great Britain', in CSO, *Social Trends*, no. 6, op. cit., Table IV, p. 39

Table 3.17 shows. These are also the areas with high infant mortality rates, child accidents, morbidity rates and low school attainment rates.

It is also worth remembering that since it is the older type of housing that lacks basic amenities, elderly people are more likely to live in such accommodation. Thus, government data for England show that almost half of households in England where the head is over 65 lack at least one basic amenity – a figure that is nine times greater than the figure for the whole population.[74] Since women outlive men in substantial numbers, inadequate housing is more a problem for elderly women than for elderly men. Furthermore, it is more than likely that it is the elderly of working-class background who are inadequately housed, rather than the elderly in general. A similar situation exists in relation to one-parent families. The Finer Report showed not only that housing conditions of one-parent families were worse than those of two-parent families, but also that those one-parent families headed by women were worse off than those headed by a man.[75] Other studies have shown that social class is as important a factor in the housing conditions of one-parent families as it is in the two-parent families.[76]

The adverse housing conditions of ethnic minorities are well known and not unexpected. It is the result of their lower position in the occupational ladder, the pattern and timing of their migration, their family size and household structure, as well as the result of the discriminatory practices of British society. Ethnic minorities suffer more than the general population from all the main housing disadvantages – overcrowding, sharing of dwellings, lacking basic amenities, older housing, etc., as Table 3.18 shows. As expected, they are also less likely to own or to be buying their house, less likely to be living in council

TABLE 3.18
Ethnic group and housing conditions, England, 1979 (%)

			Ethnic group of head of household			
	White	West Indian	African	Indian/Pakistani/ Bangladeshi	Other	All households
Tenure:						
Owner-occupier	54.6	35.9	22.6	69.9	48.3	54.4
Council-rented	30.0	45.2	29.0	10.1	18.0	29.8
Other rented	15.4	18.8	48.4	20.0	33.7	15.7
Basic amenities:						
Sole use of all	91.8	86.8	69.4	75.9	81.3	91.4
Some shared, none lacked	2.4	8.6	28.2	12.6	13.3	2.8
At least one lacked	5.8	4.6	2.4	11.5	5.4	5.8
Age of property/building:						
Pre-1919	26.6	46.8	58.9	61.7	39.7	27.3
1919-39	23.8	15.3	16.2	20.1	25.0	23.7
1940-64	27.0	18.6	12.9	9.6	19.0	26.7
1965 or later	22.6	19.3	12.0	8.5	16.3	22.3
Difference from bedroom standard:						
2 or more below	0.5	2.2	2.3	8.3	2.6	0.6
1 below	3.9	16.1	14.0	21.2	9.3	4.3
Equal to standard	32.2	53.9	59.0	39.4	48.3	32.7
1 above	40.1	21.5	17.5	24.3	28.1	39.5
2 or more above	23.4	6.4	7.1	6.9	11.7	22.9

Source: DOE, *National Dwelling and Housing Survey*, HMSO, 1979, Table 8, p. 33

accommodation and more likely to be renting furnished accommodation. While all these comments are correct as generalisations, it needs to be remembered that, as Table 3.18 shows, there are also substantial differences in the housing conditions of the different ethnic minorities.

Housing is a basic need and it is therefore to be expected that the lower income groups will pay a higher proportion of their income to meet housing costs than the higher income groups, in spite of the fact that they live in less adequate accommodation. Housing subsidies are far from egalitarian in their effects. They take two main forms, each of which is designed to promote different goals: income tax relief for mortgage payments designed to promote house ownership, with the result that the higher the mortgage and the higher the salary, the greater the income tax relief received as well. Rent and rate rebates have the opposite effect, i.e. they benefit more the low-paid. Council tenants also receive an indirect subsidy as a result of the central government grants to local authorities for housing which enable them to set rents below the level that would otherwise have been needed. The government's Green Paper on housing provided data which showed that the average amount of subsidy received by all local authority tenants, including rent rebates, was £69 in 1972/3 and £214 in 1975/6; income tax relief per mortgage was £76 and £174 respectively.[77] As expected, the data show that income tax relief is highly regressive in absolute terms but slightly progressive relative to one's income. On the other hand, subsidies to local authority tenants are progressive in absolute as well as relative terms. Clearly changes in interest rates and in government subsidies affect the relative benefit of the two main tenure groups. Thus for 1981/2, the average tax relief was £335 while the average council house subsidy was £234.[78] Briefly, the available evidence shows that the benefit they confer on the various socio-economic groups changes according to government policies and they do not always give greater benefits to those living in council accommodation, as is often assumed. In fact, the opposite is correct today.

That housing is unequally distributed today is obvious to all. What is not so obvious is whether the vast sums of money that have been spent by central government and the local authorities on housing over the years have had much effect on reducing housing inequalities. The provision of council housing has had an equalising effect both as regards reducing overcrowding and improving housing amenities among working-class people. This, however, has to be seen in conjunction with the recent widespread public rejection of certain types of council housing — new tower blocks and old slum blocks of flats. Rent subsidies have also benefited working class people more than non-working class groups in society. Rate subsidies may be equally beneficial to all socio-economic groups but there is no doubt that mortgage income tax relief has benefited the upper socio-economic groups far more than the lower socio-economic groups. The overall effect of all these measures has been a reduction of inequalities in the basic standards of housing enjoyed by the various socio-economic groups. The same claim, however, cannot be made in relation to the social aspects of housing — central heating, play space, garden, location of housing, garage, etc. The social standards of housing reflect market criteria far more than the basic physical standards.

Clearly, the most direct way of reducing housing subsidies to the better-off sections of the community is the abolition of income tax relief on mortgages. This may be a desirable policy from the egalitarian point of view, but it is not likely to lead directly to any substantial reduction of housing inequalities as the evidence from countries such as Canada, without mortgage tax relief, shows.[79] The basic reason for housing inequalities is income inequalities and as long as the latter exist, the former will do, too.

Employment and income

The way people earn their incomes has important implications for many other aspects of their life. As Brown observes: ' "What does he do?" remains the most illuminating question to ask about someone met for the first time.'[80] The previous sections of this chapter have shown that the influence of social class on education, health and housing is both strong and lasting. In this section an attempt is made to examine the impact of social policy on the costs and benefits accruing to different socio-economic groups from work and whether these have changed over the years. Wherever possible, the relevance of the data to sex and ethnicity will also be discussed.

Unemployment, notice of redundancy, industrial discipline, hours of work and accidents are the main costs to be examined here. There is abundant evidence from government and private research which shows quite clearly that manual workers, and particularly the unskilled, are more likely to suffer from both short-term and long-term unemployment than the non-manual groups. There has been no change in this over the years. The disparities in the rates of unemployment between socio-economic groups widen during periods of high unemployment. The same applies to women and various ethnic groups. During the 1970s, when unemployment rose substantially, women suffered relatively more than men, and ethnic minorities have suffered more than other workers. The various government measures — regional policies, anti-discrimination legislation, etc. — have been far too weak to counter the impact of market forces that affect more adversely the industrially weak groups in society.

Not only are manual workers more threatened by unemployment than non-manual workers, but they are also given less time to find other employment. Daniel's work in 1974 showed that though 50 per cent of managers and professionals were given at least three months' notice by their employers, the corresponding proportion for the unskilled was a mere 9 per cent. Vice versa, the proportion given one week or less notice was 54 per cent for the unskilled and only 12 per cent for the professionals and managers.[81] Though data are not available, it may well be that socio-economic disparities were narrower in 1974 than before as a result partly of the Contract of Employment Act, 1963, which required employers to give their employees notice of one to four weeks according to length of service, and partly of the increased power of trade unions.

Industrial discipline has always been harsher for manual than non-manual workers. Craig and Wedderburn showed that while almost all industrial workers have to clock in, almost all managers do not have to do so; while 90 per cent of workers had their pay reduced for lateness, none of the management employees suffered in the same way. As Craig and Wedderburn conclude:

> Discipline, therefore, tended to be stricter for manual workers than for staff, immediate penalties more severe, and the amount of discretion allowed both to the employees and their supervisors much more limited. In the case of discipline, there was a heavy reliance upon the 'rules' to control manual workers; for staff there was personal consideration, even in some cases counselling and guidance.[82]

Since no legislation has been passed to reduce socio-economic inequalities in industrial discipline and since trade union activity has not been concerned with such issues either, it is almost certain that little change has taken place in the years since this study. It is more than likely that any changes in industrial discipline are related to the demand for labour, i.e. stricter discipline for workers during periods of high unemployment, and easier discipline at times of full employment or particular local or industrial labour shortages.

Manual workers have always worked longer hours than non-manual workers — 45.3 hours per week in 1976 compared with 38.5 hours for non-manual workers.[83] In spite of the decline in the number of average basic hours per week for manual workers from 46 in 1946 to 40 in 1970, the number of average actual hours which include overtime, declined only by one hour from 47½ to 46½ during the same period. Overtime is very much a manual worker's way of increasing his basic wage. Shift work is even more a manual group activity and the trend has increased over the years. Thus, a government report in 1970 concluded that, for the period 1954-68, 'the underlying upward trend in the percentage of the manual labour force on shifts in manufacturing has been about 1 per cent per annum.'[84] Shift-work hours are not merely inconvenient but they can be disturbing to the functioning of the whole family. As the same government report pointed out: 'Shift work involves basic and far-reaching changes in the way of life of the individual and his family and the shift worker may also suffer the disadvantages of working considerable amounts of overtime. . .'[85]

Though government data on accidents at work do not distinguish between manual and non-manual workers, they differentiate according to industries. A closer look at this data supports the obvious view that not only are there different rates of accidents among manual occupations but also that rates of accidents are higher in occupations with high proportions of manual than non-manual workers. The rates of both fatal and other accidents have fluctuated over the years and it is not possible to reach any conclusions concerning long-term trends in socio-economic differences.

The picture on the costs and deprivations of work is fairly clear: manual workers suffer more than non-manual workers and the differences between the two groups appear to have changed little over the years. We now turn to the economic benefits derived from work. For the sake of convenience, these are divided into two groups: benefits derived directly from the workplace and benefits derived indirectly as a result of workplace participation. The first includes earnings, occupational sick pay and retirement benefits, and holidays. The second group includes the various social security benefits provided by the government.

The literature on the distribution of earnings is massive and no attempt will be made here either to summarise or evaluate it.[86] Rather, an attempt will be made to summarise the main trends that are relevant to the discussion. The first clear trend is that the dispersion of gross earnings among male manual workers has changed very little during the last hundred years. The wages structure has proved extremely rigid with the lowest decile of the distribution being at around two-thirds of the median wage, as Table 3.19 shows. A similar picture emerges in relation to the distribution of gross earnings among female manual workers. The second important trend has been the slight narrowing of the differentials between male and female workers in full-time occupation. The median gross weekly earnings of women in full-time manual occupations was 50.2 per cent of those of men in manual occupations in 1906, 47.4 per cent in 1938, 53.5 per cent in 1960, 54.0 per cent in 1974 and 63.1 per cent in 1978. A similar picture emerges from a comparison of the salaries of men and women in non-manual occupations — the

TABLE 3.19
Dispersion of gross weekly earnings of full-time manual men,
1886-1977, Great Britain

| Year | Median weekly earnings (£) | Lowest decile | As % of the median | | |
			Lower quartile	Upper quartile	Highest decile
1886	1.21	68.6	82.8	121.7	143.1
1906	1.47	66.5	79.5	126.7	156.8
1938	3.40	67.7	82.1	118.5	139.9
1960	14.17	70.6	82.6	121.7	145.2
1970	25.60	67.3	81.1	122.3	147.2
1977	68.20	70.6	83.1	120.3	144.4

Source: Trends in Earnings, 1948-77, *Department of Employment Gazette*,
May 1978, Table A, p. 520

slight narrowing of the gap taking place during the last decade. Third, the gap between the gross earnings of manual and non-manual workers has also narrowed slightly during recent years. Thus the median wage of male manual workers as a proportion of the median wage of male non-manual workers was 80.6 per cent in 1968, and 85 per cent in 1978. For female workers the corresponding proportions were 76.5 per cent and 87.5 per cent respectively. A similar picture emerges if the gross earnings of the lowest decile of manual workers is compared with those of the highest decile of non-manual workers, i.e. if the two extremes of the earnings distribution are compared. For male manual workers the proportion was 30.4 per cent in 1968 and 35.9 per cent in 1979; for women the corresponding proportions were 31.0 per cent and 38.3 per cent respectively.

A growing feature of the employment contract over the years has been the provision of occupational pension schemes for retirement and sickness. Thus the number of employed persons covered by occupational retirement pensions increased from 2.6 million in 1936 to 4.4 million in 1956, 12.2 million in 1967, and fell slightly to 11.5 million in 1975. The sexual and class inequalities in this form of retirement pension have always been substantial. Women accounted for 19 per cent of all those covered in 1936 and 24 per cent in 1975. Social class differences are equally stark: in spite of the fact that manual workers are the majority of the working population, they make up a small proportion of those covered by retirement pensions. Moreover, their proportion has declined over the years despite an absolute rise in the number of people covered by retirement pensions, as Table 3.20 shows.

TABLE 3.20
Social class and occupational pensions

Year	Non-manual		Manual		Total	
	Number	%	Number	%	Number	%
1956	2.0	45	2.4	55	4.4	100
1967	6.4	52	5.8	48	12.2	100
1975	6.3	55	5.2	45	11.5	100

Sources: Surveys by the Government Actuary, *Occupational Pension Schemes*, HMSO, 1958; 1968 and 1975

It is not, of course, mere coverage of pension shemes that distinguishes manual from non-manual groups. The amounts that are paid in pension are higher for non-manual groups and the qualifying conditions are still more favourable though the qualifying conditions for manual workers have improved in recent years.

Occupational sick pay schemes have increased very substantially during the last twenty years. A recent government survey showed that while in 1961 only 57 per cent of the total workforce in full-time employment was covered, the proportion increased to 73 per cent in 1970 and by 1974 it reached 80 per cent of men and 78 per cent of women in full-time employment. As expected, there were occupational variations as well as social class variations.[88] Thus, while the proportion of both male and female non-manual workers in full-time employment covered exceeded 90 per cent, the corresponding proportion for male manual workers was about three-quarters and that for female manual workers was less than 60 per cent. Moreover, manual workers tended to be paid benefits for shorter periods of time and they received smaller amounts than non-manual workers. Over the years there has, however, been a narrowing of the difference in the coverage of manual and non-manual workers, though not necessarily in the generosity of the schemes.

Holidays with pay are another feature of the employment contract. Data are not very adequate but they suggest that there has been a reduction of inequalities in this area even though the advantages of the non-manual over the manual groups are still substantial today. Townsend's data shows that a higher proportion of the non-manual groups — 19 per cent — received paid holidays of five weeks or more compared to a very negligible proportion of the manual groups — 1 per cent.[89]

This brief examination of the main benefits derived directly from work leaves out the significance of various lesser benefits — cars, interest-free or low interest loans, subsidised lunches, private school fees assistance, expense allowances, etc. The Royal Commission on the Distribution of Income and Wealth documented all these and showed that the higher an employee's wages or salary, the greater too is the benefit derived from such schemes, not only in absolute amounts but in relative terms as well. Thus all the fringe benefits derived directly from work constituted an addition of 29 per cent to the top salaries compared with 18 per cent to the average salaries.[90] This agrees with the estimates arrived at by Townsend who concluded as follows:

> Households of professional status had a mean non-asset income of 252% of that of households of unskilled manual status but the percentage rose to 369 when the annuitized value of assets was added and to 382 when the value of employer welfare benefits in kind was further added.[91]

A person's entitlement to insurance benefits as well as the amount of benefit is linked to the person's work history. Thus the payment of an adequate number of insurance contributions is a necessary pre-requisite to both the entitlement to and the amount of benefit. Though the available data on the contribution record of workers from different socio-economic groups is inadequate in several ways, it can be justi-fiably claimed that members of the lower socio-economic groups are more likely than members of the higher scoio-economic groups to be among the non-qualifiers and, in the years when they existed, to be receiving lower-earnings-related benefits. The degree to which this

TABLE 3.21
Social security expenditure by groups of beneficiaries, 1980-1, Great Britain

Group of beneficiaries	% of total expenditure
Elderly people	53
Families	18
Unemployed	11
Disabled or long-term sick	11
Widows and orphans	4
Short-term sick	3
Total	100

Source: *First Report of the Social Security Advisory Committee*, 1981, HMSO, 1982, Table 1.1, p. 3

applies varies from one type of benefit to another: it is highest for unemployment benefit followed by disability and retirement pensions in that order. Table 3.21 gives a picture of the expenditure on the various social security benefits in Great Britain for 1980. It is clear that expenditure on old people dominates all other items, followed by expenditure on the unemployed.

As Table 3.22 shows, entitlement to unemployment benefit among male workers decreased substantially during the late 1970s when the rate of unemployment was high. The same table also shows that the proportion of women qualifying for unemployment benefit increased over the years so that it surpassed that of men. This, however, is a misleading picture because many unemployed married women do not register with the employment exchanges because they do not qualify for any benefit. Though the table does not differentiate according to social class, it is evident that a higher proportion of unemployed manual than non-manual workers are among those receiving unemployment benefit. On the other hand, it is more than likely that those who do not qualify for unemployment benefit are disproportionately from the ranks of unskilled manual workers.

The majority of applicants qualify for sickness and disability benefit and it is to be expected that the proportion of manual workers receiving such benefits is higher than their corresponding proportion in the general population. The opposite is the case for the non-manual groups. It is simply a reflection of the incidence of disability and is not due to any unduly favourable treatment by the social security system. Indeed, because of the insurance contribution condition, the opposite is the case, particularly in relation to the unskilled. Table 3.23 below shows that the unskilled and the semi-skilled manual workers made up a higher proportion of those receiving sickness or invalidity benefit than their size as a population group warranted; the opposite was the case for the non-manual workers; while the skilled manual workers' position as beneficiaries reflected their size as a group among the general population. Sickness and disability mean not only varying rates of entitlement to social security benefits for different socio-economic groups but also different possibilities of being able to return to work. A study of persons who suffered accidents resulting in paraplegia and tetraplegia showed that 75 per cent of the professional group found similar employment two to three years after the onset of disability and the remaining 25 per cent were unemployed. For the other groups, the chances were almost reversed; only one-quarter to one-third found similar employment with the remainder still not at work.[92]

Half of the total expenditure on social security is on retirement pensions and, apart from 5 per cent of the retired men, the remainder receive a full pension. The issue of socio-economic inequalities in

TABLE 3.22
Unemployed persons registered on first Monday of May, analysed by benefit entitlement, Great Britain (%)

Type of benefit	1961		1971		1980	
	Males	Females	Males	Females	Males	Females
Flat-rate benefit only	42.7	41.75	21.9	31.8	16.5	29.3
Flat-rate plus earnings-related benefit	–a	–a	19.0	10.0	17.7	16.6
Flat-rate plus supplementary benefit	11.1	3.3	11.6	5.5	7.4	2.5
Flat-rate plus earnings-related plus supplementary benefit	–a	–a	2.1	0.9	2.4	0.8
Supplementary benefit only	26.1	13.2	25.1	18.2	39.5	31.6
No flat-rate or supplementary benefit	20.1	41.75	20.3	33.6	16.5	19.2
Total	100.0	100.0	100.0	100.0	100.0	100.0

a Earnings-related benefits were introduced in 1966
Source: DHSS, Social Security Statistics, 1982, HMSO, 1982, Table 1.32, p. 14

TABLE 3.23
People in receipt of sickness or invalidity benefit by their previous
occupation, 1972 (%)

Socio-economic group	Receiving benefit for				% of general population
	1 month	3 months	6 months	12 months	
Professional and managerial	9	11	11	9	21
Other non-manual	13	12	13	16	18
Skilled manual	47	45	41	39	40
Semi-skilled manual	21	20	21	21	17
Unskilled manual	10	12	14	14	5
Total	100	100	100	100	100

Source: OPCS, Prolonged sickness and the return to work, HMSO, 1975,
Table 2.9, p. 20

relation to benefit from retirement pensions is not so much one of differences in entitlement but rather involves class differences in survival
to old age and in the length of time for which a pension is drawn. There
is substantial evidence showing that the chances of surviving to old age
are lower among the manual than non-manual groups and that this also
applies, though to a lesser extent, to the number of years people live
beyond retirement.[93] Wilensky's conclusion in relation to health
services applies equally well to retirement pensions.

The poor die young — before they can contract the chronic diseases
that dearly cost national health schemes. The more affluent citizens
live to a riper age, chronically collecting health services paid for by
the lifelong taxes of the deceased poor.[94]

Data are not available about changes in socio-economic access to
social security benefits over the years. Since there has been no important relaxation of the qualifying conditions over the years, it is more
than likely that social class access to benefit has remained the same. The
introduction of the earnings-related retirement pensions scheme is
bound to favour the better-paid sections of the community because it
is not financed wholly by employee contributions.

Means-tested benefits, by their very nature, appear to favour the
low-paid. Thus supplementary benefit and family income supplement

are more likely to benefit manual than non-manual groups. There must, however, be some doubt about this in relation to supplementary benefit since two-thirds of those in receipt of this benefit are retirement pensioners. It is known that the majority of this population group are women, that the likelihood of receiving supplementary benefit increases with advanced age and that those of the elderly living alone are more likely than married couples to receive this benefit. In other words, a large proportion of the elderly receiving supplementary benefit are elderly women living alone and apart from those belonging to the very top socio-economic group, such women may be in receipt of supplementary benefit irrespective of the socio-economic background of themselves or their deceased husbands. This may, however, change by the end of the century when most married women in employment will be drawing retirement pensions reflecting their previous earnings.

Concluding this section, it can be said that manual workers not only suffer more from the costs and deprivations of the workplace than non-manual workers but they also receive lower compensation and rewards in terms of pay, fringe benefits and, in some instances, even of social security benefits. These inequalities have changed a little in some aspects as regards both the costs and rewards over the years but the striking feature is their extreme rigidity.

A different approach to estimating the distributive effects of public expenditure hass been used by the Central Statistical Office (CSO). For the last twenty years, it has used the data provided by the Family Expenditure Surveys to estimate the net benefit which different income groups derive from public expenditure. All the studies have shown that there is a redistribution of income from the higher to the lower income groups. A number of methodological criticisms have been made of these studies which cast serious doubt on the validity of their findings.[95] Moreover, the usefulness of the findings of the CSO studies for the present discussion is limited because all the published data refer to income groups and not to socio-economic groups. Thus the redistribution in favour of the lowest 20 per cent shown in Table 3.24 is mainly but not exclusively for retirement pensioners. In other words, the studies do not distinguish between horizontal and vertical redistribution of income.

An assessment of the prospects of equality/equity

So far this chapter has attempted first to document the range of inequalities existing today in the areas of education, health, housing, work and income maintenance services after more than thirty years of welfare state policies; and second, to estimate the trends in these inequalities during the same period, and the effects of social policies

TABLE 3.24
Percentage distribution of original and final income (after payment of taxes and receipt of benefits) in 1980

Quantile group	Original income	Final income
Top 20%	45	39
21% - 40%	27	24
41% - 60%	19	18
61% - 80%	9	12
81% - 100%	0.5	6.8
Total income	100.0	100.0

Source: CSO, *Economic Trends*, no. 339, Jan. 1982, Table H, p. 100

upon them. There can be no disagreement about the fact that inequalities in all four areas are still substantial today, though there can be differences of opinion as to whether these are excessive, just about right, or even too small. It is in relation to post-war trends that the data are not adequate enough to warrant making definitive conclusions. Only tentative conclusions can be reached and they are open to challenge and criticism.

In education and health, social class inequalities in the geographical distribution of services have declined slightly over the years, apart from the inner areas of the large cities where these inequalities may have widened. The use of education services has become more equal during the years of compulsory schooling. Before and after this, however, inequalities have remained the same. In other words, pre-school attendance and university education are as unequally distributed today, as they were in the 1940s. The use of health services by the different socio-economic groups has become slightly less unequal during this period. In spite of this, however, differences in infant and adult mortality rates between social classes have widened. In housing, inequalities in basic standards have narrowed but the same cannot be said in relation to the social standards of housing. Earnings from work of manual and non-manual workers have become slightly less unequal though the same cannot be claimed for the value of such fringe benefits as sick pay, retirement pensions, subsidies for cars, private schooling, house purchase, etc. The trend in social security benefits is uncertain because of the introduction of several new benefits, the modification of others, and the replacement of flat rate contributions, and, to a lesser extent, flat rate benefits, with earnings-related contributions and earnings-related benefits for retirement and widowhood.

In brief, inequalities have been reduced slightly in some areas, remained the same in others and even widened in some other areas. It is a conclusion that need not worry supporters of inequality but which should cause concern to those who believed that social services could and would create a more equal society. In trying to provide answers to the questions why have social policies failed significantly to reduce social class inequalities, it is best to look at each of the three steps in the process separately — access, use and outcome.

What would policy attempting to equalise access be like? Inevitably it will include strong elements of positive discrimination. The last forty years have shown that simply increasing the volume of services does not necessarily reduce social or geographical inequalities. Governments must take measures to ensure that the deprived areas receive more in services than other areas both as regards buildings and equipment as well as staff. Leaving aside the question of costs for the time being, what kind of problems will a government anxious to promote positive discrimination policies have to face? In the case of buildings and equipment there do not seem to be any special problems other than space and cost. The position is more difficult in relation to attracting more professional staff to work in deprived inner city areas or in isolated rural areas. So far governments have adopted two measures in relation to education and health personnel: incentives, i.e., paying higher salaries, and sanctions, i.e. restricting employment in the desirable areas. Neither measure has proved very effective partly because governments have been half-hearted. The additions made to the salaries of teachers or doctors working in undesirable areas have been far too small to have the intended effect. Similarly, the policy of refusing employment in the desirable areas to general practitioners has not been very effective because even these areas have not had their government quota of general practitioners.

If these twin policies are to have any effect in reducing geographical inequalities, they need to be pursued more vigorously than they have been in the past. This means not only spending substantially larger amounts of money but also providing the administrative framework for ensuring such policies are pursued uniformly and consistently. It also requires that working conditions for the staff in such areas are improved, work loads are lessened, research facilities improved and other similar measures adopted that would make working in such areas satisfying and challenging.

Even with a more aggressive policy of positive discrimination, it is doubtful whether geographical inequalities can be overcome. Some Eastern European countries — the USSR, for example — have attempted to deal with this problem by directing professional staff to work in certain areas for a limited number of years, as well as providing them with incentives in terms of higher salaries, pension rights, housing,

etc. Such a policy would be resisted in this country by some professional bodies and by some other groups on the grounds that it is against
individual freedom. Finally, even if a government was prepared to use
positive discrimination measures more vigorously and adopt a policy
of staff direction in employment, it will need to make private provision
illegal if it is to succeed in equalising the geographical distribution of
services. Without such a measure, professionals in education and health
can ignore government plans by setting up in private practice wherever
they choose, with the active support of other sections of society.

An alternative approach to the equalisation of the geographical
distribution of services is to concentrate on improving the physical and
social standard of the 'undesirable' neighbourhoods. Such an approach
is not without its difficulties, but it has a great deal of potential, particularly in relation to inner city areas. It is likely to be a very expensive
policy, for it implies the improvement of housing, schools, social
amenities, etc. Even with these environmental improvements, for the
policy to succeed it must attract residents of all socio-economic groups
— and there is not much that governments can do about this. Moreover,
it is far less of a real alternative in the case of isolated rural areas. The
two policy approaches — attracting staff to deprived areas and
improving the standard of deprived areas — are not mutually exclusive.
In fact, they are both necessary and they complement each other.

The task, then, of any government attempting to reduce inequalities
in the geographical distribution of services is very difficult. But these
difficulties pale into insignificance when compared to those involved
in equalising the use that different socio-economic groups make of the
services. Clearly an equitable geographical distribution of services is a
necessary but not a sufficient precondition for an equal, let alone an
equitable, use of services. Other policy measures are needed, both
negative involving sanctions and positive involving rewards.

The reasons why the lower socio-economic groups make less use of
the education and health services are complex and only a brief comment can be presented here. They are, however, of three types: cost,
culture and service ethos. Cost is used here in its widest sense involving
payment of fees, loss of earnings, loss of time and so on. Thus any
services which involve the payment of fees will be under-used by the
lower socio-economic groups — dentists' services is a good example.
Staying on at school beyond the school-leaving age involves loss of
earnings or benefit, and the absence of grants to 16-18 year olds at
school inevitably means that the lower socio-economic groups will be
under-represented in this stage of education. A mother with three
young children, with no car and living a long way from a general practitioner's surgery is almost certain not to consult the doctor as often
as she should. These are a few examples where cost is an important

113

reason for the under-use of services by the lower socio-economic groups. No doubt there are many others.

Culture is used here in the sense of sub-culture. It is the constellation of those beliefs, attitudes and values that influence sub-groups in society to behave differently from the generally expected norms of behaviour. It is a difficult concept, for it raises questions about the forces that account for its formation, as well as its modification and change. For the purposes of this discussion, however, several examples can be cited to illustrate the importance of sub-cultural factors to the use of services: attitudes towards education influence the expectations as well as the interest which parents take in the school progress of their children. Attitudes towards pain and discomfort influence the use one makes of medical services. A general tradition in a neighbourhood that children leave school as soon as possible affects the decision of individuals to stay on at school beyond the compulsory school leaving age; and so on. These beliefs, attitudes and values obviously come about as a result of the pressures stemming from material, economic, political and other forces, but, once they are in existence, they exert an influence of their own on people's behaviour.

Service ethos refers to the formal and informal social climate prevailing in a social service agency which influences the extent of use made by different groups of people. Thus if teachers' expectations in a school or class are low, in relation to the potential educational performance of working-class children, it is quite possible that the latter will respond accordingly. Professional education and training inevitably create such a social and educational gap between the providers of the services and working-class users that unless efforts are made to narrow it or close it, working-class people will make less adequate use of services.

These three types of reasons are inter-related, which makes any half-hearted attempts by government to deal with specific issues in isolation ineffective. To take one example: the under-use of ante-natal and post-natal clinics by mothers of the lower socio-economic groups. A serious government effort to rectify this would involve measures directed at cost, culture and service ethos reasons. It would mean a more equitable geographical distribution of such clinics; transport facilities provided for those mothers who, because of distance or number of children, find it difficult to get to the clinic; more concerted educational campaigns to inform mothers of the use and role of such clinics; the harsh attitudes of some health visitors and other professionals towards 'inadequate' mothers must be changed where they exist; and so on. Only when these are done, as Graham points out, should policy attempt to improve attendance by lower socio-economic group mothers through such financial sanctions as withholding or paying a reduced amount in maternity or child benefit to those mothers who do not attend such clinics or attend irregularly.[96]

Clearly, the government policies required to make the use of education and health services equitable are a daunting package. They are very costly and they are likely to be resisted by various sections of the community, including some of those who stand to benefit from such policies. Obviously, too, they are policies which will take years of consistent application before they can bear fruit. Taking the discussion one step further to the reduction of inequalities in outcome, one is faced with even more intractable problems. As far as health is concerned, it requires not only the equitable distribution and use of medical services, but also the reduction of inequalities in working and living conditions. The health of individuals is affected not only by the use they make of medical services but by their working conditions, housing, diet, leisure-time activities, and so on. Clearly no government can legislate for such a wide array of circumstances, let alone attempt to enforce such legislation. But there are areas where governments could profitably intervene in a more positive and co-ordinated way. The Black Report,[97] for example, showed that the main explanation for the higher accident rate among children of manual families lies in their residential environment: overcrowding in the house, lack of safe playing facilities in the vicinity of the house and a consequent tendency to play in the streets. Governments anxious to reduce socio-economic differences in mortality rates among children have therefore to tackle the problems of housing and urban decay, as well as providing better health services to such families. Similar arguments apply to the equalisation of the outcomes of education. It is a point made so many times by so many people that it has almost lost its meaning: even if all children went to the same nursery, primary and secondary schools, their examination performance and hence their entry to higher education establishments and eventually to well-paid jobs will still vary according to their family background. This is obviously not an argument for not equalising the use of schooling. Far from it — it is an argument for policies extending beyond the school to the areas of work and income, if government attempts to equalise the outcome of education are to stand any serious chance of succeeding.

In brief, government policies to equalise access to services are more feasible, more politically acceptable and less costly than policies designed to equalise use, let alone outcome, of services. It is not, therefore, unexpected that governments since the last war in this country have confined their efforts largely to this aspect of equality. The restructuring of the social services in the 1940s aimed primarily at making them universal, i.e. free or low-cost access to all. As mentioned earlier, it was vaguely hoped that somehow access and use of services would be equalised. Nevertheless, apart from the geographical distribution of general practitioners, there were no explicit policies to equalise either access to or use of services. It was not until the 1960s that governments acknowledged that inequalities of access and use in health, education and housing were as strong as ever. Thus the various hospital plans, the community care plans, the comprehensive school reorganisations, the positive discrimination policies, the community development projects, the urban aid programmes, etc., were intended in one way or another to reduce inequalities primarily of access to a greater or lesser extent. Similar policies were pursued in the 1970s, particularly in relation to health services, culminating in the Report of the Resource Allocation Working Party in the mid-1970s. In all these, policies were directed at geographical inequalities not at socio-economic inequalities. The concept of social class is markedly absent from government white papers and legislation.

Apart from these various policies of positive discrimination for deprived areas, a series of Acts of Parliament during the 1960s and 1970s sought to strengthen the rights of workers against unfair dismissal, the rights of tenants against unfair eviction, and the rights of immigrants and women against discrimination in the areas of employment, finance, housing, etc. Both sets of policies were weakly enforced and, as far as the positive discrimination policies were concerned, very small amounts of money were spent. The economic recession of the late 1970s has meant not only that government funds have become even more scarce for such policies but also that government and public concern has shifted away from issues of inequality to concentrate on the problems of productivity and economic growth. Emphasis has been placed on increasing income inequalities as a means of boosting incentives for more work effort on an individual and corporate level. In brief, policies towards equality have been directed mainly towards geographical inequalities, they have been haphazardly applied, they have involved very small amounts of money and, during the present economic depression, they have, to all intents and purposes, been abandoned.

What conclusions can be drawn from the failure of social services to reduce substantially socio-economic inequalities of access, use and outcome? The first conclusion must be that this failure is not unexpected because social services were not designed to reduce such inequalities. Conservative governments have never been concerned with reducing such inequalities, while Labour governments have been, at best, unclear and lukewarm and, at worst, as hostile or indifferent as Conservative governments. Our second tentative conclusion is that social services may have reduced people's subjective sense of inequality. The existence of substantially one education and one health service for the whole country reduces the obvious and blatant forms of inequality even if social class differences in opportunity survive substantially within it. The third conclusion is that the reduction of socio-economic inequalities of use and outcome depends as much on government policies relating to the areas of work, the environment, income, etc., as on social policies. The importance of the inequalities in the work environment and in the incomes of people has been under-estimated in social policy debates. Such inequalities have a pervasive effect on the power, attitudes and lifestyles of people, which have a strong bearing on their use of the social services. As Goldthorpe expressed it, any attempt to reduce inequalities via social policy reforms alone 'grossly misjudges the resistance that the class structure can offer to attempts to change it'.[98] The fourth conclusion is that any government which is anxious to reduce the socio-economic inequalities discussed in this chapter will inevitably meet wtih resistance from the powerful groups in society whose economic and social privileges will be threatened. It will also meet with resistance from some of the groups that stand to gain from such policies because of the grip that the ideology of inequality has on British society. Le Grand, for example, insists that for egalitarian policies to succeed, 'it is necessary to reduce the hold of the ideology of inequality on people's values and beliefs and this can only be done by challenging the factual underpinnings of that ideology.'[99] He hopes that in the ensuing battle of ideas, the weakness of the arguments for inequality will be exposed and young people in particular will be converted to the idea of equality. While there is a great deal of merit in this argument, it over-estimates the importance of what individuals say or write on the shaping of ideology. People's values and attitudes arise out of their material environment and daily experiences as much as out of what they hear or read. The fifth and final conclusion, is that, left to itself, capitalism has an inherent tendency to exacerbate inequalities of condition. The road to an egalitarian society, therefore, lies not so much through the social services, even broadly defined and purposefully designed, but through changes in the economic and political institutions of the country which generate and shape inequality. This line of attack on inequality is not any easier than the social services approach. It is, indeed, politically more difficult for it threatens the very essence of capitalism. It is not a panacea either — it simply provides an economic and political frame-work, where co-operation between the various groups in society is less conflict-ridden, a fact which makes the possibility of government egalitarian measures more possible. In the last analysis, egalitarian policies will only succeed if they are desired and supported by the general public. Without such public support, egalitarian governments have to resort to excessive authoritarianism which can destroy the very notion of true equality that it hopes to achieve.[100]

4

Social policy and the encouragement of economic growth

Social services are a form of both consumption and investment at the individual as well as at the aggregate level. They contribute to the enrichment of the quality of life of individuals and contribute to the general economic development of society. It is not a very fruitful exercise to indulge in a long debate as to which of these two functions is the more important. Without increased economic growth, the funds available for the provision of social services inevitably suffer; ultimately, however, the main reason for increased economic growth is to raise the level of personal consumption.

In this chapter, the discussion focuses on the contribution social policy can make to economic growth. This contribution takes several forms, all of which are complex and contested. They can be grouped under three headings: improvement of the quality of labour; promotion of the mobility of industry and labour; encouragement of production and employment through increased consumption. Since the third function has often been presented as a negative contribution to economic growth, it is also discussed in the following chapter.

Improvement of the quality of labour: the human capital theory

The 'human capital' theory as applied to education epitomises this aspect of the relationship between social policy and economic growth. But it is not only education but all the social services that may help to improve the quality of labour in varying ways and degrees. A well-housed, adequately fed, healthy and educated labour force is a necessary

118

– if not a sufficient – prerequisite for industrial advance. Most of the literature, however, has concentrated on the potential of education and health services and it is on these that this section will focus. Supporters of the human capital theory are to be found among both Marxist and non-Marxist schools of thought. Most of the detailed exposition and verification of the theory, however, has come from non-Marxists, and this is reflected in the discussion in this chapter. Following Marx, many contemporary Marxists maintain that one of two main functions of public expenditure is to enable and assist private capital to remain profitable. Such government services as transport and aid to industry directly help to increase profitability of capital while other services such as education, health and housing lower the reproduction costs of labour to private capitalists and hence increase profitability. O'Connor refers to the first group of services as social investment and to the second as social consumption[1] – a classification adopted by many other contemporary Marxists.

Historical overview

Important concepts in the social sciences are largely the product of their political and socio-economic environment and the human capital theory is no exception. As an economic concept, its fortunes have waxed and waned in response largely to the demand for labour by industry and the availability of labour reserves in the general population. At times of high demand for labour and low population reserves to meet this demand, the human capital theory was at its strongest. Vice versa, at times of high rates of unemployment, or at times of low rates of unemployment but with abundant population reserves, the human capital theory was on the sidelines of mainstream economic thought. The human capital concept is not new, even though it reached its apotheosis in the 1960s. Economists and others who have considered the human capital notion over the years can be divided into two groups: those who have argued that human beings increase national wealth; and those who went a step further to argue that improving the quality of human beings through health, education and other services increases their productivity as labourers and hence adds to the national wealth. According to the first, and the largest group, all labourers are part of the capital; according to the second group, it is, as Kiker points out, 'the skilled individual who is the capital'.[2] More broadly, it is the educated, skilled and healthy individual who is the human capital. It is with this second group of writers that we are primarily concerned here.

Sir William Petty, writing at the end of the seventeenth century, argued that excessive morbidity and mortality rates were not only a human but an economic tragedy. For this reason, government-provided services which reduced such high rates would contribute to raising the national wealth. There would, in other words, be more workers as well as healthier workers, adding to the wealth of the country through their labour.[3] Petty's writings were influenced, on the one hand, by the prevailing high death rates and infant mortality rates and, on the other, by the rising economic prospects of the country as a trading nation. It was a period of increasing demand for labour and declining or stagnant population.

The eighteenth century witnessed a substantial rise in population which accelerated even further at the beginning of the nineteenth century. 'In Great Britain, the growth of numbers over the whole century', wrote the Royal Commission on Population, 'was of the order of 50 per cent. Moreover, by the beginning of the 19th century, the rate of growth had become really fast — well over 10 per cent in ten years.'[4] During the nineteenth century, the population of the country grew by three and a half times. This was also a period of rapid industrialisation, and hence a period of high labour demand. It was, therefore, not surprising that the great economists of this period either ignored or made only brief and passing references to the quality or quantity of labour as an important factor in economic growth. Adam Smith made the most explicit statements in support of the idea that education improves the quality of labour and hence raises economic growth. Even this, however, was neither central to his thinking nor set out in any detail. He merely postulated that an educated and skilled worker was more productive than an illiterate and unskilled labourer and that this explained the difference in their wages.[5] Several other economists of the nineteenth century shared this view to a greater or lesser extent. Most, however, did not even refer to education as relevant to economic growth. Ginzberg points out, in relation to Ricardo, for example, that since labour was plentiful, there was no objective pressure for economists to place too much value on human capital. 'There was a great number of rural workers at the doors of the new factories looking for employment. The mills of that day had no difficulty in absorbing illiterate, unskilled workers so long as they were able and willing to submit to discipline.'[6]

The epidemics of the mid-nineteenth century, with their high mortality rates, revived the interest in the potential of health services to contribute to economic growth. In his report as a Poor Law Commissioner, Chadwick estimated that inadequate sanitation leading to excessively high death rates was costing the country £14 million a year in lost production, apart from the social costs in terms of crime, delinquency, and the like. Like Petty, he reckoned that health services were a paying proposition in economic terms. It was, however, the work of William Farr in the latter part of the nineteenth century that added statistical precision to estimates of the importance of the health services to human capital. Farr calculated the contribution of workers to economic growth by estimating the future net earnings of labourers dying at different ages.

The neo-classical economists and, particularly Alfred Marshall, took a more positive view of education's contribution to economic growth than the classical economists, including Adam Smith. Marshall referred to education 'as a national investment' and supported technical education in particular as a means of training the specialists in industry. His view that 'the most valuable of all capital is that invested in human beings'[7] has been quoted as evidence that his support of human capital was stronger than that of any other economist. Nevertheless, the fact still remains that education was not built into his analysis of economic growth in any more substantial way than it appeared in Adam Smith's work.

The same half-hearted recognition of the concept of human capital can be detected in government education policies during the nineteenth century. It was not until 1880 that elementary education became compulsory and the main drive behind the legislation, according to Landes, was not so much the desire to instruct and educate but rather 'to discipline a growing mass of disaffected proletarians and integrate them into British society. Its objective was to civilise the barbarians.'[8] Introducing his elementary education bill to the House of Commons in 1870, W.E. Forster, too, acknowledged both the economic and the political reasons for elementary education: 'Upon the speedy provision of elementary education depends our industrial prosperity. It is no use trying to give technical teaching to our artisans without elementary education . . . Upon this speedy provision depends also, I fully believe, the good, the safe working of our constitutional system.'[9] Technical and scientific education beyond the elementary stage was seen with even more scepticism. The country had done quite well without it — it had industrialised and prospered with the use of self-made men of minimum education. To quote Landes again, 'Here was a nation that had built its economic strength on practical tinkerers — on a barber like Arkwright, a clergyman like Cartwright, an instrument-maker like Watt, a professional "amateur inventor" like Bessner, and thousands of nameless mechanics. . .'[10]

The first half of the twentieth century brought no important changes in thinking on education or health as forms of national investment, apart from the public concern about the health of children and young people at the beginning of the century and the implication of this to both the industrial and military strength of the country. 'Health services', writes Hay in his discussion of social reforms during this period, 'would ensure that the worker was returned to the labour force as soon as possible after illness. More generally, by raising the standard of health of the community, especially among children, such services would yield an economic return outweighing their cost.'[11] Significantly, the National Health Insurance scheme of 1911 only covered insured workers. The health of their families was clearly seen as less important to society. For most of the period up to the beginning of the Second World War, labour was plentiful and unemployment rates varied from moderate to the very high rates of the depression. Keynes saw the contribution of government-provided services to economic growth as lying in their influence on consumption. It was increased consumption, not the improvement in the quality of labour, that was the prime mechanism for invigorating a stagnant economy. Government reports made few important references to the human capital concept and on the rare occasion that they did, there was division of opinion. The Minority Report of the Royal Commission on National Health Insurance, 1926, stressed the economic returns to the country of a satisfactory system of health services:

> The whole question of national health is bound up with that of efficiency and output and it is impossible to rank as a 'burden' on industry or on the community an outlay which safeguards wellbeing and (to put it no higher) conduces to the efficiency of the machine.

In a Note of Reservation, however, two members of the Majority Report took the opposite view:

> The case for expenditure on health is not in fact furthered by what we are convinced, is the fallacious suggestion that expenditure on health may indirectly help to rehabilitate the finances of the country ... Everyone who is sick and recovers lives to be sick later on.[12]

The various White Papers of the early 1940s argued for the reorganisation of social services on ethical, egalitarian and humanitarian grounds. There were passing references to social services as investment but primarily they were seen in consumption terms. It was not until the 1950s that the investment role of the services began to play a greater part in government debates while the 1960s are the period par excellence of the human capital theory and theorists. Social, political and economic factors account for this new development. These were the years when unemployment rates in all advanced industrial societies were low, demands for labour were high, economic prospects were bright and the belief in science and technology was strong. Added to these socio-economic factors was the general feeling in advanced capitalist societies, and particularly in the USA, that the successful space programme of the Soviet Union, as well as its rising economic standards, were related to its improved education system. Investing in people through the social services became both a respectable and a popular policy among governments.

Thus the Report of the Guillebaud Committee acknowledged that 'the National Health Service is a wealth producing, as well as a health producing service.'[13] The first major government report on wastage of ability in education after the war referred to 'the general shortage of trained scientists and technologists' in the country and urged the expansion of secondary education to meet this 'most pressing need'.[14] The second government report on the same issue drew attention to the wastage of very able working-class school-leavers who did not proceed to higher education. It acknowledged that education was both a consumption and investment.

> Primacy must be given to the human rights of the individual boy or girl. But we do not believe that the pursuit of national efficiency can be ranked much lower – not least because without it the human rights themselves will not be secure.[15]

This sentiment was repeated a few years later by the Newsom Report in relation to average ability working-class adolescents. The Report declared that 'the country cannot afford this wastage, humanly or economically speaking,' and therefore 'in human justice and in economic self-interest we ought as a country to give that help' to working-class youngsters who under-achieve at school.[16]

It was, however, the Robbins Report in 1963 on higher education that made the strongest case for investment in education to aid economic growth. The report acknowledged that education performs many functions and the facilitation of economic growth was only one of these functions.

> To devote resources to the training of young people may be, *au fond*, as much entitled to be considered a process of investment as devoting resources to directly productive capital goods. Judged solely by the test of future productivity, a community that neglects education is as imprudent as a community that neglects material accumulation.[17]

The Committee's arguments and recommendations were accepted by the government and higher education was expanded considerably in the 1960s and early 1970s.

It was also this same period – primarily the 1960s – that witnessed the academic upsurge in the human capital theory. Though several

economists in the late 1950s began to look at the economics of education, it was Schultz's presidential address to the American Economic
Association in 1960 that heralded the arrival of the human capital
theory on the international academic scene. His main thesis was that
the rapid rise in earnings in advanced industrial societies was due to a
large extent to improvements in the education and skills of workers.
It followed that further improvements would result in even higher
earnings. Increased expenditure on education was sound economic
investment for both the individual and the country. Moreover, reductions in inequalities of earnings could be brought about by additional
expenditure on the education and health of children from poor
familiies:

> No small part of the low earnings of many Negroes, Puerto Ricans,
> Mexican nationals, indigenous migrating farm workers, poor farm
> people and some of our older workers reflects the failure to have
> invested in their health and education. Past mistakes are, of course,
> bygone, but for the sake of the next generation, we can ill afford
> to continue making the same mistakes over again.[18]

He prescribed the same remedy for the inequalities between developed
and developing societies. Inevitably, his thesis appealed to a wide
spectrum of the academic and political community; to both the
conservatives who valued economic growth and to the progressives who
emphasised reductions of inequality at home and abroad. Education,
in particular, was the avenue to both greater economic growth and
greater income equality.

If Schultz set the scene for the acceptability of the human capital
theory, Denison provided the detailed, methodological framework for
empirical studies to test the claim that the development of education or
health services promotes economic growth. Denison's work became
extremely influential and was adopted by scholars in other countries
and by such international bodies as UNESCO, OECD and others. Along-
side the Denison-type study, there were many other studies providing
evidence on the statistical correlation between educational standards
and economic development on an historical comparative basis.

The fortunes of the human capital theory began to decline as the
growth in the economies of the advanced industrial societies began to
slow down or stagnate in the mid-1970s. A more detailed appraisal of
the human capital theory is presented in the following section. Suffice
it to say here that unemployment rates in all advanced industrial
societies rose substantially during this period; the optimism of the
1950s and 1960s was replaced by general pessimism about future
economic prospects in individual countries and in the world in general;

and all this after a period of unprecedented growth in public expenditure on education and health in all advanced industrial countries. Not only was the value of education and health to economic growth seriously questioned but fears were being expressed that high public expenditure in these areas was acting rather as an obstacle to economic growth. These services were taking much-needed capital away from industrial investment and they were, some claimed, creating attitudes and styles of living that were inimical to hard work and increased productivity — a claim discussed in the following chapter.

Appraisal of the human capital theory

Before examining the statistical evidence linking education and health to economic growth, it is useful to review briefly the ways in which these two services are said to facilitate economic growth. Beginning with education, there is general agreement that it is not just any kind of education which will encourage economic growth. As Miller puts it: 'Education is a source of economic growth if it is anti-traditional to the extent that it liberates and stimulates as well as informs the individual and teaches him how and why to make demands upon himself.'[19] He then gives four 'growth developing capacities' of education which overlap with the four ways in which Denison suggests education increases labour productivity.

First, on average, a better-educated person is likely to do the same job better than one who is less educated. Second, education reduces resistance to new ideas and new ways of doing things. Third, additional education makes for a more rational labour market by improving information and choice of occupation. Fourth, advanced industrialisation and automation have shifted 'the occupational structure of the labour force, a shift predominantly from occupations requiring little education to those requiring more'.[20]

All these four reasons are subject to varying degrees of criticism: Unskilled manual jobs may well be done just as well, if not better, by the less educated; resistance to change in employment can be affected more by the alternative job opportunities that are available than by levels of education; advanced industrialisation has so atomised and de-skilled the production process that for many workers further or higher education is not necessary in their jobs, etc., etc. Berg's summary of the evidence on the contribution of education to individual productivity in the USA is pertinent. More highly educated employees were not more productive than others and this applied to a variety of employees — factory workers, white collar workers, and managers. It must, however, be remembered that in all the studies he reviewed, all the employees had completed at least primary education.[21] Writing from a similar perspective, Collins attributes the higher salaries of the more educated employees to the certification process rather than to their higher productivity, i.e., the increasing tendency by employers to select and promote employees according to the education credentials they hold.[22] Yet it is difficult to see why employers in all countries would behave in this way if it was not to their advantage.

Education and health services are related in several obvious ways that have implications for economic growth. Children who suffer from prolonged ill-health inevitably benefit less from education than healthy children. Vice-versa, an educated general public is likely to make better use of health services than an illiterate public. Professional training of medical personnel is impossible without a sound general education system. High death rates among children reduce the value that parents place on education; and so on. There are, however, several important differences between education and health in relation to economic growth which Mushkin narrows down to four. First, while education influences the quality of labour only, health services affect both the quality and the quantity of labour, particularly in developing societies. Second, quality improvement is far more difficult to define and measure in health than it is in education. Years of schooling, types of schooling, are the indices of quality change in education. The indices for health are negative — death rates, life expectancy rates, morbidity rates — and they refer mainly to quantitative rather than to qualitative changes of the labour force. Third, it is far more difficult to calculate the economic return to the individual on investment in health services than is the case with education. There is ample data relating earnings to years of schooling with and without consideration of such factors as IQ, family background, sex, race, etc. This is not the case in relation to health. 'We now have no similar indexes', writes Mushkin, "of differences in income associated with gradations in health. More particularly, we have no indexes of differences in earnings reflecting such gradations.'[23] Fourth, education brings out and develops a person's abilities. All children are compelled to attend school and young people are encouraged to stay on at school in order to maximise this process of self-fulfilment. Health programmes, on the other hand, are concerned, in the main, with reducing the impact of ill-health on individuals. Education can make people *more* productive while health can only prevent them from becoming *less* productive. The general effect of these four differences between health and education in relation to economic growth is that it has proved far more difficult and controversial to measure the impact of health on economic growth and where it has been attempted the effects have been estimated to be lower than those resulting from education. The situation is further complicated by the fact that improvements in health are as much the result of better diet, cleaner air, more sanitary conditions, etc., as of the health services.

With all these qualifications in mind, how do health services influence economic growth? Weisbrod and his associates list three direct and four indirect effects, all of which are questionable, particularly the indirect effects.

The direct effects are: (i) increases in 'outputs' due to the decline in absenteeism from work and school because of illness; (ii) output increases associated with the rise in efficiency because of greater physical and mental ability of children and adults; and (iii) output increments due to extension of working lives. Indirect effects include: (i) reductions in the goods and services required to *care* for the sick; (ii) increases in output resulting from freeing of resources previously used by healthy people to *avoid* sickness; (iii) the output resulting from any population increase due to a rise in the birth rate, as might result from better health conditions; (iv) any net output resulting from changes in attitudes and in social and political organisation that might be a consequence of better health conditions.[24]

Apart from the dubious nature of several of these claims, no mention is made of the possible ill effects of health services on economic growth. Increased longevity results in increased dependency in old age, while on the other hand, increased investment in health has been accompanied not by falling but by rising rates of sickness absenteeism from work. The complexity and uncertainty of these trends is well summarised by the Jewkes in their study of the NHS:

Absence from work due to sickness has certainly not been falling; on the other hand, but for the increased spending on medicine, it is conceivable that it might have risen. Longer life for the individual has probably brought some gains to the community, although perhaps less than is often believed; yet improvements in longevity in very recent years have been small and the prospects of further improvements do not, at the moment, appear very promising.[25]

The various studies attempting to measure the link between education and economic development can be divided into two groups: the statistical correlation studies and the production function studies. The statistical correlation studies have been many and varied and they have been examined in detail by both Blaug and Bowman and there is no need to repeat the discussion here.[26] Most studies have shown that there is a strong, though not perfect, correlation between levels of education and level of economic development. Economic growth is usually measured in terms of GNP and though this presents some problems they pale into insignificance when compared with the problems involved in the definitions of education which have included literacy rates, school enrolment rates, university attendance rates, expenditure on education, and so on.

The study by Anderson and Bowman which examined literacy rates in 1950 and GNP per head in 1955 in eighty-three countries is typical of many similar studies. It found that countries could be divided into three groups: First, those countries (thirty-two in number) with adult literacy rates below 40 per cent had per capita income below $300; second, those countries (twenty-seven) where literacy rates ranged from 30 per cent to 70 per cent and in which no correlation could be established between literacy and income; third, the rich countries (twenty-four) with literacy rates above 70 per cent and per capita incomes of $500. Anderson and Bowman, though careful not to speak of causal relationships, tentatively suggest that a literacy rate of 40 per cent was a necessary, but not a sufficient, condition for economic development.[27] They also acknowledge the possibility that high education levels may well be the result of economic affluence but they still feel that a certain minimum level of education is a necessary prerequisite to the take-off stage of industrialisation. The implication of this study is that developing societies need to improve their elementary school system before their economies can hope to have a secure foundation for industrialisation. If this is the case, can it be substantiated by evidence from the history of developed societies? If it is assumed that this country had achieved the minimum level of industrial development by 1850, then the available circumstantial evidence suggests that by then about 70 per cent of the working class had achieved basic literacy rates. It is this evidence that led West to the cautious conclusion that 'it is reasonable to assume that in the nineteenth century education played *some* part in economic growth.'[28] Similarly, using historical data from several advanced industrial European countries, Anderson confirmed the finding that a 40 per cent literacy rate is the threshold for economic development. Similar statistical correlations have been found to exist also between GNP per head and school enrolment rates. In an often-quoted and much-criticised comparison of seventy-five countries in 1960, Harbison and Myers found a high statistical correlation between GNP per head and what they called the Index of Human Resources which was based primarily on school enrolment rates.[29]

Finally, Bennett's study is a step forward from previous studies because it differentiates between general secondary education and vocational secondary education. He collected data from sixty-nine countries (but excluded all countries in Africa) on such economic variables as GNP per head, calories consumed per head, and gross energy consumed per head and compared these to years of secondary schooling – general and vocational. As expected, he found a higher correlation between the economic indicators and vocational schooling than general secondary schooling – but only in the developing and not in the affluent countries.[30]

From these and many other similar studies, it can be concluded that there is a strong but by no means uniform statistical correlation between educational indicators and economic growth. What cannot be claimed is that education is always the cause and economic growth the effect. The relationship between the two is a two-way process, an illustration of the commonsense view that education is both a consumption and an investment good. In developing societies, primary education appears to be more of a social investment than individual consumption, while in affluent societies the demand for education may not come so much from the needs of the economy as from the demands of individual people.

In an effort to clarify the direction of the causality between education and economic development, Peaslee looked at historical trends in education for developed countries. Using 1920 as the base year for education and 1958 as the corresponding year for economic development, he found that 'sustained growth generally starts when primary enrolment is in the neighbourhood of 30% to 50% of the school-aged population.'[31] Of the richest thirty-five countries in 1958, all but six had the required level of primary education in 1920; vice versa, of the fifty countries that had not achieved the minimum level of primary education in 1920, only one was among the developed countries in 1958. This finding was not supported by Walter's study, in which she estimated the effects of increases in national primary and secondary education during 1950-60 on economic growth during 1960-70. Her general conclusion was that 'neither primary nor secondary educational expansion from 1950 to 1960 is positively related to 1960-70 economic development.'[32] One of the crucial issues in such studies is whether the time-lag allowed is the right one and had Walters allowed twenty instead of ten years, she might have reached different conclusions.

A more useful, but by no means non-problematic, analysis of the relationship between education or health and economic growth is the aggregate production function studies. A number of such studies have shown that economic growth rates cannot be explained completely by changes in capital and labour inputs. A certain proportion remains unaccounted for and it is part of this that is claimed to be the product of investment in education and health. Neither education nor health is an independent factor of production as capital and labour are. Rather, they affect production through their influence on labour quality and, to a lesser extent, labour quantity.[33]

Because of the importance of Denison's work, it is described here in some detail. Many other studies have been conducted, either in exactly the same or a very similar way. Denison examined the growth rates in real national income of the US during two periods 1909-29 and 1929-57. The overall growth rates for the two periods were 2.82 per cent and 2.93 per cent per annum respectively. Of these overall rates, growth of capital stocks accounted for 0.73 per cent and 0.43 per cent respectively. Changes in the labour force accounted for 1.53 per cent and 1.57 per cent respectively. The remaining 0.56 per cent and 0.93 per cent were attributed to a variety of residual factors. Where does the contribution of education come in? It emerges in relation to the contribution made by labour and the variety of residual factors. The 1.53 per cent and 1.57 per cent growth rates attributed to labour during the two periods consisted of quantitative changes (increase in the size of the labour force and decrease in working hours per week) and qualitative changes of labour of which education was the most important, an estimate of 0.35 per cent and 0.67 per cent respectively. As far as the contribution of the residual factors is concerned, Denison estimated that for the period 1929-57, economies of scale at the national and local level accounted for 0.35 per cent and advances in knowledge for 0.58 per cent. Obviously, one cannot add the two figures of 0.67 per cent and 0.58 per cent to arrive at the total contribution of education, since there is an overlap between the two, i.e. advances in knowledge must have affected advances in the education of the labour force and vice versa. The conclusion then must be that the *minimum* contribution of education to economic growth during the two periods was 0.35 per cent and 0.67 per cent respectively. In other words, education accounted for at least 12 per cent of the total economic growth during the first period and 23 per cent during the second; if the overlap between educational improvements in labour and advances in knowledge is not complete, then the contribution of education to economic growth is higher for both periods.[34] This was a higher contribution to economic growth than that made by capital stocks.

In a later study of economic growth in the USA, and Western European countries during the period 1950-62, Denison found the minimum contribution of education to economic growth to have been of far less importance: 15 per cent for USA, 13 per cent for UK and Belgium, and the rates for the remaining six countries varied from 7 per cent for Norway and Italy, to 2 per cent for West Germany.[35]

Denison's work on education covered also the contribution of reduced death rates and disability to economic growth. Taking the period 1960-80 for the United States, he estimated that if during these twenty years no-one died (a most extreme assumption) before reaching the retirement age of 65, then the labour force would be 4.8 per cent bigger than projected and the growth rate of national product would be 0.20 per cent higher per annum. If death rates declined by 10 per cent during the same period (a more realistic assumption) then the growth rate would be only 0.02 per cent higher per annum. He also estimated that if the number of working days lost through illness and injury was reduced by a quarter during the same period, another 0.05 per cent in growth rate per annum could be added, representing a rise of 1.1 per cent in the size of the labour force.[36]

Denison refrained from any estimates of the impact of health status on economic growth for the period 1900-60, the period he used for his education estimates. Mushkin attempted this by using the same methodology that Denison used in relation to education and in relation to health for the period 1960-80. She estimated what the size of the labour force in the United States would have been in 1960 by making two assumptions: (a) if death rates had not declined since 1900, the labour force would have been over 13 million less in 1960; (b) if death rates had declined from 1900 to 1920 but remained the same level after that, the labour force would have been 6 million smaller in 1960. Reduction in death rates during the sixty-year period meant a larger labour force and hence a higher rate of economic growth.

National income [she concludes] was increased by an amount equivalent to 0.3% per annum due to the decline in mortality rates, from the 1900 level (assuming, as does Denison that a 1% rise in the number of workers, other factors held constant, yields a 0.73% rise in national income for this period). The decline in death rates in the past sixty years thus accounts for 10% of the overall 3% growth rate in the economy.[37]

Though the production function approach was subjected to a great deal of criticism from the start, this criticism increased very substantially in the 1970s as the economies of the world began to stagnate. The criticisms have been both technical and ideological and some of them apply just as much to the statistical correlation studies. First, there are the methodological and conceptual criticisms. A point of general agreement among the critics has been the arbitrary allocation of the influence of the unaccounted residual factors to education. Ambramovitz aptly termed the residual factors as 'a measure of our ignorance'.[38] Though one can question the exact proportion allocated to education, it is impossible to argue that a certain proportion should not be so allocated. Disagreements, therefore, centre round the exact proportion of the residual factors that is accounted for by education. Such factors as incentives, motivation, perseverance, and the like may account for some of the proportion allocated to education; and these factors may be partly the effects of education and partly its causes. In abstract areas like these, statistical calculations, however sophisticated they may be, do not do justice to the complex web of inter-relationships. In a sense, this criticism is an extension of the issue of causation discussed earlier in relation to the statistical correlation studies.

Second, none of the studies takes account of any possible ill-effects of education and health expenditure on economic growth. Particularly controversial has been the argument of human capital theorists that a number of economic variables must be held constant in calculating the economic effects of education and health services. Thus, the effects of reduced mortality rates and of improved life expectancy rates on unemployment rates or hours of work are ignored on the grounds that the effects of such factors on economic growth must be considered separately. It is difficult to accept such an argument, however, much as one admires the zeal of human capital theorists. This is particularly the case in developing countries and Malenbaum's comment on this is a correct, if rather harsh, appraisal of the situation.

> However much the supply of labor [he writes] may gain in numbers or in quality from improved health and reduced death rates, there may be no corresponding gain in output. Thus, improved health in poor societies can lead to larger population, greater poverty, and eventually deterioration in health.[39]

Third, there has been substantial criticism of the implication of the human capital theory that income inequalities both within nations and between nations are reduced through increased investment in education. Several writers, including Jencks and his associates have provided ample evidence showing that increased education provision does not abolish poverty or reduce income inequalities substantially.[40] It must be pointed out, however, that rejection of this aspect of the human capital theory does not necessarily imply rejection of its main claims, i.e. that education or health contribute to economic growth. The same applies to the situation between nations: inequalities between developed countries have not declined but this does not necessarily mean wholesale rejection of the basic claims that a certain level of education is a necessary prerequisite to industrialisation. What can be added, however, is that structural aspects of the world capitalist economy make for the dependency of developing on developed countries — a fact which tends to perpetuate inequalities.[41]

Fourth, there has been criticism of the failure of the human capital theory to distinguish sufficiently between the contribution made to economic growth by different levels of education or by different subjects which, it has been claimed, has meant an unwarranted expansion of university education and of non-technical subjects. This is particularly relevant to developing countries, where higher education has led to graduate unemployment and to the 'brain drain' of qualified staff to developed countries. This criticism was valid in the early days of the human capital theory but not later when attempts were made to be more specific. The failure to arrive at any detailed results is a reflection of the complexity of the issues involved rather than of the failure of the protagonists of the human capital theory to recognise the problem.

Fifth, there is a mixture of theoretical and ideological objections from some Marxist writers. Bowles and Gintis criticise the human capital theory as providing 'a good ideology for the status quo' and for the fact that 'the contribution of schooling to growth over the last half century may on balance have been negative.'[42] And yet, in a separate discussion of education in Cuba since the revolution, Bowles claims the exact opposite: 'There is every indication', he writes, 'that the allocation of a sizeable fraction of the nation's resources to education has made a major contribution to the forces of production.'[43] There seem to be two reasons for this differential response to the human capital theory: education in Cuba extends beyond the classroom to the fields and the factories, while in capitalist countries it is restricted to the classroom. Moreover, the socialist ideology of Cuba meant a different motivation for pupils and workers from that existing in capitalist countries — 'to work for collective rather than personal objectives' — with the result that education in Cuba became both a technical and an ideological force for greater productivity. This is in contrast to the situation in capitalist countries where education reflects the authoritarian and exploitative values of the factory system with the result that it helps to reproduce the capitalist system of production which is inherently inefficient. The first argument has some merit for it is akin to the argument of non-Marxists that education should be related to the needs of the economy. It may, however, result in a less interesting and self-fulfilling system of education from the individual's point of view. The second argument is more complex and more difficult to evaluate. It is true that the capitalist system of production with its inherent conflicts between workers and management makes for inefficiency but it is not necessarily true, as they claim, that collectivism is a more powerful force for productivity than individualism.

It is not surprising that in view of all these criticisms and, more important, at a time of economic recession, the human capital theory is on the retreat. Even its long-standing strong supporters are cautious in their appraisals today. Thus Sorel in an interesting historical evaluation of the theory concludes that 'The human capital engine of analysis is performing most adequately, albeit not spectacularly, and the movement is alive and well.'[44] It is rare, indeed, to find today the original zealous approach though it is not altogether lacking. In a recent defence of investment in education, Stonier brought back memories of the early 1960s.

> Knowledge now is more important [he wrote] than the traditional land, labour, and capital, and even inputs of materials and energy. This reflects the fact that with enough technological and/or organisational expertise, you can either greatly reduce the requirements for these inputs, find substitutes, or actually create them *de novo*.[45]

What then can be concluded from this debate? In the first place, no-one has claimed that education is the only factor making for economic growth, and vice versa, no-one has argued that education makes no impact whatsoever on economic growth. Even Illich's onslaught is directed at formal schooling and not at education as such.[46] Second, there is general agreement that a minimum level of literacy is a necessary but not a sufficient condition for the process of industrialisation. This level, however, has been achieved by many of the developing countries today and expansion of their secondary and further education sectors will not by itself solve their economic problems. Third, there is substantial evidence showing that economic growth and education in advanced industrial societies are correlated, though there is equally substantial disagreement about the direction of the causality. It appears that post-primary education is both a cause and a result of economic prosperity but most circumstantial evidence points to primary education being more of a cause than a result in this relationship. Fourth, scientific and technical education is more conducive to economic development than other types of education though there are problems of identifying the appropriate mix between these different forms. Education performs political, social, as well as economic functions and it is thus too important to be made the slave to the needs of the economy even though it has no option but to be its servant. Finally, in their ceaseless pursuit of economic growth, advanced industrial societies have to rely on their scientific know-how for most of them have no vast untapped natural resources left. Thus, in spite of the problems involved in clearly identifying and measuring the contribution which education makes to economic growth, the balance of the available evidence suggests that an advanced industrial society which neglects its educational system does so at its own economic peril.

The present economic recession has highlighted the growing problems of financing an expanding education system and it has revived the debate on the contribution of education, and particularly higher education, to economic growth. There is government concern in all advanced industrial societies of how to restructure higher education so that it is made more directly relevant to the needs of the economy. There are also more vigorous attempts to relate education to industrial training, particularly for school-leavers. In a sense it is an acknow-ledgement of the potential of education to economic growth, but a questioning of the liberal tradition. It remains to be seen how successful this drive will prove because governments have to convince young people of the attractions of scientific and industrial education vis-à-vis the humanities and the social sciences as well as of the advantages of employment in industry and trade rather than in other sectors of the labour market. The danger in this new drive that is a feature of many advanced industrial societies lies not only in raising unrealistic expecta-tions from these areas of study but also in denigrating the contribution of the social sciences to economic growth and in neglecting the non-economic functions of education which are just as important to the well-being of individuals and of society at large.

Social policy and mobility of work and labour

Though this section looks only at government regional policies and labour mobility policies, it is worth mentioning that these represent only a small proportion of government expenditure on aid to industry. Denton has classified the various forms of aid to industry under three headings: general incentives provided under various programmes to all industrial firms in all parts of the country; industrial restructuring which again is universal in scope and geographical area and which is intended to encourage industrial efficiency; and regional aid which is limited to firms in the deprived regions of the country.[47] Labour mobility programmes are in an important sense different for they pro-vide aid to labour rather than to industry. In another sense, however, they are part of the same package for they are part of government attempts to bring employment and labour together irrespective of whether the aid is given to industry or to labour.

We begin the discussion with regional policies for they have featured more prominently in government initiatives than labour mobility pro-grammes, both as regards expenditure and public debate. The argu-ments for and against a government regional policy in industry are old and well-rehearsed. On the economic front, there are two pro-regional arguments. Regional unemployment and regional recession are an economic loss to the whole nation and they will not rectify themselves on their own. Government aid is necessary to counter market forces which operate in favour of the affluent regions where maximum profits can be made quickly, irrespective of long-term national considerations.

Thus the first important government report on depressed areas in the early 1930s concluded that such areas 'can only escape from the vicious cycle, where depression created unemployment and unemployment intensified depression by means of some positive external assistance'.[48] This became both the cornerstone of future government policy and the unquestioned assumption of subsequent government reports, including the Barlow Report in 1940 which made the strongest and most comprehensive case for regional development.[49] The second pro-regional policy argument emerged in the 1960s. Aid to depressed regions should be seen in regional as well as national terms: regional recovery is part of, and it assists national recovery, for it utilises the reserves of idle labour. A government report in 1963 concluded on this issue: 'A national policy of expansion would improve the regional picture; and, in turn, a successful regional development programme would make it easier to achieve a national growth programme.'[50]

Monetarist opponents of these views point out that the fact that industries in certain regions are unprofitable is evidence enough of either the fact that such industries are not in line with modern production methods or with demands in the international market; or that their location imposes additional costs on production compared with similar industries elsewhere in the country; or both factors may apply. Thus Burton concludes from his discussion of employment subsidies in general that they are

> likely to increase rather than reduce the rate of inflation. The jobs that they are claimed to save or create will be at the cost of labour under-utilisation or unemployment elsewhere in the economy. Furthermore, from a long-term viewpoint, they are likely to distort and hinder economic progress, and to induce changes in labour market behaviour that raise the natural rate of unemployment in the economy and the costs attaching thereto.[51]

For government to pursue a regional policy either by offering incentives to industries to move into depressed areas or by not allowing them to expand in the affluent parts of the country is tantamount to impeding economic growth and wasting resources.

Social reasons have also been important in the debate on regional policies. Without government aid, argue the pro-regionalists, depressed areas disintegrate socially, with the young and the skilled moving away and leaving the old and the unskilled behind; families and communities thus suffer socially. Vice versa, substantial immigration into growth areas causes social problems of crime, mental illness, etc., at least during the initial period of settling down. This social dislocation at both the depressed and the growth area is costly in economic terms too: schools are abandoned in the depressed areas and new schools are needed in the growth areas; housing suffers in similar ways; and so on. Monetarist opponents of regional policies are sceptical of how true many of these fears are. After all, they argue, there have been massive population movements within the country over the last two centuries with no apparent long-term ill-effect. They may concede that there may be frictional teething problems lasting a few years or even a few decades but argue that these are overcome eventually.

Finally, there are political reasons: people do not, on the whole, enjoy moving away from their communities and politicians find it hard to ignore these feelings. As McCrone put it: 'whatever government is in power in the United Kingdom, it ignores the regional problem at its own peril.'[52] This is particularly the case for Labour governments, for, if for no other reason, depressed areas contain more Labour than Conservative voters. The anti-regionalists have no real answer to this apart from arguing that governments must put the long-term economic interests of the country above short-term expedient considerations. The weakness of this argument is that there is no agreement, as mentioned above, about the economic implications of regional policy.

Marxists, too, have been critical of regional policies but for different reasons. Unlike monetarists, Marxists favour government regional policy in principle but they are sceptical of its effectiveness and anxious of its political consequences. They make three main criticisms: Regional policy has been too weak to counteract the tendency of large capitalist enterprises to move where it is most profitable from the immediate point of view and irrespective of social consequences on the local community. Only substantial government control and ownership of industry can hope to deal with regional inequalities of employment. Second, regional policies play an ideological role favourable to private capital: they present the economic recession as a problem of geographical distribution of jobs rather than what it is – a problem of simply insufficient jobs on a national level. By doing this, 'they have helped to set one area and one group of workers against another in the struggle to obtain a higher share of the inadequate number of jobs available.'[53] Third, regional policies have eased the process of restructuring old industries by promising new jobs. The result, however, has been that the number of jobs created has been far smaller than the number of jobs lost. For these reasons, 'the task of the left, in relation to the "regional question", should be to demonstrate the class nature of regional problems and state policy and institutions, and expose the use of spatial ideology as a dominant class strategy to split the labour movement.'[54]

McCallum divides the development of regional policy since the war into five periods: 1945-7 was a period of substantial growth; 1947-58 was the 'lull' in regional policy; 1958-64 was the re-activation; 1964-70 represented the boom; 1970-4 witnessed the unsuccessful counter-revolution; and 1974-8 was an age of uncertainty. To these a sixth can be added: 1979-82, which signalled the demise of regional policy both in ideological and economic terms.[55] The favourable labour conditions and the strong commitment of the Attlee government to regional policy resulted in substantial progress in this field: development areas gained 51 per cent of the total new industrial building during the two-year period 1945-7. The public expenditure cuts forced on the government in 1947 and the false sense of security that enough had been done led to less vigorous reinforcement of regional policy programmes. What the Labour government considered unfortunate, the Conservative government welcomed, and regional policy remained in decline all through the 1950s. This was a period of steady economic growth with demand for labour almost everywhere in the country. For regionally balanced economic growth, this neglect of regional policies was most unfortunate because regional policies are more effective when pursued during periods of labour demand than during periods of high unemployment. Yet it was the relatively high unemployment rates of 1958 and the worsening national economic situation that prodded the Conservative government in 1958 to re-activate regional policy. The Labour governments of 1964 and 1966 expanded the scope of regional policy, both as regards the areas covered, the number of programmes designed to promote regional policy and the administrative machinery needed to implement it. The return of a Conservative government in 1970 signalled a reversal of policies: the new government was anxious to disengage from both national and regional economic policies. Minimum government intervention was the new ideology. The economic recession and the sharp rise in unemployment of that year forced the Conservative government to change its policies before they had got off the ground. Regional policy was once again espoused and promoted. The Labour government of 1974 continued and expanded regional policies by establishing a multiplicity of job creation schemes in an effort to stem the rising tide of unemployment. As the economic recession continued to worsen, however, the government, in 1976, reduced very substantially its regional programmes and began to give more emphasis to encouraging economic growth in the prosperous regions. The return of the Conservative Party to power in 1979 simply accelerated the collapse of regional policies; they were now seen as unhelpful both in theoretical as well as pragmatic terms. Regional measures under the then Conservative government, wrote the Cambridge Economic Policy Review in 1980, 'are increasingly limited to areas with the worst social problems, implying greater reliance on the operation of market forces to produce "convergence" '.[56]

TABLE 4.1
Government expenditure on regional policy

Year	Government expenditure in real terms[a] (£ million)	IDC refusals[b] (%)
1960-1	34	17
1964-5	75	26
1969-70	612	16
1972-3	493	10
1975-6	612	12
1979-80	322	2

[a] At 1975-6 prices
[b] Government refusals for industrial developments in the Midlands and South

Source: *Cambridge Economic Policy Review*, vol. 6, *No. 2*, July 1980, Table 1, p. 1

Table 4.1 gives an indication of government expenditure under the various changing schemes of regional policy. The most striking feature is that expenditure in the 1970s was at a far higher level than during the 1950s and 1960s. The significant changes initiated in 1976 have led to a reduction in government expenditure. Before looking at the outcomes of regional policy, it is worth stating again that financial incentives are only one of the two strands of regional policy – the other is the industrial development certificate system through which the government can refuse applications for industrial expansion in prosperous areas thus encouraging firms to move into development areas.

Evaluating the effects of regional policy bristles with the same difficulties as the evaluation of any other large-scale government policy. It is never possible to be certain what the situation would have been in the absence of any such policy nor is it possible to know what the outcome of a different policy might have been. Nevertheless, attempts have been made to get as near the truth as possible as the brief account given here indicates. Various criteria evaluating the outcome of regional policies have been used. None is perfect, but they are useful indicators. Four such criteria are examined here. First, the number of firms which moved during the post-war period. Table 4.2 shows that both the total number of moves as well as the proportion of moves to development areas were at their highest during the two most pro-regional policy periods discussed above. Second, growth rates. Table 4.3 shows that during pro-regional policy periods, the development areas performed quite well vis-à-vis other areas in relation to manufacturing industries, which are the main beneficiaries of regional policies. Referring to their statistical findings, Moore and Rhodes conclude:

TABLE 4.2
Number of industrial establishments 'on the move', UK (annual averages)

Period	1 Total movement	2 Movement to the develop-ment areas	3 Movement to the non-development areas	Col. 2 as pro-portion of col. 1 (%)
1946-51	224	99	125	0.44
1952-9	146	28	118	0.19
1960-5	223	65	158	0.29
1966-71	264	102	162	0.39

Source: B. Ashcroft and J. Taylor, 'The Effect of Regional Policy on the Movement of Industry in Great Britain', in D. MacLennan and J. Parr, *Regional Policy*, Martin Robertson, 1979, Table 2.1, p. 45

TABLE 4.3
Differences in employment growth between development areas and non-development areas

	Difference in growth rates between development and non-development areas		Differential per-formance[a] between 1951-63 and 1963-70
	1951-63	1963-70	
Total difference	−0.74	−0.05	+ 0.69
Selected declining industries	−0.41	−0.55	−0.14
General manufacturing	−0.07	+ 0.41	+ 0.48
Services other than transport	−0.31	−0.03	+ 0.28
Construction and residual	+ 0.05	+ 0.12	+ 0.07

[a] plus sign indicates a *relative* improvement in the development areas in the period of active regional policy 1963-70 compared with the earlier period, 1951-63

Source: B. Moore and J. Rhodes, 'Evaluating the Effects of British Regional Economic Policy', *The Economic Journal*, vol. 83, March 1973

The most striking feature, however, is the very favourable differential performance of manufacturing industries in the active policy period — accounting for over two-thirds of the overall relative improvement in Development Areas. This is an important result because it is to these industries that regional policy has been primarily applied. There was also some relative improvement in the growth of construction and service industries in the more active policy period but this was smaller than that in manufacturing industries: it is consistent with a priori expectations about the multiplier effects of increased manufacturing activity, the increasing differential government expenditure in Developing Areas on health, education, and items of infrastructure and the adverse effect of continued decline in the declining industries sector.[57]

Third, there is the number of jobs created directly and indirectly as a result of regional policies. The direct effect is the number of jobs created as a result of the growth in employment in those firms assisted by the government. The indirect effect is the number of jobs created in other enterprises as a result of the growth of employment in the manufacturing sector — what is known as the multiplier effect. The generally accepted view is that, in the short-term effect, the multiplier is 1.2; in the medium term, it is 1.4; and in the long-term it is 1.7. A number of estimates have been made of the effects of regional policy in terms of new jobs created directly and indirectly. Table 4.4, which

TABLE 4.4
*Estimates of increases in the number of people employed in
development areas as a result of regional policies in Great Britain*

Study	Period	Number of workers	Area covered
Brown	1958-68	380,000	UK
Sant	1945-71	520,000	GB
Hardie	1961-70	326,000	GB
Moore, Rhodes and Tyler	1960-76	540,000	UK

Sources: M. Sant, *Industrial Movement and Regional Development*, Pergamon Press, 1975, p. 189

J. Hardie, 'Regional Policy', in W. Beckerman, *The Labour Government's Economic Record, 1964-1970*, Duckworth, 1972, Table 604, p. 234

A.J. Brown, *The Framework of Regional Economics in the United Kingdom*, Cambridge University Press, quoted in M. Sant, op. cit., p. 188

B. Moore, J. Rhodes and P. Tyler, The Impact of Regional Policy in the 1970s, *Centre for Environmental Studies Review*, no. 1, July 1977 summarises the main studies, shows that they all agree that regional policy has had an important effect on job creation though they disagree on how important it has been. The differences are small, varying between 32,000 jobs a year being the lowest estimate, to 38,000 being the highest estimate. These differences are due partly to the different periods covered by the various studies, to the different areas covered and to the importance attached to the indirect effects on employment in the non-manufacturing sector that new jobs in the manufacturing sector have.

Fourth, reduction in unemployment. The use of unemployment rates as a criterion of the effectiveness of regional policies is of limited value. During the periods of active regional policy, emigration from development areas declines and there is also the possibility that during such periods firms may make more people redundant, in the knowledge that the chances of finding employment are greater. Moreover, during such periods, new sources of labour — particularly women — may be tapped. Thus Moore, Rhodes and Tyler conclude that 'for every 100 jobs created by regional policy, unemployment in Development Areas may only be reduced by perhaps 30.'[58] With these qualifications in mind, it can be said that regional policies have moderated the relative but not the absolute differences in the unemployment rates of development and non-development areas, as Table 4.5 suggests. Clearly the improvement of the unemployment situation in Scotland during the 1970s owes a great deal to the new employment opportunities created by the discovery of North Sea oil, whereas the political troubles in Ireland have had an adverse effect on the local employment situation there.

More recent work has concentrated on the impact of regional policy on investment in the areas. Rees and Miall examined investment data in industry which was assisted in the various regions for the period 1959-78 and concluded that the three regions — Scotland, Wales and the North — which received most government assistance under regional policy initiatives also experienced a noticeable shift of investment in their favour. 'Moreover, the amount of the shift', they conclude, 'appears to have been fairly responsive to the different phases of regional policy.'[59] This positive shift in investment occurred not only in one or two large industries but for all industries — a fact which strengthens the view that the shift was due to regional policy rather than to other factors. Thus the evidence concerning the impact of regional policy on industrial investment reinforces the evidence in relation to employment.

The general conclusion that can be drawn from the evidence presented here is that regional policy has an improving effect on the employment and investment situation of development areas. Monetarist critics of regional policy, however, will find this evidence unconvincing.

TABLE 4.5
Absolute and relative[a] unemployment rates in the UK

Period	Scotland Absolute (%)	Relative (%)	Wales Absolute (%)	Relative (%)	N. Ireland Absolute (%)	Relative (%)	North Absolute (%)	Relative (%)	Merseyside Absolute (%)	Relative (%)	S. West D.A. Absolute (%)	Relative (%)	UK Absolute (%)
1951-5	2.8	175	2.6	163	7.7	481	2.3	144	n.a.	n.a.	n.a.	n.a.	1.6
1956-60	3.4	189	3.0	167	7.5	417	2.3	128	3.1	172	2.5	139	1.8
1961-5	3.7	195	2.9	153	7.2	379	3.4	179	3.4	179	2.4	126	1.9
1966-70	3.7	161	3.8	165	7.1	309	4.2	183	3.1	135	3.3	144	2.3
1971-5	5.3	156	4.6	135	7.2	212	5.6	165	6.2	182	4.2	124	3.4
1976	7.0	121	7.5	129	10.4	179	7.6	131	10.8	186	10.5	181	5.8

a The relative unemployment is the ratio of the unemployment rate in the development area to that of the UK

Source: B. Moore, J. Rhodes and P. Tyler, op-cit, Table 3

They will argue that such job creation as may have taken place is temporary and artificial, that the cost of achieving even this was too high and that it would have been cheaper and industrially more advantageous if people from development areas had been forced or encouraged to move to the prosperous areas. We do not yet have any significant evidence regarding the permanence of the jobs created by regional policy and we will look at labour mobility programmes below. As far as the efficiency argument is concerned, there are serious conceptual and empirical problems in evaluating it. If, however, one uses output per employee, the picture is encouraging for development areas. Comparing the assisted and non-assisted areas, Cameron concluded that

> the assisted areas do not appear to operate at a disadvantage. Indeed, they tend to have a higher net output per employee than two of the major non-assisted areas (the east Midlands and the West Midlands) though the South-East and also East Anglia had higher productivity than all the assisted areas in 1971.[60]

The claims for regional policy, however, should not be pressed too far to avoid giving the impression that regional policies are the answer to the country's current need for more jobs. Under the present conditions of economic recession, regional policies are fighting a losing battle. They are more effective when the national economy is expanding fast and when national rates of unemployment are low.

Labour mobility policies have not featured very prominently in this country. They have been criticised by both those who accept active government intervention in economic affairs and by those who do not. A large-scale labour mobility programme, it is argued, would result in the economic and social degeneration of the out-migration areas and would create economic and social costs to the in-migration areas. This is simply an argument for regional policies. Moreover, a labour mobility policy will not achieve a different result from the one achieved by unassisted labour mobility. In other words, the same people who would have emigrated on their own will be assisted by government programmes. In addition, there is no guarantee that the assisted emigrants will not return to their communities after a short period. This is an argument for governments leaving migration to the pressures of the market.

The introduction of the Resettlement Transfer Scheme in 1948 was the beginning of post-war labour mobility policies. The scheme was intended to provide financial help to unemployed workers in depressed areas who were prepared to move to other areas. As with regional policy, labour mobility policy was left to decline during the 1950s and improved in the late 1950s, when the economic situation was beginning to worsen. During the 1960s the scheme was widened to include more categories of workers and the financial assistance it provided was also considerably raised. Nevertheless, the scheme still affected a small number of workers only – almost 3,500 grants were made in 1960 rising gradually to 8,500 in 1971. The rise in unemployment in the early 1970s brought about even more improvements in the scheme which was renamed the Employment Transfer Scheme in 1972. The coverage of the scheme was widened further and new incentives were provided including a rehousing grant. The number of grants awarded increased rapidly so that by 1977 the number stood at 27,500. The economic recession of the late 1970s brought about a decline in the scheme similar to that in regional policy.

Clearly the labour mobility programmes have transferred fewer workers than the number of jobs created by regional policies. The cost of the two programmes, however, indicates clearly that labour mobility policy is far cheaper than regional policy both in absolute terms and, more important, per job created or worker transferred. Moreover, there is no reason to believe that, with improvements, particularly in relation to housing, labour mobility programmes could not affect a larger number of workers. In a survey of 551 labour migrants in four very different areas of England in 1971, Salt emphasises the severity of the housing problems facing migrants. Reviewing the difficulties facing migrants seeking entry to the public or private rented sectors, he concludes that:

> it is in those sectors of the housing market where government has taken most control and which provide cheap accommodation, that there is most restriction on entry for migrants. Yet, at the same time, these are the sectors that are most likely to provide for those workers (the lower paid and the unemployed) at whom the government's migration policies, operating through the Employment Transfer and Job Search Schemes, are aimed.[61]

As against this, however, it has to be remembered that a great deal of assisted labour mobility takes place within regions and, as Johnson and Salt point out, it is difficult to know 'how many transferees occupy jobs created as a result of regional policy'.[62] This is another indication that regional and labour mobility policies are not always in conflict with each other.

The question still remains, however, as to whether the assisted migrant workers would have moved anyhow without the financial aid of labour mobility programmes. Beaumont's study of assisted migrants in Scotland in 1976 showed that 88 per cent of his sample said they would have wanted to move in the absence of government assistance and, even more important, 69 per cent of the sample said they would have been able to move without government assistance. The main effect of government aid, according to his respondents, was to bring about an earlier move for 25 per cent of the group.[63] In another study in Scotland, Beaumont attempted to calculate the success of the Employment Training Scheme by finding out the proportion of migrants who remained employed in the destination areas for at least twelve months. His main findings were that 51 per cent had left employment in the destination area at some stage during the twelve-month period, most of these had returned to their area of origin and that 75 per cent of those who left the destination area had done so within the first ten weeks.[64] A study by Parker, however, using a national sample, reached conclusions which were slightly more supportive of labour mobility programmes: Only 13 per cent of his sample said they would not have moved without a grant but 56 per cent said they would have found it difficult to move without a grant.[65] These studies lend support to the thesis that labour mobility policies as presently constituted do little more than act as a mild incentive to a very small proportion of migrant workers.

Social policy and the encouragement of consumption

Until recently there would have been little dispute with the Keynesian view that the maintenance of demand in the economy was one of the central responsibilities of governments. In recent years, however, monetarist and related theories have questioned this with claims that government attempts to manage the economy and the consequent high levels of public expenditure are counter-productive – they are responsible for the economic decline of the country. We shall be discussing these views at length in the following chapter. In this section we merely want to put forward briefly the three main ways in which social policy has made and can make a contribution to increased consumption, investment, employment and hence to economic growth.

The payment of social security benefits to millions of people, most of whom would otherwise have little or no income, injects massive amounts of money into the economy. It is generally accepted that most of this is, of necessity, spent rather than saved, and hence the consumption of household goods is either increased or prevented from falling. The contribution of this to full employment is obvious, particularly at times when demand in the economy is generally low. This was clearly understood by both Keynes and Beveridge and it was one of the main considerations for the reorganisation of the social security system at the end of the last war. 'The placing of adequate purchasing power in the hands of the citizens so that they will spend more', wrote Beveridge in 1944, 'should be the main instrument of a full employment policy.'[66] In such a policy, the social security system was to play a major role since 'the income provided by the scheme to persons who are sick, unemployed, injured or past work will almost invariably be spent to the full.'[67] The social security system is the most obvious mechanism through which governments inject more money into the economy but there are, of course, other ways. Rent and rate rebates, tax relief to owner-occupiers, and exchequer subsidies to local authorities for housing purposes all make a contribution. Table 4.6 shows that government expenditure on the social services increased from

TABLE 4.6
Government expenditure on the social services, UK

Social service	1970-1		1980-1	
	£ million	% of GNP	£ million	% of GNP
Education	2,638	5.11	12,324	5.47
National Health Service	2,071	4.01	12,010	5.35
Personal social services	274	0.53	2,301	1.02
School meals, milk and welfare foods	176	0.34	500	0.22
Social security benefits	3,927	7.60	23,461	10.40
Housing	1,339	2.59	6,791	3.01
Total	10,425	20.18	57,397	25.45

Source: CSO, *Annual Abstract of Statistics*, no. 118, HMSO, 1982, Table 3.1, p. 56

one-fifth of GNP in 1970 to one-quarter in 1980. The largest single item as well as the one with the largest growth was expenditure on social security which absorbed one-tenth of GNP in 1980. Table 4.7 shows the number of recipients of the main social security benefits and gives some idea of the large number of people who rely almost totally on social security benefits for their livelihood. If double counting is discounted, but the number of dependants of recipients of benefits is taken into account, then at least one-quarter of the population in Britain relies almost totally on social security benefits. It gives an indication of the effects this has on the volume of consumption and hence on employment rates in the country.

Second, the prosperity and even the survival of many private enterprises depends largely on the workings of the social services. Schools are major consumers of books, the National Health Services is the major

TABLE 4.7
Number of persons receiving major benefits, GB (thousands)

Benefit	Month and year of survey	Number
Retirement pension	Sept. 1981	9,062
Sickness and invalidity benefits	May 1980	1,169
Unemployment benefit	Feb. 1981	1,165
Widow's benefit	Sept. 1981	423
Supplementary benefit	May 1981	3,347

Source: DHSS, *First Report of the Social Security Advisory Committee, 1981*, HMSO, 1982, Fig. 2, p. 6

consumer of drugs of all kinds, the personal social services are important clients of aids for the physically handicapped, and so on. In 1979-80, for example, the total expenditure on pharmaceutical services by the National Health Service was £989 million, while the total expenditure by universities and local education authorities in England and Wales on books and educational equipment was £314 million. New houses, new schools, new hospitals, new local authority residential establishments help to keep the building and furnishing industries going. When current and capital expenditure in these areas is substantially reduced, private enterprise inevitably suffers, for it cannot make up the loss by diverting its activities to other private sectors. These are just a few examples where public expenditure in the social services has direct implications for a number of private enterprises and, through them, for the entire national economy. What applies to social service expenditure applies equally well to such forms of public expenditure as road building, railway modernisation programmes, and so on.

Third, social services provide jobs for a large section of the labour force of all socio-economic groupings. The argument that public sector employment has expanded so much that it has absorbed too much labour and it has thus had an adverse effect on the national economy will be examined in the next chapter. Here the modest claim is made that without the social services, a section of the population will be permanently unemployed because in advanced industrial societies 'we cannot expect industry to create many extra jobs because of the speed of technical change and job-saving investment.'[68] Jobs have to be created in both the private and public sectors of the economy if full employment is to be maintained.

In these three main ways expenditure in the social services helps to maintain full employment, private profit and economic growth. This argument is a necessary corrective to the nowadays fashionable view which 'many Labour leaders share with the Conservatives . . . that the private sector produces and the public sector consumes.'[69] If, by some political catastrophe, government social services were abolished, they would soon have to be recreated in private form. They are simply essential to the economy. The crux of the debate, therefore, is not whether social service expenditure encourages consumption and hence economic growth but rather at what stage and under what economic conditions it uses up so much labour, capital and other resources that it 'crowds out' the manufacturing industries. There must be a limit beyond which expenditure on the social and public services is detrimental to economic growth; there is, however, a corresponding point below which social service expenditure is equally damaging to economic development. We return to these issues in the following chapter.

Conclusion

In this chapter we have discussed the main ways in which social services encouraged economic growth. The list is not exhaustive. We have not, for example, looked at government training schemes because until very recently they did not feature very prominently in government policies.[70] The general conclusion that emerges from this chapter is that social policy has been a positive force in economic growth though not as powerful a force as some of its protagonists have claimed over the years. There is no doubt that both education and health services improve the quality of labour and in doing so they assist economic growth. Government regional and labour mobility policies have also proved their economic worth even though they have not been pursued vigorously and at the most appropriate periods. Government expenditure also encourages consumption and hence economic growth even though they may also have detrimental effects if they exceed certain high levels — a claim that will be discussed in the following chapter.

Apart from these very specific ways, there are also the more general and non-quantifiable ways through which social policy may assist economic growth. It is quite possible that by taking care of the old, the very young, the sick and others 'public services replace the old-fashioned enlarged family and make the adults more available for employment, particularly the women who were traditionally responsible for household work and bringing up children.'[71] It is also likely that by providing minimum standards of living, social services reduce public apathy and dejection and thus maintain the will to work. In a more positive way, by raising public expectations, social services may, for better or for worse, reinforce the general belief that economic growth is and must remain the paramount objective of any government. These are mere speculations but they are, in fact, no more so than some of the anti-welfare state 'theses' referred to in the next chapter.

5

Does social policy undermine economic growth?

Public expenditure in general and social expenditure in particular are said to undermine economic growth in a variety of major and minor inter-related ways. 'Public expenditure', declared a government White Paper in 1979, 'is at the heart of Britain's economic difficulties.'[1] It is a view held not only by expert bodies and individuals but also by a substantial proportion of the general public who are not necessarily able to explain why and how this process takes place. As far as social policy is concerned, four main ways of different importance and popularity have been cited: expenditure on the social services has used up labour and capital which would have otherwise been employed in the wealth-creating manufacturing industries – this is the de-industriali-sation thesis. Second, the payment of social security benefits to workers on strike has both encouraged more and longer strikes and it has enabled trade unions to exact excessive wage rises which have damaged the economy. This is the state subsidy theory of strikes. Third, high social service expenditure has resulted in high taxation rates which, in turn, have undermined both work incentives and business initiative and fuelled inflation. Fourth, social security benefits are so generous that many people are financially better off out of work than at work. Incentives for work have, therefore, suffered. We shall examine each of these four claims separately though recognising that they are inter-related and that there are also other claims for the undermining effects of social policy on economic growth – the poverty trap and its damage to incentives, the encouragement of a general attitude favouring leisure and pleasure rather than work and saving, the lack of enthusiasm generated for profit in a welfare state, and so on.

Does social policy undermine economic growth?

The de-industrialisation thesis

The term de-industrialisation has several meanings[2] but in this section it refers to the argument that public expenditure pulls human and capital resources out of the manufacturing sector of the economy. It is the meaning attributed to the de-industrialisation process by the influential work of Bacon and Eltis in the mid-1970s. They begin their analysis by producing evidence which shows that

> Britain's growth rate has been one of the lowest of any major Western economy since 1961, that Britain's share of investment has been one of the two lowest, that Britain's share of world trade has been falling while others have had rising shares and that Britain's rate of inflation has been one of the fastest in the Western world.

Though this process had started long ago, it had accelerated recently.[3]

During the decade 1965-75, industrial production in Britain increased by less than half the level achieved in the previous decade 1955-65, i.e. a rise of 17 per cent, compared with 35 per cent. Yet the position was exactly the reverse in relation to productivity during the same two decades: productivity, i.e. output per man hour in manufacturing industry, increased by 4 per cent per annum during 1965-75 compared to only 3 per cent per annum during the decade 1955-65. In other words, during the decade 1965-75, industrial production should have increased by 40 per cent, rather than 17 per cent had the same man hours been worked. Since the overall size of the labour force was similar during the whole period, the conclusion seems inescapable that

> it is not the rate of growth of productivity that has let Britain down. What has let Britain down is that this has been allowed to produce growing numbers of redundancies instead of the increase in employment, and growth in the availability of real resources that should have resulted.[4]

In other words, firms prodded and assisted by governments, were becoming more productive and were making many of their workers redundant with the result that the numbers employed in manufacturing industry fell by 14 per cent between 1965 and 1975. What, then, happened to the redundant workers?

The answer is that they were simply being absorbed by the non-industrial sector of the economy, i.e. services and public services. It is true that all advanced industrial societies have witnessed this shift but none to the same extent as this country. During the period 1961-74, according to Bacon and Eltis, the ratio of non-industrial to industrial employment changed by 33.9 per cent in favour of the non-industrial sector in the UK, and by only 18.6 per cent in France, with the other industrial countries showing lower percentage changes.[5] Further analysis showed that during 1961-74, employment by local authorities increased by 53.7 per cent, central government employment rose by 9.4 per cent and employment in private services, such as retail distribution, banking, leisure and so on, by 13.2 per cent.

Why were so many workers absorbed by public services in such a short period? Three reasons are given by Bacon and Eltis: both Conservative and Labour governments, because of their adherence to Keynesian economics, were anxious to deal with unemployment quickly by tinkering with the economy; because of the public demand for improved social services; and because extra jobs in the public services could be provided cheaply and quickly since no extra capital investment was necessary as would be the case in industry.

The situation was made more serious by the fact that public employees, during this period, demanded and were granted substantial rises in their wages and salaries. The result was that what had been a small-sized cheap labour force became a large well-paid labour force. Thus a shrinking industrial sector had to produce enough to finance an expanding non-industrial sector. It is true that other countries managed this, but the situation in Britain was different in two important ways: productivity per man hour was lower in Britain than in other industrial countries and the shift to non-industrial employment was greatest in Britain.

The assumption behind the Bacon and Eltis thesis is that only industrial production can maintain and improve the standard of living in the country. The private sector service industries make only a small contribution while the public services make none. They divide economic activities 'between those that produce marketed outputs and those which do not. Almost everything that industry produces is *marketed*, that is, it is sold to someone. The private sector services are sold, so they are marketed.'[6] Non-marketed services include all those public services which are provided free of charge at the point of consumption – health, defence, civil service, most schools, police, etc. Public services which are sold – electricity, coal, etc. – are, however, marketed. Vice versa, private industries which are heavily subsidised by governments have only partially marketed outputs. They highlight the importance of the marketed sectors by pointing out that 'the marketed output of industry and services taken together must supply the total private consumption, investment and export needs of the whole nation.'[7]

As the shift to the non-marketed sector took place and since productivity in the shrinking marketed sector did not increase substantially, it meant that a smaller proportion of the net output of the marketed sector was left to be used by industrialists and their workers. A situation like this could have been resolved by either the workers in the marketed sector accepting lower wages, or the employers accepting lower profits or a combination of the two. The power of trade unions ensured that it was not the workers' wages that suffered but the employers' profits. Employers could not pass on the extra costs to the consumers either at home or abroad because of international competition – British goods would have been even more expensive than foreign goods. The British public was not prepared either to pay for the higher cost of the non-marketed sector through higher taxation rates. When taxes were increased, wages and benefits were also increased accordingly. The ball was, so to speak, back in the industrialists' court – the cost of the public services had to be disproportionately born by private capital which resulted in a reduction in business profitability.

A lower profit margin meant that industrialists could not afford to invest enough either to expand or to modernise their plant. It also meant that there was little incentive for them to invest in Britain since it was more profitable for them to invest in countries where profit margins were higher. The implications of this are increased unemployment, since the government cannot continue indefinitely expanding the non-marketed sector. If it does, it will mean increased taxation and even lower profits leading to less and less investment in industry. This spiral effect or vicious circle can best be broken by reducing public expenditure on a permanent basis. This can only be done by massive redundancies in the public sector and reductions in the level of benefits and services. Bacon and Eltis reject the neo-Keynesian solution that relies heavily on incomes policies because they think such policies do not work. They also reject left-wing solutions involving greater nationalisation of industries and import controls because, again, they do not feel they will be effective.

Criticisms of the Bacon and Eltis thesis are of two types: theoretical and empirical. Thirlwall, writing from a Keynesian standpoint, rejects the basic argument that the growth of the non-marketed sector was the cause of the decline of the marketed sector. He maintains that both these changes – expansion of the non-marketed sector and contraction of the marketed sector – are symptoms

of a much more basic malaise and structural phenomenon, namely the inability of the marketable output (largely industrial) sector to grow as fast as productivity growth without the economy coming up against a balance of payments constraint, due to a high U.K. income elasticity of demand for imports, coupled with a much lower world income elasticity of demand for U.K exports.[8]

He agrees that if public services expand then something in the industrial sector must decrease — profits or investment — but 'it does not follow that the former is the cause of the latter'; rather they are both the joint results of the non-competitiveness of British goods in the international market. In a subsequent article he sums up the reasons for de-industrialisation as follows: 'The most convincing explanation', he writes, 'of progressive de-industrialisation in the U.K. is the weakening of the foreign trade sector with a slow growth of exports relative to other countries, and in relation to the propensity to import.'[9]

Sleeman, again from a Keynesian standpoint, adopts an equally critical position. He points out, first, that Bacon and Eltis underestimate the effects of demographic changes on public expenditure — the rise in the proportion of old people in the community, the increased demand for places in higher education, and so on. He feels that the Bacon and Eltis thesis

> does not explain why the rate of investment and innovation in British industry were so low to begin with. Why was it that British industrialists took advantage of rising labour productivity to reduce their labour force, rather than to develop new forms of production using more sophisticated techniques and making improved products to sell at home and abroad? The problem of Britain's relatively slow rate of growth in the post-war period, compared with other industrial countries and in particular its failure to diversify and innovate competitively, is a very deep rooted one, about which there has been much controversy. Government policy in the late 1960s and early 1970s in diverting labour and other resources into the public sector may have exacerbated this, but it did not create it.[10]

Gough, writing from a Marxist perspective, finds the de-industrialisation thesis wanting on two counts. First, the reasons for the expansion of the social services are not simply the desire and anxiety of successive governments to reduce unemployment, cheaply and speedily, as Bacon and Eltis claim. Rather the expansion of the social services is the result of two major factors: '(i) the requirement of the capitalist economy as mediated by the state structure and state policies; (ii) the class balance of forces within capitalist society'.[11] In other words, working-class pressure and the needs of private capital, jointly and separately, account for the growth of both public and social service exenditure. Second, not all social services are unproductive. He follows O'Connor — as mentioned in the previous chapter — in dividing government services into 'social consumption' and 'social expenses', and concludes that the effect of growing social expenditure depends on its type (whether transfers, purchases or state produced services), its nature (the department or production or, in the case of transfers, the class to which it is directed), the manner in which it is financed and the final incidence of taxes.[12]

In other words, the effects of government expenditure on private profit is a far more complicated process than Bacon and Eltis imply and it does not always work to the detriment of private capital and private profit. In brief, the economic crisis of capitalism in Britain is not due to the extension of social welfare but to far deeper contradictions of British and international capital. It is acknowledged, however, that in its efforts to support the capitalist system, politically and economically, the capitalist state creates and expands public and social services only to find that it does not have the required resources to meet the growing cost of the public sector. The root of the problem, however, lies in the capitalist form of production which generates these conflicting tendencies.

The empirical criticisms of Bacon and Eltis are twofold, as far as the supply of labour is concerned. First, all the evidence that is available shows that the expansion of the social services did not so much rely on the workers made redundant from the industrial sector but rather it drew on new sources of labour — mainly women. Klein et al. showed that the number of full-time male employees of local authorities increased by only 13 per cent during the critical period of 1964-74 while the number of part-time women in local authority employment rose by 86 per cent during the same period.[13] Similarly, Thatcher provides abundant evidence which shows that while most of the workers made redundant in the industrial sector were men, most of the expansion in the public services was in female employment. Table 5.1 makes this abundantly clear, while Table 5.2 shows that while full-time employment declined overall, part-time employment increased substantially, particularly among women.

The second criticism is that though public expenditure and public employment have been reduced during the last five years, this has not resulted in any upsurge of employment in the marketed sector. Far from it: rising unemployment in one sector has been accompanied by rising unemployment in the other sector. It can therefore be argued that not only do social services not pull labour out of the manufacturing sector, but also if they are not expanded the redundant labour from the manufacturing sector simply remains unused and joins the existing long-term reserve army of labour. Looking back at the decade of 1965-75, which Bacon and Eltis consider critical for the economic health of the country, one can see that there was no shortage of labour

TABLE 5.1
Changes in UK employment, 1966-77 (thousands)

Employment in	Males	Females	Total
Production industries	−1,438	− 536	−1,975
Other industries:			
Private sector	− 385	+ 213	− 171
Public sector	+ 367	+ 1,065	+ 1,432
Total	−1,456	+ 742	− 714

TABLE 5.2
Changes in UK employment, 1971-6 (thousands)

| Employment in | Full-time | | Part-time | | Total |
	Males	Females	Males	Females	
Production industries	−585	−296	+ 11	+ 34	− 836
Other industries	+ 142	+ 186	+105	+820	+1,253
Total	−443	−110	+116	+854	+ 417

Source: R.A. Thatcher, 'Labour Supply and Employment Trends', Tables 2.4
and 2.5 respectively, in F. Blackaby (ed.), De-industrialisation,
Heinemann, 1979, p. 31

because unemployment increased during this period.

It can, however, be claimed that though the expansion of employment in the public sector was not directly responsible for the decline in
the number of people employed in the manufacturing sector because it
did not use the same labour sources and because there was no labour
shortage anyhow, it was, nevertheless, indirectly responsible because it
led to a decline in private profit and hence to a shortage of capital for
investment in the manufacturing industries. The question of business
profitability is both crucial and difficult. A distinction must be made
between pre-tax and post-tax profits as well as between the two main
methods of measuring profitability. These are profit share, i.e. profit
income as a proportion of the total income of an enterprise and profit
return, i.e. profit as a proportion of the capital invested in the
enterprise.

There is general, though not unanimous, agreement that profitability
in British industry has declined since the early 1950s. In a review article
of the findings of Marxist, Keynesian and monetarist scholars, Burgess

and Webb concluded in 1974 that, first, 'there has been a marked and persistent decline in pre-tax profit shares since the mid-1950s. However, the acceleration in the rate of decline which appears to have occurred in the second half of the 1960s has been lessened by the payment of investment grants.' Second, that 'post-tax figures indicate that the share of profit was fairly constant up until the mid-1960s but there was a decline during the latter 1960s.' Similar conclusions applied if the rate of return on capital was used as the yardstick of profitability.[14] A more recent summary of profit trends arrived at similar conclusions and also showed that the decline in profitability in the UK was sharper than that in other countries, as Table 5.3 indicates.

Thus the conclusion must be that profitability of British industry declined, though not on the pattern suggested by Bacon and Eltis. The decline of profitability started in the 1950s, when the public sector was small. In other words, the decline in profits preceded rather than followed the expansion of the public sector as regards both employment and expenditure.

The reasons for the decline in profitability are lucidly and cogently analysed in an influential Marxist work by Glyn and Sutcliffe in 1972. 'We conclude', they wrote, 'that the basic reason for the decline in the profit share was the squeezing of profit margins between money wage increases on the one hand and progressively more severe international competition on the other.'[15] The full employment situation of the 1950s provided trades unions with the power to extract wage rises from employers which were higher than increased productivity. Employers could not pass on in full these extra costs to the consumers because of the competitive international situation, with the result that profitability fell. These two tendencies may have been exacerbated by the rise in public expenditure in the 1960s, as Bacon and Eltis suggest, but they were not the cause of it, since they preceded it.

The decline in profitability may have resulted in an unwillingness of British business to invest in industry in this country, but it did not lead to any scarcity of capital for investment. Thus the Treasury in its evidence to the Wilson Committee stated that 'there is no evidence that there have been real constraints on the supply of funds to industry.'[16] Similarly, the evidence of the London Clearing Banks to the same committee stated: 'There is certainly no evidence to suggest that the availability of bank finance has been even a remotely significant factor holding investment back.'[17] The Wilson Committee itself summarised the evidence it received on this issue as follows:

Few in industry or the institutions believe that the way the financial institutions operate has deprived firms of funds they should have had, or has constrained investment. Low productivity, low

TABLE 5.3
International comparisons of profitability in manufacturing industry, 1955-78

Averages per year	UK		Canada		USA		West Germany	
	Profit shares[a]	Net rate of return[b]	Profit shares[a]	Net rate of return[b]	Profit shares[a]	Net rate of return[b]	Profit shares[a]	Net rate of return[b]
1955-9	28	17	30	22	21	29	–	–
1960-2	26	15	28	19	20	27	32	29
1963-7	24	14	28	18	23	36	29	21
1968-71	21	11	25	16	19	26	28	22
1972-5	16	7	27	17	17	22	21	16
1976-8	13	5	23	13	19	24	21	–

a defined as net operating surplus as percentage net value added
b defined as net operating surplus as percentage net capital stock of fixed assets (excluding land)

Source: W.E. Martin, The Economics of the Profit Crisis, HMSO, 1981, Tables B.4a and B.4b, pp. 26 and 27 respectively

profitability, low demand and problems caused by government policies are regarded as far more important factors behind our industrial performance.[18]

In brief then, there was no shortage of capital nor were there any institutional barriers to its being invested in the manufacturing industries in Britain. The point should not be missed either that a great deal of capital for investment comes not from profits in industry but from the vast and growing capital of pension funds and other financial institutions relying on personal savings, which, as we shall show below, have shown an upward trend in recent years. What was therefore happening during the period reviewed by Bacon and Eltis was that British capital was being invested either abroad, where profit returns were higher and easier to achieve, or in finance companies in this country where again profitability was higher than in industry.

To sum up this section: the Bacon and Eltis thesis that the public sector crowded out the manufacturing sector cannot be substantiated. The expansion of the public sector, as Harris points out, merely filled the gap left by the private sector and, what is more, 'there is no evidence that private sector output would have been substantially higher than it actually was if the output of the public sector had been lower.'[19] It is quite possible that the expansion of the social services may have used up some of the labour that could have been absorbed by the manufacturing sector but there was no scarcity of labour as such in the 1960s and 1970s. It is also quite likely that the social services consumed some of the capital that could have been invested in industry, but again there was no scarcity of capital during this period. Finally, the expansion of the social services may have contributed slightly to the unprofitability of capital but the roots of the decline in profitability lie elsewhere whether one adopts one of the various Keynesian or Marxist perspectives.

The state subsidy theory of strikes

We are not concerned here with the various theories attempting to identify the causes of strike activity. This literature is very substantial and far more sophisticated than the state subsidy theory of strikes.[20] What we are concerned with in this section is to examine the claim that government financial assistance to strikers both encourages the propensity to strike and prolongs strikes. No-one has claimed that this is the only cause of strike activity — merely that it is one of many factors that have a bearing on strike activity.

Gennard sets out six propositions which make up the theory in its strongest version. They are as follows: first, the system of government financial assistance to strikers reduces 'the financial cost of striking in terms of income forgone' and it therefore reduces 'the incentive for workers to resist calls for strike action'.[21] Second, because of the rules governing the payment of supplementary benefit to strikers (to be discussed below) the present system results 'in short strikes developing into long strikes'.[22] Third, since supplementary benefit can be paid indefinitely, long strikes are prolonged into longer strikes. Fourth, until 1981, trade unions could evade having to make any payments to their members on strike since they were in receipt of supplementary benefit. The result is that 'there is no economic incentive for the union to act as a moderating influence on its members and so induce a settlement.'[23] Fifth, since the amount a striker can receive in income tax rebate is greatest during the end of the financial year, i.e. March, the incidence of strikes is highest during that period. Sixth, the employer's will to resist trade union demands is weakened and he therefore 'settles closer to the union's minimum acceptable increase than to his own maximum acceptable offer'.[24]

Before looking at the different propositions of the theory, it is necessary to describe briefly the two forms of government financial assistance: income tax rebates and supplementary benefit. The amount of income tax rebate depends on the person's previous income and the time of the year when it is paid. It increases with income and with the passage of months during the tax year. It is paid irrespective of any other income coming to the striker or his family. Supplementary benefit is a means-tested weekly allowance which is not normally paid for the striker himself, but for his family only. A number of observations follow from this: the number of single strikers who receive supplementary benefit is very small — during the five-year period 1970-5 it ranged from 100 to 400, or an average 240 per annum.[25] Single strikers receive supplementary benefit at the discretion of the supplementary benefit officer only in very exceptional circumstances. Payment of supplementary benefit to the family of a married striker will depend on any other income the family may have. Thus if the wife is in employment her earnings will be taken into account and the family will normally be disqualified. Similarly, any amount of income tax rebate or trade union strike pay will be considered and may have a similar result. A disregard of £4 per week is granted after which any other income is taken fully into account. Finally, any wages payable to the striker by the employer during the strike are fully taken into account. The result of this is that most strikers are disqualified from receiving supplementary benefit during the first two weeks of a strike. There are, of course, many who are disqualified for shorter or longer periods depending on their employer's method of paying them.

Attempts to test the state subsidy theory of strikes have been of two kinds: studies attempting to show the correlation, if any, between levels of benefits and strike activity over the years; and studies exploring the views of strikers in relation to benefits and strike activity. We begin with the first type of study. From the long-term point of view, there does not seem to be any relationship between strike volume, on the one hand, and the level or terms of provision of government financial assistance to strikers. The payment of means-tested benefits to the families of strikers was part of the poor law system from the end of the nineteenth century, but it was not until after the National Assistance Act, 1948, that the conditions for the payment as well as the level of the benefit were improved. Yet various studies have shown that the volume of strikes was far higher before than after 1950.[26]

Table 5.4 covers the post-war period and provides detailed data concerning strike activity and payment of supplementary benefit. The number of strikers receiving supplementary benefit has always constituted a very insignificant proportion of the total number of persons on strike — the lowest figure was 0.12 per cent in 1962 and the highest was 14.46 per cent in 1972 which was the year of the miners' strike. Even as a proportion of the number of workers on strike for two weeks or more, the figures are still very small — 4.4 per cent in 1965 and 36.8 per cent in 1971, the year of the post office workers' strike. During that year, 70 per cent of all supplementary benefit paid to strikers went to post office workers, partly because of their greater knowledge of the workings of the supplementary benefit scheme.

Two main conclusions can be drawn from Table 5.4 in relation to the state subsidy theory of strikes. First, there is no consistent trend in the number of strikers who receive supplementary benefit as a proportion of either those who are 'eligible', or as a proportion of the total number of strikers in any one year. Second, there is no consistent pattern over the period covered by the table between, on the one hand, the level of supplementary benefit, and the proportion of 'eligible' strikers, i.e. those involved in strikes lasting for more than two weeks when supplementary benefit is normally payable. The amount of supplementary benefit for a wife and two children constituted 47 per cent of net average earnings of male manual workers in 1957; it was 53 per cent in 1964; and 65 per cent in 1975. In spite of this improvement in the level of the benefit, the percentages of 'eligible' strikers were lower in the 1960s than the 1950s. It is, however, correct that these percentages were at their highest in the 1970s when the number of strikers was also at its highest.

The amount of the tax rebate is at its highest during the last quarter of the tax year and it is obviously at its lowest during the first quarter. Duncan and McCarthy examined data for the period 1956-70 and

TABLE 5.4
Supplementary benefit and strike activity

Year	Col. 1 Number of strikers 'eligible' for supplementary benefit[a]	Col. 2 'Eligible' strikers as % of all strikers	Col. 3 Number of strikers who received supplementary benefit	Col. 4 Col. 3 as % of Col. 1	Col. 5 Col. 3 as % of all strikers
1954	101,000	22.6	11,200	11.7	2.64
1955	138,000	21.0	18,700	13.5	2.83
1956	46,000	9.1	3,700	7.9	0.72
1957	212,000	15.6	42,000	19.8	3.09
1958	96,000	18.4	11,700	12.2	2.24
1959	149,000	23.1	8,000	5.3	1.22
1960	109,000	13.3	8,000	7.3	0.97
1961	134,000	17.4	9,500	7.1	1.24
1962	40,000	0.9	5,700	12.8	0.12
1963	34,000	5.8	3,000	8.7	0.50
1964	42,000	4.8	4,600	11.0	0.53
1965	130,000	15.0	5,700	4.4	0.66
1966	72,000	13.5	8,000	11.0	1.48
1967	78,000	10.6	19,800	25.3	2.68
1968	104,000	4.6	19,200	18.4	0.85
1969	417,000	25.2	67,300	16.1	4.06
1970	556,000	31.0	102,400	18.4	5.70
1971	345,000	29.4	126,900	36.8	10.82
1972	768,000	44.5	249,700	32.5	14.46
1973	296,000	19.5	36,000	12.1	2.36
1974	686,400	42.4	157,100	22.9	9.75
1975	205,300	26.0	26,200	12.8	3.33
1976	113,400	16.9	10,100	8.9	1.50
1977	366,300	31.7	54,400	14.8	4.69
1978	378,800	37.7	45,200	11.9	4.49

a Eligible refers to the number of workers directly and indirectly involved in trade disputes lasting over twelve working days.
The figures for 1979 refer to over ten working days
Source: For the period 1954-74 J. Gennard, *Financing Strikes*, Macmillan, 1977, Table 2.1, p. 26. For the period 1974-9 various issues of
Department of Employment Gazette and Supplementary Benefits Commission, *Annual Report 1979*, Cmnd 8033, HMSO, 1980, Table 10.1, p. 95

found that 'strike activity peaked, as expected, during the last quarter of the financial year but it was also at a very high level (not expected) during the first quarter.'[27] It is, however, generally known that many trade unions choose the winter months for strikes because they can exert more pressure on employers than during other periods of the year and not so much because their members can claim tax rebates.

Perhaps what is interesting and puzzling is not why a minority of 'eligible' strikers' families receive supplementary benefit, but why the majority do not. Wives' earnings from work must be one reason and ignorance or reluctance to apply is another. In a study of strikes during 1970-2 lasting for more than two weeks, Gennard and Lasko found that the number of people involved in a strike, the duration of the strike and whether it was official or unofficial affected the payment of supplementary benefit. Strikes that are more likely to attract supplementary benefit are those involving large numbers, which last long and which are official. The most important criterion, however, was the official status of the strike. 'In every case, whatever the length or size, benefit was about twice as likely to be paid out in official strikes as in unofficial strikes.'[28] The backing of the union is not only important because of the information and clerical services it provides to strikers applying for supplementary benefit, but also, perhaps, because it evokes a more sympathetic treatment from the supplementary benefit officers.

The second approach to verifying the state subsidy theory is through interviews with strikers. If supplementary benefit is an inducement to strike activity, then knowledge of how the system operates and reliance on it as a source of livelihood must enter into workers' plans before embarking on strikes. In another study, Gennard and Lasko interviewed fifty workers from each of two long and large strikes in 1971 and 1973. They also supplemented the personal interviews with over 500 postal questionnaires making a total of just over 600. In both strikes, a great deal of confusion prevailed: most people had no clear idea when they would be entitled to supplementary benefit or how much they could claim. Indeed, in one of the strikes, the union paid the strikers so much strike pay that most strikers became ineligible for supplementary benefit. Moreover, most strikers did not see themselves relying on supplementary benefit during the strike — rather they envisaged getting by on their savings and their spouses' wages. Most strikers also underestimated the length of the strike, anticipating it to last for a far shorter period and the continuation of the strike was not something they enjoyed.[29] They also provide evidence of the various sources of income of the strikers: spouses' job and savings were the two most important sources; tax rebates were an important source for both strikes, but supplementary benefit was insignificant for one strike because of their union's practice of providing strike pay. All strikers had to resort to some extent to borrowing, credit, casual work and other ways and means of managing.

A similar picture emerges from Cole's study of a small number of strikers in the building industry in the Midlands. The main sources of their average weekly income during the strike were personal savings constituting 45 per cent of all income, wives' earnings 17 per cent, supplementary benefit 16 per cent and tax rebates 10 per cent.[30]

In conclusion, the evidence from both the statistical correlation and the personal interview studies does not substantiate the state subsidy theory of strikes but it does not refute it either. The only tentative conclusion that can be drawn from all these studies is that government financial assistance to strikers may play some minor part, not so much in starting, but in prolonging a strike, but it is an insignificant factor compared to the complex web of economic and political reasons that generate and sustain strike action. Social policy, however, is not usually shaped by research evidence. The view that state subsidies encourage strike activity in a variety of ways is strongly held in advanced industrial societies,[31] and it is part of the Conservative Party folklore on industrial relations. It was not therefore unexpected that the Thatcher government introduced legislation which reduced the amount of supplementary benefit payable to strikers and which made their trade union responsible for paying a higher amount of strike pay.

Taxation and incentives to work, to save and to invest

In any examination of the supposed detrimental effects of social policy on economic growth, the tax system must be included if for no other reason than that social policy consumes around half of all public expenditure today and therefore substantially affects rates of taxation. Concern with the disincentive effects of taxation has, however, been a continual theme during the whole period covered by this study irrespective of the prevalent rates of taxation or the level of public expenditure. Writing in 1947, Hogg (later Lord Hailsham), presenting the Conservative Party case against the reforms introduced by the Labour government, felt that the rate of income tax 'has become a potent cause of social harm as well as a source of revenue'.[32] Twenty years later, in an article in *The Times*, Treasure was even more categorical: 'I believe the tax system is the single most important cause of the lack of desire to improve efficiency that exists in our economy today.'[33] Just over ten years after that, the Conservative government's Chancellor of the Exchequer, Sir Geoffrey Howe, repeated the same sentiment in his budget speech on 12 June 1979. 'Excessive rates of income tax', he told the House of Commons, 'bear a heavy responsibility for the lack lustre performance of the British economy.'[34]

The tax system of any country has to perform several functions which are not always compatible. It has to provide the financial resources for at least a minimum number of services — defence, roads, education, income support, etc. — which are generally deemed to be necessary for the survival of any modern society. Most governments, too, have used the taxation system in their efforts to influence the growth of the economy — either to control inflation or to encourage consumption. An egalitarian government may also wish to use the tax system as a means of redistributing resources from the rich to the poor. All governments, to a lesser or greater extent, will also be anxious that the rates of taxation do not undermine work incentives.

Inevitably there are conflicts between these various functions: a highly progressive tax system may well undermine work effort among the small minority of large wealth-owners; a strong anti-inflation policy may well mean high levels of taxation which can have effects — positive and negative — on work incentives; and so on. Finally governments have also to bear in mind taxation rates in other countries when framing their own policies.

In the language of the economists, taxes have an 'income effect' and a 'substitution effect'. On the twin assumptions that workers act rationally and that time is divided between work and leisure, it follows that if taxation encourages more leisure then it discourages more work, and vice versa. Thus when direct taxes are increased, they reduce people's net incomes — the income effect — with the result that people have to work harder if they want to maintain, let alone improve, their standard of living. At the same time, however, increased taxes on income mean that people derive less income for each hour they work and they may therefore decide to prefer leisure to work, i.e. work less — the substitution effect. There is, therefore, no reason why taxation always encourages people to work less hard rather than harder, as so many have claimed. It depends on the individual's attitudes, needs and priorities which clearly vary from person to person and from time to time.

There are, obviously, a multitude of factors that affect people's work effort apart from taxation rates. The individual's personal circumstances, the demand for labour in the economy, restrictive practices, the opportunities offered by employers for more work effort, and so on. Some of these factors are beyond the control of the individual worker; others are his own to decide; and others represent situations where the individual can exert only a minor influence. It is thus important to see the influence of the taxation system on work incentives in this wider perspective. When the issue is examined in this way, one cannot but agree with Brown's conclusion that 'at best (or worst) taxation should have a relatively minor impact on the supply of labour, or work effort.'[35] Moreover, whatever methodological approach is adopted, there will be serious difficulties in separating the effect of taxation on work effort from that of other factors.

The incentive/disincentive effects of taxation can be direct and indirect and they can be seen in either broad or narrow terms. In their broadest terms they refer to the whole issue of the supply of labour: do taxes affect the choice of occupation, the individual's drive for promotion, the number of hours worked, the rate of productivity, labour mobility, the decision to retire from work, to emigrate, and so on? More narrowly defined they refer to work effort, i.e. the number of hours worked and the effort per hour worked. These are the direct effects of taxation; indirect effects go beyond the area of possible measurement into the realm of sheer speculation. Thus a worker who increases his hours of work, as a result of higher taxation (direct effect), may use the extra income to buy consumer items, the manufacture and use of which increase pollution of the environment (indirect effect). In this section we are concerned with the direct effects rather narrowly defined. We begin with studies base on personal interviews and we distinguish between working-class and professional samples.

The first study during the period covered by this study was conducted in 1952 by the Government Social Survey for the Royal Commission on Taxation. It covered 1,429 industrial workers and supervisors in England and Wales who could vary their work effort either through working overtime or by producing more in piece work. Unfortunately the way in which the issues were formulated and the phrasing of the questions were such[36] that no credence can be given to the findings of the survey or to the general conclusion of the Royal Commission that 'there was no evidence from this enquiry of productive effort being inhibited by the income tax structure within its present limits.'[37]

The second main study of industrial workers' attitudes was carried out by Brown and Levin in the early 1970s, with a national sample of over 2,000 weekly-paid workers. Table 5.5 provides a summary of the results. It shows that about three-quarters of the male respondents replied that the tax system had no influence on their work effort, 15 per cent replied that it made them work more and 11 per cent that it made them work less. Over 90 per cent of the women in the sample felt that tax rates did not influence their work behaviour, with the remainder being about equally divided between the other two options. Married men with children were the group most likely to reply that taxation made them work more hours. After a more detailed and refined analysis of their results, Brown and Levin concluded as follows: 'The evidence clearly suggests, therefore, that the aggregate effect of tax on overtime is small; it may perhaps add about 1% to the total

TABLE 5.5
Reported effects of taxation on hours worked (%)

Group of male workers	Less hours	No effect	More hours
All men	11	74	15
Single men	13	77	10
Married men	12	73	15
Married men with children	9	72	19

Source: C.V. Brown, *Taxation and the Incentive to Work*, Oxford University Press, 1980, Table 4.1, p. 36

hours worked, since, on balance, tax has made people work more rather than less overtime.'[38]

Turning now to the views of professional employees on taxation, we confine ourselves again to British studies. The first such study was conducted by Break in 1956 and covered 306 self-employed lawyers and accountants in England — two groups of professionals who are in a position to vary their work effort, and who are also liable to high rates of taxation because of their high incomes. Again, the vast majority, 77 per cent, felt that their work effort had not been affected by taxation rates; 13.1 per cent reported disincentive effects and 10.1 per cent reported the opposite. Break's conclusion was that the net effect of taxation rates 'be it disincentive or incentive, is not large enough to be of great economic or sociological significance'.[39] As expected, personal circumstances influenced respondents' views with the result that disincentive effects were greatest among the single, those married without children, those living in rural areas, and among those with high incomes from property.

Thirteen years later, Fields and Stansbury did a follow-up study of Break's work but with some changes in the research methodology which were likely to increase the proportion of those reporting disincentive effects.[40] Their findings were that 18.9 per cent of the sample reported disincentive effects and 11.2 per cent experienced incentive effects — a difference which was statistically significant. Moreover, the rise in the proportion of respondents experiencing disincentive effects from 13.1 per cent in Break's study to 18.9 per cent was statistically significant. What is puzzling, however, is that this increase occurred in spite of the fact, as Beenstock points out, that 'marginal tax rates were lower in 1968 than they were in 1956.'[41] It is likely that the methodological differences account for this.

Opinion surveys suffer from various drawbacks, the most important of which is that they reflect opinion and not necessarily behaviour. What people say and what people do is not always one and the same thing. For this reason, econometric studies have been used to explore actual behaviour. These studies collect statistical data on a number of items considered important to the hours worked by employees who are free to vary their work effort — wage rates, family size, unearned income, type of employment, etc., etc. They then analyse the inter-relationship of these data using various statistical techniques in an effort to isolate the importance of the various factors for the number of hours worked. Clearly there are numerous technical and conceptual problems involved in such studies,[42] and the general applicability of the findings of such studies 'will depend on how far these numerous factors have been incorporated in the original economic theory and how representative are the data used'.[43] Most of these studies refer to the United States and the major British study refers to the situation in 1971. In a national study of weekly-paid married male workers in Britain who could vary their work effort, Brown, Levin and Ulph found that higher rates of taxation tended to have an incentive effect on the hours worked.[44]

The authoritative review of the theoretical and empirical literature from a number of countries conducted by Godfrey for the OECD con-cluded that all the various methods used to measure the incentive/disincentive effects 'indicate that taxation does not have a large and significant effect in the total supply of work effort and that, in parti-cular, the net effect on the labour supply of male family heads is likely to be very small'.[45] The general conclusion, therefore must be that the overall effect, whether negative or positive, of existing taxation rates on the work effort, and hence on economic growth, is negligible in spite of the apocalyptic assertions and rhetoric from various quarters.

It may well be, however, that for the very small minority of very high income-earners where the maximum rates of direct taxation apply, taxation may have disincentive effects. It was with this in mind that in 1979 the government reduced the maximum rate of income tax from 83 per cent to 60 per cent. It may also be equally true that disincentive effects operate for the very low and the low income-earners where any increase in earnings is counter-balanced — sometimes more than counter-balanced — by a corresponding loss of benefits. This is the phenomenon generally known as the poverty trap. Unless low income-earners can achieve, at a stroke, a very large rise in earnings and jump right out of the trap, it is virtually impossible for them significantly to improve their situation. One of the main reasons for the poverty trap is the decline of tax thresholds over the years, as well as the rela-tively heavy rates of direct taxation on low incomes. Thus, while a two-child family would have begun paying income tax at about average earnings in the mid-1950s, its liability to income tax began at about half average earnings by the mid-1970s. The same government that reduced substantially the taxation rates for the very rich did very little, apart from reducing the basic rate of tax from 33 per cent to 30 per cent, for the low-income groups. Moreover, the increasing emphasis on indirect taxation may have little impact on work incentives, but indirect taxes inevitably weigh more heavily on the low income groups. The excessive concern with disincentive effects has resulted in a less equitable system of taxation.

Another aspect of the debate on taxation and labour participation is the claim that taxation rates in the UK are higher in relation to those prevailing in other industrial countries, with the result that they encourage the professional and the well-paid to emigrate to other lower-taxed countries. There are always severe difficulties in comparing the tax systems of different countries because taxes and tax allowances take various forms in different countries. Nevertheless, most studies suggest that these fears are largely groundless. A recent government study showed that out of twelve advanced industrial countries, the UK was fourth in 1971 and seventh in 1978, on a table estimating taxes and social security contributions as a percentage of GNP. Looking at the same issue from another angle — percentage of total taxation (including social security contributions) derived from taxes on household incomes — the UK was joint second in 1971 and fifth in 1978 out of ten countries. The recent shift towards indirect taxation would have lowered even further the position of this country in the comparative scene.[46] The Meade Report provided data which showed that in 1975 the maximum rate of taxation on earned income in this country was the highest among ten advanced industrial countries. Again, the recent reduction of the maximum rate of 83 per cent to 60 per cent has changed the situation substantially.[47]

The issue of emigration of professionals and management executives was examined by a government working group in 1967 and its report concluded as follows: 'It is popularly believed that income tax plays a dominant part in the decision to emigrate from Britain. This is a half-truth.' It went on to add that 'the effect of taxation (if properly understood) is unlikely to sway a decision to emigrate.'[48] The major financial reason for emigration was the higher salaries, pre-tax as well as post-tax, that could be earned by professionals in some other countries.

The last issue to be discussed in this section concerns the effects of taxation on personal savings. It is claimed that high taxation rates reduce personal savings which are an essential ingredient in the moral character of a nation and which are also an important source of funding for investment in private industry. The Beveridge Report referred to both of these consequences when it argued that social security benefits should be of subsistence level only, allowing the individual, if he so wished, to make his own provision for higher benefits through voluntary insurance – which should also be positively encouraged by the government through tax allowances.[49]

Before examining the evidence it is important to point out the political assumptions of such claims. The argument that high taxes reduce the flow of private savings for investment in industry is only important if one believes that the ownership of industry should be in private hands. If one believes that industries should be owned by the government then one will argue that the level of taxation should be such that, taken with the government's other financial resources, it should provide capital for investment wherever the government considers it necessary. Nevertheless, even taking the argument as it stands, there does not seem to be much evidence to support it. As we showed earlier in this section, there has not been any serious shortage of capital for investment during the period covered by this study. Moreover, the available data on personal savings show that there has been a rise rather than a fall during the 1970s when taxation rates were higher than at any time before. As Falush points out, there are various reasons for this, but the taxation system does not feature among them.[50] Table 5.6 shows that the personal saving ratio, i.e. personal saving as a percentage

TABLE 5.6
Personal saving ratio in the UK, 1963-80 (%)

Year	Ratio	Year	Ratio
1963	7.5		
1964	8.2		
1965	8.5	1973	11.7
1966	8.5	1974	13.5
1967	8.0	1975	12.7
1968	7.5	1976	11.9
1969	7.8	1977	10.8
1970	9.3	1978	12.7
1971	7.6	1979	14.1
1972	9.7	1980	15.1

Source: CSO, *Financial Statistics*, Annual Returns

of total personal disposable income, was above 10 per cent for most of the decade in the 1970s – well above the rates prevailing in the 1960s. Even if, however there had been a decline in the personal savings ratio, it would have been difficult to attribute it to taxation rates. Advanced industrial societies are consumer-oriented societies. The mass media and the financial institutions encourage maximum consumption of goods which are often so manufactured that they have a very limited life. Consumption rather than saving has become the central feature of contemporary societies. Substantial personal saving is not only difficult but can be disfunctional to production and economic growth. In this social and economic climate it is idle to attribute the decline of personal saving, when it occurs, to the taxation system.

Social security benefits and work incentives

Government concern about the disincentive effects of social security benefits is not new. Such concern has been expressed all through the centuries — from the very early days of the Poor Law system to the present day. The language has changed and the emphasis has varied but the essential point has remained constant: the level of benefits must be kept low so as not to make it more profitable for people to stay out of work than to be at work. The principle of less eligibility that was enshrined in the Poor Law Amendment Act, 1834, exemplifies the nineteenth-century concern: 'The first and most essential of all conditions', stated the Act, 'is that the situation of the individual relieved (in the workhouse) shall not be made really or apparently so eligible as the situation of the independent labourer of the lowest class.' This was necessary, declared the Royal Commissioners, because 'we do not believe that a country in which that distinction has been completely effaced, and every man, whatever be his conduct or his character, ensured a comfortable subsistence, can retain its prosperity, or even its civilisation.'[51] Though the harshness of the principle of less eligibility had been softened over the years, it remained part of the post-war social security system under the wages-stop rules. The aim of the wages-stop, according to the Supplementary Benefits Commission, was 'to ensure that an unemployed man's income is no greater than it would be if he were in full-time employment.'[52] Otherwise, people in low-paid jobs would lose the incentive to work. The wages-stop rule was abolished in 1973, partly because of the introduction of the Family Income Supplement and partly because of its inevitable conflict with one of the other aims of social security — the abolition of subsistence poverty. The introduction of the family income supplement meant that low wages of family heads were supplemented by the government with the result that the number of people who would be affected by the wages-stop was drastically reduced. The abolition of subsistence poverty was impossible so long as the wages-stop rule was in existence because the rule meant that the income of thousands of families should be kept below the supplementary benefit level lest work incentives be undermined.

In addition to the wages-stop rule of the supplementary benefits scheme, the Social Security Act, 1966, required that the amount of flat-rate and earnings-related insurance benefit paid to the unemployed, the sick and other groups should not exceed 85 per cent of their previous gross earnings from work. This remained in force until 1982, when earnings-related insurance benefits for the unemployed, the sick, and other groups were abolished, partly because of the government's fears that they encouraged work disincentives and partly because of its desire to reduce public expenditure.

The charges against the social security system are many and varied and several of these defy rational discussion, let alone verification. We will examine the two most common charges in this section: first, benefit levels are too high in relation to the wages of many people with the result that they encourage workers both to leave their jobs too easily and to stay out of work longer than is necessary. Second, social security benefits discourage both labour mobility and work effort for many of those at work. The first charge relates to the unemployed while the second is directed against the low-paid in employment.

A brief review of the benefits payable to the unemployed as at the end of 1981 and the conditions under which they are paid is necessary to facilitate the understanding of both the claims and the evidence for the disincentive effects. Until the end of 1981, a person becoming unemployed received a flat-rate unemployment insurance benefit for himself and his wife and children, if any; he also received an earnings-related unemployment benefit, the amount of which depended on his previous earnings and not on his family responsibilities. Being insurance benefits, they are only payable if the unemployed satisfied the necessary contribution conditions. In addition to these two insurance benefits, an unemployed person can claim supplementary benefit. This is a means-tested benefit and the amount payable, if any, depends on the applicant's income, the spouse's income, their family responsibilities and their housing costs. A number of regulations are used to control abuse of the system. If a person leaves his job voluntarily, or if he is dismissed through misconduct, he may lose his entitlement to unemployment benefit, for a period of up to six weeks. He can apply for supplementary benefit and, even if he qualifies, he will receive only 60 per cent of the amount he would normally be entitled to. Unemployed persons who refuse offers of suitable employment or who refuse training are similarly dealt with. Moreover, the Department of Health and Social Security employs various officials – the unemployment review officers, fraud officers, and others – to pressurise the unemployed to return to work and to detect and prosecute those who commit fraud against the social security system.[53] In brief, the social security system is so designed as to enforce work discipline, minimise work disincentives and reduce fraud as far as possible.

The various assessments and studies of the willingness of the unemployed to go back to work can be divided into 4 different types: professional assessment, the speculative benefit-earnings replacement ratio inferences, econometric studies, and studies of the actual behaviour of the unemployed. Each of these different types of studies will be discussed separately even though they overlap at times.

The National Assistance Board carried out several investigations into the attitudes of the unemployed towards work – in 1951, 1956, 1958, 1961 and 1964. Its officers were asked to express their professional opinion on whether unemployed recipients of benefit were workshy. The conclusions of all these studies were similar and the quotation from the 1956 study is typical of the findings of all the studies.

> The results disclose many problems, but do not support any sugges-
> tion that workshyness is extensive since three out of four of those
> interviewed, and more than four out of five of those who had been
> out of work for three or more years, were found to be under some
> sort of physical and/or mental handicap.[54]

In all, the officers concluded that 7 per cent of the unemployed recipients of benefit could be considered as workshy although most of these were either physically handicapped or suffered from ill-health. The weakness of such studies is that they are all based on the subjective judgment of government officials who used what evidence was available to them. The Supplementary Benefits Commission discontinued these studies but a similar study was carried out in 1973 when the local office staff were asked to gather information on the attitudes of the unemployed towards work rather than express their judgment about the workshyness of individual claimants as in the previous studies. The study concluded: 'Although in the assessment of the local office staff a third of unemployed men appeared "somewhat unenthusiastic for work" this does not mean that those men would in practice refuse a job if one was offered.'[55] The report rightly pointed out that there are sanctions against those refusing jobs and that most of these 'unenthusiastic for work' claimants lived in areas of generally bleak job opportunities. Moreover, when the 'unenthusiastic' claimants were interviewed again, six months later, it was found that 35 per cent had been employed for at least part of that intervening period.

The benefit-earnings replacement ratio studies are more recent than the professional assessment studies. They claim that the improvement in the level of benefits for the unemployed resulting from the introduction of earnings-related benefits and the liberalisation of the supplementary benefit scheme in 1966 substantially improved the benefit-earnings replacement ratios. When the gap between earnings and benefit levels narrows, incentives for work suffer. The problem with all these studies is that there is no agreed level beyond which the replacement ratio definitely discourages return to work. Kay, Morris and Warren, for example, feel that 'a replacement ratio of 70 or 80 per cent retains a significant incentive to seek employment;' that 'a replacement ratio below 50 or 60 per cent, implies that unemployment causes considerable financial hardship;' that a replacement ratio in excess of 100 per cent makes it 'financially disadvantageous to take employment'; and for replacement ratios of 80 to 100 per cent there can be legitimate differences of opinion.[56]

The Royal Commission on the Distribution of Income and Wealth provided data which showed that in 1965 a married couple, with two children and on average earnings would have been entitled to unemployment benefit worth 49.3 per cent of the husband's net earnings plus family allowances. After the introduction of the earnings-related unemployment benefit in 1966, unemployment benefit for the same family constituted 68.6 per cent of the husband's earnings in 1966, increased to 77.9 per cent in 1971 and then declined to 68.4 per cent in 1977.[57] Clearly the benefit-earnings replacement ratio appears to have increased dramatically after 1966.

There are, however, three very important considerations which, when taken into account, reduce substantially the force of this argument. In the first place, the improvement is more nominal than real since many of the unemployed who received earnings-related benefit simply lost all or part of their supplementary benefit. Thus in 1975 a man on average earnings, with a wife and two children under the age of five, received supplementary benefit which was equivalent to 64.8 of his net earnings when average rent and rates were taken into account.[58] The same man would have received unemployment benefit − flat-rate and earnings-related − equivalent to 67 per cent of his net earnings. The primary reason for this is that supplementary benefit takes rent into account while unemployment benefit does not. The result is that for many of the unemployed, the amount of income derived from benefits has remained the same, though they have received their benefits under different administrative programmes. Second, the earnings-related benefit lasts for only six months and, third, only a small proportion of the unemployed at any one time receive earnings-related benefit.

Table 5.7 shows that only one-fifth of the men registered unemployed in May 1971 and in May 1980 received earnings-related benefit. What is also clear from Table 5.7 is the large proportion − almost one-fifth − of the unemployed who receive no benefit at all and of the even larger proportion who rely solely on supplementary benefit. Since the earnings-related benefit has now been abolished and since we shall be

TABLE 5.7
Registered unemployed men by type of benefit received,
Great Britain (%)

	May 1961	May 1971	May 1980
Flat-rate unemployment benefit only	42.73	21.88	16.43
Flat-rate plus earnings-related unemployment benefit	–	19.01	17.72
Flat-rate plus earnings-related unemployment benefit plus supplementary benefit	–	2.08	2.45
Flat-rate unemployment benefit plus supplementary benefit	11.11	11.66	7.37
Supplementary benefit only	26.06	25.08	39.49
No benefit	20.10	20.29	16.54
Total	100.00	100.00	100.00

Source: DHSS, *Social Security Statistics, 1981*, HMSO, 1981, Table 1.32, p. 14

referring to it again below, we will concentrate here on that section of
the unemployed who rely on supplementary benefit.

Clark's survey of 1,535 unemployed men receiving supplementary
benefit in 1974 showed that 12 per cent had incomes below the supplementary benefit level. As one would expect, the proportion in poverty
varied according to family responsibilities: 2 per cent of lone claimants,
6 per cent of claimants with wife only, 13 per cent with one or two
children and 34 per cent with three or more children. 'For most unemployed men on supplementary benefit', she wrote, 'careful budgeting,
paying for costly items by instalments and cutting down on basic items
and social expenditure were not enough to make ends meet.'[59] As far as
the issue of incentives is concerned, Table 5.8 shows that only 12 per
cent had a replacement ratio of 90 per cent or above and these were
predominantly men with large families who had been in low-paid jobs.
This is a higher proportion than that established in other studies
because Clark concentrated on the long-term unemployed who relied
mainly on supplementary benefit for their support, with the result that
the sample included a high proportion of low-paid men with large
families.

The Supplementary Benefits Commission explored the problem of
work incentives for the unemployed with considerable care during the
period 1975-80. Its estimates at the end of 1975 suggested that only
about 1 per cent of families without children where the head was

TABLE 5.8
Replacement ratio of unemployed men on supplementary benefit (%)

Supplementary benefit income[a] less than 60% of net work income[b]	53
Supplementary benefit income less than 60%-69% of net work income	12
Supplementary benefit income less than 70%-79% of net work income	12
Supplementary benefit income less than 80%-89% of net work income	11
Supplementary benefit income less than 90%-110% of net work income	7
Supplementary benefit income more than 110% of net work income	5

[a] Supplementary benefit income = Supplementary benefit + unemployment benefit + family income supplement + child benefit + any other

[b] Work income = Usual take-home pay + regular overtime + family income supplement + child benefit

Source: M. Clark, 'The Unemployed on Supplementary Benefit', *Journal of Social Policy*, vol. 7, part 4, Oct. 1978, Table 5

self-employed or in full-time work could be financially better off drawing supplementary benefits; the proportion rose to 2 per cent for families with children. Obviously, the proportion increased for families with a large number of children but, as the report pointed out, in December 1975 there were only 45,000 unemployed claimants with four or more children and this represented only 7 per cent of all the unemployed receiving supplementary benefit. Moreover, these were the very families who found it hardest to manage on the amount of supplementary benefit they received.[60]

The final report of the SBC summarised the findings of a report by a review team specially set up to examine the issue of work incentives for the unemployed in 1978. It is worth quoting this in full:

(a) the proportion of the unemployed who actually get more money in benefit than in work is very small. They are mainly men in the early months of unemployment for which higher benefits have been deliberately designed and when the disincentive effects seem small anyway; or men on supplementary benefit with low earnings potential and large families;

(b) this latter group are among the poorest on supplementary benefit and many of them are in poor health and have other personal problems;

(c) financial incentives cannot be considered in isolation, and in many cases may not be the major determinant of whether someone works. Of far more importance in present circumstances is whether jobs are available and are offered;

(d) means-tested benefits for those in work are now of considerable significance and can make all the difference to the standard of living of low earners. Nevertheless, there is much ignorance about them and reluctance to claim them.[61]

We conclude the discussion on replacement ratios by looking at the findings of the study by Kay et al., which was based on the data of the Family Expenditure Survey, 1977, but updated to 1980. They found, first, 'few households for whom the replacement ratio exceeds 100 per cent'; second, 'under half the population have ratios below 50 per cent;' third, for more than four-fifths of all heads of households the long replacement ratio is below 70 per cent; and fourth, there was a 'substantial minority for whom the short run replacement ratio is high. More than a third of all households will have short run ratios above 70 per cent even after the disappearance of earnings-related supplements to national insurance benefit.' In other words, Kay et al. acknowledge that these disincentives exist for short periods of unemployment only and that

the net income of almost any household which is unemployed long-term will be lower than if it contains at least one worker. As the job market becomes more difficult, the likelihood that anyone will gamble on finding a new job in a short period is quite low.[62]

They were also aware of the fact that few people have the knowledge and the skills to arrange their tax benefit and work affairs in such a way that they get the best possible deal out of the existing relationship between benefits, taxes and earnings.

We turn now to the various econometric studies. As mentioned earlier, they followed the introduction of earnings-related benefits in 1966 and they took various forms of complexity and sophistication. Gujarati sought to explain the changed relationship between the number of people unemployed and the number of vacant jobs in the country before and after 1966. Since unemployment after 1966 rose faster than one would have expected from the pre-1966 experience, in spite of the availability of vacancies, this must have been due to the introduction of the earnings-related benefits and redundancy payments which influenced the supply of labour, i.e. unemployed people's willingness to re-enter the labour market. His overall conclusion was that for the five years 1966-71, unemployment was 44 per cent higher than one would have expected from the pre-1966 experience.[63] Gujarati's study is obviously simplistic because on the one hand it assumes that all the unemployed received the new benefits and on the other it does not take into account such variables as age, occupation, region, etc. which have a bearing on an individual's ability to find a job. In a rejoinder, Taylor argues that Gujarati misinterprets the situation by ignoring the changing pattern of demand for labour in the years after 1966. Taylor sees unemployment as the product of changes in the demand for labour — what at the time was euphemistically described as 'shake-out' rather than the product of factors affecting the supply of labour.[64]

A study by the Department of Employment adopted a similar methodological approach but took more safeguards than Gujarati. It covered the period 1966-74 and noted that unemployment rose faster than the number of vacancies by 300,000. During the same period, however, a number of economic changes had taken place in addition to the introduction of the new benefits. The Department also took into account the fact that only a small proportion of the unemployed received these benefits. Its general conclusion was that 'statutory redundancy payments and earnings-related supplement could have accounted for only a small part of the observed shift. The relative impact on male unemployment was probably less than 20,000 and 50,000 respectively.'[65] Thus the Department of Employment's estimate of the impact of benefits on unemployment is only about half of the figure arrived at by Gujarati. Basically, however, neither Gujarati nor the Department of Employment can produce any real evidence to justify their statistical findings.

A slightly more sophisticated methodological approach is found in the study by Maki and Spindler. Their statistical calculations tried to take into account not only the introduction of new benefits but also structural and cyclical factors in the economy which could have affected the rate of unemployment for the period 1967-73. Their conclusion was that during this period the overall unemployment rate in the UK was 30 per cent higher because of the introduction of the earnings-related benefit, i.e. an increase of 110,000 in the number of unemployed.[66] Thus their estimate of 'induced unemployment' falls half-way between the figures arrived at by Gujarati and the Department of Employment.

There have been various studies critical of the methodology and findings of Maki and Spindler. Sawyer, for example, argues that the comparison between the earnings-related unemployment benefit after 1966 and the flat-rate unemployment benefit prior to 1966 is mistaken for the reason we gave earlier. Maki and Spindler should have taken into account the amount of national assistance paid to the unemployed before 1966 because what the earnings-related unemployment benefit did for significant numbers of unemployed was simply to replace or reduce the national assistance payment. Sawyer also broadens the discussion to include factors affecting employment which are not

179

measurable by statistical studies.

> The general work ethic, [he writes] the impact of unemployment on
> future job prospects, the withdrawal of benefits from those who
> voluntarily quit their jobs, poor information on the level of benefits
> are some of the reasons for thinking that there is little impact on the
> work decision.[67]

Moreover, Maki and Spindler do not take into account any of the
factors mentioned earlier — occupation, education, region, family
responsibilities, amount of benefit, etc. — which affect both people's
willingness and ability to find a new job.

Basically, the weakness of aggregate time-series studies is that they
do not take enough into account the individual characteristics of the
unemployed. Studies which do this come up with results which show a
far lower disincentive effect of benefits. MacKay and Reid analysed the
experience of 613 men made redundant in 1968 in the Midlands. They
took into account such variables as the amount of the weekly benefit,
the amount of redundancy payment, the search for work, age, marital
status, etc. Their conclusion was that unemployment may have been
increased by only 12,000 for the years 1966-8 as a result of earnings-
related benefits — a far weaker effect than that found by other studies.
They concluded that 'while unemployment benefit may have had some
impact in raising the level of unemployment, the small partial regression
co-efficient does not indicate that workers were "living off the state"
for long periods.'[68] Moreover, they assert the fact that the unemployed
bear the burden of labour market changes and the small compensation
they receive is not such a high price to pay by those who benefit from
these changes.

Nickell's analysis of data for the period 1967-76 shows that though
unemployment increased between 1967 and 1976, the flow into unemployment hardly changed. In fact, it was slightly higher in May 1967
than in May 1976, though unemployment was twice as high in 1976.
So, if the numbers of people becoming unemployed had not changed,
the more favourable benefit earnings ratio after 1966 cannot have led
to an increase. But the earnings-related benefit had affected the duration of unemployment so that it may have increased unemployment
by about 10 per cent — a third of the increase calculated by Maki and
Spindler.[69]

What then can be concluded from these various econometric studies?
In an authoritative review of such studies, Atkinson drew attention to
the substantial difficulties 'of representing the impact of benefits in a
single factor, and of separating it from other trended variables'.[70] The
three most competent studies he reviewed showed that even the

estimates of the Department of Employment cited above may overstate the impact of benefits on unemployment considerably. His general conclusion was: 'There does, however, seem to be little ground to suppose that the introduction of Earnings Related Supplement led to an "avalanche" of claims or that its abolition will dramatically reduce the level of unemployment.'[71]

We turn now to the studies which explore the actual behaviour of unemployed people in their search of employment. Such studies tend to look at the totality of the situation of the unemployed and though their statistical sophistication is modest, they are a corrective to the attempts to pin-point the effects of one variable — benefits — on unemployment. Hill's study of the unemployed showed how complex an individual's situation was, and hence how difficult it was to isolate the impact of one factor. His analysis of unemployment duration by the payment of earnings-related benefit 'produced no evidence in support of the hypothesis, and in fact, in one area, Newcastle, there was a statistically significant tendency for those without earnings-related supplement to remain unemployed the longest'.[72] He points out, of course, that those receiving earnings-related benefit are likely to have better employment records, to be, by definition, short-term unemployed, and generally to be more employable than the long-term unemployed who are not receiving such benefit.

A more recent government study also showed the same complexity of factors affecting an unemployed person's ability of finding a job. Moylan and Davies interviewed a large national sample of unemployed men twice — one month after registration as unemployed and three to four months later. We are not concerned with the first round of interviews except to note that the low-paid unskilled workers are over-represented among the unemployed.[73] Their second round of interviews covered 1,750 men, representing 55 per cent of the original sample or 76 per cent of those who were first interviewed: over half of whom were still unemployed, over a third had found employment and the remaining were sick, etc. Age, health and previous employment history were important factors in finding new employment. Family status did not prove so important apart from the fact that having a large family — four or more children — tended to act against finding employment. Assuming that these were predominantly low-paid unskilled workers, there is indirect evidence that benefits may have acted as a disincentive though the authors do not comment on it. Those who found jobs were prepared to change both industry and occupation and on balance 'more moved to a job at a lower skill level than moved to a job at a higher skill level'.[74] Similarly there was a greater tendency to accept jobs with lower pay than they had earned from the jobs they held before the study. Those who were still unemployed exhibited similar tendencies: about half were prepared to accept a job which paid less than their previous job, and very few insisted on a job that paid them more. Even fewer gave up the search for a job at that stage and those who did were realistic about the negligible chances they stood of employment. The general message of Moylan and Davies is that in spite of all the difficulties, the unemployed were anxious to find another job, they looked hard for one, and they were more than flexible in the kind of job and pay they were prepared to accept. The payment of benefits did not appear to influence the unemployed person's willingness to search for a job.

The payment of redundancy allowances has also been mentioned as another added disincentive but it has not received the same extensive attention by either politicians or researchers. Showler summarises the evidence on the effect of redundancy payments on incentives to resume employment and concludes that, if patterns of job search behaviour and length of unemployment following redundancy are taken as indicators of any disincentive effects, there is no significant effect on incentives.[75] A number of research studies[76] have found that those receiving larger redundancy payments tend to spend longer unemployed but this has been shown to be due to age. Older workers tend to draw larger redundancy payments because of the importance of length of service in the calculation of the benefit and they also tend to find it more difficult to find alternative employment. So age rather than the size of the payment is the crucial factor.

The available evidence presented so far suggests that the level of and the conditions of paying benefits to the unemployed do not constitute a major threat to work incentives. They may, however, affect the willingness to work of a small number of men with very large families in semi-skilled and unskilled occupations. The social security system, however, cannot cope with this problem in punitive ways, because by doing so it will create even more serious problems for larger groups of claimants. The issue can only be settled satisfactorily through the improvement of child benefits and low wages. Intelligent people must be concerned not only with why some prefer to live on benefits rather than work, but with why so many more people prefer to work in difficult, low-paid jobs rather than rely on social security benefits.

Fraud is another reason cited to explain why the pressure on the unemployed to look for employment is lessened. There are two main types of fraud that may be committed by the unemployed: receiving benefit while still in full-time or part-time employment; and drawing benefit for working wives. There is very little reliable information about the extent of fraud by the unemployed, or indeed by other groups of claimants. The Fisher Committee provided very little reliable evidence on the type or extent of fraud but nevertheless felt that 'abuse by wrongful claims is a serious problem. Although *the percentage of claims which are known to be fraudulent is not great, substantial sums of money are misappropriated each year.* [77] The total amount of over-payment this Committee found during the year 1971-2 was £1.5 million for all groups of claimants. The Department of Health and Social Security has since provided more detailed figures and Table 5.9 summarises these for the year 1978/9. It will be seen that both in terms of the total number of claims and the total amount of social security expenditure, fraud is insignificant.

TABLE 5.9
Extent of fraud, Great Britain, 1978-9

Type of benefit	Fraud as % of all claims for benefits	Fraud as % of all expenditure on benefits
Child benefit	0.042	0.639
Unemployment benefit	0.563	0.664
Retirement pension	0.127	0.001
Sickness and invalidity, maternity benefits	} 0.061	0.051
Widows benefits		0.025
Industrial injury benefits		0.012
Supplementary benefit	0.596	0.138
Total	0.273	0.027

Source: F. Field, 'Scroungers: crushing the invisible', *New Statesman*, 16 Nov. 1979, Tables 2 and 3

Detected fraud, it is sometimes argued, is only the tip of a large ice-berg and the real extent of fraud is far bigger. The recent Rayner Report found it just as hard to document the extent of fraud as the Fisher Report. Nevertheless, it accepted rather uncritically what frag-mentary evidence it could find and hastily concluded that 7 per cent to 8 per cent of all the claims by the unemployed were fraudulent. [78] It therefore recommended a very substantial increase in the number of fraud officers, a recommendation which the government implemented with a blaze of publicity. The government's over-zealous attack on 'scroungers' was criticised not only by the poverty lobby but by its own Supplementary Benefits Commission on the grounds that

this is likely to discourage genuine claimants from seeking their rights and failure to take up benefits is a much bigger problem than fraudulent take-up, both in terms of the amount of money involved,

183

and in less obvious ways because of the hardship it can cause. We must not forget that most claimants are without work through no fault of their own.[79]

In brief, the evidence on fraud by the unemployed is inadequate for any definitive conclusions. Nevertheless, it suggests that the number of 'scroungers' as a proportion of the number of unemployed is very small indeed and the amount of money fraudulently claimed is even less significant, particularly when compared with the amount lost through income tax fraud. Deacon's conclusion that 'the degree of popular concern is out of all proportion to its (scrounging) extent, and may be fairly termed "scroungerphobia" ' aptly sums up the situation.[80]

We turn now to the issue of benefits affecting work incentives among the employed population. The discussion will be limited to the specific charges that the payment of Family Income Supplement to low-paid workers reduces their incentive to work longer hours and to change their jobs. The Family Income Supplement scheme, introduced in 1971, provides additions to the wages of heads of families depending on the family income and family size. The number of families receiving FIS has fluctuated between 60,0000 and 95,000, about half of which are one-parent families. In one sense the payment of FIS is an incentive to work for low-paid workers with large families because without it these workers would be financially better off giving up their job and relying on supplementary benefit.

What evidence is there that workers receiving FIS limit their hours of work or avoid taking up better-paid jobs for fear of losing it? The DHSS has conducted two studies of the Family Income Supplement scheme: the first looked at the position of two-parent families in 1972 and the second at the position of fatherless families in 1974. The first study showed 13 per cent of the two-parent families in receipt of FIS had incomes which were still below the Supplementary Benefit level; without the FIS, the proportion of families in poverty would have been 29 per cent. The corresponding figures found by the second study on fatherless families were 13 per cent and 24 per cent. The question of work incentives was discussed at length in the first study because it involved men at work, and its general conclusion was that the payment of FIS 'did not seem to figure strongly in people's motivation to increase earnings'.[81] Those few who had the opportunity to change jobs but did not explained it as being due to such factors as housing problems, familiarity with their present job, etc. and not because of fear of losing FIS. The question of work disincentives did not arise in the case of fatherless families. In fact, the opposite was the case — FIS was seen as a means of encouraging lone mothers to combine full-time work with parenthood rather than stay at home and rely on Supplementary

Benefit. For most mothers, work provided the necessary social contacts and despite their low-paid position, 'the majority of the respondents declared themselves satisfied with their present job.'[82] In general, then, there does not appear to be a problem of disincentives for either male or female workers on FIS. This is no surprise, since the regulations governing the payment of FIS were so drawn up as to minimise its possible disincentive effects: the amount of FIS payable is only half the applicant's legal entitlement and even this must not exceed a maximum amount.

There is also the evidence from the Negative Income Tax experiments in the United States. The best known experiment was that carried out in several urban centres in New Jersey covering 1,374 families, 724 as experimental and 650 as controls. The experimental families were further sub-divided into a number of groups receiving different amounts of subsidy. The aim of the experiment was to find out what effect these payments had on work incentives in terms of hours of work, employment, unemployment and earnings. Evaluation of the experiment by different authors reached contradictory conclusions, partly because different criteria were used to estimate disincentives, partly because of different items included in the regression analyses, and so on. Haverman and Watts found no difference in the work effort between the experimental or treatment group and the control group: 'The most striking features of the results for husbands', they write, 'are that all of the differentials are quite small in both absolute and relative terms . . . All are statistically insignificant.'[83] Hall's re-analysis of the results, however, show that for white husbands there was a reduction of hours of work among the experimental group in comparison to the hours worked by the control group. He found no such disincentive effects, however, among the black and the Spanish-speaking samples: there was little change in hours worked by men in the experimental group and there was, in fact, a rise in the hours of work by the control group. Hall, however, rejects these findings on the grounds of very high attrition rates among the non-white groups.[84]

Conclusion

The claims that social policy undermines economic growth have always come to the forefront of public debate when the economy is in difficulties. Yet the main reasons for the economic decline of the country relative to some other advanced industrial societies are to be found outside the area of social policy because social services have always been provided in ways in which the needs of the economy, or rather the needs of private capital, are taken into account as far as possible. This is not to deny that the evidence reviewed in this chapter suggests that social service expenditure may have slightly exacerbated an already adverse economic situation. This, however, must be seen in line with the positive contribution of social policy to economic growth reviewed in the previous chapter. Moreover, many of the minor disincentive effects of social policy are not inherent in government policies; they are the product of over-emphasis on means-tested benefits. Finally, social services are only one of many forces that affect people's willingness to work and the same volume of social service expenditure can be found in countries with high, medium and low rates of economic growth. Work provides people with social contacts, often personal satisfaction and a structure to their life as well as financial support. Excessive concern with possible disincentive effects of social policy distracts attention from its positive aspects and creates a climate of opinion for reductions in social service provision. It also tends to blame the individuals for their unemployment rather than government policies and structural factors which are beyond the individuals' control.

6

Social services and political stability

Social services and social policy have always been seen as having a role to play in promoting social and political stability. Such ideas were a factor in the development of the Elizabethan Poor Law and in the surge of social policy development in the 1830s. In more recent times José Harris emphasises how the contribution social services could make to social and political integration was central to Beveridge's thinking.[1] It was also a preoccupation to which Titmuss returned again and again and it was a main theme in his last major work, *The Gift Relationship*.[2] Mishra has stressed the same theme in T.H. Marshall's work emphasising the weight Marshall lays on 'the part social services can play in creating and maintaining solidarity in conditions of modern society'.[3]

The discussion suffers, however, from three central weaknesses. Terms are left undefined and the issues are discussed at a level of generality which makes it extremely difficult to know exactly what it is that is being discussed. Second, the argument has proceeded by assertion. There has been little attempt to gather, let alone review, evidence. 'The welfare state', says Shirley Williams, to quote just one example, 'has been a crucial element in maintaining the political stability of the Western world in the turbulent post-war years.'[4] But she does not pause to provide any evidence for such a bold statement. Third, the value assumptions implicit in discussion of social and political stability have been left unexplored. It has been assumed as self-evidently obvious that integration and stability will be approved by all thinking citizens. It needed the Marxists to expose the fact that integration and stability, at one level the product of consensus, can at the same time be the fruit of successful domination and the basis of

187

exploitation by powerful minorities.

There are various ways in which a discussion of the impact of social services on political stability could be tackled. It could concentrate on the impact of social services on key social and political values — for example, attitudes to authority, to hierarchy, to inequality or to the work ethic. Or it might focus on the impact on political behaviour — voting patterns, trade union activities, political compaigning. We have chosen to focus on what we see as the five most important ways in which social services contribute to political stability — their contribution to the easing of potentially disruptive problems, their adoption of definitions of social problems which do not challenge the economic and social order, the way they encourage, reward and punish certain values and certain forms of behaviour, the support they provide for authority and hierarchy in society, and the way in which they help transform class conflict into less threatening group conflict.

To try to make such an assessment of the impact of social policy is not easy. Political stability is difficult to define and even more difficult to measure. We define it as a situation in which there is general acceptance in society of the legitimacy of the existing economic, social and political systems. Measuring stability can be tackled in various ways — none of them very satisfactory. We see stability as dependent on the continuance of certain core values, beliefs and patterns of behaviour and we take these as, in a sense, proxies of stability. In any case, sophisticated indices of stability would not be very helpful in a discussion of the impact of social services since there is a dearth of empirical evidence on the political impact social services have. The best that can be done at the moment is to bring together what little evidence is available, to show the connections which can be plotted, albeit tentatively, between social services and political order and to attempt a hopefully constructive use of the sociological imagination.

Before embarking on a consideration of the five ways in which we suggest social services contribute to political stability it may be helpful to clarify four other points. We are both in favour of political stability and opposed to it — a dilemma shared by all radicals. We are in favour of it when stability is the alternative to anarchy or disorder; we are against it when it means the survival of a system which we regard as inequitable. Second, though we regard social services as a conservative force in society, that does not mean that we are hostile to them. Promotion of stability is only one of the many consequences of the development of social service — and many of those other consequences we regard as highly desirable. Third, social services are only one of many stabilising elements in society. The economic market can be a powerful instrument of economic, social and political integration and so a force for stability. Some right-wing thinkers are hostile to social services because they see them as damaging to the market system and so, in this way, as dysfunctional to political stability in spite of the stabilising contribution they may make in other ways. Fourth, while we stress the tendency for services to promote stability we do not rule out their ability to make for change. Tawney regarded social services as vital to 'the creation of a population with the nerve and self confidence to face without shrinking the immense task of socialist reconstruction'.[5] We share some part of that vision of the possibilities of social services while exploring and stressing in this chapter another aspect of their impact.

Social services ease potentially disruptive problems

The first and perhaps most important way in which social services contribute to political stability is through the amelioration or solution — or seeming attempt at amelioration and solution — of problems which could provoke serious discontent and might be used as an indictment of the existing economic and political order.

The easing of social problems has an impact on political stability in three different ways. It reduces suffering and so presumably discontent among the victims of such problems. Second, social services greatly reduce the ammunition available for would-be critics of the established economic and political order seeking to challenge its ability to respond to human needs and make good the ravages of its economic orthodoxies. Third, the easing of social problems through social service provision shows the existing political order in a new light. It appears as benevolent and caring, not concerned simply for profit, growth and order, but as concerned, too, for individual citizens and their needs. The established order assumes a new legitimacy and so attracts new sources of loyalty.

> The provision of medical care [Doyal writes] often comes to represent the benevolent face of an otherwise unequal and divided society. People who are sick are extremely vulnerable and the ultimate demonstration of concern on the part of the state is to care for its citizens when they are ill, or even to save them from death.[6]

What is proclaimed by deed as well as by word is that this is indeed a welfare state concerned for the good of all. This aura legitimates its existence and its authority.

The unemployed, for example, are given an income which obviously makes their plight less intolerable than it would otherwise be — and allows the rest of society to feel that those without work are being protected. Deacon is probably right in his judgement that 'the

189

unemployment insurance scheme was extended in the 1920s because Ministers were convinced that such a concession was essential if a serious threat to political stability was to be avoided.'[7] Piven and Cloward explain the development of public welfare in the United States in similar terms, arguing that 'relief arrangements are initiated or expanded during the occasional outbreaks of civil disorder produced by mass unemployment, and are then abolished or contracted when political stability is restored.'[8] Mass unemployment in Britain, however, did not see any increase in government generosity towards the unemployed in the early 1980s. Efforts are made by governments to find work for those without it and to provide opportunities for training and retraining. There are also programmes to provide work experience for young people, to encourage firms to keep on workers who might otherwise become redundant and so on. The aims of government policy in relation to the unemployed — as also with other large groups in need — are threefold: to ease their plight, to avoid the possible growth of discontent among those suffering and to preempt criticism of its handling of the problem from those sympathetic to the casualties of economic and social life.

As we saw in Chapter 2 successive governments since 1945 have tried, with varying degrees of enthusiasm and success, to ease the poverty of the poorest members of society. Wages councils exist to act as watch dogs in industries with traditionally low wages. Family incomes supplement tops up the incomes of the low-paid — as do a range of means-tested benefits. There is a quite bewildering variety of benefits for the disabled. The aim is to ease the plight of the casualties of a competitive economic system and to cushion them against its unpleasant, if invigorating, rigours. Such policies clearly do ease the condition of the worst off. Certainly, some individuals and groups slip through the net, but their plight is less noticeable than the efforts of government to tackle the needs which they present.

Similarly, government housing policy has been directed to easing the key elements in the housing problem. Dwellings have been built to combat the housing shortage. They have been let at subsidised rents to bridge the gap between rent-paying capacity and the minimum rent at which physically satisfactory housing could be let — a gap which has historically destined the poor to bad housing. Policy has been directed, too, at clearing slums and improving unsatisfactory housing judged to be capable of modernisation, even if privately owned.

At times, discontent with bad housing conditions has been seen as threatening by governments. It was concern at the political implications of rent increases on Clydeside in 1915 which led to the introduction of statutory rent control. The strong connection between industrial unrest and bad housing established by the Commission on Industrial Unrest in

1917 was certainly one of the pressures underlying government commitment to Exchequer aid for house building in 1919. The riots in some major British cities in the summer of 1981 persuaded the government of the seriousness of the inner city problem and led to the direction of more resources to certain key urban areas.

It may be that people do not have any sense of their housing problem till they are told about it, but failure to make available housing judged to be reasonable, at rents which the majority can afford, could easily become a dangerous charge against an economic and political system. If the system rather than the characteristics of individuals was seen to be the cause of homelessness, even the most moderate would be driven to pose awkward questions about it.

The sale of council houses is an interesting example of a policy aimed explicitly at tackling a situation which the Secretary of State for the Environment saw in 1981 as problematic in relation to political stability. He spoke of his 'principal motive' in pressing forward with council house sales as being 'to reverse the polarization of society between home owners and council tenants'. That, he said, 'was far more important than any savings that might accrue to tax payers and rate payers'.[9] Polarisation threatened stability; sales could restore stability by reducing polarisation.

The provision of health care free at the point of use avoids the politically damaging situation of citizens with a desperate need for health care, but unable to secure it because they lack the means to pay for it. In the National Health Service, shortages remain and waiting lists lead to delays, but the problem of access to health care has been eased or solved for most people. By divorcing access to health care from ability to pay, care and treatment, albeit often less than adequate, are provided for the most vulnerable and needy — the chronic sick, geriatrics, the mentally ill and mentally handicapped and the physically handicapped.

One of the tasks of the personal social services is to ease the problems produced by the uneven processes of change in society — social, demographic, economic and medical. To retain loyalty and legitimacy the political order has to show itself able to respond to the problems which follow from the increase in one-parent families, in the number of dependent elderly and in the number of severely handicapped preserved by medical science. The political system has to show itself capable of responding to such problems if it is not to become the target of criticism from large and potentially vocal groups and if it is not to provide causes for those who seek to indict its inability to respond to basic needs.

One of the historic problems at which social services are directed is the problem of social injustice. To win support, governments need to present themselves as concerned for justice. 'Individuals', said Hirsch, 'can be expected to restrain the exercise of their individual power in the interests of protecting the fabric of their society if, but only if, they believe the society as a whole to be a just one.'[10] Rawls supports Hirsch's argument when he speaks of justice as 'the first virtue of social institutions'.[11]

The development of social services suggests a planned redistribution of the national product on the basis of principles of equity — from rich to poor, from working to non-working, from those without children to those with children, from healthy to sick, from whole to handicapped. If the task of government is indeed a work of justice social services seem a mechanism designed for and achieving this purpose.

Most of the stated aims of social services are to do in some way with justice. The Health Service aims to make available treatment according to need. It seeks an equitable distribution of general practitioners and other resources. The education system again aims at securing education according to age, aptitude and ability for all children. There is special education for those with special needs and a modicum of positive discrimination for areas with special difficulties. The social security system seeks to take account of groups with special needs — the disabled are perhaps the most obvious example where there has been a proliferation of benefits developed in response to pressure to meet needs which governments have found it difficult to resist. A new and potentially threatening problem of social injustice to which the state has responded in recent years is that of discrimination. As the evidence accumulated in the 1960s about the extent and degree of discrimination on grounds of race and sex, so governments responded in a series of measures designed to show their commitment to equality of opportunity and to defuse a potentially threatening situation. Clearly government action has had an impact. Women's pay has risen relative to men's, women have gained legal rights against discrimination and certain tangible rights in employment. The impact of policy to combat racial discrimination is more difficult to assess. But what government has clearly achieved in both areas is a measure of protection from the charge of ignoring injustice and discrimination. Laws have been passed; bodies to monitor their operation have been set up. Government seems to have done its best. Middle England can see little cause for critcism or for further action. A problem may remain but government action has ensured that it is only tortured liberals, those of a militant tendency, and those actually affected by discrimination who believe that significant problems still exist. Offe has pointed out that 'the existence of a capitalist state presupposes the systematic denial of its nature as a capitalist state.'[12] Redistribution of national resources and opportunity on grounds of justice and need can be a powerful element in this process of denial. The unequal rewards of capitalism become less obtrusive and objectionable.

Social services thus give an added legitimacy to the political order.

Social services are historically both a response to poverty and a response to economic growth. They grow to make available to the poor — for all kinds of reasons — goods and services which have become or are becoming the norm for the better-off. They are also a response to growth and change in the economy and are designed to ease problems which are a consequence of such developments — through providing support for the elderly because of the increased geographical mobility required of families by the economy, through expanding the provision of education as education becomes a crucial means of access to greater opportunity, through the provision of alternative job opportunities as manufacturing industry becomes less labour intensive. Equally, social services can be important at times of non-growth through mitigating the impact of recession. As Klein suggests, 'The welfare state can . . . be seen as an essential instrument for making the consequences of economic decline socially and politically acceptable.'[13]

The easing of potentially disruptive problems has also contributed to the growth and flowering of the consensus politics which characterised the first thirty years of the post-war period. The seeming possibilities offered by social services and managed capitalism blurred the philosophies of the two major political parties because a middle way seemed a realistic possibility. The Labour Party accepted the mixed economy in 1945, retreating from more radical possibilities. The Conservatives endorsed their decision in 1951. This *rapprochement*, according to Beer, 'left the two parties occupying the common ground of the Welfare State and the Managed Economy'.[14] Certainly, differences remained between the parties. But what is striking, as Beer emphasises, is 'the massive continuity'[15] between Labour policies before and Conservative policies after 1951.

In 1955 R.T. McKenzie went so far as to argue that 'the "agreement on fundamentals" is very nearly as great as it has ever been in the modern history of British parties.'[16] Bogdanor and Skidelsky stress that 'consensus is a fundamental idea in understanding the politics of the 1950's.'[17] There was consensus about the necessity for a broad sphere of government action in economic and social affairs and about its general aims and direction. Both parties were united by a new confidence in the possibilities of government action and in its legitimacy. State action seemed to involve fewer principles, to be no more than a pragmatic approach to dealing with observed social ills. Ideology seemed to be dead. Welfare state policies were simply practical system maintenance, promoting solidarity and cohesion in society to the benefit of all social groups, the product of the general will and the public interest.[18]

Consensus politics contributed to political stability by narrowing and limiting the terms of economic and political debate. Hayek and Friedman and their obscure counterparts on the Left were stranded like dinosaurs, survivors, so it seemed, of a previous age and long-dead debates, voices crying feebly in the wilderness. The agenda of politics was clear. So were the terms and methods of action. Debates were about issues of technique and degree rather than about underlying principles.

Keynesian welfare state policies set the terms of political debate in narrow channels. Debate ceased, while those ideas were dominant, to be about principles of economic and social arrangements, about the ends and purposes of politics and human societies. The welfare state provided a permanent, if limited, political agenda, because in such a web of complex and benevolent activity there were always real and pressing problems calling out for the resolution which seemed so easily achievable through the refining of institutional arrangements, the modification of qualifying conditions, a modicum of well-directed research or improvements in the training given to key workers.

In this atmosphere, accompanied as it was by economic growth, welfare state policies seemed the ideal lubricant of the political machine. To the vast majority the new order offered very tangible benefits and almost equally tangible possibilities. The minorities who gained less remained generally passive in their deprivation. The uncertainties, challenges, and instability of the inter-war years seemed a long way off.

Whatever their critics may say and think social services do ease problems which could prove socially and politically disruptive. Discontents are allayed, potential critics are mollified, the legitimacy of government and the existing political order is enhanced. Political debate centres on the middle ground and challenges to the political consensus are easily dismissed. Stability is therefore enhanced.

Social services adopt non-challenging definitions of social problems

The second way in which social services contribute to political stability is through the adoption, and so reinforcement, of definitions of social problems which see such problems in individual, family, or group terms rather than in terms of the malfunctioning of the economic or social system. Challenge to the existing political order is thus minimised or avoided. Dominant values and problem definitions are strengthened.

In this section we look in turn at the major social services and explore the problem definitions which they have adopted and express. We then look at the significance of these definitions for the maintenance of political stability.

194

The social security system operates on the basis that claimants are in need because of individual factors, rather than as the result of the operation of the economic system. The treatment of the unemployed illustrates this argument very clearly. A contributory system which produces only short-term benefits and which is surrounded and protected by tightly-drawn rules and regulations emphasises the individual nature of the experience and suggests the importance of individual factors in its continuance. The fact that unemployment benefit only lasts for twelve months suggests and propagates the notion that self-helpful individuals should be able to find work by then. The ways, subtle and less subtle, in which the unemployed are encouraged back to work — through the limited length of benefit, the abolition in 1982 of earnings-related benefit, the fact that the unemployed on supplementary benefit never become eligible for the long term rate of benefit (worth an extra £7.50 per week in 1983 for a single person) all suggest to public opinion, and to the unemployed themselves, that there *is* work for those who want it and look hard enough.

> Unemployment insurance programmes in most Western countries [says Disney] embody an individualistic conception of eligibility, requiring individual contribution conditions or means testing of personal income and wealth which both stems from and reinforces social perceptions of unemployment as an individual experience resulting from personal failure in a competitive labour market.[19]

Other parts of the social security system convey similar messages. Pensions, for example, could be described in terms almost identical to those Disney uses of unemployment insurance. Means testing means that there is no right to benefit because of the claimant's condition — sickness, unemployment, handicap. Individual need has to be proved because of the presumption of the system that the causes of need are individual and not to do with the way the economic system functions.

The personal social services reinforce a personal definition of many problems which would widely be regarded by those who have explored them as ultimately and essentially structural. The problem of old age, for example, is defined in terms of the needs of particularly vulnerable individual elderly people for home helps, meals on wheels, day and residential care and so on. Focus on age as the basis of need and on need in terms of a very limited range of services usefully narrows the problem. The message conveyed by the organisation of services is that the problems of the elderly are the problems of individuals and a particular age group rather than the problems of a class. The implication is also conveyed that if we are to look beyond the individual for explanations of need we should look not at the economic and social system, but at changes in family and community and in the care and support they provide.

Similarly, the focus on child-care services is on the individual and immediate needs of families and children. How and why families reach the situation in which social services departments become involved is less relevant than assessing what needs to be done and can be done. The latter is what tends to determine the definition of the problem adopted by the personal social services. What can be provided is invariably personal — support and counselling, a modicum of day care, advice, co-ordination of services, some minimal financial help. The pre-disposing conditions underlying non-accidental injury or family break-down are not directly relevant to departments. They are part of a past which has happened. Inevitably individual definitions depoliticise problems. In Simpkin's words 'individual helping is used to mask need.'[20] There is little or nothing the personal social services can do about low pay, unemployment, insecure employment or bad housing. They tackle what they can hope to do something about but that perpe-tuates a definition of the problem which suggests individual causation and the irrelevance of structural factors.

The role of social workers in defining problems is extremely impor-tant, though it is relevant too to stress how varied the work of social workers actually is. They are key message-carriers in personal social services. What confronts them in their work and the only thing they can hope to do much about is the personal needs of individuals or families. Pritchard and Taylor stress the need for a politicised and radical social work but their final and predictable word is that 'At the same time social work must never sacrifice its primary concern with the welfare of the individual to other ideological concerns.'[21]

The principles and skills of social work as outlined in key textbooks reflect the way social workers see the problems which confront them. Client self-determination, task-centred casework, family therapy, behaviour modification and so on, all reflect a primary orientation to individuals as the focus of work and this inevitably gives currency to individual definitions of problems in spite of the very different views held by many social workers. Immediate care for individuals is clearly vital, but when pursued in isolation from concern for broader needs, such a focus contributes to political stability because it supports a definition of problems which spares the political order the questioning and criticism which it would receive if the causes of problems were located in the very nature of society.

One of the classic examples of the definition of a structural social problem in community terms is the definition of the problem of urban deprivation set out in the early Home Office documents on the role and function of the Community Development Projects. The roots of the problems afflicting the run-down areas of the great cities were seen as lying within the areas themselves. Given such an assumption it was by no means unreasonable to hope that a few community workers, better co-ordination of services and a decent injection of moral fibre from outside would solve the problem. The Community Development Projects, of course, turned such a definition on its head, located the source of urban deprivation in the economic and political structure, and gave a long, hard and painful bite to the hands that were feeding them.

Since 1979 government policy on housing has been to stress more explicitly the residual role of local authority housing. Normal people, the argument runs, will organise their own housing provision through the market system. That is better and more natural. The role of the Local Authority is then to provide for special needs groups — the very poor, the homeless, problem families, one-parent families, the elderly. Within such a policy is a very clear implicit definition of the housing problem. It is a relatively small problem; its causes lie in the character-istics of individuals not in the operation of the housing market or the economic system generally; 'normal' people face no problem in providing for their housing needs. Such an approach stigmatizes those who fail to provide adequately for their own housing and gives them an identity which they have to transcend before they can criticise a system which has failed them while providing adequately — or so it seems — for the majority.

The most serious housing problem in its impact on individuals, if not in its size, is homelessness. The fact that at any given moment thousands of people in our society are physically homeless while hundreds of thousands of houses lie empty could be seen as an indict-ment of the way we organise the provision and allocation of housing. Homelessness has, however, been defined convincingly by the policy-makers, in spite of research to the contrary, as a problem with its origins in individual characteristics rather than in the nature of the housing system. Such a definition functions to distract attention from what, if it could successfully be attributed to the housing market, could open up serious criticism of the whole economic system. The fact that until 1977 responsibility for homelessness belonged, not to housing departments, but to welfare departments and then to social services departments, shows all too clearly how the problem was defined and regarded.

The goal set for the education system in 1944 was the achievement of equality of opportunity. Education policy-makers had therefore to adopt a view of the causes of inequality of opportunity — they had to define the problem — if they were to devise policies to combat it. The problem also had to be defined in ways which gave educational policy a viable role in the struggle against it. Educational policy-makers could not reasonably or usefully define it as a problem to be ameliorated only by, for example, changes in the distribution of income. Policy-makers were, therefore, eased towards a definition of the problem of educational inequality which saw it as susceptible to action by the educational system itself — the expansion of higher education, secondary reorganisation, the development of pre-school education, the inauguration of educational priority areas and so on. Such policies have been tried but have made little difference. Inequalities survive — of class, race and sex — not greatly diminished. But the educational system has gone along with a definition of the problem which poses no threat to the basic structures of society. The notion that equality of opportunity can be a reality in an unequal society is given added currency. And if it can be solved through a little judicious educational engineering awkward questions can be avoided.

Just as the education system gives an educational definition of the problem of inequality of opportunity, so the National Health Service supports an individual, medicalised definition of illness. Navarro sums up the significance of the victory of individualist conceptions of disease over environmental views in the late nineteenth century.

> At a time [he writes] when most disease was socially determined due to the conditions of nascent capitalism, an ideology that saw the 'fault' of disease as lying with the individual or that emphasised the individual therapeutic response clearly absolved the economic and political environment from the responsibility for disease and channeled potential response and rebellion against that environment to an individual and thus less threatening level. The ideology of medicine was the *individualization of a collective causality* that by its very nature would have required a collective answer.[22]

Medicine's focus on the individual causation of ill-health is presumably a reflection of the strength of individualist ideologies in the nineteenth century when the medical profession was forging its identity. It is in the individual that the problem becomes manifest but the contribution of environmental and social structural factors to the causation of much disease is now clear.[23]

Medicine still proceeds however with an essentially individual approach. Ill-health and disease are individualised, medicalised and depoliticised. Bad genes, bad habits and bad luck are defined as the essential causes — and they can only be tackled in their individual manifestations.

The individualisation of problems leads logically and obviously to the individualisation of solutions. In current medicine such solutions embrace two elements — cure and self-care. Doyal points out the significance of giving primacy to curing. 'In so far', she writes, 'as curative medicine appears to deny, or at least to minimize, the need for such preventative measures, it serves to protect existing economic interests.'[24] The other recently emergent medical ideology which also contributes to the stability of our political order is self-care. Stress on self-care as the royal road to health is based on a number of assumptions — that the causes of sickness lie in the individual not in the economic and social system, that the solution therefore has to be primarily his, that he has it within his power to care for his own health in an unhealthy environment. Navarro emphasises that it is in fact the economic and social structure which conditions and determines unhealthy behaviour in the first place — the advertising of the tobacco companies and the food conglomerates and so on.[25] The individual is not therefore as free and as able to change his lifestyle as the self-care enthusiasts tend to suppose.

This approach to the problem of ill-health is functional for the stability of capitalism in two obvious ways. If ill-health is the product of individual way of life factors, then the individual has only himself to blame for his sickness. Ill-health can be very satisfactorily explained in terms of individual moral failings and a lack of a proper sense of responsibility. Secondly, if changes in lifestyle can be paraded as the solution then there is no need for expensive and disruptive changes in methods of production, health and safety and environmental regulation or the provision of more and more health care and so on. Conflict between interest groups is avoided. Production can continue confident in the new individualism of health. Individualisation and medicalisation, cure and self-care fuse together to make an ideology which provides no challenge to what Illich called the health-denying elements of our society.

What is the significance of the way in which social services reflect and support particular definitions of social problems? We see the significance as fourfold. First, those definitions tend to reflect individual definitions and explanations of problems which 'blame the victim' in a way which places the economic and political order above blame or question. As Butrym puts it, 'If society can justify another's predicament in terms of its resulting from that person's own shortcomings or misdeeds, then it can feel safer.'[26] Awkward questions about the nature and ordering of society are avoided; they are irrelevant. Serious-minded citizens will concentrate on the outward and visible manifestations of human need and not ask irrelevant and unhelpful questions. So social services provide useful support to definitions of problems which pose no awkward questions about the economic and political order. The very provision of social services makes it look as though the needy have only themselves to blame for their need.

The second point to be made is that the social services contribute to definitions of problems which seem to make them susceptible to ameliorative solutions. Poverty can be vanquished by moderately minor improvements in the social security system, ill-health can be tackled by changes in personal habits, the problems of fracturing families by social work and advice about welfare rights – and so on. There is quite simply no need to ponder the question of radical changes in economic, social or political arrangements.

The third way in which the definitions adopted by social services are significant is in the way they contribute to a segmented and fragmented view of problems. The problem of social deprivation or social inequality is seen in terms of homelessness or poor housing, high rates of sickness or high perinatal mortality rates, slum schools or under-achievement and educational failure or high rates of unemployment. The totality of the problem is obscured by the way in which social services encourage a perspective which views one aspect of deprivation at a time rather than exposing the problem in its shocking totality. C. Wright Mills saw the problem forty years ago.

> Present institutions [he wrote] train several kinds of persons – such as judges and social workers – to think in terms of situations. Their activities and mental outlook are set within the existing norms of society; in their professional work they tend to have an occupationally trained incapacity to rise above 'cases'.[27]

Concentration on cases conceals the true nature of problems. *In and Against the State* makes the same point in the comment that

> Although the state may appear to exist to protect us from the worst excesses of capitalism, it is in fact protecting capitalism from our strength by ensuring that we relate to capital and to each other in ways which divide us from ourselves, and leave the basic inequalities unquestioned.[28]

The inequalities are unquestioned because they are not seen as a whole but partially as problems of health, housing, education, income or sex rather than from a holistic perspective. The class-based nature of problems is obscured when we look at them through the refracting lens of social service provision. The services can only adopt a social work perspective or an educational perspective or a health perspective. The ultimate causes of problems and the ultimate nature of the political order are both usefully, if not intentionally, obscured.

The fourth point to be made about the significance of the definitions of problems encapsulated in social service provision is in a sense a summary of earlier points. It is that social services thereby contribute to the deradicalisation of political protest. The easing of problems contributes to this but so too, more importantly perhaps, do definitions of problems which locate their causes in individuals, groups and communities rather than in the very nature of the economic and social system. Such definitions give a new credibility to policies of amelioration. By promising solutions without fundamental change, the teeth of radical protest are drawn. If the obstinate problems which afflict capitalist society can be solved within a capitalist framework of economic and social relations, demands for radical, root and branch social change become an irrelevance to practical men.

Social services encourage, reward and punish certain values and certain forms of behaviour

Any society needs to encourage and reward socially desirable behaviour and to punish behaviour which conflicts with established values and norms. There are two kinds of behaviour and values — those required by almost any society such as regard for authority or commitment to work and those required by particular forms of society such as capitalism or socialism. A point which is perhaps worth emphasising is that it is only in regard to certain types of behaviour and certain values that capitalist and socialist societies will differ. They share, as do all human societies, a common, if limited, core of values. Our contention in this section is that social services function in this way, encouraging and rewarding certain attitudes, values and types of behaviour and punishing values and behaviour judged by those with power in society to be in conflict with vital norms. 'Social services', says Pinker, 'are used to impose sanctions as well as to confer benefits.'[29]

Social security systems have always been concerned to influence citizen attitudes and behaviour. They are best regarded as a form of institutionalised self-help. Help is provided for those who have not paid their contributions but in a manner which is designed to make them feel its inferiority. Bismarck, says Thane 'quite explicitly saw the insurance legislation (which he introduced in the 1880's) as a means of winning working-class allegiance and of destroying socialism'.[30] Beveridge's interest in social security, Harris has pointed out, stemmed from his conception of society 'as an increasingly complex organism in which it was desirable to foster social solidarity and feelings of identification with a benevolent state'.[31] He was concerned about attitudes conducive to political stability. Piven and Cloward's study of social security policy in the United States, suggestively entitled *Regulating the Poor*, led them to the conclusion that 'expansive relief policies are designed to mute civil disorder, and restrictive ones to reinforce work norms.'[32]

The social security system also stigmatises economic failure. By implication the individual is to blame for his need and the way he is treated, in many cases, is to discourage him from further applications and to deter other potential applicants. Some benefits, of course, seem to involve no stigma — child benefit for example. There is less stigma attaching to insurance benefits earned by contributions than accompanies the supplementary benefit scheme. For many, supplementary benefit is felt to stigmatise — because of the terms under which help is given, because of the way in which it is given, and because of the low level of benefit provided. The system is also successfully characterised by the media as the resort of scroungers and layabouts, the feckless and the fraudulent. The terms on which benefit is given suggest the presumption of fraud in the close investigation of reason for need, of the applicant's resources and domestic arrangements. The way in which help is given can be equally stigmatising — long waits in seedy offices, curt treatment by overloaded staff, the association in waiting rooms of rough and respectable claimants, for example.

Stigmatisation of claimants is the product of a range of values and beliefs seldom made explicit but powerfully influencing policy — that self-helpful, responsible citizens should have no need of such artificial props, that claiming is the product of individual failure, that if claiming became too easy the number of claimants would leap up, that those unable to work should, and must, be worse off than those working. A latent function of the system is to destroy the credibility of claimants whose plight stands as an implicit indictment of the economic and social system.

The social security system also operates in various ways as part of the system of labour discipline designed to produce and sustain a compliant and diligent working class committed to the value and practice of hard work. First, unemployment benefit is not payable for a period of up to six weeks to those who leave their jobs voluntarily, who are dismissed for industrial misconduct or who refuse employment without good reason. In Kincaid's words, 'the national insurance system is used to back up the disciplines exercised by employers, by imposing further sanctions against disobedience and negligence.'[33] Second, specialist officers are employed to track down fraudulent claims for unemployment benefit. Third, Unemployment Review Officers interview claimants who, it is felt, are not seeking re-employment as actively as they might. Fourth, claimants can be required to attend Re-establishment Centres for the acquisition of the habits and attitudes deemed likely to speed their return to work. Finally, financial benefits are kept at a level designed to provide incentives to return to work as rapidly as possible.

As the Fisher Report put it,

> there has to be a certain amount of pressure on claimants to find
> work and stay in it and it is a matter of hard fact that this involves
> letting it be known that state money is not there for the asking for
> anyone who is able to work but unwilling to do so.[34]

The rightness or wrongness of such pressure depends on a range of
factors — how real the opportunities are for finding work, how the
pressure is applied and how vigorously — and so on. What is not
arguable is that there are, within the social security system, a whole
battery of mechanisms designed to preserve work discipline as one of the
foundations of our society.

The buoyant programmes of the Manpower Services Commission
bear witness to the government's concern for the damaging effect of
long-term unemployment on young people and for the potentially
explosive effects on society of large numbers of young people without
work or the resources to realise their aspirations. A central concern of
the MSC is with 'the importance of moulding and controlling the sub-
jectivity of the young worker'.[35] Properly tackled such activities can be
of inestimable benefit to young people and 'the cheapest and most
efficient mode of labour discipline'.[36]

What effect the social security system has on values or behaviour
remains a mystery. Figures for claimants seen by Unemployment
Review Officers who then speedily return to work or for the percentage
of those leaving Re-establishment Centres who subsequently secure
re-employment do not, without further examination, tell us much
about the success of such processes in changing values or behaviour.

On its own the social security system can only have a weak
influence. The important fact is that it functions to support rather than
to challenge dominant values. What impact it has is therefore conservative. It reinforces the shame of the unemployed and dependent. It
exalts achievement and success. Its method of financing provides, as the
Phillips Committee put it 'an important measure of social discipline
since everyone is aware that higher rates of pension must at once be
accompanied by higher contributions'.[37]

In one respect the social security system seems to challenge
dominant values and patterns of behaviour — in providing benefits for
strikers' families. Strikes, of course, are usually about earnings or conditions of work so they constitute no direct challenge to the basic
political order. It has always been very clear that no benefit is paid to
cover the man or woman actually on strike and benefit is now abated
by a sum for assumed strike pay. But strikes are still supported, albeit
indirectly and very modestly from public funds. The gain for the state

is perhaps the reinforcement which is thus given to the notion of the neutrality of the state in the struggle between capital and labour.

What effects does government housing policy have on values and behaviour? The consultative document *Housing Policy* stressed the desire for owner-occupation as 'a basic and natural desire' and assumed its superiority as a form of tenure.[38] There is much talk about owner-occupation encouraging a greater sense of responsibility than renting by providing people with a stake in the country. Owner-occupation also fits with and reinforces a belief in private property. But there is little evidence for such arguments.

A move to owner-occupied housing does, however, seem to be associated with changes in voting patterns, which support the view that attitudes change when people own property. Butler and Stokes reported striking movements in political party preferences among voters changing their type of housing between 1963 and 1970. Movement to owner-occupied housing, whether from the private rented sector or from local authority housing, was strongly associated with a decline in Labour voting.[39] Whether the political impact of change in housing tenure is due to the formation of new class self-images, or to connections with the economic institutions linked to type of housing, or to the influence of neighbourhood it is impossible to say, but Butler and Stokes conclude that electoral change is partly, at least, 'housing driven'; changes in housing do have direct or indirect effects on party preferences and prospects.

It might also be argued that owner-occupation means, for most people anyhow, large debts and regular repayments for as far ahead as the eye can see. Such responsibilities might be assumed to be a stimulus to work discipline and job stability and a deterrent to any action likely to prejudice job security or to interrupt earnings. But again we have no evidence that owner occupiers are less militant and more committed to work than those who do not own property.

Local authority housing certainly functions to encourage particular sorts of behaviour. High standards of housekeeping and a good record of rent-paying may be a precondition of access to local authority housing. They are certainly a prerequisite of access to the more desirable local authority dwellings and to success in the important transfer market. Low or eccentric standards of housekeeping can mean that offers of re-housing are limited to problem estates and subsequent application for a transfer elsewhere yields nothing. Housing management policies, 'whilst purporting to be for the good of the majority, do in fact assist the "respectables", and discredit and stigmatize the less fortunate.'[40] The discrediting and stigmatising of certain groups encourages conforming behaviour in those who aspire to local authority tenancies and those who seek transfers.

For many people, being an applicant for local authority housing or a local authority tenant can only create doubt and lack of confidence in public provision of goods and services. Treatment of tenants can be arbitrary and can seem inequitable because of the mystery surrounding allocation policies. As Lambert and his colleagues put it when describing the allocation system in Birmingham in the early 1970s, 'the most important features of the system are its apparent randomness, arbitrariness and "unfairness" or simply that no explanation can be given.'[41]

The nature of much local authority provision is far removed from the kind of housing most people ideally want. While the dwellings may be physically satisfactory it is the type of housing and the social environment which most tenants complain about. Local authority management policies too can be bureaucratic and inefficient. The overall impact can well be to encourage the belief that public provision is inevitably and inherently inferior to provision through the market. Emphasis on the public subsidy to local authority tenants, though in fact many tenants pay a full market rent and few are subsidised more generously than owner occupiers, increases the stigma of being a local authority tenant.

The twin arms of post-war housing policy – the extension of owner-occupation via massive tax subsidies and the expansion of the local authority sector – can both be seen as furthering values and behaviour functional to economic and political stability – saving, materialism, achievement, a belief in private property, respectability, regular rent-paying, a belief that private provision is superior to public provision and a healthy suspicion of the efficiency, fairness and practicality of meeting a basic need through the bureaucratic procedures of public bodies.

Claims made about the role of the education system in inculcating the values and patterns of behaviour required for political stability are numerous and far-reaching. Marxists see the education system as one of the instruments by which the ruling class imposes and perpetuates its cultural hegemony. Others see formal education as a mechanism for passing on agreed social values to the next generation and confirming the socialisation necessary for individual and social harmony. All see the school as important. 'The policeman is looked on as a friend of everybody in a great city like London', wrote Sir Cyril Norwood in 1929, 'because he represents a system of order which the elementary school teacher has taught the nation to respect.'[42] Hess and Torney, on the basis of a major empirical study, concluded that 'The public school appears to be the most important and effective instrument of political socialisation in The United States'[43], though there has been much criticism of the evidence on which Hess and Torney base this claim.[44]

Nevertheless, confident assertions about the role of the school still appear — 'Schooling is not just one among many of the social institutions which contribute to the perpetuation of the capitalist mode of production,' the authors of one well known study assert, 'it is arguably the most important.'[45] Marxists see the education system as a key element in the reproduction of capitalist social relations through the values and patterns of behaviour inculcated by the school. For Althusser education is the dominant element in the Ideological State Apparatus.[46] Those wanting change in society on the other hand — the Fabians for example — have always seen the education system as a means of inculcating a new social ethic.

There are at least three important questions which need to be posed about the contribution of education in this field — What is the contribution? How is it made? How important is it?

There is a mass of historical evidence that governments have thought the school could teach the virtues of achievement, individualism, hard work, respect for authority, the inevitability of inequality and so on.[47] There is however little evidence as to how successful the schools have been in this — apart from the fact that such virtues still flourish and the proletariat has been contained. To isolate the contribution of the school from other agencies of socialisation and value transmission is difficult if not impossible.

Any education system will reflect the basic beliefs and values of the society in which it is set. Teachers will share those values to a greater or lesser extent and so will the education policy-makers. Part of the school's job is to prepare children for adult life in the world outside which means passing on certain key values and inculcating certain types of behaviour — in informal alliance with the family, the mass media and so on. Our society must socialise each generation to a belief in individual responsibility, competition, self help and achievement because the continuance of our economic and political system depends on such values. It must also pass on a belief in the rightness and fairness of democratic procedures and an acceptance of authority as exercised for the good of all.

A number of writers have shown how the conflict elements of politics are kept out of the classroom through their elimination from school histories and from civics text books. Litt has shown how, in school, politics is presented as a harmonious search for the common good rather than as a way of regulating group conflict.[48] Abrams's review of British textbooks comes to similar conclusions.[49] The result is to make for an acceptance of authority as legitimate and exercised impeccably for the common good.

What is also clear is the strong stress on individual achievement and competition which characterises the British education system.[50] That is the way to success for individuals and for schools and to make equality of opportunity a reality. It also prepares young people for the world of work in a free enterprise economy.

Early research in the USA tended to focus on the impact of manifest attempts at political socialisation through civics teaching. Research has suggested, however, that the impact of such teaching on political attitudes is small, though Merelman argued that it could be important in providing what he called 'compensatory political socialisation' — that is, socialisation for minority groups and duller students[51] so extending a political consensus among groups which previously did not share it.

Ehman has argued on the basis of American research that schooling 'is more closely linked as an important socialization agent in the acquisition of political knowledge and awareness than as a shaper of political attitudes'.[52] He goes on to stress however the importance of what he calls the latent curriculum in schools in the development of political attitudes, seeing school and classroom climate as more significant than the actual curriculum.[53] Hess and Torney also lay stress on the importance of the symbolic indications of loyalty displayed in schools in America and the emphasis, implicit and explicit, on compliance with laws and the demands of authority at the expense of discussion of citizens rights.[54] Davies sums up this more general approach to the role of the school.

> Pupils 'learn' in school [he writes] a significant proportion of what they know about their own 'worth', their relation to others and to the political, economic and stratification systems. They gather this from the explicit messages of the curricular content presented to them and the manner of its presentation and evaluation, as well as from the more general 'noise' surrounding these communications.[55]

Schools reward certain forms of behaviour which in the world outside the school would often seem absurd but what is really being rewarded is conformity, achievement, effort, hard work, acceptance of failure, of being 'a good loser' and of others' success. Other kinds of behaviour are punished through formal sanctions, through loss or absence of privileges, through ritual forms of degradation — for example, rejection of school rules, lack of effort, lack of commitment to the school, refusal to compete, lack of aspirations, lack of deference to authority. The whole stream of life of the school is directed inevitably at the explicit and implicit inculcation of certain values through formal teaching and through rewarding and punishing certain types of behaviour.

This is the situation even in supposedly progressive and child-centred establishments. Sharpe and Green's study of a progressive British primary school shows how even a supposedly child-centred approach to education is constrained by the wider society which demands certain kinds of knowledge and skills and certain attitudes and patterns of behaviour. The teachers in Sharpe and Green's school saw themselves as operating on different lines from traditional teachers but at the end of the day their outputs were not very different. 'Publicly, the school operates as a progressive educational establishment', the authors conclude, 'while in the practice of these teachers and in the private views of the headmaster, it is also a socialising institution, civilising a deprived portion of the population.'[56]

How important, at the end of the day, is the contribution of the education system to the encouragement and reinforcement of values and patterns of behaviour which make for political stability? As has been indicated earlier, to separate the role of education from that of other socialising institutions is practically impossible. Most commentators are clear that the family is a more important influence than the school. Merelman argues for the school as an independent influence on the inculcation of the political values which make for stability on the basis of his finding that during the period of schooling the values of working- and middle-class students do converge. He thinks that one factor in this is the way history, civics and other textbooks slide over conflict in economic and social life, so creating the impression that economic and social development constitute progress through consensual action. Such educational practices, he thinks, 'have undoubtedly reduced the potential for class warfare in industrial society'.[57] He sees the school as a significant element in the creation of consensus in society and stable democracy, in legitimating class cleavage in educational achievement and in the creation of 'an allegiant, compliant, subordinate working class'.[58]

No writers see the school as a radicalising force in society but many have blamed higher education for producing students fundamentally at odds with the society in which they live. In the late 1960s the higher education system in many countries seemed to have detached itself from dominant values and to be generating an independent critique of society. Those who challenged the economic, social and political order in those heady days were ultimately only a minority but for a time higher education looked like a destabilising force.

What part do personal social services play in the task of inculcating stabilising values and behaviour? The services have a heavy and explicit responsibility in the area of socialisation and resocialisation – the socialisation of children for whom the normal mechanisms have broken down temporarily or permanently, the resocialisation of actual or potential delinquents, the support and resocialisation of families whose style or patterns of child-rearing seem seriously to threaten their children's well being, the resocialisation of the mentally ill and mentally handicapped on discharge from institutions.

Social work is often about conformity. Social workers work in agencies which are part of the machinery by which society seeks to induce conformity in its members, what was described above as socialisation and resocialisation. At the same time client self-determination is a central tenet of social workers – clients have the right to make up their own minds about how they shall live and how they will extricate themselves from the situation which has brought them into contact with social workers. The emphasis depends, of course, on the type of client and the nature of the relationship. Some social work is clearly and explicitly about control and conformity – social work with delinquents by local authority social workers or probation officers for example. In other types of social work – with the elderly, for example, self-determination can and should play a larger part in the relationship.

Derek Morrell raises another conflict for social workers in this area. 'It is part of the social worker's function', he says, 'to help people adjust to the expectations of the society in which they live, it is equally part of their function to criticize those expectations.'[59] Social workers must not see their task as simply and solely to fit people to society's demands – the shoe-horn role. In the real world, however, it is the immediate, pressing task – adjustment – which is always going to get priority in practice, and therefore also in training, rather than the vaguer, less tangible, more long-term task with a dubious beginning and an uncertain end.

In recent years, social work has become more obviously and intrinsically an instrument of social policy and so social workers have become more involved in the social control elements of child-care legislation, dealing with delinquents, the provision of a fall-back income maintenance system, the rationing of scarce resources, such as day care. The dangers of this position – and its possibilities – are obvious. Handler pointed out some years ago that the extension of social workers' control over 'hard' goods increased their potential power over clients. Access to 'hard' goods could be made conditional on acceptance of the casework plan.[60] Jordan has suggested that such control over material goods is an obstacle to establishing the relationships required for productive social work.[61] That may be so, but it also increases the social worker's ability to influence behaviour if material help or day care become conditional on improved standards of housekeeping, a better work record, a greater willingness to accept advice about child care, greater concern about children's school attendance, a more regular attack on debt repayments – and so on.

At the end of the day, and it may be quite a long one, the central concerns of the social worker are going to be with social stability rather than with individual well-being through self-determination. In Pritchard and Taylor's words, 'For clients who are seen as actually or potentially "deviant" or "disruptive" the social worker's role is fundamentally integrative.'[62] In Corrigan and Leonard's words, 'There is no place in dominant state definitions for practice which contributes to transforming the private problem into a class experience.'[63] Integration is to be achieved through the inculcation and acceptance of key values and patterns of behaviour — self-reliance, individual responsibility, regular work, acceptance of authority. They are advanced through rewarding conformity and through the stigmatisation of unacceptable behaviour, such as dependency or failure in parental responsibilities, and the long stop legal powers available to social workers.

Two areas of social work where the inducement of conformity to accepted values and types of behaviour is central are residential work with children and young people and traditional probation work. Children's homes and community homes are centrally concerned with socialisation, because other methods of providing it have been found wanting, and with resocialisation for those whose previous socialisation has been ineffective. As agents of the wider society residential establishments will propagate accepted values and norms.

The probation officer has the clearest social control role of any social worker. The aim is explicitly to help clients adjust to society and to adopt more conforming attitudes and patterns of behaviour. The Morison Report spoke of the work of the probation officer as being to help the offender to see that 'his interests and those of society are identical'.[64] The Home Office booklet, *The Probation and After Care Service in England and Wales*,[65] describes the probation officer's task as being to 'help the probationer to develop qualities which will enable him to adjust to the demands of society and become and to remain a happy and useful citizen'.

We have been considering the more explicit aims and functions of social work. What of its actual effect on those with whom social workers come in contact? Simpkin writes of social work having 'the effect of marking out individuals, families or groups as being in some way outside the normal functioning of society'.[66] The process of stigmatisation marks out need as the product of individual failure. It acts as a deterrent to others seeking help and makes those seeking help feel guilt and shame rather than anger at their plight.

Personal social services, of course, only come into contact with a tiny minority of the population but for some of their clients concern with encouraging more acceptable values and patterns of behaviour and discouraging unacceptable attitudes and lifestyles is central and explicit. Personal social services can seek to persuade through the ministrations of social work. They can reward through the provision of desirable goods and services and through acting as advocates with bodies such as housing departments, social security officers and electricity boards. They can punish through the non-provision of services, through the threat of or actual removal of children, through allowing eviction or electricity disconnection. Social workers have powerful weapons in their armoury. Inducing and encouraging conformity is only one of the varied tasks but it can make a significant contribution to encouraging 'right' behaviour in the most deviant. And, whatever the claims of radical social work, such encouragement is in the direction of political stability.

There is one important area of behaviour which is best considered in conclusion rather than in relation to the impact of specific services on values and behaviour. That is the way in which the social services function to confirm the pattern of sex roles in our society and the outcome of such a process is, of course, the perpetuation of women's subordination. Some feminists would see women's subordination as an integral element in capitalist society and patriarchy as one of capitalism's central organising principles.[67] If that interpretation is correct then institutions and services which help to perpetuate women's position in society are making for political stability.

Sharpe draws out just how social services function in this way. A vital factor is women's position in the family. 'Women's central position in the family', Sharpe writes, 'connects them closely with the workings of the state and their dependence on welfare constantly reminds them of the "correct" and moral assumptions made about their role as women, wives and mothers.' Nurseries are organised so as not to cater effectively for women in full-time work. The cohabitation rule assumes and asserts women's dependence. The school perpetuates the notion of boys and girls as different in attitudes and interests. In the health services used by women, male doctors are usually the key figures. 'In all these areas', Sharpe suggests, 'women and children are directly dependent on the state and each encounter reinforces the implications of female status and role. It is also working class women who are most affected because of their greater dependence on welfare.'[68]

The whole stream of economic, social and political life functions to reward certain kinds of values and behaviour and to discourage others. Social services are only one element in that pattern of institutions and activities. Their role is varied but significant.

Social services support authority and hierarchy in society

There is considerable controversy among political sociologists as to what makes for order and stability in society. Some argue that the crucial bonding element is value consensus. Others argue that the pragmatic acceptance by the working class, racial minorities and women of their subordinate role is the crucial component of order. These two explanations can be synthesised. Acceptance of subordination could be pragmatic in the sense that there seems no alternative to so doing. Or it could be normative – the subordinate groups could have internalised the values of dominant groups and accept their inferior position as entirely legitimate and appropriate.[69]

Mann's conclusion after reviewing all the relevant studies is that evidence favours the pragmatic explanations because there is little evidence of value consensus among subordinate groups.[70] If this is so, it is important to examine the social system for the mechanisms and processes which lead to this pragmatic acceptance of authority and hierarchy in society. We argue that social services play a not unimportant role in this. In a democratic society, the state needs to establish two points if it is to gain support – that the exercise of power by those wielding it is legitimate, and that power is exercised for the good of all. Social services perform a useful role in respect of both these points.

Authority and hierarchy become legitimate if based on principles generally accepted in society. The school also helps to this end by legitimating the inequalities which underlie authority and hierarchy. Tapper and Salter speak of the legitimation of inequality as 'the most important political function of formal schooling'.[71] It does this by providing a supposed equality of opportunity. All have equal chance of rising to positions of success and authority. If that is so, then those who gain positions of power or wealth must be assumed to enjoy extra gifts or talents and so to be particularly fitted by merit for the positions they have reached. Opportunity for individual advancement contributes to the stabilising notion that society is open and it is also likely to discourage pressure for collective mobility by offering an individual solution to status problems.[72]

If society is open, then failure can have nothing to do with economic or social structure but all to do with individual ability and character. Success and power are therefore legitimated. The existing economic and political order is sanctified. As Bourdieu puts it:

'By making social hierarchies and the reproduction of these hierarchies appear to be based upon the hierarchy of "gifts", merits or skills established and ratified by its sanctions, or, in a word, by converting social hierarchies into academic hierarchies, the education system fulfils a function of legitimation which is more and more necessary to the perpetuation of the "social order" as the evolution of the power relationship between classes tends more completely to exclude the imposition of a hierarchy based upon the crude and ruthless affirmation of the power relationship.'[73]

Inequality, then, has all to do with individual effort and ability, nothing to do with the way society functions. 'The educational system', as Miliband puts it, 'thus conspires to create the impression, not least among its victims, that social disadvantages are really a matter of personal, innate, God-given and insurmountable incapacity.'[74]

Another way in which the school helps toward an acceptance of authority is in its own pattern of authority relations. Eckstein has argued that a necessary feature of stable political systems is a high degree of congruence between patterns of authority at the political system level and in other social institutions such as schools. He goes on to argue that in school less able children are subjected to patterns of authority which correspond to the non-participatory role they are expected to play at work and in politics.[75] They are socialised for subordination. Bowles and Gintis argue along similar lines in a way which seems to close off the possibility of any kind of progressive social change.

> The educational system [they write] helps integrate youth into the economic system, we believe, through a structured correspondence between its social relations and those of production. The structure of social relations in education not only inures the student to the discipline of the work place, but develops the types of personal demeanour modes of self presentation, self image, and social class identification, which are the crucial ingredients of job adequacy.[76]

Hess and Torney point out that they found that compliance to rules and authority was the major focus of civics education in the American elementary schools they studied. The citizen's right to participate in government was very little stressed in the school curriculum.[77] Barlagli and Dei also argue the importance of the carry-over effect from authority relationships in school to the acceptance of authority in the larger society on the basis of empirical work in Italian schools.[78]

Social services can also reflect and reinforce patterns of sexual, racial and class domination. The Ehrenreichs describe the doctor-patient relationship as constituting intimate dominance by upper-class white males. The ideological impact of such a relationship, they argue, must be important. 'A relationship of dominance and dependency, of intimacy and authority', they write, 'between a person and a member of the upper class can only act to promote acquiescence to a social system built on class- and sex-based inequalities in power.'[79] Leeson and Gray quote research which shows how the medical profession endorses, explicitly and implicitly, prevailing ideologies about sex roles in a whole variety of ways. The ideologies therefore get embedded in the way the profession reacts to women and in the medical assessments and judgments made about women's needs — which all contributes unwittingly to the perpetuation of women's subordination.[80]

The same charge could be laid against other services. Education prepares boys and girls for different roles in society. Because of the historic pattern of the division of labour in our society, that means preparation for unequal roles — which contribute to the perpetuation of inequality of opportunity for women.[81] Similarly the social security system reflects — and so helps to perpetuate — the traditional social position of women — dependence on men. Personal social services, by stressing family and community care as the natural and proper way to care for the dependent, help to perpetuate women's imprisonment in traditionally female caring roles. As Finch and Groves have argued, community care means family care, family care means care by women, care by women means the perpetuation of a discriminatory division of labour.[82]

Working-class women and racial minorities are also disadvantaged in the education system. Their subordinate position is legitimated by their failure and perpetuated. Traditional patterns of superiority and subordination are preserved and justified by the meritocratic principle which, as Bowles and Gintis put it, is etched deep into popular culture as a seeming step towards equality but as in fact a major prop to the existing distribution of power and authority.

We argued above that social services can endow the social order with a new legitimacy. Another way of looking at the same point would be to argue that social services contribute to political stability by obscuring the fundamental nature of society. Its competitive, inequitable, exploitative, profit-centred politics are concealed behind a facade of social service provision suggesting a nature far different from the reality. Plant makes an interesting point relevant to this argument.[83] Marxists, he points out, would stress the ideological function of casework concepts. The notions of respect for persons or client self-determination deeply embedded in social work ideology have the function of suggesting that these are basic principles of life in liberal democratic societies. They contribute to a picture of society which Marxists would see as totally false since there is no respect for individuals in capitalist society except as actual or potential producers. Self-determination is equally mythical when most people are bound to the engine of capitalism. Key social work concepts contribute to a notion of society quite other than it is, they contribute to a notion of society as people would like to think it is, to the picture of a society above and beyond criticism, to an obfuscation of its real nature. Criticism is diverted; critics are silenced.

The final way in which social services support the existing pattern of authority in society is the way they treat too many of their clients. In the social security system, in housing departments, in the health service, in personal social services and in education there is an abundance of evidence that those using services are treated with scant courtesy and consideration. They are kept waiting as if their time was valueless, they are not vouchsafed explanations of their condition or the likelihood of help or why no help is likely, little credence is given to their view of their situation. The relationships of the world of work are complemented and confirmed by the subordinate status accorded to those seeking their rights as citizens in the welfare state. Leeson and Gray have a delightful and revealing chart describing 'How the Pregnant Woman Becomes a Patient'. Her condition is successfully medicalised and through a series of interventions she becomes ever more dependent on the medical profession. She ceases to be able to determine how the pregnancy is to be managed. She becomes a patient. Expert upper-class men have reasserted a traditionally and socially important pattern of authority relations.[84]

It is in the social services that most people have their closest and most important experience of government authority. For most it is an experience which confirms their own subordination and reinforces the existing patterns of authority in society — and so political stability.

Social services contribute to the replacement of class conflict by group conflict

Class conflict is the type of social conflict most threatening to society because it is deep, pervasive and along one axis. Welfare state policies are seen by some as part of a truce situation, a compromise settlement making for social harmony. We would argue that social services also contribute importantly to an underlying political stability through the way in which they institutionalise group conflict. Social services divide society in new and significant ways — into claimants and non-claimants, into wealth creators and wealth consumers, into tax-payers and the dependent, into local authority tenants and owner-occupiers — and so on. Different needs groups are very clearly in competition with each other — the elderly with children, the unemployed with the employed and with other dependent groups, the healthy with the ill, universities with schools, nurses with teachers, nurses with other health service workers, social workers with nurses. Welfare state policies create group conflicts because the conflicting claims made by groups can only be resolved through conflict. Because of the nature of the welfare state such conflicts are often transformed into political conflicts.

Schattschneider suggested some years ago that 'government in a democracy is a great engine for expanding the scale of conflict.'[85] An expansion in the scale of conflict, odd though this may appear, may make it less threatening to political stability. If conflict can be politicised, that is, if it can be directed and confined to the political sphere, then it can be conducted within boundaries prescribed by political convention. This may well limit its effects. Second, it is important to distinguish between the scope and intensity of conflict — a point which Zeigler and Peak emphasise. They argue that it is intensity of conflict which really threatens political stability. Increasing the scope of conflict does not *per se* make conflict more dangerous.[86]

> Multiple group applications of individuals [says Coser] make for a multiplicity of conflicts criss-crossing society. Such segmental participation, then, can result in a kind of balancing mechanism preventing deep cleavages along one axis. The interdependence of conflicting groups and the multiplicity of non cumulative conflicts provide one, though not, of course, the only check against basic consensual breakdown in an open society.[87]

Claus Offe also produces arguments relevant to this thesis. One way, in his view, in which social services function to reduce social conflict is by the way in which they contrive to turn political debate and conflict to the issue of the distribution of the national product rather than the mode of production — which according to Marxist analysis is the crucial determinant of economic and social relations. The significance of such a change in the pattern of conflict is that conflict about distribution is twofold. First, such conflict can be processed on the political plane through conventional party competition because it involves questions of more/less or sooner/later rather than yes/no. Second, such conflict becomes group conflict rather than class conflict because it is detached from the basic class cleavages of society. It can therefore be contained within the existing political system and poses no fundamental threat to its continuance.[88]

Mishra argues along similar lines stressing how the welfare state has increased the complexity of social stratification. Class interests and class conflict are fragmented by new interests which cut across class divisions and create divisions within classes.[89] Working-class owner-occupiers may come, for example, to have stronger links with middle-class owner-occupiers than with working-class council tenants.

Our argument is that the development of social services contributes to the replacement of class conflict by group conflict. This is less threatening to political stability because less fundamental and so more susceptible to resolution through compromise and less likely to lead to a head-on challenge to the existing political order. Fragmentation of conflict leaves existing authority more secure.

We have said little in this chapter so far about whether or not social services also make a contribution to political instability − partly because we think there is less to be said, partly because we treat this issue from a rather broader perspective in the next chapter. At this point we would want to do no more than indicate that such charges can be made against all the main services albeit less convincingly than the charge that they contribute to reinforcing the political *status quo*.

It can be argued, for example, that the NHS stands as a unique challenge to the basic principles which govern the distribution of goods and services in our society. Distribution of most goods is according to market power; distribution of health care, in contrast, is according to need not according to ability to pay. Such a principle could pose a challenge, and so a threat, to market principles − if health is distributed on this basis why should other essential goods and services not be distributed in the same way?

The threat, however, is more apparent than real. It is reduced by various factors. Health, it is argued, is 'different', so distribution of health care according to need does not mean that there is a case for the distribution of other goods − housing for example − on a similar basis. The principle of a service financed by taxation, freely available according to need is also continuously attacked as leading to waste and inefficiency and an inadequate standard of service provision because of people's reluctance to pay taxes. Private provision is asserted by many powerful voices to be more efficient, more responsive to individual need, and productive of higher quality service. So the threat which the NHS could, or might, pose to market principles is contained and muted.

A second way in which the NHS might be charged with contributing to political instability is the way it affects attitudes. It could be charged with contributing to the socially damaging notion that 'the state will provide', that something really can be obtained for nothing, that state provision releases the individual from the invigorating and effort-inducing responsibility for providing for his own and his family's essential needs. The individual loses something which is an important element in mature citizenship and which is therefore conducive to political stability.

The most serious charge which can be laid against the social security system is that it weakens work incentives and so undermines the basic discipline which work provides in society. By providing a subsidy to the idle and the feckless, the argument runs, the basis of the productive system and so of social and political order is gradually undermined. We saw in Chapter 5 that the evidence hardly supports such sweeping charges.

The social security system can also be charged with contributing to the suspicion and hostility which underlie the fiscal crisis of the state. Any welfare system is open to abuse. Governments and public opinion have always been more sensitive to anxieties about the abuse of social security than abuse of other services. Critics of social security provision build on public anxieties. The fruit of their efforts is a hostility to social security provision, or more particularly to certain types of provision and certain categories of claimant. The feeling that abuse is widespread encourages a hostility to welfare state policies in general and to the levels of taxation required to sustain them — so contributing to the fiscal crisis of the state and threatening the viability of welfare capitalism. Some of the links in the argument are tenuous but it is significant that those hostile to welfare state policies build on the alleged abuse of social security to fuel a broader discontent. They are, in fact, using the system to contribute to a legitimacy crisis.

Three relevant accusations are made against government housing policy. First, that it encourages the polarisation of society, dividing the population into the two camps of owner-occupation and local authority tenants with sharply divergent interests and fed with hostility-inducing stereotypes of each other by the media. Government housing policy in such a situation can only create hostility among one or other of the major interests because of the impossibility of satisfying both of them simultaneously. Second, the expansion of owner-occupation has exposed many more people to close involvement with some of the central financial institutions of capitalism — banks and building societies in particular. What this involvement exposes is the way in which these institutions are at the mercy of incomprehensible financial trends and money market movements. Interest rates rise and fall and the owner-occupier's mortgage repayments go up and down in a way he or she can neither understand or anticipate. The irrationality of such a system is nakedly obvious — which can do the broader economic order nothing but damage. Critics of capitalism have always inveighed against the irrationality of capitalism — and here it is displayed nakedly to an ever expanding group of often struggling owner-occupiers. Third, the expansion of owner-occupation has fuelled the movement for greater citizen participation — initially in planning, which was where the owner-occupier's interests were immediately and clearly affected by local and national planning decisions, but then extending to other areas. The movement for participation encouraged a more critical perspective on central and local government decisions. The standing of government suffered as the irrationality and interest-bound nature of many decisions was exposed. Government was revealed as a fallible activity pursued with regard for special interests rather than always for the general good as governments would wish people to suppose.

Three relevant charges are levelled at the education system. First, schools have been charged with producing young people ill-equipped for life in the real world — that is with basic skills and attuned to low-paid, routine work. In the same way, the whole educational system — school, further and higher — has been accused of failing to produce the young people with the more advanced skills required by an advanced economy. Students somehow prefer dysfunctional subjects rather than subjects functional to economic development.

Second, the schools are charged with failing to induce a proper regard for authority in their pupils. Modern methods are blamed for a weakening of authority and discipline in school and community alike. A generation has grown up without experience of firm authority in the school and society suffers as a result — a belief close to the heart of Dr Rhodes Boyson, for example.

The third charge is one which we have referred to already, the charge made against the higher education system that it produces young people disaffected with the society which has nourished them and provided them with extended and expensive educational opportunities. Certainly, the development of the New Left movement and the renaissance of Marxism took place, and have been sustained, in the higher education system. Society itself indirectly provided hospitality for those seeking to develop and expound a philosophy which sought its replacement by a new social order.

Personal social services came under fire from the critics for their supposed role in undermining the family, the basic building-block of stable political systems, by removing from it basic responsibilities which have helped bind families together in the past. Such removal of responsibilities weakens the family and encourages a morally debilitating dependency on public institutions and services. People lose the independence and the individual sense of responsibility which are a corollary of vigorous citizenship and a healthy social and political life.

Personal social services are accused more specifically of helping to undermine individuals' sense of responsibility for their own actions. Attempts to explain law-breaking behaviour as something for which individuals are somehow not fully responsible degrades them and weakens the moral bonds of law and order. Social workers are seen as colluding with delinquents in such explanations and as failing to express the condemnation and need for punishment which such behaviour evokes in other citizens. The general aspect for law and authority is thereby weakened.

We sketch these charges about the politically destabilising role of social services simply to indicate that a case can be argued on those lines. We believe, however, that the evidence suggests a stabilising, rather than a destabilising, impact for social services. The furtherance of political stability is one of the aims and functions of social services. It is, however, only one of many and varied aims and social services are only one of a range of social institutions functioning to promote stability. That services have an impact of this kind is clear, and when the role of social services in society is being discussed, it needs to be considered whether the concern is with stability or with change.

7

The legitimation crisis of the welfare state

Introduction

We argued in the previous chapter that social services have contributed more to political stability than instability. Nevertheless, there is considerable discussion of an alleged crisis in the welfare state − in part the product of hope, in part the product of fear. In this chapter we explore this supposed crisis from a broad political perspective. We are not concerned here with the problems and crises of particular social services but with the supposed legitimation crisis of that form of polity known as the welfare state.

'Legitimacy', says Lipset, 'involves the capacity of the system to engender and maintain the belief that the existing political institutions are the most appropriate ones for the society.'[1] Lane is more specific.

A system is regarded as legitimate [he writes] when the claims to rightful power of its leaders, the procedures which they employ, and the outcomes of their acts are regarded as morally appropriate; to grant legitimacy is to engage in an act of moral evaluation.[2]

Today, in spite of all the powerful system sustaining institutions and pressures which inhibit criticism there is a strong sense of crisis in the welfare state. Seemingly insoluble problems afflict the economic, social and political systems alike and it is this co-existence of problems which contributes to the sense of crisis. Two factors, in particular, underlie it. First, the economic growth which made public policy 'almost costless in political terms'[3] has ended. Social policy now clearly costs money and can be financed only by the painful forgoing of other desirable purchases whereas growth meant painless financing. The end of growth means debate about the pros and cons of different types of expenditure private and public, a debate which continuing growth had obscured.

Second, the absence of a strong, positive philosophy underlying the welfare state has become more obvious and more significant. In a situation of growth and painless financing there was no need for its supporters to set out to build a strong basis of political support. It seemed that their aims could be achieved without that effort. The welfare state developed, but was kept in motion not

> by the 'pull' of a conscious political will, but rather by the 'push' of emergent risks, dangers and bottlenecks, and newly created insecurities or potential conflicts which demand immediate measures that avoid the socially destabilizing problem of the moment.[4]

The ending of growth opened up debates about the role of the state in welfare which had never taken place until the ending of growth posed sharper choices and threatened established programmes. We approach the crisis first by exploring the evidence for the existence of a threatened or actual disturbance to the system of welfare capitalism and then by reviewing the debate about the causes and nature of the crisis and attempting to give it a measure of order.

Is there a legitimation crisis?

There is abundant evidence that welfare capitalist societies are experiencing significant economic, social and political difficulties and that those difficulties have increased in the 1970s and 1980s. What is less clear is precisely how people see these difficulties and the extent to which they blame the economic, social and political system for them, rather than the traditional incompetence of governments. There is also the problem of deciding when difficulties can be deemed to constitute a crisis. We come to these issues later in the section.

Welfare states were beset by economic difficulties in the 1970s and 1980s. The rate of economic growth slowed down and in some countries the economy ceased to expand altogether. Rates of inflation and unemployment both increased, reaching unprecedented post-war levels. For thirty years governments had confidently asserted their ability to control the workings of the economy. Now their incapacity stood clearly revealed. In 1970 nearly 60 per cent of the population of the UK felt a government could do a lot to check rising prices. Four years later only a quarter of the electorate felt that way.[5]

Alt makes another important point about the economic aspects of the crisis. From the early 1960s he discerns an increasing trend to see the personal aspects of the economic problem as the most important rather than its more general dimensions. What people emphasise is prices and taxes rather than, for example, unemployment.[6] This is significant for what it says about economic and social solidarity. Inflation too, in part at least, is the product of groups pursuing their own economic interests without regard for what governments tell them is the national interest. The benefits of restraint are of course public goods; there is no obvious, immediate pay-off for the groups showing self-restraint. Inflation is then, in some measure, an index of declining regard for the general good. It is both a source of economic, social and political disruption and an index of an absence of cohesion in society. Crozier goes as far as to describe inflation as 'a direct result of the ungovernability of Western democracies',[7] in that it indicates the failure or inability of government to assert the general good.

Another way in which analysis of the economic problems of welfare capitalism suggest problems which are more than simply economic is the way in which public spending is blamed for economic difficulties. When public expenditure is arraigned as the cause of low growth rates, inflation and high unemployment what is, in fact, being blamed is the economic system of welfare capitalism as such. The role of the state in managing the economy, state aid to industry and to declining regions, redistribution of income via the tax system and social and public services are being questioned. An economic philosophy and a generation of economic arrangements are being questioned. Much more is at issue than simple levels of spending on social services as we tried to show in Chapter 5.

Finally, there is the evidence on tax evasion and tax avoidance and the growth of the black economy. Inevitably evidence is uncertain but some of those in the best position to know the situation speak warningly of 'the growing threat of avoidance and evasion'.[8] Estimates of the size of the problem are disconcertingly variable. Some analysts put the size of the black economy at 10-15 per cent of national income, others at between 3 and 8 per cent. The head of the Inland Revenue recently suggested a figure of 6 per cent which implies a tax loss of some £4,000 million per year.[9] Rose and Peters conclude that tax evasion 'is already substantial or becoming significant in every major Western nation.'[10] There are, however, those who dispute the evidence that the problem is increasing.[11]

Tax avoidance and evasion are most obviously of financial and economic importance. They are also a significant index of attitudes to government. 'Reaction to taxation, more than any other legislative policy', argued the General Secretary of the Inland Revenue Staff

Federation in 1979, 'may be seen as indicative of the people's attitude to government itself.'[12] Taxation, Christopher argues, implies two things in a democracy. 'Firstly, it implies recognition of community and interdependence. Secondly, it acknowledges the right of properly elected governments to redistribute the revenue they raise with a degree of discretion.'[13] Evasion shows a weakening of the sense of legitimacy of levels of taxation and government authority and as knowledge of evasion spreads in the community it feeds suspicion and distrust and a reluctance by even the most law-abiding to pay more taxation than they should be paying because of the evasion and avoidance of others. It helps feed resentment about the level of taxation on which welfare capitalism depends, so contributing directly to the fiscal crisis of the state.

There are two elements in what might be called the social evidence for the legitimation crisis — the decline in enthusiasm for the welfare state and the increase in social conflict. In the 1960s social welfare problems became less salient to people asked about the most important problems facing government and economic problems and problems of taxation came to loom much larger.[14] In the autumn of 1964 77 per cent of the population felt the government should spend more on pensions and social services and 20 per cent felt spending should stay as it then was. By the summer of 1969 only 43 per cent were in favour of further spending and 52 per cent felt spending should stay as it was.[15] The age of massive majority support for more welfare spending of all kinds had passed. By 1979 opinion is evenly divided, as Table 7.1

TABLE 7.1
Opinions on government (Gallup survey, 21-6 March, 1979).

People have different views about whether it is more important to reduce taxes or keep up government spending. Which of these statements comes closest to your own view?

Taxes being cut even if it means some reduction in government services such as health, education and welfare.	34%
Things should be left as they are.	25%
Government services such as health, education and welfare should be extended even if it means some increases in taxes.	34%
Don't know.	7%

shows, between those wanting cuts in taxes even at the cost of reductions in some services and those wanting to extend services even if it meant some increase in taxation. A quarter of the sample still stand by the *status quo*.[16]

A Marplan poll carried out for the *Guardian* in early September 1982 found a predictable 83 per cent of a national sample who felt taxes should be reduced when faced with the simple question 'Do you think taxes ought to be increased or reduced?' Only 36 per cent supported such reductions if they resulted in falling standards in social services.[17] Much seems to depend on, for example, how questions are phrased, whether respondents' belief that somehow they can have lower taxes without effect on standards of services is really confronted, whether social services and benefits are differentiated one from another, but clearly there is a sizeable group which wants cuts in taxes even at the cost of reductions in some services even though 'welfare spending is still popular amongst the great majority of the electorate.'[18]

Over-Ruled on Welfare provides further evidence. In 1963 41 per cent of a national random sample were willing to pay higher taxes in return for an improved National Health Service. By 1978 the percentage who were so prepared had fallen to 20.[19] Similarly in 1963, 51 per cent of the sample were willing to pay higher taxes for better state education. By 1978 this proportion had fallen to 15 per cent.[20] By the mid 1970s it was only among strong Labour supporters that there was any large measure of support for more spending on social services.[21] By the mid 1960s a majority of Conservative supporters were against further social service spending.[22] In 1979, for the first time since the war, the idea of cutting back existing welfare programmes got firmly on to the political welfare agenda.

Not only does there seem to have been a decline in support for the principle of welfare spending in the 1960s and 1970s. There was also an increase in dissension and social conflict.

> What has become clear [says Heclo] is that far from achieving a sense of domestic solidarity, British social policy has been accompanied by more intense clashes of interest . . . Far from becoming one nation, post war Britain seems to have become a nation that is increasingly divided against itself.[23]

Commenting on why Britain has become harder to govern, John Mackintosh picked out what he described as 'a decline in the sense of common purpose among the various sections of society'.[24] Society then comes to be regarded not as a vehicle for the achievement of common goals but as 'an orange to be squeezed by those with the strength or the nerve to extract more juice for themselves'.[25] Certainly the 1970s were marked by increased organisation and militancy in pressing sectional claims among all groups of workers and notably and noticeably among welfare state employees — doctors, teachers, hospital workers and social workers.

The welfare state had seemed to promise a new measure of social consensus and altruism. By the 1970s increased militancy in pressing wage claims, increased crime and violence, increased problems of race relations made such hopes and promises look very thin. By 1977 the median Briton reckoned there was an almost 50-50 chance of civil disorder in the years ahead.[26] In the summer of 1981 such anxieties were shown to have been well-founded when serious riots swept parts of London, Liverpool, Manchester and other major cities. There had, of course, been riots before in the late 1950s in Notting Hill and Nottingham but on a considerably smaller scale.

In its period of expansion and consolidation after the Second World War the welfare state reflected a new sense of national solidarity. Many of those who supported its development believed it could help to preserve such a consensus because of 'its potential for evoking such moral commitment to the common welfare'.[27] By the 1970s, whether or not due to the failings of the welfare state, that sense of national solidarity was clearly in shreds. Questions about what had gone wrong inevitably promoted ideas about the failure of the welfare state.

What political evidence is there for a legitimation crisis? Four issues need to be considered. First, there is the general political mood. Commentator after commentator speaks of 'a politics of quiet disillusion',[28] 'the extent of the pessimism about British government',[29] 'the general background of disillusion with parties and governments that has been evident in recent years',[30] 'a growing and more public scepticism about the capacity of governments to solve the major problems of the day',[31] 'substantial and persistent causes of discontent which may contain the seeds of more serious trouble'.[32] There is considerable evidence, at the level of the informed judgments of students of the political scene, of a public mood of pessimism and disillusion.

A second index of a decline in political stability is the weakening of attachment to political parties which has been a feature of politics in many European countries in the 1970s. Parties are important to political stability for various reasons. They encourage identification with the existing political system. They function as a mediating element between the governors and the governed. They give credibility to the essential belief that the individual's interests are taken care of in the political process.[33] Between 1950 and 1970 the average number of MPs unconnected with the Conservative or Labour Parties was ten. The number never rose above fourteen. In February 1974 it leaped up to thirty-seven. At that election the Conservative and Labour share of the vote which had never fallen below 89 per cent since 1945 fell to 76 per cent.[34] Not since 1922 had the two major parties suffered substantial losses of votes at the same time. In the election of October 1974 the number of minority party seats rose from thirty-seven to thirty-nine.

The Labour government's share of the poll was the lowest for any majority government since 1922 and the Conservative Party's share of the vote — 36 per cent — was the lowest in its history.[35] Just before the election one in five Labour voters showed their dissatisfaction and apprehension with their own party by confessing to the opinion pollsters that they thought a Labour government would behave less sensibly if it had a large majority.[36] At the 1979 election things were a little less abnormal. Nevertheless, the Conservative vote at 44 per cent showed the lowest level of support for any post-war government except that elected in October 1974. But what is really striking is the long-term trend. Crewe and his colleagues suggest that the important statistic is the Conservative and Labour share of the electorate rather than their share of the actual vote. In 1951 the two parties shared the votes of 80 per cent of the electorate. In 1959 the share was down to 74 per cent, in 1970 to 65 per cent and in 1974 it fell to 56 per cent, rising to just over 60 per cent in 1979.[37]

This change is not peculiar to Britain. Wolfe notes that in the United States 80 per cent of voters in 1950 cast straight party votes whereas in 1970 the figure was 50 per cent.[38] Bell notes how the index of such partisan dealignment is minority governments and he points out that in 1974 no party held a majority in the legislatures of Norway, Sweden, Denmark, France, West Germany, the Netherlands, Belgium, Italy or Britain.[39] There is clearly a widespread sense of dissatisfaction with established parties, with the way they have exercised power when in government and with the pledges and promises they have made to secure election and re-election to office.

A third issue which is relevant is the sense of frustration and powerlessness which emerges from surveys of public attitudes to government. This was a major theme of the Memorandum of Dissent submitted by Lord Crowther Hunt and Professor Alan Peacock to the Royal Commission on the Constitution. They commented on what they described as a decline in this century in the extent to which we as a people govern ourselves[40] and stressed what they saw as a direct result — 'a sense of powerlessness in the face of government'[41] and 'a growing alienation from the government system'.[42] Crowther Hunt and Peacock write of 'today's widespread and justifiable belief' that the country is becoming less democratic, that people do not have enough say on issues that affect them, that government has become too centralised and too congested.[43] Such a feeling, if it is widely prevalent and strongly held, can deprive the actions of government of the legitimacy which derives from popular endorsement. There is evidence — votes for minority parties, low turn-outs at general elections, derisory turn-outs at local elections, the development of issue-based movements for participation and protest — that confidence in the ability of established political institutions to mediate popular opinion has declined.

The three points made so far all point towards the final indication of political discontent – a decline of confidence in government and politics generally. Almond and Verba asked a sample of voters in different countries in the early 1960s what they would do to influence local government. Only 1 per cent in Britain, Italy and the United States said they would work through a political party; about the same percentage as said they would engage in political violence.[44] Wolfe quotes figures showing the proportion of the general public expressing various views about the United States government at various dates between 1964 and 1970. What is plain is an increasing distrust of governmental morals and competence. In 1964 27.4 per cent of the sample felt that 'the people running the government don't know what they are doing.' By 1970 68.7 per cent held this view. In 1972 38 per cent of the population said their political leaders regularly lied to them. In 1975 68 per cent felt this way.[45]

In Europe 44 per cent of a sample taken from EEC countries in 1975 said they were dissatisfied with the working of democracy in their country.[46] What data on changing opinion and attitudes in the 1970s shows, says Kaase, is not 'mass publics disenchanted with their governments to the point of revolution or exodus into indifference' but that 'there are signs of a considerable amount of strain, value conflict, and a rather critical distance from the world of politics.'[47]

Evidence for the existence of a legitimation crisis is essentially of three kinds – informed comment by experts, information about the values and attitudes of the citizenry, and evidence about citizen behaviour. In the economic, social and political spheres most developed societies currently face strains and problems. There can be no dispute about that. The issue for discussion is whether and when such problems can be deemed to constitute a crisis.

Lane is helpful in setting out criteria by which to judge whether responses to public opinion polls constitute a crisis of legitimacy. Such views, he suggests, would have to satisfy five conditions. They would have to

(a) be directed at the system and not at the incumbents or policies;
(b) be directed at the rationales or values underlying the system, and not merely serve to identify villains or even criticize system performance;
(c) persist over some long duration and not be merely ephemeral;
(d) be rooted in some structural property of the system such that a group, or set of groups, is systematically deprived of crucial values and
(e) enlist a sense of personal malaise related to system performance

> . . . people contented with their own lives do not act upon or
> act out their beliefs in system inadequacy.[48]

These are extremely important points. Much of the research which pur-
ports to support the notion of a legitimacy crisis fails to distinguish
satisfactorily between dissatisfaction with a particular government or
particular institutions of government and dissatisfaction with the basic
system and the philosophy underpinning it.

Kaase, for example, looks at the alleged breakdown of the traditional party political system in Western democracies. When the hard
evidence is explored, however, he finds a lack of evidence over time
for countries other than the USA. His conclusion is that existing data
does not reveal the consistent pattern of critical erosion of existing
party systems that might be expected on the basis of the ungovernability hypothesis.[49] Habermas supports such a view. 'We certainly cannot speak of a real crisis of legitimation,' he says, 'people continue to
vote, and in their vast majority vote for the traditional parties.'[50]
A real legitimation crisis, in his view, would signify a collapse of the
traditional party system and the formation of a new party whose aims
would transcend the existing economic system.

Lane's own conclusion, on the basis of his five criteria, and after a
lengthy review of survey evidence on dissatisfaction with the United
States government, is that the evidence does not meet his criteria for a
crisis of legitimacy. There is considerable dissatisfaction but it is compatible, he judges, with acceptance of the American *system* of government. He refers to evidence which shows that

> more than 80 per cent of the public believes 'our country will be
> strong and prosperous again', and 'the American way of life is
> superior to that of any other country', and 63 per cent agree that
> 'our government system should not be changed in any major way.'[51]

Moreover, the public may lack confidence in big business or in the
business community but it also overwhelmingly approves of the 'free
enterprise' system.

In conclusion, it can be said that public opinion survey data show
that there is substantial dissatisfaction with the political parties, governments and their leaders but there appears to be general acceptance of
the central values of parliamentary systems and private enterprise.
Whether this constitutes a crisis of legitimacy in welfare capitalism
depends on one's views of what constitutes a crisis and what is legitimacy. The definitions accepted in this chapter lead to the conclusion
that welfare capitalist societies are experiencing severe difficulties but
these have not reached crisis dimensions. It seems as if the public sees

no alternative system to welfare capitalism or rather that what it sees is not very appealing. Denitch rightly concludes a debate on welfare state capitalism by making the point that 'the crisis of legitimacy of the capitalist West is therefore simultaneously a crisis of modern socialism.'[52]

Theories of the crisis

The various theories identifying a deep crisis in welfare capitalism can be divided into three broad groups – the 'overload in government' thesis propounded by neo-conservatives and others, the 'state contradiction' thesis argued by a largely Marxist following, and a group we have called the pragmatists who see the crisis as a complex of problems which can be resolved by appropriate government action, rather than as a situation which cannot be resolved within present institutional arrangements. These classifications are by no means watertight. The Marxist thesis of the fiscal crisis of the state is in a real sense a theory of government overload but the explanation given by Marxists for the fiscal crisis roots it in the state contradiction theories. Again, Hadley and Hatch's argument about the failure of the state[53] is in a sense a theory about overload but for reasons we hope to make clear later we think it is more properly located among the pragmatist group.

Government overload
There is an influential group of thinkers who see the root of the political problems of welfare capitalism as lying in government over-load. For various reasons they see government as having become over-loaded with duties and responsibilities and they see this as threatening to political stability and to the legitimacy of welfare capitalism. Over-load means different things to different people. Some protagonists of the theory – King is the obvious example[54] – define the problem essen-tially in terms of *administrative* overload. People expect and demand that governments do many more things than in the past and problems result, leading to fundamental questions being asked about the political system. Other writers – Brittan, for example,[55] – see the problem much more in terms of system overload; more is expected of our system of government – welfare state democracy – than it can deliver and the result is instability. In the discussion which follows we try to explore how it is that writers about overload explain the development of the problem and the alleged implications of overload for the legiti-macy of the welfare state.

Brittan sees the root of the problem as lying in the nature of the type of democracy which has evolved. He follows Schumpeter in viewing democracy 'neither as a method of popular participation in government nor as a means of putting into effect the people's will, but mainly as a competition for power by means of votes among competing teams'.[56] Such competition contributes to overload in a number of ways. It imparts 'a systematic upward bias to expectations'.[57] People are encouraged to expect more of everything from parties and governments. This problem of excessive expectations — as Brittan sees them — is exacerbated by the way in which voters are insulated from a full or immediate awareness of the cost implications of party promises. It thus becomes impossible for them to act as rational consumers and choose between alternatives. The elector comes 'to favour all worthy objects at the same time'.[58] Competitive democracy generates the belief that everything is possible — now.

'What has gone', says Brittan, 'is the tacit belief in limiting the role of political decision: and this is likely to put a burden on democratic procedures which they are not designed to bear.'[59] When 'an excessive burden is placed on the "sharing out" function of government' competitive democracy is stimulated as parties and interest groups strive to outdo each other in their promises to gain support and further their interests. King, too, stresses the enormous expansion in the past ten or twenty years in the range of matters for which British governments hold themselves responsible and for which they believe the electorate holds them responsible. Government, he writes has 'come to be regarded, in Britain at least, as a sort of unlimited-liability insurance company'.[60]

Competitive democracy is one element in this expansion but other factors are also significant. There is the enormous prestige with which the state emerged from the Second World War — a point on which Middlemas lays great stress in his analysis of the nature of the politics which emerged after 1945.[61] Governments seemed to be able to do almost anything. Government prestige in the first twenty-five years was increased by two other factors — one was the way in which it seemed to be able so to manage the economy as to secure economic growth. Such growth in turn contributed to overload by encouraging the belief that there was nothing governments could not undertake and afford, and of course it made the financing of new government activities relatively painless.

More important, perhaps, in the eyes of Brittan and other neo-conservatives was Keynesianism. Keynesianism is accused of contributing to overload in a number of ways. Keynes's repudiation of the balanced budget as the outward and visible sign of financial and economic rectitude freed government from a historic constraint on widening its sphere of activities. Government borrowing to ensure full employment and to further a desirable range of social objectives was given a new respectability. Keynes also, it is argued,[62] simply expected too much of the political system. He thought that once the political managers were converted to his ideas all would be well. Such a belief depended, however, on two vital but implicit assumptions — that government economic policy could be insulated from political demands which conflicted with economic rationality and that government policy was immune to undermining by actions from trades unions or employees.[63] Skidelsky's argument is that in the 1940s climate of consensus about ends and purposes such assumptions had a certain plausibility. More recently, however, governments have been less and less able to manage the economy rationally and more and more have been driven to buy off potentially hostile voters and over-powerful interest groups to ensure short-term survival. Keynes assumed an authority and independence for government which it has not been able to sustain. Democracy was overloaded with responsibility, not simply at the administrative level where adaptation and reform may be possible without excessive difficulty, but at the more crucial system level where a political-economic order finds itself unable to sustain the role on which the survival of that order depends.

Finally, economic recession gives a further push to overload. As economic growth slows down pressure increases for government to do something. Governments have trumpeted about their ability to fine-tune the economy; they are now pressed to avert disaster by rescuing ailing industries and regions, by controlling wages and prices, by providing programmes for the unemployed, by encouraging growth points in the economy. New demands are made upon them when the political solvent of the fiscal dividend is drying up and such initiatives can no longer be financed painlessly. In recession, in Offe's words 'the *conflict-generating* potential of the institutions of the democratic polity by far outweighs their *conflict-resolving* capacity,'[64] an aspect of competitive democracy which has previously been obscured by the fact that economic growth made it possible to provide something for almost everyone. The ability of liberal competitive democracy to provide consensus was revealed as an overload in expectation which the system could not meet. This is one of the arguments outlined by Usher. If the assignment of income is attempted through the political market, that is by voting, the result will be a divided society with little hope of reconciling its various elements.[65]

King focuses his attention much more on the overloading of the actual machinery of government rather than on the more macro-level issue of system overload. He examines four reasons put forward for this kind of overloading. First, governments sometimes attempt to achieve the physically impossible given the current knowledge base. Though this happens sometimes, it is not common and it cannot be considered an important reason. Second, and equally insignificant, is the argument that governments lack the necessary resources to meet their multifarious duties. This lacks plausibility, King argues, because resources 'were far scarcer forty years ago when Britain seemed almost the only country that was relatively easy to govern'. Third, and most important, 'the number of dependency relationships in which government is involved has increased substantially, and because the incidence of acts of non-compliance by the other participants in these relationships has also increased substantially.' In other words, production, distribution and service industries are today far more inter-dependent, with the result that a government attempting to cope with problems in one area finds itself enmeshed in a web of inter-relationships that are beyond its ability to untangle. This growth in inter-dependence is the result of such structural factors as 'the division of labour, the increase in standards of living, the increases in the scale and complexity of international trade'. Fourth, and it is a point closely related to the previous one, there has been a lack of knowledge and understanding of how to cope with increasingly complex problems.[66]

Essentially, then, King locates the source of the problem in structural changes in society which have put strong pressure on governments to expand the range of their activities. The same changes, however, have also reduced governments' ability to deal effectively with the problems which are pressed upon them.

What then are the implications which the overload theorists see for the legitimacy of the welfare state? By his location of the problem in the very nature of what he calls liberal representative democracy Brittan is driven to pessimistic conclusions. The problem, as he sees it, is systemic, not to be solved by judicious piecemeal social engineering. He is, however, quite clear that 'the present situation is unsustainable' and that democratic welfare capitalism has lost legitimacy. Although unwilling to commit himself on how the present order will collapse, Brittan suggests 'a gradual disintegration of traditional political authority and the growth of new sources of power' and he adds that 'a continuation of present trends might lead to a situation where nothing remained of liberal democracy but its label.'[67]

King pin-points the most obvious general result of overload as being a decline in the ability of governments to carry out their responsibilities effectively. He then lists four other consequences for government 'of a world at once more demanding and more intractable'. First, 'policies of government more often fail.' Second, there is the risk that 'mass dissatisfaction with the consequences of our present political arrangements could grow to the point where the arrangements themselves were seriously called in question.' King sees this as a very real possibility.

Although no one has produced a plausible scenario for the collapse of the present British system of government [he writes] the fact that people are talking about the possibility at all is in itself significant, and certainly we seem likely in the mid or late 1970's to face the sort of 'crisis of the regime' that Britain has not known since 1832, possibly not since the seventeenth century.

Third, overload in government means a larger and ever more complex government machine which gets increasingly difficult to direct, co-ordinate and control. Finally, there is the possibility of 'a quite radical change in the nature of government, and in our conceptions of it', in the direction of more 'authoritative' government, that is a situation in which people expect ' "They" will deal with it.' But ('they') — the state — could find itself 'merely one among a number of contenders for wealth, power and influence'.[68] What King seems to be hypothesising, though through a glass rather darkly, is a situation in which government gains power but loses authority; the citizen loses power to government, but overload creates a situation in which other centres of power can threaten and thwart the policies of government.

Douglas in his review of the overload thesis draws out two important reasons as to why overload should be a cause for concern. 'The "over-load" analysis', he writes, 'seems to me without doubt correct.'[69] His first reason for concern, which he judges to be the more important, 'is that at each swing of the pendulum the whole two party system loses some of its legitimacy'.[70] Voters find that neither party can deliver its promises and their respect for parliamentary democracy, as such, drops at each swing of the pendulum. 'I would argue', Douglas writes, 'that the absence of popular support must undermine the authority of government and ultimately the authority of Parliament and the whole parliamentary system.'[71] Second, political party competition for votes tends 'to push the whole political/economic system towards an unduly short run perspective'.[72] Politicians need to act in a way which will maximise the long-term growth of the economy. Party competition, however, overloads the system with pressure to respond to immediate demands and long-term interests and needs get pushed into second place.

All overload theorists see overload as leading to a loss of government authority. Brittan sees competitive democracy as the product of a loss of stability in society, of the decline in power of norms and values of self-restraint, respect for government, acceptance of inequality and as giving a push to the decline of those stabilising factors. King sees the link as more between overload, ineffectiveness and loss of credibility and standing. The result is pessimism, disillusion and the politics of recrimination.

Overload also contributes to alienation. As governments expand their responsibilities, their organisation becomes more complex and, in Britain, more centralised and more bureaucratic. There is also an increased risk, as Rose has pointed out that 'big government' will threaten popular consent to the extent that it 'implies an increasing risk of impropriety, or justification by values more appropriate to authoritarian or totalitarian regimes than to Western societies today'.[73] One example of overload is the way central government has been pressed to take action to remedy inequalities in social service provision by local authorities. Such inequalities, even though they might be judged as a natural and inevitable sign of a healthy local government system responding to local concern (or lack of it) and local priorities, have come to be regarded as unacceptable. The concept of territorial justice has been forged as a battle cry. But the concept has profoundly centralising implications.[74] Overload is the product of centralisation and therefore leads to that sense of powerlessness in the face of government which Crowther Hunt and Peacock discuss in their dissenting note to the Report of the Royal Commission on the Constitution.

Neither Brittan nor King discuss O'Connor's theory of *The Fiscal Crisis of the State*.[75] Although we consider O'Connor as one of the state contradiction theorists because of the way he grounds his analysis in a Marxist theory of the state, at the superficial level the fiscal crisis is the product of overloaded demand on government. People expect more of government than they will or can, without damage to the economic system, pay for.

Brittan and King have no clear prescriptions for avoiding disaster. Brittan's main hope seems to lie in persuading opinion makers in society to cease propagating an ideology of equality. People, Brittan feels, should be encouraged to compare their own standard of living not with that of other individuals and groups, but with what their's was in the past. In this way egalitarianism could be soothed away, competitive politics could be weakened and the system might survive. Detailed policy programmes will not save liberal democracy but 'it could yet be saved if contemporary egalitarianism were to lose its hold over the intelligentsia.'[76]

King discusses two possibilities for reducing overload and its damaging implications. First, the range of government activities might be reduced. Second, the ability of government to tackle problems might be boosted. Neither alternative strikes King as particularly promising. He thinks it unlikely that government can be made more effective. Certainly, our understanding of problems will increase — but not necessarily faster than the problems or the complexity of the measures required to deal with them. As regards reducing the range of government activities, 'it is almost impossible in a competitive democracy to make the political non-political or prevent the potentially political from becoming actually so.' King is therefore as pessimistic as Brittan about the possibility of finding a solution to the overload problem. As Brittan, like a good journalist, turns to the opinion formers, so King, as a student of politics, turns to the political scientists urging them to begin to 'be concerned more with how the number of tasks that government has come to be expected to perform can be reduced',[77] but having encouraged them with the advice that this is almost impossible.

State contradiction theories

Marxists are in agreement with neo-Conservatives about the facts of the crisis. They agree about government overload and about the increase in welfare expenditure which makes it difficult for governments to pay their bills. They agree about a fiscal crisis and about a broader crisis of legitimation. Where Marxists and those we have called overload theorists differ is in their analysis of the causes of the crisis and possible solutions. Marxists see the causes of the crisis as rooted and grounded in the inherent contradictions of capitalism as an economic system. They see excessive expectations and the difficulties generated by competitive politics as no more than symptoms of an underlying disorder in the economic, social and political system which is capitalism.

Four writers have contributed most significantly to this debate: O'Connor in *The Fiscal Crisis of the State*, Wolfe in *The Limits of Legitimacy*, Jurgen Habermas in *Legitimation Crisis*,[78] and Claus Offe in a number of scattered and often rather inaccessible publications. We concentrate on the work of O'Connor, Wolfe and Habermas. The first concentrates more particularly on the economic contradictions of welfare capitalism, the second on the political contradictions, whereas Habermas has a more holistic, synthesising perspective. We deal with the work of each in turn and then draw out certain general points.

In essence O'Connor's argument is a simple one – that welfare capitalist societies cannot raise in taxes the money they need to provide the services which will ensure their survival. The explanation for this is to be found in the nature of capitalist society. Capitalism, O'Connor argues, is inherently unstable as an economic system. Its booms and slumps, if allowed to continue unmodulated, are likely to produce working-class pressure for its abolition. The state has to come to the rescue and must 'try to fulfil two basic and often mutually contradictory functions – accumulation and legitimation'.[79] The state must, in other words, try to maintain or create the conditions in which private capital can remain profitable. But at the same time it must also try to create or maintain social harmony. If the state goes all out to support private capital it will lose its legitimacy and weaken the loyalty and support on which any state depends. On the other hand, if it ignores the need to assist capital, it risks finding itself without the resources on which its power depends.

The state seeks to achieve a profitable capitalism and social harmony by three kinds of expenditure which, as mentioned in Chapter 4, O'Connor describes as social investment concerned primarily with increasing labour productivity, social consumption directed to lowering the reproduction costs of labour, and social expenses designed to maintain social harmony and fulfil the legitimation function. The mixture only succeeds in the short term; in the longer term it simply exacerbates the crisis it was designed to prevent. The essence of the problem is that though the state has to pay for these services it does not reap all the benefits which accrue from the increased profitability of private capital. There comes a point, therefore, when it cannot raise the revenue needed to meet the rising cost of public services. 'The socialisation of costs and the private appropriation of profits', writes O'Connor, 'creates a fiscal crisis, or "structural gap", between state expenditure and state revenues. The result is a tendency for state expenditures to increase more rapidly than the means of financing them.'[80] Private appropriation of the benefits of state expenditure exacerbates the crisis by threatening the legitimacy of such expenditure. And the state's failure to raise the revenue required to meet its commitments both undermines its standing and shows its weakness.

O'Connor's contribution is that he locates the explanation for the fiscal crisis in the nature and needs of capitalism. Overload theorists are talking of a fiscal crisis – though they use other terminology – but they locate the root of the problem as lying in party competition, lack of political will, or administrative weakness. O'Connor is not arguing that private capital is the sole beneficiary of state spending. He is simply arguing the primacy of the economic needs of capital. The final contradiction is that because of the nature of capitalism, the capitalist state cannot provide what the economic system requires for its survival.

Wolfe builds on O'Connor's ideas and adds to his analysis an emphasis on the political contradictions of democratic welfare capitalism. He starts from the hypothesis that the history of politics in capitalist societies is the history of tensions between liberal and democratic notions of the state.

> Liberal political arrangements [he writes] may be defined as those that attempt to facilitate the accumulation of capital by removing traditional encumbrances to the market in labour power, encouraging a conception of man based on self-interest, and creating a governmental structure that facilitates control over the system by those with ability in economic affairs rather than social standing.[81]

For Wolfe democracy is 'a political ideal that advocates the maximum participation of all citizens in order to create a community based upon the mutual and respectful interaction of all toward commonly agreed upon goals'.[82] Thus the ethos of liberalism and the ethos of democracy are antithetical.

The political history of democratic capitalist societies is the story of the struggle to find solutions to this conflict. Six solutions were developed in turn as one after another each proved unworkable. The heart of the problem, as Wolfe sees it, is the reconciliation of the twin functions of accumulation and legitimation — and here he draws on O'Connor's ideas. Liberalism is the philosophy produced by a need to facilitate accumulation and to legitimate the economic and social arrangements which characterise such a system. Democracy is the product of the system's need to legitimate economic, political and social arrangements and to secure popular acceptance and obedience. But a democratic system generates notions quite at odds with the earlier liberal ones. Instead of legitimating accumulation it challenges it.[83]

The economic stagnation of late capitalism can be attributed, partly at least, to this conflict. Recession exacerbates the problems and the political system is no longer capable of resolving the tasks which the economy imposes on it. Expenditure increases but problems are not removed. The state becomes immobilised by the contradictory demands made upon it by groups who can no longer resolve their differences outside the state. Following Habermas, Wolfe also sees a weakening of the cultural symbols which used to strengthen loyalty to the state. Serious problems of legitimation arise. 'The more the state does . . . the less it can do'[84] and Wolfe sees only 'the exhaustion of political alternatives'.[85]

The fundamental cause of the crisis for Wolfe is class struggle. The divided nature of society and the power of the working class make it impossible for the state to adopt policies which would resolve the contradiction in favour of the capitalist class and the accumulation function. Equally the democratic elements in society are unable to resolve the dilemma in favour of labour. If the state does more to aid accumulation, as it must if private capital is to remain profitable, it must, at the same time, spend more on welfare and social control if its legitimacy is to be safeguarded. Recession means the circle cannot be squared any longer. 'Damned if it does and damned if it doesn't, the state approaches the point at which its utility for reproducing social relationships is nil.'[86]

Wolfe also sees a cultural element in the crisis — drawing on Habermas.

The legitimacy crisis [he writes] is produced by the inability of the late capitalist state to maintain its democratic rhetoric if it is to preserve the accumulation function, or the inability to spur further accumulation if it is to be true to its democratic ideology.[87]

The state cannot meet the need for accumulation without contravening the liberal, democratic values which it asserts. The accumulation function is critical but capitalism is legitimated by those very democratic values which must be discarded if capital is to remain profitable.

For Wolfe there is only one way to resolve the contradictions which underlie the legitimacy crisis. That is to apply the principles of democracy to both accumulation and legitimation 'to give people the same voice in making investment and allocation decisions as they theoretically have in more directly political decisions'.[88] In other words, society should become socialist in both its economic and political systems.

Habermas attempts to provide a theory of the crisis of the state in advanced industrial societies which takes into account both the economic, political and cultural systems.[89] He sees a susceptibility to crisis as intrinsic to capitalism and he outlines four possible crisis tendencies – the economic system fails to produce the required quantity of goods, the administrative system fails to produce the requisite quantity of rational decisions, the legitimation system does not provide the requisite quantity of generalised motivations and the socio-cultural system does not generate the requisite quantity of action-motivating meaning.[90]

Like O'Connor, Habermas sees the state in advanced capitalist society as faced with two tasks – the avoidance of crisis-ridden disturbances in growth and the provision of goods and services to satisfy the system's need for legitimation.[91] In other words, government activities have to promote both capital accumulation and the acceptability of capitalism.

Private capital, however, has to pay a price for this state protection – in fact there are three prices. First, government intervention on the scale required means that economic issues of all types become politicised. They become clearly matters for political decision rather than issues decided by mysterious and unalterable economic processes. In a democratic system, the public can influence government decisions through the electoral process and is able, therefore, to make demands for the satisfaction of needs which can be in conflict with the requirements of capital accumulation. Second, government action can produce a crisis in rationality by which Habermas means a situation in which the administrative system fails to fulfil the imperatives received from the economic system.[92] As the range and sphere of government activity widens in late capitalism such failures to achieve objectives become more likely. Third, there is the price which results from the fact that expansion of state activity to solve the problem of accumulation leads to a disproportionate increase in the need for legitimation.[93] Here Habermas echoes Brittan's anxieties. 'The formal democratic type of legitimation', he writes, 'might involve expenses which cannot be covered if it compels the competing parties to outbid one another in their programmes, thus winding popular expectations to a higher and higher pitch.'[94] When such conflicts rise, the state can only meet the requirements of capital by refusing to satisfy some of the public demands for services to meet public needs. It can do this by authoritarian means but this will be contrary to the dominant ideology which proclaims that people must have a say in government affairs. This solution, therefore, creates difficulties for a parliamentary system. If, however, the government allows the public to decide, it may well decide in favour of the provision of government services. Habermas is confident that 'genuine participation of citizens in the processes of political will-formation, that is, substantive democracy, would bring to consciousness the contradiction between administratively socialized production and the continued private appropriation and use of surplus value.'[95] Thus the capitalist state has to look for a third alternative: the encouragement of a value system that stresses 'civic privatism — that is, political abstinence combined with an orientation to career, leisure, and consumption'.[96] Civic — or civil — privatism is vital to Habermas because it is an ideology that discourages participation in politics and thus 'corresponds to the structures of a depoliticized public realm',[97] which would reduce one of the destabilising influences in advanced capitalism. He sees little chance of achieving this because the socio-cultural processes generating civic privatism are in decline.

The net result of all this is that the state is unable to justify to the public the carrying out of the imperatives of capital accumulation when they are in conflict with the provision of services that meet human needs. This is the legitimation crisis of advanced capitalist societies. Unlike some other Marxists, Habermas sees parliamentary democracy, not as a mere façade, but as a new source of the legitimation crisis of capitalism, an argument which Wolfe expands and develops. Faced with such a basic contradiction, it is not unexpected that whatever the capitalist state does creates difficulties for the capitalist system. The contradiction requires

> the mutually contradictory imperatives of expanding the planning capacity of the state with the aim of a collective-capitalist planning and, yet, blocking precisely this expansion, which would threaten the continued existence of capitalism. Thus the state apparatus vacillates between expected intervention and forced renunciation of intervention, between becoming independent of its clients in a way that threatens the system and subordinating itself to their particular interests. Rationality deficits are the unavoidable result of a snare of relations into which the advanced capitalist state fumbles and in which its contradictory activities must become more and more muddled.'[98]

Do the legitimation problems of advanced capitalism constitute a legitimation crisis? Are the problems so insoluble that they lead inevitably to the prediction of a crisis? Habermas is cautious. He points out, as we saw earlier, that the traditional party system survives and there is no sign as yet of a new party whose aims transcend the existing economic system.[99] His conclusion is that 'as long as the welfare state program, in conjunction with a widespread technocratic common consciousness . . . can maintain a sufficient degree of civil privatism, legitimation needs do not have to culminate in a crisis.'[100]

The conclusion does seem, however, to mark something of a retreat from the logic of the argument Habermas has been deploying. He marshals a mass of evidence about the crisis. He locates the fundamental causes of the crisis in the economic and social system of capitalism. Even if economic growth could be achieved it would be growth shaped by private goals of profit maximisation not by concern for the general good. The pattern of priorities in the use of such growth is shaped by the class structure and 'in the final analysis, *this class structure* is the source of the legitimation deficit.'[101] These difficulties look fundamental and in the long term irresolvable.

Elsewhere, Habermas argues that democratisation, greater popular participation and decentralisation of the policy-making process are essential because the market and government activity as now carried on cannot satisfy a whole series of collective needs.[102] As quoted earlier, Habermas is convinced that greater democracy would pose a more serious threat to the legitimacy and stability of the present systems.

Marxists, then, explain the legitimation crisis of welfare capitalism in terms of the inherent contradictions of such a union of opposites. They see capitalism as inherently unstable as a economic system, though given temporary stability at different times by periods of growth, by war, or by Keynesian techniques of economic management. That economic instability is increased by democracy, the kind of political system to which capitalist values lead, but a system which, in the end, highlights and exacerbates the clash between capitalism's need for accumulation and legitimation. Growth and welfare state policies have obscured the fundamental contradictions for a generation. Recession has exposed them.

Other groups also stress the contradictions of welfare capitalism. Right-wing thinkers would stress the damage done to the capitalist economy by welfare spending, that rather than harmonising the conflicts of a market economy welfare-state policies, in fact, sharpen them by reducing the rate of growth and by politicising issues previously resolved by impersonal forces. Those on the right would agree happily with O'Connor about the reality of the fiscal crisis of the state — though they would see it as caused by the contradictions of welfare spending rather than as rooted in the capitalist system. Right-wing thinkers too — Buchanan and Wagner, for example[103] — see a conflict between democracy and a healthy capitalism — though given their belief in market principles they see such tension as damaging rather than in the positive terms in which Wolfe views the contradiction.

There are other less committed critiques of the inherent conflicts and contradictions of welfare capitalism. Goldthorpe suggests, for example, that sociologists tend to view the market economy as exerting 'a constant destabilizing effect on the society within which it operates'.[104] Inflation, regarded by the right as the product of the excessive expectations generated by competitive party politics and of one-eyed Keynesianism is seen by Goldthorpe as simply 'the monetary expression of distributional conflict'.[105] Skidelsky points out how the ethic of capitalism has removed restraints on social conflict by reducing social relations to the cash nexus, so destroying earlier notions of an organic society and by initiating a powerful assault on social hierarchy, so weakening traditional authority.[106] Bell argues on rather similar lines that whereas classic political theory sought to justify the primacy of the *polis*, liberalism, the ideology of capitalism, justified the individual pursuit of private goals free of restraint. In welfare capitalism individuals and groups pursue private wants and the redress of inequities politically. But the twentieth-century public household, as Bell calls it, is not a community because there is no bonding philosophy, but an arena in which competing private claims are fought and resolved. Market relations are transferred — destructively — to the political sphere.[107]

Where these non-Marxist commentators differ from the writers whose work we have reviewed is in their analysis of the causes of the contradictions they describe and in their views about their solution. The Marxists see the cause of the contradictions as lying in the very nature of the system and as therefore to be resolved only by its abolition or transcendence. The other commentators see possibilities of amelioration and reform without recourse to fundamental change.

The pragmatists
The group we describe as the pragmatists differs from the other two groups of theorists of the legitimacy crisis in three important respects. First, they do not see the crisis as rooted in the workings of democracy or in the contradictions of capitalism; they do not, in other words, see the crisis as systemic but rather as the product of a number of trends, errors and developments. Second, although they talk about 'crisis' they do not see the problem they describe as unresolvable within the present economic and social system. They believe — with varying degrees of conviction certainly — that a way can be found to ease or solve the problems. It might be more accurate to see them as talking of problems

of legitimacy rather than of a legitimacy crisis. Third, it is more difficult to classify the pragmatists politically. Overload theorists tend to be
on the right of the political spectrum, the state contradiction theorists
are Marxist, the pragmatists occupy a broad area of rather muddy
middle ground.

How then do the pragmatists see and explain the legitimation crisis?
Some of them would lay great stress on economic difficulties as the
major factor. As Rose and Peters put it, 'the greatest challenge facing
the governors of every Western country today is the maintenance of
political authority in the face of economic difficulties.'[108] The Trilateral
Commission made the same point when it argued that 'the governability
of democracy is dependent upon the sustained expansion of the
economy.'[109] Klein emphasises that 'the most successful Welfare States
— such as Sweden's and Germany's — tended to develop precisely in
those countries with the best growth record.'[110] Aims could be
achieved, standards could be high, conflicts of objectives could be
avoided. The argument has a number of strands. In part recession is
seen as a cause of problems. It reduces the ability of governments to
achieve their objectives, for example because they lack the necessary
resources and so reducing their effectiveness. It sharpens conflicts
between groups seeking higher rewards or improved services. Recession
is also seen not so much as the cause of political difficulties but rather as
exposing and exacerbating difficulties which were present all the time.
As Dahrendorf puts it,

> Democracy worked as long as the contest for higher expectations
> built into its structures promised some success. As long as a
> governing party could deliver at least some of the goods, all was well.
> But once economic growth — the necessary condition of the ability
> of governments to respond to expectations, the increase of which
> they themselves had to stimulate — became more difficult, demo-
> cratic governments were in trouble.[111]

Rose and Peters emphasise one particular result of the failure of
economies to grow which they regard as crucial to maintenance of the
authority of government. 'If successive British governments', they
write, 'whatever their party, continue to reduce the take home pay of
ordinary citizens, then political bankruptcy threatens.'[112] Political
bankruptcy is the fate that faces a government which so mismanages its
economy that it loses popular consent as well as economic effectiveness. Such bankruptcy is reached in stages. The first is

> when a government progressively overloads its political economy,
> allocating more money for public programmes and take home pay

than the national economy produces. This can be a consequence of
a nation's economic growth rate declining, or of a continuing and
unrestrained demand by citizens for more of everything. . . . A
government reaches a second stage in the progress to political
bankruptcy if the overloading of the economy faces a steady fall
in the take-home pay of most of its citizens . . . citizens are not
prepared to finance additional government programmes by accepting
a cut in the absolute value of their take-home pay. . . . The final
stage in the undermining of political authority is reached when
masses of citizens realise that their government no longer protects
their interests as they wish.[113]

In the contemporary welfare state governments enter into policy commitments which anticipate the continuance of economic growth so
risking political bankruptcy if growth ceases.

Rose and Peter's analysis is both political and economic. They assert
the centrality of the maintenance of take-home pay to the maintenance
of political authority and indict governments for failing to grasp this
as a central political fact. Then they argue, with a wealth of supporting
evidence, how declining rates of growth have left governments unable
both to honour policy commitments and to increase take-home pay.
Real take-home pay, they point out (writing in 1978), fell in Britain in
1975, 1976 and 1977.[114]

Some explanation is needed, however, for the lack of enthusiasm for
welfare spending and the concentration of the citizenry on take-home
pay. Klein is helpful here. He points out that the welfare state contains
within itself the seeds of declining support. As it eases and ameliorates
problems, or seems to do so, so people will inevitably become less keen
to pay taxes to deal with issues which strike them as less important.
The appeal of the poor has never been strong, but it gets even weaker as
their plight seems less desperate. By 1974 only 34 per cent of a
National Opinion Poll sample were prepared to pay extra tax 'in order
to help people who do not earn so much money as yourself'.[115]
Furthermore, as the public sector expands it can no longer be financed
simply by taxing the rich. The burdens increasingly fall on Middle
England. Imposing burdens on others is always more attractive than
assuming them oneself.

Political authority depends on two interconnected aspects — effectiveness and consent. Government needs to show itself as effective in
securing its objectives. To be effective in democratic society it needs
consent. The pragmatists lay great stress on how ineffective policies
have undermined the authority and legitimacy of government. Our
political system, they point out, was designed to deal with a much more
limited range of responsibilities than it now assumes. As Rose and

Peters put it, by expanding their commitments Western governments have exchanged the authority of command for the uncertainties of influence. Growth in responsibilities has not been matched by any equivalent growth in capabilities.[116] Governments now engage in activities where they lack the knowledge to secure the goals to which they are committed – the tackling of the causes of a range of social problems, for example. The more government does, the greater will be the problem of co-ordinating the various strands of government policy.[117] The more government does the more it depends on the co-operation of other groups and interests in society to achieve its objectives – and dependence means that effectiveness cannot be guaranteed. As we argued in the previous chapter, the National Health Service shows government as caring and concerned, which increases legitimacy. On the other hand, as Klein sees it, 'securing the consent of the medical profession has meant giving it power of veto over large areas of policy in the NHS.'[118] If and when such weakness becomes apparent, government's authority and legitimacy are damaged.

Another line of argument adopted by the pragmatists is to stress how centralisation and bureaucratisation have led to the failure of welfare-state policies, the loss of public support, and so to a loss of authority for government. Hadley and Hatch, for example, set out four charges against collectivist and centralised welfare policy – that such a system suffers from non-compliance, that is a deflection from the pursuit of stated goals because of employee influence, that such a form of organisation is inherently inefficient and ineffective, that it will suffer from bureaucratic ossification and will be unable to adapt to change and finally that, by its nature – remote, inaccessible, inflexible – such a pattern of organisation will fail to gain or sustain public support.[119] Failure to grasp the important truth that support for welfare policies depends on motives which can only be generated at a local, personal level of involvement builds in to the welfare state a time bomb. Recession reveals how little support for the current system actually exists as cuts fail to generate the protest which interest groups expect.

Pragmatists see the search for efficiency in welfare – designed to maintain the legitimacy of such expenditure – pursued through centralisation and bureaucratisation, the supposed routes to efficient government, as doomed to fail. Dahrendorf emphasises this element in the decline of legitimacy. Larger organisations, he argues, have been less effective, planning has been clumsy, bureaucratisation has proved costly and centralisation has weakened local support and denied participation.[120] Horowitz, in an interesting discussion, emphasises what he calls the 'stretching out effect of representational government', that is, the increasing sense of distance between rulers and ruled as 'in large part the source of the legitimacy crisis in the West'.[121] This stretching-out effect can be seen as the outcome of a particular philosophy of government and welfare.

Finally the pragmatists stress the debilitating effects on the legitimacy of government authority of the failure to create a philosophy to sustain democratic capitalism. A new dynamic collectivist ethic of public responsibility for private need has not emerged. Therefore, there is no solid ideological underpinning for the massive welfare programmes of government. They remain reactive and *ad hoc* rather than the expression of firm social purposes. 'The growth of the welfare state', Rose suggests, 'reflects a calculating individual desire for collective insurance to meet individual needs as much as it expresses a collective sense of community care.'[122] At the end of the day there is no philosophy which expresses the commitments of welfare capitalism and legitimates them. Rather, there are conflicts of philosophy which may be undermining. Mackintosh suggests that the welfare state has nourished attitudes which have contributed to crisis. 'The building of a social atmosphere which regards profit as sordid', he writes, 'and which suspects private enterprise has, over time, weakened and demoralised the private sector to the extent that it no longer provides the necessary growth to keep the whole economy moving.'[123]

The pragmatists acknowledge the problems of welfare capitalism as serious and deep-seated but they see them as soluble — partly because they do not see them as rooted in the very nature of the system and partly because they see government as more capable of autonomous action than do the overload or state contradiction thinkers. Rose and Peters express the pragmatist viewpoint. Political bankruptcy can be avoided, they argue, and government needs only to put a brake on future spending.[124] Easy to say; not quite so easy to do — but possible.

In his assessment of the seriousness of the problem of ungovernability[125] Rose argues that the biggest danger is not violence or dramatic collapse of government but rather the growth of civic indifference. That may be an equally serious challenge but if that is the nature of the crisis then governments have more time in which to respond and save themselves.

Discussion

Clearly welfare capitalism is beset by problems — economic, social and political. The authority and capacity of governments to solve the problems which confront them are being questioned. Government no longer seems to be able to draw effectively on any of Weber's classic sources of legitimacy — tradition, charisma, or rationality and legality.

The era of consensus politics and near-universal support for the mixed economy and the welfare state is over. Students emphasise increasingly the degree to which the welfare state was a product of a peculiar coincidence of circumstances — a post-war sense of solidarity, economic growth, Keynesian principles of economic management, a confidence in government's ability to right wrongs. Now, the stress is all on the limited capacity of governments, on a politics of imperfection, on the way the welfare state has failed in its central objectives — the reduction of inequality, the abolition of poverty, the forging of a new social unity. More is spent but problems survive. Issues of welfare have become less important to voters; there is a sense that enough has been done. There is a stress on abuse and scrounging, inflated bureaucracies, overweening professionals and a need to cut expenditure to rescue the economy. *The Perception of Poverty in Europe*[126] shows how harsh — and distinctively harsh — are British attitudes towards poverty and economic failure. People in Britain were much more likely than people in the rest of the EEC to blame individuals for their poverty and cite reasons such as laziness, lack of will-power and drink. They were also more likely to think that too much was done for the poor. Golding and Middleton's work produced comparable conclusions. When asked about the reasons for poverty, 'far more than any other reason poverty was seen to result from the failure of the poor to control money going *out* of the home, rather than from society's failure to get a decent income *into* the home.' Only a quarter of respondents accepted structural explanations of poverty.[127]

Interpreting the situation is not easy. The assumptions of the Titmuss or Butskellite years, Donnison wrote in 1979, 'are disintegrating .... Middle England is not ready to be convinced by research and blue books that benign public services will — or should — create a more humane and a more equal society.'[128] Taylor-Gooby, on the other hand, on the basis of his empirical work on attitudes to state welfare in 1981, concluded that 'the pattern of public opinion about welfare issues does not suggest that there is a tendency towards "legitimation crisis".' His data did not support the view that 'there is a general unwillingness to fund state welfare expenditure.'[129]

How helpful are our three groups of theorists in explaining this situation? The overload theory as argued by Brittan and King has been the subject of strong criticism. The argument is not about the existence of overload — Conservatives, Marxists and pragmatists are all agreed about that — but rather about its causes. Brittan's thesis is based on a number of important assumptions which have been sharply challenged. Skidelsky has pointed out that there is no inevitable connection between democracy and an overburdened economy. Nineteenth-century party politics were highly competitive but fiscally conservative.

Brittan also assumes governments respond to citizen preferences rather than themselves determining the pattern of political debate. If it is democracy which pushes up public expenditure on social services, then we should expect expenditure levels in non-democratic countries to be lower – and the evidence shows no great differences.[130]

Brittan's assumptions about excessive expectations underlying overload have also been challenged. Alt has pointed out that empirical evidence suggests that people are much more sceptical of politicians' claims than Brittan allows. He also shows that people's expectations are much more realistic than Brittan assumes and criticises Brittan for confusing desires, demands and expectations.[131] Alt, in contradiction to Brittan, characterises the story of the 1970s as 'the story of a politics of declining expectations' and speaks of 'a politics of quiet disillusion'.[132] Rose argues along similar lines.[133]

The central criticism which can be levelled at the overload theorists is that they do not search for fundamental causes. They do not ask why democracy should lead to damaging competition between parties or why expectations should be excessive. They write without exploring the nature of the economic and social system which underlies this particular political system. They do not look further. And no political system can be understood except as a manifestation of a particular economic and social order. Because of the myopic nature of their analysis, overload theorists look for solutions within the framework of political behaviour. Political behaviour, however, is the product of economic and social relations and cannot usefully be studied, and certainly cannot be dramatically changed, without changes in the system which underlies it. Overload theorists look only at the assumed precipitating causes of the problem. They neither verify those with due care or probe behind them for predisposing strains and tensions. They stop short at symptoms. This is because they see the political system as autonomous and fail to appreciate the close relationship between the economic and political order, made most visible in the economic dependence of capitalism on government.

The state contradiction theorists explain the legitimation crisis in terms of the fundamental contradictions of capitalism, of the increasing demands which late capitalism makes on government and on government's inability to meet those demands. The contradictions of capitalism lead inevitably to destructive contradictions in the welfare state. Gough sees it as torn between public pressure for more social services which taxpayers are nevertheless unwilling to finance, and demands from capital for more support which capital then insists it cannot afford to pay for through increased taxation.[134] The welfare state is, of course, further torn by contradiction in its simultaneous concern for welfare and control, for the well-being of the working class and the prosperity of capital. The contradictions of capitalism have, of course, been stressed for a long time – and capitalism has survived. It has emerged triumphantly from recession in the past and has shown an ability to deliver economic growth. Recession, of course, highlights the difficulties and conflicts of any economic system and provokes questioning of its durability. The state contradiction theorists stress the existence of crisis; they stress its origins deep in the economic and social system; they say little about the historic resilience of capitalism – or about how and when alternative systems will emerge.

The pragmatists are ultimately only interested in explaining the crisis in so far as that will help them to tackle it. Essentially their concern is with the resolution of very manifest problems. They do not look for underlying causes – Rose and Peters, for example, list a range of factors leading to increased public expenditure, but they do not attempt to weight different factors. They react to the tangible manifestations of disorder. Their concern is with problem analysis and action rather than fundamental explanation.

Is there a legitimacy crisis? In the end, the answer one gives will depend heavily on one's definition of crisis. If a crisis is a situation which cannot be fully resolved without fundamental economic and social changes, then we believe such a situation exists. If a crisis is a situation which will lead in the short term to the breakdown of the existing economic and political order then we do not see such a situation in Britain.

For most of the post-war period there has been a surprising degree of agreement among politicians and experts about the economic and social policies required to maintain and develop the economic and social systems in peace and harmony. That consensus collapsed in the face of the recession in the mid-1970s. Collapse of consensus does not constitute a legitimation crisis. Politics is about the resolution of group differences within a framework of established law and convention. Recession does not inevitably mean economic and political crisis. Neither does an emerging reduction of confidence in the welfare-state policies which have become part of the British response to the needs and costs of a mixed economy, but if Offe is correct in his view that 'the welfare state is no longer believed to be the promising and permanently valid answer to the problems of the socio-political order of advanced capitalist economies',[135] then that is significant.

What suggests an underlying disorder – benign or malignant – is the co-existence of economic, social and political problems of a serious nature. In many Western countries governments have retreated from the struggle to manage the economy to achieve social goals and have taken refuge in a reliance on impersonal forces. Growth has stopped; unemployment has risen. Social problems seem obstinately resistant to established policies and the national mood is such that gains and progress are forgotten and ignored, supposed failure is emphasised and used, not as a stimulus to the forging of new policies, but as a justification for reducing existing expenditure and limiting public involvement. The political problem is essentially one of disillusion. Politics is blamed for failing to create growth and harmony and seems to have less to offer. What is manifest is indifference rather than revolutionary fervour.

Capitalism survives for three reasons — its ability to generate wealth, the belief that it is somehow the natural and therefore the only way of organising economic relations, and the successful stigmatisation of socialism through its association with austerity, tyranny and oppression. A blow to any of these supports will be disturbing and will reverberate through the social and political systems. But if capitalism is to reach a state of crisis all three supports have to be challenged — and that is not yet the situation. We see capitalism as having a naturally destabilising impact on society because it depends on the inculcation and nourishing of relationships and attitudes which are fundamentally anti-social. We also see a fundamental conflict between capitalism and democracy. The first depends on individualism, competition and inequality, the second on co-operation, collective action and equality in certain spheres of life. At times a truce situation will exist when the economy is growing. Recession will highlight the fundamental conflict between self-interested economic relationships and the solidaristic social relations on which the public household depends. Crisis therefore is to be expected in a capitalist system. Order and harmony and stability may be achieved — as they were substantially between 1945 and 1970 — but that was due to an exceptional co-existence of circumstances. What has become more apparent in recent years is the natural tendency to disorder in economic, social and political relations produced by capitalist economic relations. The temporary and fragile stabilising forces have disappeared. Normality has returned. As long as the present economic system and its dominant ideology of individualism persist, so long will the crisis continue in its manifest or latent form.

8

Conclusion

The impact of social policy on society is wide-ranging. We have discussed what we think are the main areas of impact but there are obviously others which we have not mentioned. It is hoped, however, that these can be fitted into our framework, for while it is necessary to discuss specific consequences in isolation, it is equally important to fit them into some kind of framework that seeks to combine their significance with that of other factors of similar type and to trace their collective impact on society.

On the whole, social policy expenditure has been fairly successful in establishing minimum standards of living below which people do not fall. It is important to see the failures and shortcomings of social policy within this context. There are still minorities, sometimes sizeable, sometimes small, whose incomes are below the government's own poverty line, who are homeless or who live in unsatisfactory housing conditions, who attend schools, hospitals or doctors' surgeries which provide a low-quality service in comparison with the standards enjoyed by the majority. The bulk of the population, however, receive services which reach the minimum standards or guidelines set by successive governments. Minimum standards, however, are relative, and the achievement of yesterday's minimum standards is only a step towards the establishment of more generous levels. Whether official minimum standards are adequate will always be the subject of debate, particularly in an era of rising standards of living such as Britain enjoyed in the thirty years which followed the Second World War. There is no doubt either that without the existence of universal social services, the proportions of the population whose standards of living fall below the various minimum levels

251

would have been greater. The current political proposals for increased privatisation in the social services, if implemented, will have this effect. The smooth rhetoric for increased 'partnership' between the private and the public sectors, or for greater emphasis on 'the mixed economy of welfare' does not change this fact.

Supporters of the establishment of national minimum standards in social service provision have traditionally argued that it is the responsibility of central government to make sure that minimum standards are achieved. Local authorities have been seen as the unwilling partner to be coaxed, cajoled or coerced by a more enthusiastic central government. We have seen that this has not been totally true even during the period of consensus politics, let alone during the last few years of Thatcherism. Central government ministries have not been more successful in achieving minimum standards in the services they administer themselves than in the services administered by local authorities. Their greater enthusiasm for minimum standards has often been nothing more than rhetoric. It can, nevertheless, be argued that national minimum standards can only be achieved if central government sets explicit standards in all social services, provides the inspectorate and legal machinery to enforce them, and also makes available to local authorities the necessary funds. Such a policy, even if judged desirable in terms of social service goals, would, of course, have profound effects on local government and on central-local relations. In the real world of politics, however, such a policy is unlikely to be adopted for obvious financial and political reasons.

The alternative strategy of allowing local authorities full autonomy to decide their own minimum standards has its own problems. There would inevitably not only be variation in standards as there is today, but differences between authorities would inevitably become even greater. Autonomy means freedom to provide the very best as well as the very worst. The only curb on the meanness of local authorities would be the power of pressure groups and the risk of losing the support of the electorate. Neither of these can be effective checks on a determined, residualist-prone local authority. Even pressure groups as potentially powerful as NALGO and the NUT have not yet shown the power to prevent damaging cuts in the services they provide and the mass of the electorate can be apathetic as well as influenced by crudely simplistic programmes of lower rates and streamlined service provision. In brief, there is no magic administrative formula for ensuring that minimum standards in all social services are simply and fully achieved.

The failure of governments to achieve minimum standards in full is too serious an issue to be attributed to administrative reasons. It is rather the result of the lack of political will by successive governments which were, in theory at least, committed to the establishment of such standards. Political will implies government determination to provide the necessary funds, adequate encouragement to local authorities as well as the required monitoring services. Such a determined approach inevitably means moving resources from some groups of society to others but it is not of a scale that renders it incompatible with the ethos and practice of welfare capitalism. It can be of a scale, however, that raises open or veiled opposition from various interest groups whose influence on government is stronger than that exerted by pressure groups of and for those in need.

The overwhelming body of evidence shows that inequalities in the areas of the social services have remained fairly constant during the period covered by this study. Minor changes in the geographical distribution and in the use of services may have taken place in a patchy and haphazard way but the overall picture remains the same: the higher socio-economic groups have easier access to services than the lower socio-economic groups; and they often have access to better services. They make as much use and sometimes more use of services than the lower socio-economic groups; and at the end of the day they derive as much and often more benefit from the use of services. It is always misleading to summarise a complex situation and the reader must refer back to Chapter 3, but it is clear that the welfare state does not redistribute income and resources from the rich to the poor. It is an institutional arrangement for providing services free or almost free at the point of consumption to all paid for by a system of taxation which is essentially unprogressive. Those with the best know-how and social power make more use of social services. The welfare state may not be the poor man's burden but it is not a millstone grinding down the rich and prosperous either.

The substantial achievement of minimum standards, however, has meant that these inequalities in access to and use of basic services have lost their pre-war starkness and political salience. The retirement pensioner who relies completely on supplementary benefit today is clearly worse off than the retirement pensioner who receives the various types of government pensions plus occupational pensions and private insurance pensions. Nevertheless, the difference between the two is not near-starvation and affluence, as was the case in pre-war days. The same can be said of the situation of the council tenant, vis-à-vis the richest house-owner, between the user of state schools and the best independent schools, or the user of the poorest NHS hospital and the finest BUPA private palace. Differences between socio-economic groups have persisted but they are not as blatant and stark — they have been blunted to the point where they no longer cause widespread public indignation by the general rise in standards of provision.

The main reason for the persistence of inequalities in the areas of

253

social services has been the substantial indifference shown by governments and public opinion to this issue. Social services were not designed and planned in the 1940s to reduce inequalities because inequalities were seen as less important than the securing of a national minimum, and because the nature and resilience of inequalities was not fully grasped. Only in recent years, for example, has there been a genuine government attempt in the area of health services to combat geographical inequalities. Social class has not entered into the vocabulary of government social service planning. Clearly only a massive and sustained shift of government policy can hope to have any effect on inequalities. As it was pointed out in Chapter 3, inequalities of access are less intractable than inequalities of use and outcome; their reduction is also more morally compelling. An egalitarian government could pursue equality of access to services without being seriously censured for either pursuing a Utopia or sacrificing individual freedom. Whether, however, there will be a government in the near future prepared to grasp this nettle remains a moot point but the task is by no means an impossibility. What clearly is an unrealistic expectation is that there will be a direct and serious assault on inequalities of outcome. They remain beyond the scope of reformist governments, for such an attack is an assault on the very basis of the economic and political system. Policies for the reduction of inequalities of use pose no serious and direct threat to the capitalist system but they can raise serious threats to individual freedom if pursued over-zealously. These problems and difficulties involved in the pursuit of reductions in inequality are not presented as an argument against such a policy, but rather to sound a cautionary note against excessive expectations and as a reminder that a great deal of thinking still needs to be done on how best to tackle excessive inequalities. However egalitarian a social programme may be, however, it is important not to forget Durbin's warning forty years ago that social policy 'deals with the consequences of inequality . . . without changing the basic principle of administration in the capitalist system, or the distribution of executive power between the classes in it'.[1]

Economic growth has always been the primary concern of governments in this and other countries. As a broad generalisation, when economic growth rates have been high, social policy has been seen in positive terms and as conducive to such growth. Vice versa, at times of economic recession, social policy has either been made the scapegoat or at least has been scrutinised very carefully by governments. The evidence presented in Chapters 4 and 5 suggested that, on balance, social services have either contributed positively to economic growth or have had no effect on economic performance. Britain's economic decline is due to domestic and international factors which have very little to do with social policy. What is strange and interesting, however, is that so many in the industrial and business community have voiced their antipathy to social services as they are provided today. Such beliefs may, of course, have had an adverse effect on growth even when they are contradicted by objective evidence. What people believe to be true may be just as important, if not more so, than what the real situation is. As the technological competition among advanced industrial societies intensifies, it is difficult to see how a country can benefit from neglecting the education and training of its workforce and its management. Though social service expenditure uses up roughly a quarter of GNP, there has never been any shortage of private capital for investment in industry. The problem has been the massive exodus of British capital abroad compared with only a trickle of foreign capital coming to invest in Britain. Carson and Vines note that 'in 1981, British industry (as opposed to the City) invested an extra £3.5 billion abroad (this excludes oil projects) compared with under £1 billion invested in Britain by foreign manufacturers.'[2] Figures for other years provide a similar picture. Obviously British capital is invested abroad because of the prospects of higher profits but low rates of return on investment in Britain are not the product simply of high rates of social policy expenditure in this country. The evidence clearly shows that the volume of social and public expenditure in Britain as a proportion of GNP is lower than that of most European countries whose economies are also healthier. There is no inverse correlation between high public expenditure and the rate of economic growth – if anything, the relationship between the two variables is a positive one.

The social services of this country have evolved in a piecemeal, gradualist fashion over long periods of time stretching back to the nineteenth century. They have, therefore, incorporated a diverse and complex value system ranging from remnants of the poor law philosophy to beliefs about universal, non-stigmatising forms of provision. Their pervading ethos has, by and large, been in line with the values of capitalism with a few notable exceptions such as the health services. It is not, therefore, surprising that the overall conclusion of Chapter 6 was that social services are functional to political stability. They are provided in such ways and on such conditions that they either reinforce or do not seriously question the dominant values of welfare capitalism – individualism, inequality and private profit. They do this by easing the social problems which afflict such societies, by contributing to individual rather than structural definitions of problems, by reinforcing certain values and patterns of behaviour, by supporting authority and hierarchy in society, and by helping to convert a more threatening class conflict into less dangerous group conflict.

In spite of the contribution of social services to political stability, there is a sense of crisis in many welfare capitalist societies – the so-called legitimation crisis. Some writers blame welfare state policies for the crisis through the way in which such policies have overloaded government. Others see the problem as lying deep in the inherent contradictions of capitalism. A third group see the crisis not as systemic but rather as the product of a number of problems which with thought and effort could be overcome. Whether one sees the situation as soluble within the limitations of welfare capitalism or as insoluble without radical changes in economic and political arrangements, it is clear that social policy has in some ways contributed to the crisis, while in other ways it has eased it.

What is striking is that social services are currently under attack by right-wing governments in a number of advanced industrial countries. The immediate and most obvious reason for the attack is that the collapse of economic growth means that increased public expenditure can only be financed through increases in taxation. Such increases are seen as economically and politically unacceptable — economically unacceptable because they will act as a further disincentive to effort and entrepreneurial innovation and will further reduce profits, politically unacceptable because of the opposition they will generate as they reduce real take-home pay at a time of nil growth in incomes. According to this view, it is economic factors which underlie the overload crisis by making it more difficult for government to meet expanding demands successfully and it is failure to maintain economic growth which seems to present the most serious challenge to political authority — the so-called legitimation crisis. In the short term, cutting back on social service expenditure seems to offer the best hope of curing the economy and avoiding political bankruptcy. It is a myopic view, even from a conservative perspective, because it grossly under-estimates the contribution of social policy both to economic growth and to the de-radicalisation of anti-capitalist protest in society.

Our review of the impact of social policy stops at 1980 and it, therefore, says nothing of the developments during the last few years of Thatcherite government policies. It is a chapter in the history of social policy development that merits a separate study in due course. There is no doubt that recent cuts in the social services have caused untold personal distress to many but they have not so far achieved the government's main aim of substantially reducing the volume of public expenditure. So far, the course of events has been in line with structural explanations of the forces behind the growth of the welfare state: public expenditure growth is the result of structural factors in the political economy of a country; it performs many functions and it is highly resistant to government attempts to curb it. Yet over-emphasis on structural factors runs the risk of implying that social services need no defending. It under-estimates the influence of public opinion on the nature of social policy and allows too much room to the revival of *laissez-faire* residual conceptions of social services, so ably fostered by the Thatcher government.[3]

What is abundantly clear from a study of thirty-five years of welfare state policies is that social policy can be an important instrument for enhancing social well-being and reducing the ravages of economic and social adversity. What is urgently needed at present is a re-appraisal of the relationship between economic and social policy. Up to now the latter has played a subservient role to the former — expanding during periods of economic growth, contracting at times of no growth and, at all times, being dominated by the ideology of work incentives, the necessity of economic inequality, the inevitability of authoritarian administrative structures, and so on. The present government is using the economic recession to subordinate social policy even more to economic policy. Defenders of social welfare need to develop an alternative social strategy that gives at least parity between the economic and the social goals of the country. The current debates on an alternative economic strategy need to be complemented with some serious thinking on an alternative social strategy and how the two can be combined into a coherent political programme that commands the support of the general public. Such a programme will have to take into account the experience of the social services during the post-war period and we hope our study can provide the broad backcloth against which this vital but extremely difficult task can be undertaken.

Notes

Chapter 1 The aims and consequences of social policy

1 D. Larkey, C. Stolp and M. Winer, 'Theorising About the Growth of Government', *Journal of Public Policy*, vol. 1, no. 2, May 1981.
   E.g. R. Mishra, *Society and Social Policy*, Macmillan, 1977; D. Tarschys, 'The Growth of Public Expenditure: nine models of explanation', *Scandinavian Political Studies*, vol. 10, 1975.
2 S.J. Curtis, *History of Education in Great Britain*, University Tutorial Press, 1948, Ch. 8.
3 Ministry of Health, *A National Health Service*, Cmd 6502, HMSO, 1944, p. 5.
4 V. George and P. Wilding, *Ideology and Social Welfare*, Routledge & Kegan Paul, 1976.
5 D. Gill, *Unravelling Social Policy*, Schenkman, 1973.
6 C. Benn and B. Simon, *Half Way There*, McGraw-Hill, 1970, Ch. 2.
7 For a different categorisation of the consequences of social policy, see: P. Caim-Kaudle, 'A Cross-National Evaluation of Post-War European Social Policies', paper given to the Social Administration Association Conference, July 1980, Cambridge.
8 J. Irvine, I. Miles and J. Evans, *Demystifying Social Statistics*, Pluto Press, 1979, Chs 9, 10 and 11.
9 M.D. Shipman, *The Limitations of Social Research*, Longman, 1972, Ch. 10.
10 K. Popper, *The Logic of Scientific Discovery*, Hutchinson, 1959, p. 50.
11 For an early discussion, G. Myrdal, 'The Relation Between Social Theory and Social Policy', *British Journal of Sociology*, vol. IV, Sept. 1953. For a more recent discussion: T.S. Simey, *Social Science and Social Purpose*, Constable, 1968, M. Rein, *Social Science and Public Policy*, Penguin, 1976, Chs 3 and 7.
12 V. George and P. Wilding, op. cit., Chs 1 and 6.
13 M. Rein, op. cit., *Social Science and Public Policy, Penguin, 1976*, p. 255.

Chapter 2 Achievement of minimum standards

1 M. Wright (ed.), *Public Spending Decisions*, Allen & Unwin, 1980, p. 140.
2 C.A.R. Crosland, *The Future of Socialism*, Cape, 1956, p. 148.
3 C.A.R. Crosland, 'A Social Democratic Britain', *Fabian Tract 404*, Fabian Society, 1970.
4 *Social Insurance and Allied Services*, Cmd 6404, HMSO, 1942, p. 166 (Beveridge Report).
5 W.H. Beveridge, *The Pillars of Security*, Allen & Unwin, 1943, p. 89.
6 J. Harris, *William Beveridge*, Clarendon Press, 1977, p. 414.
7 F.A. Hayek, *The Road to Serfdom*, Routledge & Kegan Paul, 1944, p. 89.
8 F.A. Hayek, ibid., p. 90.
9 F.A. Hayek, *The Constitution of Liberty*, Routledge & Kegan Paul, 1960, p. 286.
10 F.A. Hayek, ibid., p. 289.
11 F.A. Hayek, ibid., p. 203.
12 C.A.R. Crosland, *The Future of Socialism*, op. cit., p. 120.
13 W. Churchill, *The Second World War*, vol. IV, Cassel, 1950, p. 861 as quoted in K. Jones et al., *Issues in Social Policy*, Routledge & Kegan Paul, 1978, p. 48.
14 Board of Education, *Educational Reconstruction*, Cmd 6458, HMSO, 1943, p. 9.
15 Ministry of Health, *A National Health Service*, Cmd 6502, HMSO, 1944, p. 5.
16 Minister of Reconstruction, *Social Insurance, Part I*, Cmd 6550, HMSO, 1944, p. 11.
17 Minister of Reconstruction, *Housing*, Cmd 6609, HMSO, 1945, p. 2.
18 Minister of Reconstruction, *Employment Policy after the War*, Cmd 6527, HMSO, 1944, p. 3.
19 D.W. Henderson, *Social Indicators*, Economic Council of Canada, 1974, p. 20.
20 I. Illich, *Medical Nemesis*, Calder & Boyars, 1975, pp. 11 and 12.
21 Royal Commission on the National Health Service, *Report*, Cmnd 7615, HMSO, 1979, p. 26.
22 Ibid., p. 23.
23 J.C. Nicholson, 'The Assessment of Poverty and the Information We Need' in DHSS, *Social Security Research*, HMSO, 1979, p. 63.
24 A. Webb and N. Falk, 'Planning the Social Services: the Local Authority Ten Year Plans', *Policy and Politics*, vol. 3, no. 2, Dec. 1974.
25 S. Lansley, *Housing and Public Policy*, Croom Helm, 1979, p. 90.
26 P. Hall, H. Land, R. Parker and A. Webb, *Change, Choice and Conflict in Social Policy*, Heinemann, 1975.
27 M. Bulmer (ed.), *Social Policy Research*, Macmillan, 1978.
28 P. Townsend and D. Wedderburn, *The Aged in the Welfare State*, Bell, 1965.
29 DHSS, *Health and Welfare: The Development of Community Care*, Cmnd 3022, HMSO, 1966, p. 13.
30 P. Townsend, *Poverty in the United Kingdom*, Penguin, 1979.
31 DHSS, *Health and Welfare*, op. cit., p. 26.
32 DHSS, *Priorities in Health and Personal Social Services in England*, HMSO, 1976, p. 2.
33 R. Klein, 'The Welfare State: a Self-Inflicted Crisis', *Political Quarterly*, vol. 51, no. 1, Jan.-March 1980.
34 Commission of the European Communities, *The Perception of Poverty in Europe*, 1977, Table 9, p. 19.
35 P. Townsend, op. cit., pp. 237-40.

36   V. George, *Social Security and Society*, Routledge & Kegan Paul, 1973, Ch. 2.

37   R. Berthoud, J.C. Brown and S. Cooper, *Poverty and the Development of Anti-Poverty Policy in the U.K.*, Heinemann, 1981, p. 138.

38   D. Donnison, *The Politics of Poverty*, Robertson, 1982, p. 7.

39   R. Berthoud et al., op. cit., p. 142.

40   P. Townsend, op. cit., p. 249.

41   S. MacGregor, *The Politics of Poverty*, Longman, 1981, p. 76.

42   P. Townsend, op. cit., p. 915.

43   M. Ketttle and S. Lansley, 'The New Poverty Line: the necessities that millions are having to do without', *Sunday Times*, 21 Aug. 1983.

44   *Supplementary Benefits Commission Annual Report 1978*, Cmnd 7725, HMSO, 1979, p. 2.

45   *Supplementary Benefits Commission Annual Report 1976*, op. cit., para 1.11.

46   C. Walker and M. Church, 'Poverty by Administration: a review of Supplementary Benefits, Nutrition and Scale Rates', *Journal of Human Nutrition*, vol. 32, no. 1, 1978.

47   D. Piachaud, *The Cost of a Child: A Modern Minimum*, Child Poverty Action Group, 1979.

48   P. Townsend, op. cit., Table 7.2, p. 275.

49   G. Fiegehen et al., *Poverty and Progress in Britain, 1953-1973*, Cambridge University Press, 1977, Table 3.4, p. 27.

50   Office of Population Censuses and Surveys, *Family Finances*, HMSO, 1981, as reported in L. Burghes, 'Facts and Figures', *Poverty*, no. 51, April 1982.

51   R. Berthoud et al., op. cit., p. 43.

52   *Supplementary Benefits Commission Annual Report 1978*, Cmnd 7725, HMSO, 1979, Tables 12.8-12.10, p. 103.

53   Royal Commission on the Distribution of Income and Wealth, *Lower Incomes*, Report, No. 6, Cmnd 7175, HMSO, 1978, p. 97-8.

54   J. Ritchie and P. Wilson, *Social Security Claimants*, OPCS, 1979, p. 41.

55   Ibid, Table 7.2, p. 487.

56   Department of the Environment, *Housing Policy: A Consultative Document*, Cmnd 6851, HMSO, 1977, p. 1.

57   R. Mathews and P. Leather, 'Housing in England', *Roof*, May-June 1982.

58   R. Bailey, *The Homeless and the Empty Houses*, Penguin, 1977.

59   G. Burke, *Housing and Social Justice*, Longman, 1981, p. 66.

60   P. Rigby, Office of Population Censuses and Surveys, *Hostels and Lodgings for Single People*, HMSO, 1976.

61   J. Greve, D. Page and S. Greve, *Homelessness in London*, Scottish Academic Press, 1971, p. 54.

62   D. Donnison and C. Ungerson, *Housing Policy*, Penguin, 1982, p. 271.

63   R. Franey, 'Apart from the Law', *Roof*, Nov.-Dec. 1980.

64   G. Burke, op. cit., p. 79.

65   A. Block, *Estimating Housing Needs*, Architectural Press, 1946, p. 1.

66   F. Berry, *Housing: the Great British Failure*, Knight, 1974, p. 165.

67   Report of the Central Housing Advisory Committee, *Council Housing Purposes, Procedures and Priorities*, HMSO, 1969, p. 10.

68   M. Woolf, *The Housing Survey in England and Wales*, HMSO, 1964.

69   Central Statistical Office, *Local Trends*, no. 12, HMSO, 1981, p. 151.

70   D. Ormandy, 'Housing Standards', *Roof*, Jan.-Feb. 1982.

71   *English House Conditions Survey 1976*, Part I, HMSO, 1978, p. 3.

72   Department of the Environment, *Housing Policy*, op. cit., p. 7.

73   S. Lansley, *Housing and Public Policy*, Croom Helm, 1979, p. 75.

74 *And I'll Blow Your House Down*, Shelter, 1980, p. 7.
75 N. Ditch, 'Northern Ireland', *Roof*, March-April 1981.
76 Department of the Environment, *Housing Policy*, op. cit., p. 11.
77 J. Hunt and L. Heyes, *Housing the Disabled*, Torfaen Borough Council, 1980, p. 176.
78 Commons, Hansard, cols 241-2, March 1980.
79 P. Townsend, op. cit., p. 486.
80 Department of the Environment, *Housing Policy*, op. cit., Table 1, p. 11.
81 Department of the Environment, *English Housing Conditions Survey, 1976*, Part 2, p. 11.
82 Ibid, p. 24.
83 I. Shonfield and S. Shaw (eds), *Social Indicators and Social Policy*, Heinemann, 1972, p. 1.
84 The Royal Commission on the National Health Service, op. cit., p. 174.
85 Ibid, p. 211.
86 Ibid, p. 75.
87 J. Ritchie, A. Jacoby and M. Bone, *Access to Primary Health Care*, OPCS, 1981, Table 3.1, p. 14.
88 J. Butler, *How Many Patients?*, Bedford Square Press, 1981, p. 132.
89 College of General Practitioners, 'Evidence to the Royal Commission on the NHS', *Journal of the Royal College of General Practitioners*, April 1977.
90 DHSS, *Primary Health Care in London*, Report of Study Group, HMSO, 1981, pp. 12-13 (Acheson Report).
91 *Acheson Report*, op. cit., pp. 62-3.
92 Ibid., p. 32.
93 Report of the Royal Commission on the National Health Service, op. cit., p. 90.
94 J.E. Todd and A.M. Walker, *Adult Dental Health, 1968-78*, DPLS, 1980, Table 8.1, p. 46.
95 Report of the Royal Commission on the National Health Service, op. cit., p. 106.
96 Ibid, p. 126.
97 DHSS, *Report of the Committee of Enquiry into the Pay and Related Conditions of the Professions Supplementary to Medicine*, HMSO, 1978.
98 Report of the Royal Commission on National Health Service, op. cit., p. 141.
99 DHSS, *Report of the Committee of Enquiry Into Normansfield Hospital*, Cmnd 7357, HMSO, 1978, p. 399.
100 J. Gibbons, 'The Mentally Ill', in P. Brearley et al., *The Social Context of Health Care*, Martin Robertson and Basil Blackwell, 1978, p. 119.
101 DHSS, 'In-Patient Enquiries: Facilities and Services in Mental Illness and Mental Handicap Hospitals', HMSO.
102 N. Bosanquet and P. Townsend, *Labour and Equality*, Heinemann, 1980, p. 225.
103 Report of the Royal Commission on the National Health Service, op. cit., p. 13-14.
104 R. Simpson, *Access to Primary Care*, Royal Commission on the National Health Service, Research Paper no. 6, HMSO, 1979, quoted in Royal Commission on the National Health Service, op. cit., p. 14.
105 J. Ritchie et al., *Access to Primary Health Care*, OPCS, 1981.
106 Royal Commission on the National Health Service, op. cit., p. 27.
107 N. Wright, *Progress in Education*, Croom Helm, 1977, p. 16.
108 DES, *A Study of School Buildings*, HMSO, 1977, p. 6.

109 DES, *Primary Education in England*, HMSO, 1978, p. 9.
110 Ibid, p. 58.
111 DES, *Aspects of Secondary Education in England*, HMSO, 1979, p. 79.
112 Ibid., pp. 131 and 132.
113 Ibid., p. 175.
114 Ibid., p. 176.
115 Ibid., p. 178.
116 DES, *Statistics of Education, 1970, Vol. 1*, HMSO, 1971, Table 18, p. 36 and *Statistics of Education, 1979, Vol. 1*, HMSO, 1981, Table 17, pp. 35-6.
117 C.B. Cox and R. Boyson (eds.), *Black Paper 1975*, Dent, 1975, p. 1.
118 DES, *Primary Education in England*, op. cit., p. 6.
119 DES, *Aspects of Secondary Education in England*, op. cit., p. 45.
120 N. Wright, op. cit., p. 97.
121 DES, *Children and their Primary Schools*, vol. 1, HMSO, 1967, p. 187.
122 C. Burstall, 'Time to Mend the Nets: A commentary on the outcome of class-size research', *Trends in Education*, Autumn 1979.
123 A. Hopkins, *The School Debate*, Penguin, 1978, p. 139.
124 DES, *A Language for Life*, HMSO, 1975, p. 26.
125 DES, *Primary Education in England*, op. cit., pp. 44-5.
126 Ibid., p. 100.
127 C. Mabey, 'Black British Literacy: A Study of Reading Attainment of London Black Children from 8 to 15 years', *Educational Research*, vol. 23, No. 2, Feb. 1981.
128 DES, *A Language for Life*, op. cit., p. 12.
129 T.P. Gorman, 'A Survey of Attainment and Progress of Learners in Adult Literacy Schemes', *Educational Research*, vol. 23, No. 3, June 1981.
130 DES, *A Language for Life*, op. cit., p. 6.
131 DES, *Primary Education in England*, op. cit., p. 52.
132 DES, *Aspects of Secondary Education in England*, op. cit., p. 113.
133 K. Fogelman (ed.), *Britain's Sixteen-Year-Olds*, National Children's Bureau, 1976, pp. 44-5.
134 DES, *Aspects of Secondary School Education in England*, op. cit., p. 265.
135 Ministry of Health, *A Hospital Plan for England and Wales*, Cmnd 1604, HMSO, 1962.
136 Ministry of Health, *Health & Welfare: the Development of Community Care*, Cmnd 1973, HMSO, 1963, pp. 47-8.
137 Ibid., p. 48.
138 Ibid., p. 3.
139 P. Townsend, 'The Timid and the Bold', *New Society*, vol. 1, No. 34, 23 May 1962.
140 Ministry of Health, *Health and Welfare: The Development of Community Care*, Cmnd 3022, HMSO, 1966, p. 1.
141 Ibid., p. 26.
142 Ibid., pp. 23-5.
143 Ibid., pp. 1-2.
144 A. Webb and N. Falk, 'Planning the Social Services: The Local Authority Ten Year Plans', *Policy and Politics*, vol. 3, No. 2, Dec. 1974.
145 R. Hambleton and V. Scerri, 'Three Views of Need', *New Society*, 18 Oct. 1973.
146 K. Judge, 'Territorial Justice and Local Autonomy', *Policy and Politics*, vol. 3, No. 4, June 1975.
147 DHSS, *Priorities for Health and Personal Social Services in England*, HMSO, 1976, p. 3.

148 DHSS, *The Way Forward*, HMSO, 1977, p. vii.
149 Ibid., p. 15.
150 *Second Report from the Social Services Committee, 1981-82, Vol. II*, House of Commons Paper 306-11, HMSO, 1982, p. 72.
151 Ibid., p. 218.
152 Committee on Local Authority and Allied Personal Social Services, Cmnd 3703, HMSO, 1968, pp. 147 and 44 respectively.
153 P. Townsend and D. Wedderburn, op. cit.
154 A. Hunt, *The Elderly at home*, HMSO, 1978, p. 89.
155 A. Bebbington, 'Changes in the Provision of Social Services to the Elderly in the Community over Fourteen Years', *Social Policy and Administration*, vol. 13, *No. 2*, Summer 1979.
156 M. Wicks, *Old and Cold: Hypothermia and Social Policy*, Heinemann, 1978, Ch. 10.
157 B. Davies, *Social Needs and Resources in Local Services*, Joseph, 1968, pp. 64-70.
158 DHSS, *Report of a Study on Community Care*, HMSO, 1981, p. 24.
159 A.J. Norman, *Rights and Risk*, National Corporation for the Care of Old People, 1980, pp. 19-20.
160 DHSS, Residential Care for the Elderly in London, *Social Work Service*, HMSO, 1979, p. 43.
161 DHSS, *Priorities for Health and Personal Social Services in England*, op. cit., p. 38.
162 A. Walker, 'Community Care and the Elderly in Great Britain: Theory and Practice', *International Journal of Health Services*, vol. 11, *No. 4*, 1981.
163 DHSS, *Better Services for the Mentally Handicapped*, Cmnd 4683, HMSO, 1971.
164 DHSS, *Report of the Committee of Enquiry into Mental Handicap Nursing Care*, Cmnd 7468, HMSO, 1979, vol. 1, p. 37 (Jay Report).
165 E. Whelan and B. Speake, *Adult Training Centres in England and Wales*, University of Manchester, 1977.
166 J. Carter, *Day Services for Adults*, Allen & Unwin, 1981, p. 58.
167 P. Mittler, *People Not Patients*, Methuen, 1979, p. 181.
168 DHSS, *Development Team for the Mentally Handicapped, Second Report, 1978-1979*, HMSO, 1980, p. 5 and Table, p. 6.
169 *Jay Report*, vol. II, Table 29, p. 34.
170 Ibid., vol. I, p. 62.
171 Ibid., vol. II, Table 10, p. 15.
172 Ibid., Table 23, p. 25.
173 M. Rutter et al., *Fifteen Thousand Hours*, Open Books, 1979.
174 B. Davies and M. Knapp, *Old People's Homes and the Production of Welfare*, Routledge & Kegan Paul, 1981, Ch. 4.
175 DHSS, *Priorities for Health and Personal Social Services*, op. cit., p. iii.

Chapter 3 Social policy and inequality

1 S. Brittan, *Left or Right, The Bogus Dilemma*, Secker & Warburg, 1968, p. 11.
2 W. Beckerman (ed.), *The Labour Government's Economic Record, 1964-70*, Duckworth, 1972, p. 31.
3 T.H. Marshall, *Sociology at the Crossroads and Other Essays*, Heinemann, 1963, p. 107.
4 B. Webster and J. Stewart, 'The Area Analysis of Resources', *Policy and*

Politics, vol. 3, *No. 1*, Sept. 1974.

5   Ministry of Education, *Half our Future*, HMSO, 1963, p. 21.

6   Department of Education and Science, *Children and their Primary Schools*, vol. 1, HMSO, 1967, p. 50.

7   E. Midwinter, 'Education', in F. Williams (ed.), *Why the Poor Pay More*, Macmillan, 1977.

8   N. Boaden, 'Local Authorities and Education', in J. Rayner and J. Harden (eds) *Equality and City Schools*, Routledge & Kegan Paul, 1973, p. 106.

9   D. Byrne and W. Williamson, 'The Case of the North East', in J. Rayner and J. Harden (eds), ibid., pp. 139-40.

10   C. Howick and H. Hassani, 'Education Spending: Primary', *Centre for Environmental Studies Review*, Jan. 1979.

11   C. Howick and H. Hassani, 'Education Spending: Secondary', *Centre for Environmental Studies Review*, Jan. 1980.

12   S. Ball, *Beachside Comprehensive*, Cambridge University Press, 1981.

13   Ministry of Education, *Early Leaving*, HMSO, 1954, Table J, p. 17.

14   Ministry of Education, *15-18*, HMSO, 1959, p. 8.

15   Office of Population Censuses and Surveys (OPCS), *General Household Survey*, HMSO, 1978, Table 6.1, p. 121.

16   J.W.B. Douglas, *The Home and the School*, Panther, 1967, pp. 157-58.

17   A. Halsey et al., *Origins and Destinations*, Clarendon Press, 1980, p. 38.

18   A. Halsey et al., ibid., p. 203.

19   Ministry of Education, *Early Leaving*, op. cit., Table P, p. 38.

20   R. Davie, N. Butler and H. Goldstein, *From Birth to Seven*, Longman, 1958, p. 102.

21   A. Halsey et al., op. cit., p. 141.

22   E. Byrne, *Women and Education*, Tavistock, 1978, Table 4 (4), p. 129.

23   R. Kelsall, A. Poole and A. Kuhn, *The Sociology of an Elite*, Tavistock, 1972, p. 206.

24   OPCS, *General Household Survey, 1977*, op. cit., Table 5.7, p. 76.

25   G. Becker, *Human Capital*, Columbia University Press, 1964.

26   S. Bowles, 'Schooling and Inequality from Generation to Generation', *Journal of Political Economy*, vol. 80, 1972.

27   P. Taubman and T. Wales, 'Higher Education, Mental Ability and Screening', *Journal of Political Economy*, vol. 81, *No. 1*, Jan. 1973.

28   C. Jencks et al., *Inequality*, Penguin, 1975, p. 223.

29   C. Jencks, *Who Gets Ahead?*, Basic Books, 1979, p. 311.

30   G. Psacharopoulos, 'Family Background, Education and Achievement', *British Journal of Sociology*, vol. 28, *No. 3*, Sept. 1977.

31   J.H. Goldthorpe, *Social Mobility and Class Structure in Modern Britain*, Clarendon Press, 1980, p. 252.

32   R. Bouden, *Education, Opportunity and Social Inequality*, Wiley, 1973, p. 115.

33   M. Rein, *Social Science and Public Policy*, Penguin, 1976, p. 226.

34   Political and Economic Planning, 'Medical Care for Citizens', *Planning*, no. 222, 1944, June 30, p. 6.

35   J. Butler et al., *Family Doctors and Public Policy*, Routledge & Kegan Paul, 1973, p. 29; see also Table A.1, p. 157.

36   A. Cartwright, *Human Relations and Hospital Care*, Routledge & Kegan Paul, 1964.

37   R. West and C. Lowe, 'Regional variations in need for and provision and use of child health services in England and Wales', *British Medical Journal*, 9 October 1976.

38   J.T. Hart, 'The Inverse Care Law', in C. Cox and A. Mead (eds),

   A Sociology of Medical Practice, Collier-Macmillan, 1975, p. 205.

39   Quoted in DHSS, *Inequalities in Health*, Report of a Research Working Group, HMSO, 1980, p. 115.

40   *Primary Health Care in Inner London*, DHSS, 1981.

41   Quoted in M. Buxton, *Health and Inequality*, Open University Press, 1976, p. 11.

42   M. Cooper and A. Culyer, 'An economic analysis of some aspects of the NHS', in I. Jones (ed.), *Health Services Financing*, British Medical Association, 1970.

43   J. Noyce, A. Snaith and A. Trickey, 'Regional variations in the allocation of financial resources to the community health services', *The Lancet*, 30 March 1974.

44   M. Buxton and R. Klein, 'Distribution of Hospital Provision, Policy Themes and Resource Variations', *British Medical Journal*, 8 Feb. 1975.

45   DHSS, *Sharing Resources for Health in England*, Resource Allocation Working Party, HMSO, 1976.

46   A. Maynard and A. Ludbrook, 'Budget Allocation in the National Health Service', *Journal of Social Policy*, vol. 9, *No. 3*, July 1980.

47   House of Commons Debates, 21 January 1982.

48   D.P. Forster, 'Social Class Differences in Sickness and General Practitioner Consultations', *Health Trends*, no. 8, 1976; J. Brotherston, 'Inequality: Is It Inevitable?', in C.O. Carter and J. Peel (eds) *Equalities and Inequalities in Health*, Academic Press, 1976, Table x, p. 82.

49   DHSS, *Inequalities in Health*, Report of a Research Working Group, HMSO, 1980, p. 97.

50   E. Collins and R. Klein, 'Equity and the NHS: self-reported morbidity, access and primary care', *British Medical Journal*, vol. 281, 25 Oct. 1980.

51   V. Walters, *Class, Inequality and Health Care*, Croom Helm, 1980, p. 132.

52   M. Blaxter, 'Social Class and Health Inequalities' in C.O. Carter and J. Peel (eds), op. cit., p. 121.

53   A. Cartwright and M. O'Brien, 'Social Class Variations in Health Care', in M. Stacey (ed.), 'The Sociology of the National Health Service', *Sociological Review Monograph*, no. 22, 1976.

54   M. Backett, 'Health Services' in F. Williams (ed.), *Why the Poor Pay More*, Macmillan, 1978, p. 119.

55   A. Cartwright, Human Relations and Hospital Care, op. cit.

56   A. Cartwright, *Parents and Family Planning Services*, Routledge & Kegan Paul, 1970.

57   J. Brotherston, 'Inequality − Is it Inevitable?', in C.O. Carter and J. Peel (eds), *Equalities and Inequalities in Health*, op. cit.

58   Quoted in DHSS, *Inequalities in Health*, op. cit., p. 108.

59   DHSS, *Inequalities in Health*, op. cit., p. 102.

60   W. Morgan et al., 'Casual Attenders', *Hospital and Health Services Review*, vol. 70, 1974.

61   Ministry of Health, *Report of Hospital Inpatient Enquiry*, HMSO, 1967, part III, Table VI.8, p. 365.

62   *Royal Commission on the National Health Service*, Report, Cmnd 7615, HMSO, 1979, p. 8.

63   T. Ferguson and A. MacPheal, *Hospital and Community*, Oxford University Press, 1954, p. 137.

64   DHSS, *Inequalities in Health*, op. cit., p. 174.

65   Minister of Reconstruction, *Housing*, Cmd 6609, HMSO, 1945, p. 2.

66   Ministry of Housing and Local Government, *The Housing Programme, 1965-1970*, Cmnd 2838, HMSO, 1965, p. 8.

67   OPCS, *General Household Survey, 1977*, op. cit., Table 3-27, p. 35.
68   OPCS, *General Household Survey, 1978*, HMSO, 1980, Table 3.49, p. 53.
69   S. Lansley, *Housing and Public Policy*, Croom Helm, 1979, Table 6.7, p. 164.
70   C. Hamnett, *Inequalities in Housing*, Open University Press, 1976, Table 3, p. 12.
71   D. Donnison, *The Government of Housing*, Penguin, 1967, Table 17, p. 218.
72   P. Townsend, *Poverty in the United Kingdom*, Penguin, 1979, Table 13.1, p. 482.
73   P.N. Balchin, *Housing Improvement and Social Inequality*, Saxon House, 1979, p. 227.
74   Department of Environment, *National Dwelling and Housing Survey*, HMSO, 1978, p. 35.
75   DHSS, *Report of the Committee on One-Parent Families*, Cmnd 5629, HMSO, 1974.
76   V. George and P. Wilding, *Motherless Families*, Routledge & Kegan Paul, 1972, pp. 34-5.
77   Department of the Environment, *Housing Policy*, Technical vol. II, HMSO, 1977, Table VI, p. 19.
78   'Whose Featherbed?' *New Society*, 4 June 1981.
79   A. Moscovitch and G. Drover, *Inequality: Essays on the Political Economy of Social Welfare*, University of Toronto Press, 1981, Ch. 11.
80   R. Brown, 'Work', in P. Abrams (ed.), *Work, Urbanism and Inequality*, Weidenfeld & Nicolson, 1978, p. 55.
81   W.W. Daniel, 'A National Survey of the Unemployed', *P.E.P. Broadsheet*, no. 546, 1974.
82   C. Craig and D. Wedderburn, 'Relative Deprivation at Work', in D. Wedderburn (ed.), *Poverty, Inequality and Class Structure*, Cambridge University Press, 1974, p. 146.
83   Department of Employment, *New Earnings Survey, 1976*, Part A, Report and key results, HMSO, 1976, Table 1, p. 45.
84   National Board for Prices and Incomes, *Hours of Work, Overtime and Shift Working*, Cmnd 4554, HMSO, 1970, pp. 64-5.
85   National Board for Prices and Incomes, ibid., p. 91.
86   G. Routh, *Occupation and Pay in Great Britain, 1906-1979*, Macmillan, 1979; H.P. Brown, *The Inequality of Pay*, Oxford University Press, 1977.
87   Department of Employment, 'Key Results of the New Earnings Survey, 1979', *Department of Employment Gazette*, Oct. 1979, Table 15, p. 996.
88   DHSS, *Income During Sickness: A New Strategy*, Cmnd 7864, HMSO, 1980, p. 18.
89   P. Townsend, *Poverty in the United Kingdom*, op. cit., Table A.44, p. 1,027.
90   Royal Commission on the Distribution of Income and Wealth, *Higher Incomes from Employment*, Report no. 3, Cmnd 6383, HMSO, 1976, Table 49, p. 97.
91   P. Townsend, *Poverty in the United Kingdom*, op. cit., p. 360.
92   M. McLean and M. Jeffreys, 'Disability and Deprivation' in D. Wedderburn, *Poverty, Inequality and Class Structure*, Cambridge University Press, 1974, Table 8.1, p. 168.
93   DHSS, *Inequalities in Health*, op. cit., Tables 3.3 and 3.4, pp. 68 and 69.
94   H.L. Wilensky, *The Welfare State and Equality*, University of California Press, 1975, p. 96.
95   F. Field, M. Meacher and C. Pond, *To Him Who Hath*, Penguin, 1977.
96   H. Graham, 'Women's Attitudes to the Child Health Services', *Health Visitor*, vol. 52, May 1979.

97   DHSS, *Inequalities in Health*, op. cit., Table 6.7, p. 175.
98   J.H. Goldthorpe, op. cit., p. 252.
99   J. Le Grand, *The Strategy of Equality*, Allen & Unwin, 1982, p. 150.
100   M. Los, 'The Concept of Justice and Welfare Rights', *The Journal of Social Welfare Law*, Jan. 1982.

Chapter 4 Social policy and the encouragement of economic growth

1   J. O'Connor, *The Fiscal Crisis of the State*, St Martin's Press, 1973, pp. 6-7.
2   B.F. Kiker, 'The Historical Roots of the Concept of Human Capital', *Journal of Political Economy*, vol. LXXIV, Oct. 1966.
3   R. Fein, 'On measuring economic benefits of health care programmes', in Nuffield Provincial Hospitals' Trust, *Medical History and Medical Care*, Oxford University Press, 1971.
4   Royal Commission on Population, Report, Cmd 7695, HMSO, 1949, p. 6.
5   A. Smith, *The Wealth of Nations*, Encyclopaedia Britannica edn. 1952, pp. 42-3.
6   E. Ginsberg, *The Development of Human Resources*, McGraw-Hill, 1966, p. 2.
7   A. Marshall, *Principles of Economics*, 1890, p. 564.
8   D.S. Landes, *The Unbound Prometheus*, Cambridge University Press, 1969, p. 340.
9   J. Stuart Maclure (ed.), *Educational Documents, England and Wales, 1816-1963*, Methuen, 1965, pp. 104-5.
10   D.S. Landes, op. cit., p. 343.
11   J.R. Hay, *The Origins of the Liberal Welfare Reforms, 1906-1914*, Macmillan, 1975, pp. 16-17.
12   J. and S. Jewkes, *Value for Money in Medicine*, Blackwell, 1963, pp. 3-4.
13   Ministry of Health, *Report of the Committee of Enquiry into the Cost of the National Health Service*, Cmd 9663, HMSO, 1956, para. 98.
14   Central Advisory Council for Education, *Early Leaving*, HMSO, 1954, p. 49.
15   Ministry of Education, *15-18*, HMSO, 1959, vol. 1, p. 55.
16   Ministry of Education, *Half Our Future*, HMSO, 1963, pp. 3 and 5.
17   Committee on Higher Education, *Higher Education*, Report, Cmnd 2154, HMSO, 1963, p. 204.
18   Th. Schultz, 'Investment in Human Capital', *American Economic Review*, vol. 51, *No. 1* March 1961.
19   W.L. Miller, 'Education as a Source of Economic Growth', *Journal of Economic Issues*, vol. 1, *No. 4* Dec. 1967.
20   E. Denison, 'Measuring the contribution of education (and the residual) to economic growth', in OECD, *The Residual Factor and Economic Growth*, Paris, 1964, p. 37.
21   I. Berg, *Education and Jobs: The Great Training Robbery*, Penguin, 1970, Ch. 5.
22   R. Collins, *The Credential Society*, Academic Press, 1979, Ch. 1.
23   S.J. Mushkin, 'Health as Investment', in M.H. Cooper and A.J. Culyer (eds), *Health Economics*, Penguin, 1973, p. 100.
24   B.A. Weisbrod et al., *Disease and Economic Development*, The University of Wisconsin Press, 1973, p. 10.
25   J. and S. Jewkes, op. cit., p. vi.
26   M. Blaug, *An Introduction to the Economics of Education*, Penguin 1972;

M.J. Bowman in B. Cosin (ed.), *Education: Structure and Society*, Penguin, 1972.

27   M.J. Bowman and C.A. Anderson, 'Concerning the role of education in development', in C. Geertz (ed.), *Old Societies and New States*, Free Press, 1963.

28   E.G. West, *Education and the Industrial Revolution*, Batsford, 1975, p. 249.

29   F.H. Harbison and C.A. Myers, *Education, Manpower and Economic Growth*, McGraw-Hill, 1964.

30   W.S. Bennett, 'Educational Change and Economic Development', *Sociology of Education*, vol. 4. *No. 2*, Spring 1967.

31   A.L. Peaslee, 'Education's Role in Development', *Economic Development and Cultural Change*, vol. 17, *No. 1*, Oct. 1968.

32   P.B. Walters, 'Educational Change and National Economic Development', *Harvard Education Review*, vol. 51, *No. 1*, Feb. 1981.

33   W. Beckerman, *The British Economy in 1975*, National Institute for Economic and Social Research, 1964.

34   E. Denison, *The Sources of Economic Growth in the United States*, Committee for Economic Development, New York, 1962.

35   E. Denison, *Why Growth Rates Differ*, The Brookings Institute, 1967.

36   E. Denison, *The Sources of Economic Growth in the United States*, op. cit.

37   S. Mushkin, op. cit., p. 115.

38   M. Ambramovitz, 'Economic Growth in the United States', *American Economic Review*, *No. 4*, Sept. 1962.

39   W. Malenbaum, 'Health and Productivity in Poor Areas', in H.E. Klarman (ed.), *Empirical Studies in Health Economics*, Johns Hopkins Press, 1970, p. 32.

40   Ch. Jencks et al., *Inequality: a Reassessment*, Basic Books, 1972.

41   A. Amin, 'Underdevelopment and dependence in Black Africa', in J. Abu-Lughod and R. Hay (eds), *Third World Urbanization*, Maaroufa Press, 1977.

42   S. Bowles and H. Gintis, 'The Problem with Human Capital Theory – A Marxian Critique', *The American Economic Review*, vol. LXV, *No. 2*, May 1975.

43   S. Bowles, 'Cuban Education and the Revolutionary Ideology', *Harvard Educational Review*, vol. 41, *No. 4*, Nov. 1971.

44   I. Sorel, 'The Human Capital Revolution in Economic Development: its Current History and Status', *Comparative Education Review*, vol. 22, *No. 2*, June 1978.

45   T. Stonier, 'A Little Learning is a Lucrative Thing', *The Times Higher Education Supplement*, 1 May 1981.

46   I. Illich, *Deschooling Society*, Harper & Row, 1971.

47   G. Denton, 'Financial Assistance to British Industry', in W.M. Corden and G. Fels, *Public Assistance to Industry*, Macmillan, 1976.

48   Ministry of Labour, *Reports of Investigations into the Industrial Conditions in Certain Depressed Areas*, Cmnd 4728, HMSO, 1934, p. 106.

49   *Royal Commission on the Distribution of the Industrial Population*, Report, Cmd 6153, HMSO, 1940.

50   National Economic Development Council, *Conditions Favourable to Faster Growth*, HMSO, 1963, p. 29.

51   J. Burton, 'Employment Subsidies – the cases for and against', *National Westminster Bank Quarterly Review*, Feb. 1977.

52   G. McCrone, *Regional Policy in Britain*, Allen & Unwin, 1969, p. 26.

53   M. Dunford, M. Geddes and D. Perrons, 'Regional Policy and the Crisis
       in the U.K.', *International Journal of Urban and Regional Research*, vol. 5,
       No. 3, Sept. 1981.
54   Conference of Socialist Economists, *Struggle Over the State*, CSE Books,
       1979, p. 47.
55   D. McCallum, 'The Development of British Regional Policy', in
       D. MacLennan and J.B. Parr, *Regional Policy*, Martin Robertson, 1979.
56   *Cambridge Economic Policy Review*, vol. 6, *No. 2*, July 1980, p. 1.
57   B. Moore and J. Rhodes, 'Evaluating the Effects of British Regional
       Economic Policy', *The Economic Journal*, vol. 83, March 1973.
58   B. Moore and P. Tyler, 'The Impact of Regional Policy in the 1970s',
       Centre for Environmental Studies Review, no. 1, July 1977.
59   R.D. Rees and R.H.C. Miall, 'The Effect of Regional Policy on Manufac-
       turing Investment and Capital Stock within the U.K. between 1959 and
       1978', *Regional Studies*, vol. 15, *No. 6*, 1981.
60   G.C. Cameron, 'The National Industrial Strategy and Regional Policy', in
       D. MacLennan and J. Parr (eds), *Regional Policy*, op. cit., p. 309.
61   J. Salt, 'Labour Migration, Housing and the Labour Market', in A. Evans
       and D. Eversley (eds), *The Inner City: Employment and Industry*, p. 267.
62   J.H. Johnson and J. Salt, 'Employment Transfer Policies in Great Britain',
       The Three Banks' Review, no. 126, June 1980.
63   P.B. Beaumont, 'An Examination of Assisted Labour Mobility Policy', in
       D. MacLennan and J.B. Parr (eds), op. cit., Table 3.1, p. 73.
64   P.B. Beaumont, op. cit., Table 3.3, p. 76.
65   S. Parker, 'Assisted Labour Migration', OPCS, 1975, quoted in
       J.H. Johnson and J. Salt, op. cit.
66   W. Beveridge, *Full Employment in a Free Society*, Allen & Unwin, 1944,
       p. 184.
67   W. Beveridge, ibid., p. 160.
68   Conference of Socialist Economists, *The Alternative Economic Strategy*,
       Blackrose Press, 1980, p. 47.
69   D. Blake and P. Ormerod, *The Economics of Prosperity*, McIntyre, 1980,
       p. 24.
70   B. Showler, *The Public Employment Service*, Longman, 1976, ch. 5.
71   J. Delcourt, 'Social Policy – Crisis or Mutation?', *Labour and Society*,
       vol. 7, *No. 1*, Jan.-March 1982.

Chapter 5 Does social policy undermine economic growth?

1   Government's Expenditure Plans 1980-1, Cmnd 7746, HMSO, 1979, p. 1.
2   T. Sheriff, *A De-industrialised Britain*, Fabian Publications, 1979, pp. 2-5.
3   R. Bacon and W. Eltis, *Britain's Economic Problem: Too Few Producers*,
       Macmillan, 1976, p. 3.
4   Ibid., p. 11.
5   Ibid., Chart 7, p. 11.
6   Ibid., p. 26.
7   Ibid., p. 27.
8   A.P. Thirlwall, 'The U.K.'s Economic Problem: a Balance of Payments
       Constraint?', *National Westminster Bank Quarterly Review*, Feb. 1978.
9   A.P. Thirlwall, 'De-industrialisation in the United Kingdom', *Lloyds Bank
       Review*, no. 144, April 1982.
10   J.F. Sleeman, *Resources for the Welfare State*, Longman, 1979, pp. 90-1.
11   I. Gough, *The Political Economy of the Welfare State*, Macmillan,

1979, p. 123.
12   I. Gough, ibid.
13   R. Klein et al., *Constraints and Choices*, Centre for Studies in Social Policy, 1976.
14   G.J. Burgess and A.J. Webb, 'The Profits of British Industry', *Lloyds Bank Review*, no. 112, April 1974.
15   A. Glyn and B. Sutcliffe, *British Capitalism, Workers and the Profit Squeeze*, Penguin, 1972, p. 65.
16   Committee to Review the Functioning of Financial Institutions, Cmnd 7937, HMSO, 1980, (Wilson Committee).
17   W.J. Benson, 'London Clearing Banks Evidence to the Wilson Committee', *National Westminster Bank Review*, May 1978.
18   Committee to Review the Functioning of Financial Institutions, op. cit.
19   T. Harris, 'The Role of Public Spending', in D. Blake and P. Ormerod, *The Economics of Prosperity*, McIntyre, 1980, p. 34.
20   A.M. Ross and P.T. Hartman, *Changing Patterns of Industrial Conflict*, Wiley, 1960; J.E.T. Eldridge, *Explanations of Strikes: a Critical Review in Industrial Disputes: Essays in the Sociology of Industrial Relations*, Routledge & Kegan Paul, 1968; R. Hyman, *Strikes*, Fontana, 1975.
21   J. Gennard, *Financing Strikes*, Macmillan, 1977, p. 123.
22   Ibid.
23   Ibid., p. 124.
24   Ibid., p. 125.
25   Supplementary Benefits Commission, *Annual Report, 1979*, Cmnd 8033, HMSO, 1980, Table 10.1, p. 95.
26   D.A. Hibbs, Jr, 'On the Political Economy of Long-Run Trends in Strike Activity', *British Journal of Political Science*, vol. 8, *No. 2*, April 1978, Figure 2.
27   W. Duncan and W.E.J. McCarthy, 'The State Subsidy Theory of Strikes', *British Journal of Industrial Relations*, vol. XII, *No. 1*, March 1974.
28   J. Gennard and R. Lasko, 'Supplementary Benefit and Strikers', *British Journal of Industrial Relations*, vol. XII, *No. 1*, March 1974.
29   J. Gennard and R. Lasko, 'The Individual and the Strike', *British Journal of Industrial Relations*, vol. XIII, *No. 3*, Nov. 1975.
30   W.J. Cole, 'The Financing of the Individual Striker: a case study in the building industry', *British Journal of Industrial Relations*, vol. XIII, *No. 1*, March 1975.
31   A.J. Thieblot, Jr and R.M. Cowin, *Welfare and Strikes*, University of Pennsylvania, 1972.
32   Q. Hogg, *The Case for Conservatism*, Penguin, 1947, pp. 251-2.
33   J. Treasure, 'The Toll Our Taxes Take', *The Times*, 12 Jan. 1968.
34   Sir G. Howe, in *Parliamentary Debates*, 5th series, vol. 968, C. 258.
35   C.V. Brown and O.A. Dawson, 'Personal Taxation, Incentives and Tax Reform', *P.E.P. Broadsheet*, 506, 1969, p. 3.
36   C.V. Brown, 'Misconceptions about Income Tax and Incentives', *Scottish Journal of Political Economy*, vol. 15, Feb. 1968.
37   Royal Commission on the Taxation of Profits and Income, *Second Report*, Cmd 9105, HMSO, 1954, appendix I, paragraph 10.
38   C.V. Brown and E. Levin, 'The Effects of Taxation on Overtime: the results of a national survey', *Economic Journal*, vol. 34, Dec. 1974, p. 834.
39   G.F. Break, 'Income Taxes and Incentives to Work: An Empirical Study', *American Economic Review*, vol. XLVII, *No. 5*, Sept. 1957.
40   D.B. Fields and W.T. Stanbury, 'Income Taxes and Incentives to Work: Some Additional Empirical Evidence', *American Economic Review*,

vol. 61, *No. 3*, June 1971.

41 M. Beenstock, 'Taxation and Incentives in the U.K.', *Lloyds Bank Review*, no. 134, Oct. 1979.

42 C.V. Brown, *Taxation and the Incentive to Work*, Oxford University Press, 1980, ch. 5.

43 J.E. Meade, Report of the Committee chaired by Professor J.E. Meade, *The Structure and Reform of Direct Taxation*, Allen & Unwin, 1978, p. 24.

44 C.V. Brown, E. Levin and D.T. Ulph, 'Estimates of Labour Hours Supplied by Married Male Workers in Great Britain', *Scottish Journal of Political Economy*, Vol. 23, Nov. 1976.

45 L. Godfrey, *Theoretical and Empirical Aspects of the Effects of Taxation on the Supply of Labour*, OECD, 1975, p. 126.

46 K.J. Newman, 'International Comparison of Taxes and Social Security Contributions 1971-8', *Economic Trends*, no. 326, Dec. 1980.

47 Meade Report, op. cit., Table 5.16, p. 98.

48 Committee on Manpower Resources for Science and Technology, *The Brain Drain: Report of the Working Group on Migration*, Cmnd 3417, HMSO, 1967, pp. 29 and 30.

49 *Social Insurance and Allied Services*, Cmd. 6404, HMSO, 1942, p. 143.

50 P. Falush, 'The Changing Pattern of Savings', *National Westminster Bank Quarterly Review*, Aug. 1978.

51 Report of the Royal Commission on the Poor Laws, Report, 1834, p. 228.

52 Ministry of Social Security, *The Administration of the Wages Stop*, HMSO, 1967, p. 1.

53 F. Field et al., *To Him Who Hath: A study of poverty and taxation*, Penguin, 1977, ch. 8.

54 *Report of the National Assistance Board, 1956*, Cmnd 181, HMSO, 1957, p. 15.

55 Department of Employment, 'Characteristics of the Unemployed: Sample Survey, June 1973', *Department of Employment Gazette*, vol. 83, no. 3, March 1974.

56 J.A. Kay, C.N. Morris and N.A. Warren, 'Tax, Benefits and Incentive to Seek Work', *Fiscal Studies*, vol. 1, *No. 4*, Nov. 1980.

57 Royal Commission on the Distribution of Income and Wealth, Report no. 6, quoted in A.B. Atkinson and J.S. Flemming, 'Unemployment, Social Security and Incentives', *Midland Bank Review*, Autumn 1978, Table 2.

58 Supplementary Benefits Commission, *Report of the Supplementary Benefits Commission, 1975*, Cmnd 6615, HMSO, 1976, Table 10, p. 37.

59 M. Clark, 'The Unemployed on Supplementary Benefit', *Journal of Social Policy*, vol. 7, part 4, Oct. 1978.

60 Supplementary Benefits Commission, *Annual Report, 1976*, Cmnd 6910, HMSO, 1977, pp. 32-3.

61 Supplementary Benefits Commission, *Annual Report, 1979*, Cmnd 8033, HMSO, 1980, p. 39.

62 J.A. Kay et al., op. cit.

63 D. Gujarati, 'The Behaviour of Unemployment and Unfilled Vacancies, Great Britain, 1958-1971', *Economic Journal*, vol. 82, 1972.

64 J. Taylor, 'The Behaviour of Unemployment and Unfilled Vacancies, Great Britain, 1958-1971: An Alternative View', *Economic Journal*, vol. 82, Dec. 1972.

65 Department of Employment, 'The Changed Relationship Between Unemployment and Vacancies', *Department of Employment Gazette*, Oct. 1976.

66 D. Maki and Z.A. Spindler, 'The Effect of Unemployment Compensation

on the Rate of Unemployment in Great Britain', *Oxford Economic Papers*, 27, 1975, pp. 440-54.

67 M.C. Sawyer, 'The Effects of Unemployment Compensation on the Rate of Unemployment in Great Britain – A Comment', *Oxford Economic Papers*, 31, 1979, p. 136.

68 D. MacKay and G. Reid, 'Redundancy, Unemployment and Manpower Policy', *Economic Journal*, vol. 82, Dec. 1972.

69 S.J. Nickell, 'The Effect of Unemployment and Related Benefits on the Duration of Unemployment', *Economic Journal*, vol. 89, March 1979.

70 A.B. Atkinson, 'Unemployment Benefits and Incentive', in J. Creedy (ed.), *The Economics of Unemployment in Britain*, Butterworth, 1981.

71 Ibid., p. 146.

72 M. Hill, 'Can we distinguish voluntary from involuntary unemployment?', in G. Worswick (ed.), *The Concept and Measurement of Involuntary Unemployment*, Allen & Unwin, 1976, p. 172.

73 S. Moylan and B. Davies, 'The Disadvantages of the Unemployed', *Employment Gazette*, vol. 88, *No. 8*, Aug. 1980.

74 S. Moylan and B. Davies, 'The Flexibility of the Unemployed', *Employment Gazette*, vol. 89, *No. 1*, Jan. 1981.

75 B. Showler, 'Incentives, Social Security Payments and Unemployment', *Social and Economic Administration*, vol. 9, *No. 2*, Summer 1978.

76 S.R. Parker et al., *Effects of the Redundancy Payments Act*, OPCS, 1971, and M.J. Hill et al., *Men out of Work*, Cambridge University Press, 1973.

77 Committee on Abuse of Social Security Benefits, Report, Cmnd 5228, HMSO, 1973, p. 224.

78 Report of the Joint Department of Employment/DHSS Rayner Scrutiny, *Payment of Benefits to Unemployed People*, HMSO, 1981, pp. 61-3.

79 *Report of the Supplementary Benefits Commission, 1979*, Cmnd 8033, HMSO, 1980, p. 94.

80 A. Deacon, 'The Scrounging Controversy: Public Attitudes Towards the Unemployed in Contemporary Britain', *Social and Economic Administration*, vol. 12, *No. 2*, Summer 1978.

81 DHSS, *Two-Parent Families Receiving FIS in 1972*, HMSO, 1975, p.

82 DHSS, *Fatherless Families on FIS*, HMSO, 1979, p. 82.

83 R. Haverman and H. Watts, 'Social Experimentation as Policy Research: a Review of Negative Income Tax Experiments', in V. Halberstadt and A. Culyer (eds), *Public Economics and Human Resources*, Cujas, 1977, p. 248.

84 R. Hall, 'Effects of the Experimental NIT on Labor Supply', in J. Pechman and P. Timpane, *Work Incentives and Income Guarantees: The New Jersey Income Tax Experiment*, The Brookings Institute, 1975.

Chapter 6 Social services and political stability

1 J. Harris, *William Beveridge*, Clarendon Press, 1977, e.g. pp. 102-3.

2 R.M. Titmuss, *The Gift Relationship*, Allen & Unwin, 1970.

3 R. Mishra, *Society and Social Policy*, Macmillan, 2nd edn, 1981, p. 35.

4 S. Williams, *Politics is for People*, Penguin, 1981, p. 37.

5 R.H. Tawney, *Equality*, Allen & Unwin, 1964, p. 120.

6 L. Doyal, *The Political Economy of Health*, Pluto, 1979, p. 43.

7 A. Deacon, 'Concession and Coercion: The Politics of Unemployment Insurance in the Twenties', in A. Briggs and J. Saville (eds), *Essays in Labour History, 1918-1939*, Croom Helm, 1977, p. 10.

8   F. Piven and R.A. Cloward, *Regulating the Poor*, Tavistock, 1972, p. xiii.
9   Quoted in J. English (ed.), *The Future of Council Housing*, Croom Helm, 1982, p. 183.
10   F. Hirsch, *Social Limits to Growth*, Routledge & Kegan Paul, 1977, p. 152.
11   J. Rawls, *A Theory of Justice*, Oxford University Press, 1972, p. 3.
12   Quoted in V. Navarro, *Class Struggle, the State and Medicine*, Martin Robertson, 1979, p. 110-11.
13   R. Klein, 'The Welfare State: A Self Inflicted Crisis?', *Political Quarterly*, vol. 51, *No. 1*, Jan.-March 1980, p. 32.
14   S.H. Beer, *Modern British Politics*, Faber, 1976, p. 386.
15   Ibid., p. 357.
16   Ibid., p. 386.
17   V. Bogdanor and R. Skidelsky (eds), *The Age of Affluence 1951-6*, Macmillan, 1970, p. 10.
18   T. Parsons and N.J. Smelser, *Economy and Society*, Routledge & Kegan Paul, 1956, pp. 18-19.
19   R. Disney, 'Theorising the Welfare State: the case of unemployment insurance in Britain', *Journal of Social Policy*, vol. 11, *No. 1*, 1982, p. 52.
20   M. Simpkin, *Trapped Within Welfare*, Macmillan, 1979, p. 66.
21   C. Pritchard and R. Taylor, *Social Work: Reform or Revolution*, Routledge & Kegan Paul, 1978, p. 129.
22   V. Navarro, *Medicine Under Capitalism*, Prodist/Croom Helm, 1976, p. 207.
23   E.g. J. Mathews, 'The Politics of Cancer', *Marxism Today*, May 1981, pp. 19, 22; S. Epstein, *The Politics of Cancer*, Anchor/Doubleday, 1980.
24   L. Doyal, op. cit., p. 36.
25   V. Navarro, *Medicine Under Capitalism*, op. cit., p. 127.
26   Z. Butrym, *The Nature of Social Work*, Macmillan, 1976, p. 111.
27   C. Wright Mills, 'The Professional Ideology of Social Pathologists', *American Journal of Sociology*, vol. 49, *No. 2*, 1943, p. 171.
28   London Edinburgh Weekend Return Group, *In and Against the State*, Pluto, 1980, p. 4.
29   R. Pinker, *Social Theory and Social Policy*, Heinemann, 1971, p. 144.
30   P. Thane, *Foundations of the Welfare State*, Longman, 1982, p. 108.
31   Harris, op. cit., p. 102.
32   Piven and Cloward, op. cit., p. xiii.
33   J.C. Kincaid, *Poverty and Equality in Britain*, Penguin, 1973, p. 223.
34   Committee on Abuse of Social Security Benefits, Report, Cmnd 5228, HMSO, 1973, p. 109.
35   Education Group, Centre for Contemporary Cultural Studies, University of Birmingham, *Unpopular Education*, Hutchinson, 1981, p. 236.
36   Ibid., p. 238.
37   Committee on the Economic and Financial Problems of the Provision for Old Age, Report, Cmd 9333, HMSO, 1954, p. 44.
38   Department of the Environment, *Housing Policy: a Consultative Document*, Cmnd 6851, HMSO, 1977, p. 50.
39   D. Butler and D. Stokes, *Political Change in Britain*, Macmillan, 2nd edn, 1974, pp. 111-12.
40   P. Gallagher, 'Ideology in Housing Management' in English, op. cit., p. 132.
41   J. Lambert, B. Blackaby and C. Paris, *Neighbourhood Politics and Housing Opportunities*, Centre for Environmental Studies, 1975, p. 9.
42   Quoted in M.D. Shipman, *Education and Modernisation*, Faber, 1971, p. 161.
43   R.D. Hess and J.V. Torney, *The Development of Political Attitudes in*

Children, Aldine, 1967, p. 101.

44 E.g. B.G. Massialas, *Education and the Political System*, Addison Wesley, 1969.

45 R. Dale et al., *Schooling and Capitalism*, Routledge & Kegan Paul, Open University, 1976, p. 1.

46 L. Althusser, 'Ideology and Ideological State Apparatus', in B.R. Cosin (ed.), *Education, Structure and Society*, Penguin, 1972.

47 E.g. J.S. Hunt, *Education in Evolution*, Hart Davis, 1971; R. Johnson, 'Educational Policy and Social Control in Early Victorian England', *Past and Present*, 49, No. 1970; B. Simon, *Studies in the History of Education*, Lawrence & Wishart, 1960.

48 E. Litt, 'Civic Education, Community Norms and Political Indoctrination', *American Sociological Review*, vol. 28, *No. 1*, 1963, pp. 69-75.

49 P. Abrams, 'Notes on the Uses of Ignorance', *Twentieth Century*, Autumn 1963, pp. 67-77.

50 P. Abramson, 'The Differential Political Socialisation of English Secondary School Students', *Sociology of Education*, vol. 40, *No.3*, 1967.

51 R.M. Merelman, 'The Adolescence of Political Socialisation', *Sociology of Education*, vol. 45, *No. 1*, 1972, p. 150.

52 L.H. Ehman, 'The American School in the Political Socialisation Process', *Review of Educational Research*, vol. 50, *No. 1*, 1980, p. 103.

53 Ibid., p. 113.

54 H. Zeigler and W. Peak, 'The Political Functions of the Educational System', *Sociology of Education*, vol. 43, *No. 1*, 1970, pp. 115-42.

55 B. Davies, *Social Control and Education*, Methuen, 1976, p. 50.

56 R. Sharpe and A. Green, *Education and Social Control*, Routledge & Kegan Paul, 1975, p. 217.

57 R.M. Merelman, 'Social Stratification and Political Socialisation in Mature Industrial Societies', *Comparative Education Review*, vol. 19, *No. 1*, 1975, pp. 18-20.

58 Ibid., p. 21.

59 Quoted in Z. Butrym, *The Nature of Social Work*, Macmillan, 1976, p. 113.

60 J. Handler, 'The Coercive Children's Officer', *New Society*, 3 Oct. 1968.

61 B. Jordan, *Freedom in the Welfare State*, Routledge & Kegan Paul, 1976, Chs 11 and 12.

62 Pritchard and Taylor, op. cit., p. 96.

63 P. Corrigan and P. Leonard, *Social Work Practice Under Capitalism*, Macmillan, 1978, p. 102.

64 Quoted in B. Wilkins, 'The Morality of Law and the Politics of Probation', in N. Timms and D. Watson (eds), *Philosophy in Social Work*, Routledge & Kegan Paul, 1978, p. 138.

65 *The Probation and After Care Service in England and Wales*, HMSO, 1973.

66 Simpkin, op. cit., p. 70.

67 E.g. M. MacDonald, 'Socio Cultural Reproduction and Women's Education', in R. Deem (ed.), *Schooling for Women's Work*, Routledge & Kegan Paul, 1980.

68 S. Sharpe, *Just Like a Girl*, Penguin, 1976, p. 309.

69 M. Mann, 'The Social Cohesion of Liberal Democracy', *American Sociological Review*, vol. 35, no. 4, 1970, pp. 423-5.

70 Ibid., pp. 435-6.

71 T. Tapper and B. Salter, *Education and the Political Order*, Macmillan, 1978, p. 44.

72 F. Parkin, *Class Inequality and Political Order*, MacGibbon & Key, 1971.

73 P. Bourdieu, 'Cultural Reproduction and Social Reproduction', in
J. Karabel and A.H. Halsey, *Power and Ideology in Education*, Oxford
University Press, 1977, p. 496.
74 R. Miliband, *The State in Capitalist Society*, Quartet, 1973, p. 216.
75 H. Eckstein, quoted in Abramson, op. cit., p. 250.
76 S. Bowles and H. Gintis, *Schooling in Capitalist America*, Routledge &
Kegan Paul, 1976, p. 131.
77 Hess and Torney, op. cit., p. 110; Tapper and Salter, op. cit., p. 34.
78 M. Barlagli and M. Dei, 'Socialization into Apathy and Political Subordination', in Karabel and Halsey, op cit.
79 B. and J. Ehrenreich, 'Medicine and Social Control' in J. Ehrenreich (ed.),
The Cultural Crisis of Modern Medicine, Monthly Review Press, 1978,
p. 61.
80 J. Leeson and J. Gray, *Women and Medicine*, Tavistock, 1978, pp. 86-7.
81 E.g. R. Deem, *Women and Schooling*, Routledge & Kegan Paul, 1978,
Ch. 2.
82 J. Finch and D. Groves, 'Community Care and the Family: A Case for
Equal Opportunities', *Journal of Social Policy*, vol. 9, *Part 4*, 1980.
83 R. Plant, *Social and Moral Theory in Casework*, Routledge & Kegan Paul,
1970, p. 66.
84 Leeson and Gray, op. cit., pp. 126-7.
85 Quoted in Zeigler and Peak, op. cit., p. 116.
86 Zeigler and Peak, op. cit.
87 Ibid., p. 117.
88 C. Offe, *Competitive Party Democracy and the Welfare State*, Mimeo,
1981.
89 R. Mishra, *Society and Social Policy*, Macmillan (2nd edn) 1981, p. 127.

Chapter 7 The legitimation crisis of the welfare state

1 S.M. Lipset, *Political Man*, Doubleday, 1960, p. 77.
2 R.E. Lane, 'The Legitimacy Bias', in B. Denitch (ed.), *Legitimation of
Regimes*, Sage, 1979, p. 55.
3 H. Heclo, 'Towards a New Welfare State', in P. Flora and A.J. Heidenheimer, *The Development of Welfare States in Europe and America*,
Transaction Books, 1981, p. 397.
4 C. Offe, 'Advanced Capitalism and the Welfare State', *Politics and Society*,
vol. 2, *No. 4*, 1972, p. 485.
5 J. Alt, *The Politics of Economic Decline*, Cambridge University Press,
1979, p. 157.
6 Ibid., pp. 50-1.
7 M. Crozier et al., *The Crisis of Democracy*, New York University Press,
1975, p. 37.
8 Board of Inland Revenue, 120th Report, Cmnd 7092, HMSO, 1978,
para. 70.
9 *New Society*, 26 August 1982, p. 341.
10 R. Rose and G. Peters, *Can Governments Go Bankrupt?*, Macmillan, 1979,
p. 207.
11 E.g. M. O'Higgins, 'Tax Evasion and the Self-Employed: an Examination of
the Evidence, II', *British Tax Review*, No. 6, 1981.
12 A. Christopher, 'The Law is the Law is the Law', in Institute of Economic
Affairs, *Tax Evasion*, 1979, p. 79.
13 Ibid., p. 79.

14 D. Butler and D. Stokes, *Political Change in Britain*, Macmillan (2nd edn), 1974, p. 297.
15 Ibid., p. 299.
16 Ibid., p. 342.
17 *Guardian*, 23 September 1982.
18 P. Whiteley, 'Public Opinion and the Demand for Social Welfare in Britain', *Journal of Social Policy*, vol. 10, *No. 4*, 1981, p. 473.
19 R. Harris and A. Seldon, *Over-Ruled on Welfare*, IEA, 1979, p. 46.
20 Ibid., p. 51.
21 Alt, op. cit., p. 259.
22 Ibid., p. 262.
23 H. Heclo, 'Welfare: Progress and Stagnation', in W.B. Gwyn and R. Rose, *Britain – Progress and Decline*, Macmillan, 1980, p. 48.
24 J.P. Mackintosh, 'The declining respect for the law', in A. King, *Why is Britain Becoming Harder to Govern?*, BBC, 1976, p. 93.
25 Ibid., p. 94.
26 R. Rose, 'Ungovernability: Is there fire behind the smoke?', *Political Studies*, vol. XXVII, *No. 3*, 1979, p. 352.
27 G. Room, *The Sociology of Welfare*, Martin Robertson, 1979, p. 63.
28 Alt, op. cit., p. 270.
29 Rose, op. cit., p. 352.
30 D. Butler and D. Kavanagh, *The British General Election of February 1974*, Macmillan, 1974, p. vii.
31 D. Butler and D. Kavanagh, *The British General Election of 1979*, Macmillan, 1980, p. 6.
32 Royal Commission on the Constitution 1969-73, Report, Cmnd 5460, HMSO, 1973, vol. I, para. 1102.
33 M. Kaase, 'The Crisis of Authority: Myth and Reality', in R. Rose (ed.), *Challenge to Governance*, Sage, 1980, pp. 177-8.
34 D. Butler and D. Kavanagh, *The British General Election of February 1974*, op. cit., pp. 272-3.
35 D. Butler and D. Kavanagh, *The British General Election of October 1974*, Macmillan, 1975, pp. 275 and 280.
36 Ibid., p. 287.
37 I. Crewe et al., 'Partisan Dealignment in Britain 1964-74', in *British Journal of Political Science*, vol. 7, *No. 2*, 1977, p. 130.
38 A. Wolfe, *The Limits of Legitimacy*, Free Press, 1977, p. 308.
39 D. Bell, *The Cultural Contradictions of Capitalism*, Heinemann, 1976, p. 247.
40 Royal Commission on the Constitution 1969-73, op. cit., vol. II, para. 1.
41 Ibid., para. 10.
42 Ibid., para. 76.
43 Ibid., para. 79.
44 Quoted in Wolfe, op. cit., p. 308.
45 Ibid., p. 324.
46 R. Rose, *Challenge to Governance*, op. cit., p. 156.
47 Kaase, op. cit., p. 183.
48 R.E. Lane, 'The Legitimacy Bias', in B. Denitch, op. cit., p. 63.
49 Kaase, op. cit., pp. 176f.
50 J. Habermas, 'Conservatism and Capitalist Crisis', *New Left Review*, 115, 1978, p. 80.
51 Lane, op. cit., pp. 63-4.
52 B. Denitch, 'The Dimensions of the Problem', in B. Denitch, op. cit., p. 21.
53 R. Hadley and S. Hatch, *Social Welfare and the Failure of the State*, Allen

& Unwin, 1981.
54   A. King, 'Overload: Problems of Governing in the 1970s', *Political Studies*, vol. XXIII, *Nos 2 and 3*, 1975, pp. 284-96.
55   S. Brittan, 'The Economic Contradictions of Democracy', *British Journal of Political Science*, vol. 5, *No. 1*, 1975, pp. 129-59.
56   Ibid., p. 150.
57   Ibid., p. 141.
58   Ibid., p. 142.
59   Ibid.
60   King, op. cit., p. 286.
61   K. Middlemas, *Politics in Industrial Society*, Deutsch, 1979, pp. 221 and 273-4.
62   E.g. S. Brittan, 'Can Democracy Manage an Economy?', in R. Skidelsky (ed.), *The End of the Keynesian Era*, Macmillan, 1977.
63   R. Skidelsky, 'The Decline of Keynesian Politics', in C. Crouch (ed.), *State and Economy in Late Capitalism*, Croom Helm, 1979, p. 56.
64   C. Offe, 'The Separation of Form and Content in Liberal Democratic Politics', in *Studies in Political Economy*, 3, 1980, p. 7.
65   D. Usher, *The Economic Prerequisite to Democracy*, Blackwell, 1981.
66   King, op. cit., pp. 289-92.
67   S. Brittan, 'The Economic Contradictions of Democracy', *British Journal of Political Science*, vol. 5, *No. 1*, 1975, p. 155.
68   King, op. cit., pp. 294-5.
69   J. Douglas, 'The Overloaded Crown', *British Journal of Political Science*, vol. 6, *No. 4*, 1976, p. 494.
70   Ibid., p. 487.
71   Ibid., p. 488.
72   Ibid.
73   R. Rose, 'What if Anything, is Wrong with Big Government?', *Journal of Public Policy*, vol. 1, *No. 1*, 1981, p. 31.
74   R. Rose, 'From Steady State to Fluid State: the UK today', in Gwyn and Rose op. cit., p. 137.
75   J. O'Connor, *The Fiscal Crisis of the State*, St Martin's Press, 1973.
76   Brittan, op. cit., p. 159.
77   King, op. cit., p. 296.
78   J. Habermas, *Legitimation Crisis*, Beacon Press, 1975.
79   O'Connor, op. cit., p. 6.
80   Ibid., p. 9.
81   Wolfe, op. cit., p. 4.
82   Ibid., p. 6.
83. Ibid., p. 247.
84   Ibid., p. 258.
85   Ibid., p. 252.
86   Ibid., p. 259.
87   Ibid., p. 329.
88   Ibid., p. 346.
89   J. Senat, *Habermas and Marxism*, Sage, 1979, Ch. 4.
90   Habermas, op. cit., p. 49.
91   Ibid., p. 62.
92   Ibid., p. 46.
93   J. Habermas, 'Problems of Legitimation in Late Capitalism', in P. Connerton (ed.), *Critical Sociology*, Penguin, 1976, p. 377.
94   Ibid., pp. 379-80.
95   J. Habermas, *Legitimation Crisis*, op. cit., p. 36.

96   Ibid., p. 37.
97   Ibid., p. 75.
98   Ibid., p. 63.
99   J. Habermas, 'Conservatism and Capitalist Crisis', *New Left Review*, 115, 1978, p. 80.
100 J. Habermas, *Legitimation Crisis*, op. cit., p. 74.
101 Ibid., p. 73.
102 J. Habermas, 'Conservatism and Capitalist Crisis', op. cit., p. 81.
103 J.M. Buchanan and R.E. Wagner, *Democracy in Deficit*, Academic Press, 1977.
104 J.H. Goldthorpe, 'The Current Inflation. Towards a Sociological Account', in J.H. Goldthorpe and F. Hirsch (eds), *The Political Economy of Inflation*, Martin Robertson, 1978, p. 194.
105 Ibid., p. 195.
106 Skidelsky, op. cit., p. 64.
107 Bell, op. cit., p. 256.
108 R. Rose and G. Peters, op. cit.
109 Quoted in Wolfe, op. cit., p. 326.
110 R. Klein, 'The Welfare State: a Self-Inflicted Crisis', *Political Quarterly*, vol. 51, *No. 1*, 1980, p. 29.
111 R. Dahrendorf, 'Effectiveness and Legitimacy: on the Governability of Democracies', *Political Quarterly*, vol. 51, no. 4, 1980, p. 405.
112 Rose and Peters, op. cit., p. xiii.
113 Ibid., pp. 33-4.
114 Ibid., p. xiii.
115 Quoted in R. Klein, 'The Case for Elitism: Public Opinion and Public Policy', *Political Quarterly*, vol. 45, *No. 4*, 1974, p. 412.
116 Rose and Peters, op. cit., p. 21.
117 R. Rose, 'What, if Anything, is Wrong With Big Government?', op. cit., pp. 12-13.
118 R. Klein, 'Costs and Benefits of Complexity: the British NHS', in R. Rose (ed.), *Challenge to Governance*, op. cit., p. 119.
119 Hadley and Hatch, op. cit., pp. 23-31.
120 Dahrendorf, op. cit., pp. 400-1.
121 J.L. Horowitz, 'The Norm of Illegitimacy – Ten Years Later', in Denitch, op. cit., p. 25.
122 R. Rose, 'The Nature of the Challenge', in R. Rose, *Challenge to Governance*, op. cit., p. 23-4.
123 J.P. Mackintosh, 'Has Social Democracy Failed in Britain?', *Political Quarterly*, vol. 49, *No. 3*, 1978, p. 267.
124 Rose and Peters, op. cit., p. xiii.
125 R. Rose, 'Ungovernability: Is there fire behind the smoke?', op. cit., pp. 351-70.
126 Commission of the European Communities, *The Perception of Poverty in Europe*, 1977.
127 P. Golding and S. Middleton, *Images of Welfare*, Martin Robertson, 1982, pp. 195-8.
128 D. Donnison, 'Social Policy Since Titmuss', *Journal of Social Policy*, vol. 8, *No. 2*, 1979, p. 152.
129 P. Taylor Goodby, 'Mosaic to Kaleidoscope: the pattern of public opinion about legitimation issues in the welfare state', *Journal of Sociology*, May 1983, vol. 17, no. 2, pp. 165-84.
130 Skidelsky, op. cit., pp. 65-6.
131 Alt, op. cit., pp. 264-5.

131   Alt, op. cit., pp. 264-5.
132   Ibid., p. 270.
133   R. Rose (ed.), *Challenge to Governance*, op. cit., Ch. 7.
134   I. Gough, *The Political Economy of the Welfare State*, Macmillan, 1979, Ch. 7.
135   C. Offe, 'Some Contradictions of the Modern Welfare State', *Critical Social Policy*, vol. 2, *No. 2*, 1982, p. 13.

Chapter 8 Conclusion

1   E.F.M. Durbin, *The Politics of Democratic Socialism: An Essay on Social Policy*, The Labour Book Service, 1940, p. 293.
2   I. Carson and S. Vines, 'Battling To Stop the Jobs Drain', *Observer*, 11 July 1982.
3   P. Golding and S. Middleton, *Images of Welfare*, Martin Robertson, 1982.

Bibliography

Abrams, P., 'Notes on the Uses of Ignorance', *Twentieth Century*, autumn 1963.

Abramson, P., 'The Differential Political Socialisation of English Secondary School Students', *Sociology of Education*, vol. 40, *No. 3*, 1967.

Acheson, E., *Primary Health Care in Inner London*, DHSS, 1981.

Alt, J., *The Politics of Economic Decline*, Cambridge University Press, 1979.

Ambramovitz, M., 'Economic Growth in the United States', *American Economic Review*, Sept. 1962.

Amin, S., 'Underdevelopment and dependence in Black Africa', in J. Abu-Lughod and R. Hay (eds), *Third World Urbanization*, Maaroufa Press, 1977.

Atkinson, A.B., 'Unemployment Benefits and Incentive', in J. Creedy (ed.), *The Economics of Unemployment in Britain*, Butterworth, 1981.

Backett, M., 'Health Services', in F. Williams (ed.), *Why the Poor Pay More*, Macmillan, 1978.

Bacon, R. and Eltis, W., *Britain's Economic Problem: Too Few Producers*, Macmillan, 1976.

Bailey, R., *The Homeless and the Empty Houses*, Penguin, 1977.

Balchin, P.N., *Housing Improvement and Social Inequality*, Saxon House, 1979.

Ball, S., *Beachside Comprehensive*, Cambridge University Press, 1981.

Beaumont, P.B., 'An Examination of Assisted Labour Mobility Policy', in D. MacLennan and J.B. Parr (eds), *Regional Policy*, Martin Robertson, 1974.

Bebbington, A., 'Changes in the Provision of Social Services to the Elderly in the Community over Fourteen Years', *Social Policy and Administration*, vol. 13, *No. 2*, summer 1979.

Becker, G., *Human Capital*, Columbia University Press, 1964.

Beckerman, W., *The British Economy in 1975*, National Institute for Economic and Social Research, 1964.

Beckerman, W. (ed.), *The Labour Government's Economic Record 1964-70*, Duckworth, 1972.

Beenstock, M., 'Taxation and Incentives in the U.K.', *Lloyds Bank Review*, no. 134, Oct. 1979.

Beer, S.H., *Modern British Politics*, Faber, 1976.

Bell, D., *The Cultural Contradictions of Capitalism*, Heinemann, 1976.

Benn, C. and Simon, B., *Half-Way There*, McGraw-Hill, 1970.

Bennett, W.S., 'Educational Change and Economic Development', *Sociology of Education*, spring 1967.

Benson, W.J., 'London Clearing Banks' Evidence to the Wilson Committee', *National Westminster Bank Review*, May 1978.

Berg, I., *Education and Jobs: The Great Training Robbery*, Penguin, 1970.

Berry, F., *Housing, the Great British Failure*, Knight, 1974.

Berthoud, R., Brown, J.C. and Cooper, S., *Poverty and the Development of Anti-Poverty Policy in the U.K.*, Heinemann, 1981.

Beveridge, W., *The Pillars of Security*, Allen & Unwin, 1943.

Beveridge, W., *Full Employment in a Free Society*, Allen & Unwin, 1944.

Blake, D. and Ormerod, P., *The Economics of Prosperity*, McIntyre, 1980.

Blaug, M., *An Introduction to the Economics of Education*, Penguin, 1972.

Blaxter, M., 'Social Class and Health Inequalities', in C.O. Carter and J. Peel (eds), *Equalities and Inequalities in Health*, Academic Press, 1976.

Block, A., *Estimating Housing Needs*, Architectural Press, 1946.

Boaden, N., 'Local Authorities and Education', in J. Rayner and J. Harden (eds), *Equality and City Schools*, Routledge & Kegan Paul, 1973.

Bogdanor, V. and Skidelsky, R. (eds), *The Age of Affluence, 1951-64*, Macmillan, 1970.

Bosanquet, N. and Townsend, P., *Labour and Equality*, Heinemann, 1980.

Bouden, R., *Education, Opportunity and Social Inequality*, Wiley, 1973.

Bowles, S., 'Cuban Education and the Revolutionary Ideology', *Harvard Educational Review*, vol. 41, *No. 4*, Nov. 1971.

Bowles, S., 'Schooling and Inequality from Generation to Generation', *Journal of Political Economy*, vol. 80, *No. 1*, 1972.

Bowles, S. and Gintis, H., *Schooling in Capitalist America*, Routledge & Kegan Paul, 1976.

Bowles, S. and Gintis, H., 'The Problem of Human Capital Theory — A Marxian Critique', *The American Economic Review*, vol. LXV, *No. 2*, May 1975.

Bowman, M.J. and Anderson, C.A., 'Concerning the role of education in development', in C. Geertz (ed.), *Old Societies and New States*, Free Press, 1963.

Break, G.F., 'Income Taxes and Incentives to Work: An Empirical Study', *American Economic Review*, vol. XLVII, *No. 5*, Sept. 1957.

Briggs, A. and Saville, J. (eds), *Essays in Labour History 1918-1939*, Croom Helm, 1977.

Brittan, S., *Left or Right, The Bogus Dilemma*, Secker & Warburg, 1968.

Brittan, S., 'The Economic Contradictions of Democracy', *British Journal of Political Science*, vol. 5, *No. 1*, 1975.

Brotherston, J., 'Inequality — Is it Inevitable?', in C.O. Carter and J. Peel (eds), *Equalities and Inequalities in Health*, Academic Press, 1976.

Brown, C.V., 'Misconceptions about Income Tax and Incentives', *Scottish Journal of Political Economy*, vol. 15, Feb. 1968.

Brown, C.V., *Taxation and the Incentive to Work*, Oxford University Press, 1980.

Brown, C.V. and Dawson, O.A., 'Personal Taxation, Incentives and Tax Reform', *P.E.P. Broadsheet*, 506, 1969.

Brown, C.V. and Levin, E., 'The Effects of Taxation on Overtime: the results of a national survey', *Economic Journal*, 34, Dec. 1974.

Brown, C.V., Levin, E. and Ulph, D.T., 'Estimates of Labour Hours Supplied by Married Male Workers in Great Britain', *Scottish Journal of Political Economy*, vol. 23, Nov. 1976.

Brown, H.P., *The Inequality of Pay*, Oxford University Press, 1977.

Brown, R., 'Work', in P. Abrams (ed.), *Work, Urbanism and Inequality*, Weidenfeld & Nicolson, 1978.

Buchanan, J.M. and Wagner, R.E., *Democracy in Deficit*, Academic Press, 1977.

Bulmer, M. (ed.), *Social Policy Research*, Macmillan, 1978.

Burgess, G.J. and Webb, A.J., The Profits of British Industry, *Lloyds Bank Review*, no. 112, April 1974.

Burghes, L., 'Fact and Figures', *Poverty*, no. 51, April 1982.

Burke, G., *Housing and Social Justice*, Longman, 1981.

Burstall, C., 'Time to Mend the Nets: A commentary on the outcome of class-size research', *Trends in Education*, autumn 1979.

Burton, J., 'Employment Subsidies – the cases for and against', *National Westminster Bank Quarterly Review*, Feb. 1977.

Butler, J. et al., *Family Doctors and Public Policy*, Routledge & Kegan Paul, 1973.

Butler, J., *How Many Patients?*, Bedford Square Press, 1981.

Butler, D. and Kavanagh, D., *The British General Election of February 1974*, Macmillan, 1974.

Butler, D. and Kavanagh, D., *The British General Election of October 1974*, Macmillan, 1975.

Butler, D. and Kavanagh, D., *The British General Election of 1979*, Macmillan, 1980.

Butler, D. and Stokes, D., *Political Change in Britain*, Macmillan (2nd edn) 1974.

Butrym, Z., *The Nature of Social Work*, Macmillan, 1976.

Buxton, M., *Health and Inequality*, Open University Press, 1976.

Buxton, M. and Klein, R., 'Distribution of Hospital Provision: Policy Themes and Resources Variations', *British Medical Journal*, 8 Feb. 1975.

Byrne, D. and Williamson, W., 'The Case of the North East', in J. Rayner and J. Horden (eds), *Equality and City Schools*, Routledge & Kegan Paul, 1973.

Byrne, E., *Women and Education*, Tavistock, 1978.

Caim-Kaudle, P., 'A Cross-national Evaluation of Post-War European Social Policies' (a paper given to the Social Administration Association Conference, July 1980).

Cambridge Economic Policy Review, vol. 6, *No. 2*, July 1980.

Cameron, G.C., 'The National Industrial Strategy and Regional Policy', in D. MacLennan and J. Parr (eds), *Regional Policy*, Martin Robertson, 1979.

Carter, J., *Day Services for Adults*, Allen & Unwin, 1981.

Cartwright, A., *Human Relations and Hospital Care*, Routledge & Kegan Paul, 1964.

Cartwright, A., *Parents and Family Planning Services*, Routledge & Kegan Paul, 1970.

Cartwright, A. and O'Brien, M., 'Social Class Variations in Health Care', in M. Stacey (ed.), 'The Sociology of the National Health Service', *Sociological Review Monograph*, no. 22, 1976.

Churchill, W., *The Second World War*, vol. IV, Cassel, 1950.

Clark, M., 'The Unemployed on Supplementary Benefit', *Journal of Social Policy*, vol. 7, part 4, Oct. 1978.

Cole, W.J., 'The Financing of the Individual Striker: a case study in the building industry', *British Journal of Industrial Relations*, vol. XIII, *No. 1*, March 1975.

College of General Practitioners, 'Evidence to the Royal Commission on the NHS', *Journal of the Royal College of General Practitioners*, April 1977.

Collins, E. and Klein, R., 'Equity and the NHS: self-reported morbidity, access and primary care', *British Medical Journal*, vol. 281, 25 Oct. 1980.

Collins, R., *The Credential Society*, Academic Press, 1979.

Commission of the European Communities, *The Perception of Poverty in Europe*, 1977.

Conference of Socialist Economists, *Struggle Over the State*, CSE Books, 1979.

Conference of Socialist Economists, *The Alternative Economic Strategy*, Blackrose Press, 1980.

Connerton, P. (ed.), *Critical Sociology*, Penguin, 1976.

Cooper, M. and Culyer, A., 'Health Services Financing', *British Medical Association*, 1970.

Corrigan, P. and Leonard, P., *Social Work Practice Under Capitalism*, Macmillan, 1978.

Cosin, B.R. (ed.), *Education, Structure and Society*, Penguin, 1972.

Cox, C.B. and Boyson, R. (eds), *Black Paper 1975*, Dent, 1975.

Craig, C. and Wedderburn, D., 'Relative Deprivation at Work', in D. Wedderburn (ed.), *Poverty, Inequality and Class Structure*, Cambridge University Press, 1974.

Crewe, I. et al., 'Partisan Dealignment in Britain 1964-1974', *British Journal of Political Science*, vol. 7, *No. 2*, 1977.

Crosland, C.A.R., *The Future of Socialism*, Cape, 1956.

Crosland, C.A.R., 'A Social Democratic Britain', *Fabian Tract 404*, Fabian Society, 1970.

Crough, C. (ed.), *State and Economy in Late Capitalism*, Croom Helm, 1979.

Crozier, M. et al., *The Crisis of Democracy*, New York University Press, 1975.

Curtis, S.J., *History of Education in Great Britain*, University Tutorial Press, 1948.

Dahrendorf, R., 'Effectiveness and Legitimacy: on the Governability of Democracies', *Political Quarterly*, vol. 51, *No. 4*, 1980.

Dale, R. et al., *Schooling and Capitalism*, Routledge & Kegan Paul/Open University, 1976.

Daniel, W.W., 'A National Survey of the Unemployed', *P.E.P. Broadsheet*, no. 546, 1974.

Davie, R., Butler, N. and Goldstein, H., *From Birth to Seven*, Longman, 1958.

Davies, B., *Social Needs and Resources in Local Services*, Joseph, 1968.

Davies, B., *Social Control and Education*, Methuen, 1976.

Davies, B. and Knapp, M., *Old People's Homes and the Production of Welfare*, Routledge & Kegan Paul, 1981.

Deacon, A., 'The Scrounging Controversy: Public Attitudes Towards the Unemployed in Contemporary Britain', *Social and Economic Administration*, vol. 12, *No. 2*, summer 1978.

Deem, R., *Women and Schooling*, Routledge & Kegan Paul, 1978.

Delcourt, J., 'Social Policy – Crisis or Mutation?', *Labour and Society*, vol. 7, *No. 1*, Jan.-March 1982.

Denison, E., 'Measuring the contribution of education (and the residual) to economic growth', in OECD, *The Residual Factor and Economic Growth*, Paris, 1964.

Denison, E., *The Sources of Economic Growth in the United States*, New York Committee for Economic Development, 1962.

Denison, E., *Why Growth Rates Differ*, The Brookings Institute, 1967.

Denison, G., 'Financial Assistance in British Industry', in W.M. Corden and G. Fels, *Public Assistance in Industry*, Macmillan, 1976.

Denitch, B. (ed.), *Legitimation of Regimes*, Sage, 1979.

Denton, G., 'Financial Assistance to British Industry', in Corden, W.M. and Fels, G., *Public Assistance to Industry*, Macmillan, 1976.

Disney, R., 'Theorising the Welfare State: the case of unemployment insurance in Britain', *Journal of Social Policy*, vol. 11, *No. 1*, 1982.

Ditch, N., 'Northern Ireland', *Roof*, March-April 1981.

Donnison, D., *The Government of Housing*, Penguin, 1967.

Donnison, D., 'Social Policy Since Titmuss', *Journal of Social Policy*, vol. 8,

No. 2, 1979.

Donnison, D., *The Politics of Poverty*, Robertson, 1982.

Donnison, D. and Ungerson, C., *Housing Policy*, Penguin, 1982.

Douglas, J., 'The Overloaded Crown', *British Journal of Political Science*, vol. 6, *No. 4*, 1976.

Douglas, J.W.B., *The Home and the School*, Panther, 1967.

Doyal, L., *The Political Economy of Health*, Pluto, 1979.

Duncan, W. and McCarthy, W.E.J., 'The State Subsidy Theory of Strikes', *British Journal of Industrial Relations*, vol. XII, *No. 1*, March 1974.

Dunford, M., Geddes, M. and Perrons, D., 'Regional Policy and the Crisis in the U.K.', *International Journal of Urban and Regional Research*, vol. 5, *No. 3*, Sept. 1981.

Durbin, E.F.M., *The Politics of Democratic Socialism: An Essay on Social Policy*, The Labour Book Service, 1940.

Education Group, Centre for Contemporary Cultural Studies, University of Birmingham, *Unpopular Education*, Hutchinson, 1981.

Ehman, L.H., 'The School in the Political Socialisation Process', *Review of Educational Research*, vol. 50, *No. 1*, 1980.

Ehrenreich, J. (ed.), *The Cultural Crisis of Modern Medicine*, Monthly Review Press, 1978.

Eldridge, J.E.T., *Explanations of Strikes: a Critical Review in Industrial Disputes*, Routledge & Kegan Paul, 1968.

English, J. (ed.), *The Future of Council Housing*, Croom Helm, 1982.

Epstein, S., *The Politics of Cancer*, Anchor/Doubleday, 1980.

Falush, P., 'The Changing Pattern of Savings', *National Westminster Bank Quarterly Review*, Aug. 1978.

Fein, R., 'On measuring economic benefits of health care programmes', in Nuffield Provincial Hospitals' Trust, *Medical History and Medical Care*, Oxford University Press, 1971.

Ferguson, T. and Macpheal, A., *Hospital and Community*, Oxford University Press, 1954.

Fiegehen, G. et. al., *Poverty and Progress in Britain, 1953-1973*, Cambridge University Press, 1977.

Field, F., Meacher, M. and Pond, C., *To Him Who Hath: A study of poverty and taxation*, Penguin, 1977.

Fields, D.B. and Stanbury, W.T., 'Income Taxes and Incentives to Work: Some Additional Empirical Evidence', *American Economic Review*, vol. 61, June 1971.

Finch, J. and Groves, D., 'Community Care and the Family: A Case for Equal Opportunities', *Journal of Social Policy*, vol. 9, *Part 4*, 1980.

Flora, P. and Heidenheimer, A.J., *The Development of Welfare States in Europe and America*, Transaction Books, 1981.

Fogelman, K. (ed.), *Britain's Sixteen-Year-Olds*, National Children's Bureau, 1976.

Forster, D.P., 'Social Class Differences in Sickness and General Practitioner Consultations', *Health Trends*, no. 8, 1976.

Franey, R., 'Apart from the Law', *Roof*, Nov.-Dec. 1980.

Gennard, J., *Financing Strikes*, Macmillan, 1977.

Gennard, J. and Lasko, R., 'Supplementary Benefit and Strikers', *British Journal of Industrial Relations*, vol. XII, *No. 1*, March 1974.

Gennard, J. and Lasko, R., 'The Individual and the Strike', *British Journal of Industrial Relations*, vol. XIII, *No. 3*, Nov. 1975.

George, V., *Social Security and Society*, Routledge & Kegan Paul, 1973.

George, V. and Wilding, P., *Motherless Families*, Routledge & Kegan Paul, 1972.

George, V. and Wilding, P., *Ideology and Social Welfare*, Routledge & Kegan Paul, 1976.

Gibbons, J., 'The Mentally Ill', in P. Brearley et al., *The Social Context of Health Care*, Martin Robertson and Basil Blackwell, 1978.

Gill, D., *Unravelling Social Policy*, Schenkman, 1973.

Ginsberg, E., *The Development of Human Resources*, McGraw-Hill, 1966.

Glyn, A. and Sutcliffe, B., *British Capitalism, Workers and the Profit Squeeze*, Penguin, 1972.

Godfrey, L., *Theoretical and Empirical Aspects of the Effects of Taxation on the Supply of Labour*, OECD, 1975.

Golding, P. and Middleton, S., *Images of Welfare*, Martin Robertson, 1982.

Goldthorpe, J.H., *Social Mobility and Class Structure in Modern Britain*, Clarendon Press, 1980.

Goldthorpe, J.H. and Hirsch, F. (eds), *The Political Economy of Inflation*, Martin Robertson, 1978.

Gorman, T.P., 'A Survey of Attainment and Progress of Learners in Adult Literacy Schemes', *Educational Research*, vol. 23, *No. 3*, June 1981.

Gough, I., *The Political Economy of the Welfare State*, Macmillan, 1979.

Graham, H., 'Women's Attitudes to the Child Health Services', *Health Visitor*, vol. 52, May 1979.

Greve, J., Page, D. and Greve, S., *Homelessness in London*, Scottish Academic Press, 1971.

Gujarati, D., 'The Behaviour of Unemployment and Unfilled Vacancies, Great Britain, 1958-1971', *Economic Journal*, vol. 82, 1972.

Gwyn, W.B. and Rose, R., *Britain – Progress and Decline*, Macmillan, 1980.

Habermas, J., *Legitimation Crisis*, Beacon Press, 1975.

Habermas, J., 'Conservatism and the Capitalist Crisis', *New Left Review*, 115, 1978.

Hadley, R. and Hatch, S., *Social Welfare and the Failure of the State*, Allen & Unwin, 1981.

Hall, P., Land, H., Parker, R. and Webb, A., *Change, Choice and Conflict in Social Policy*, Heinemann, 1975.

Hall, R., 'Effects of the experimental NIT on Labor Supply', in J. Pechman and P. Timpane, *Work Incentives and Income Guarantees: The New Jersey Income Tax Experiment*, The Brookings Institute, 1975.

Halsey, A., Heath, A. and Judge, J., *Origins and Destinations*, Clarendon Press, 1980.

Hambleton, R. and Scerri, V., 'Three Views in Need', *New Society*, 18 Oct. 1973.

Hamnet, C., *Inequalities in Housing*, Open University Press, 1976.

Handler, J., 'The Coercive Children's Officer', *New Society*, 3 Oct. 1968.

Harbison, F.H. and Myers, C.A., *Education, Manpower and Economic Growth*, McGraw-Hill, 1964.

Harris, J., *William Beveridge*, Clarendon Press, 1977.

Harris, R. and Seldon, A., *Over-Ruled on Welfare*, IEA, 1979.

Harris, T., 'The Role of Public Spending', in D. Blake and P. Omerod, *The Economics of Prosperity*, McIntyre, 1980.

Hart, J.T., 'The Inverse Care Law', in C. Cox and A. Mead (eds), *A Sociology of Medical Practice*, Collier-Macmillan, 1975.

Haverman, R. and Watts, H., 'Social Experimentation as Policy Research: a Review of Negative Income Tax Experiments', in V. Halberstadt and A. Culyer (eds), *Public Economics and Human Resources*, Cujas, 1977.

Hay, J.R., *The Origins of the Liberal Welfare Reforms 1906-1914*, Macmillan, 1975.

Hayek, F.A., *The Road to Serfdom*, Routledge & Kegan Paul, 1944.
Hayek, F.A., *The Constitution of Liberty*, Routledge & Kegan Paul, 1960.
Henderson, D.W., *Social Indicators*, Economic Council of Canada, 1974.
Hess, R.D. and Torney, J.V., *The Development of Political Attitudes in Children*, Aldine, 1967.
Hibbs, D.A. (Jr), 'On the Political Economy of Long-Run Trends in Strike Activity', *British Journal of Political Science*, vol. 8, *No. 2*, April 1978.
Hill, M., 'Can we distinguish voluntary from involuntary unemployment?', in G. Worswick (ed.), *The Concept and Measurement of Involuntary Unemployment*, Allen & Unwin, 1976.
Hill, M.J. et al., *Men Out of Work*, Cambridge University Press, 1973.
Hirsch, F., *Social Limits to Growth*, Routledge & Kegan Paul, 1977.
Hogg, Q., *The Case for Conservatism*, Penguin, 1947.
Hopkins, A., *The School Debate*, Penguin, 1978.
Howe, Sir G., *Parliamentary Debates*, 5th series, vol. 968.
Howick, C. and Hassani, H., 'Education Spending: Primary', *Centre for Environmental Studies Review*, Jan. 1979.
Howick, C. and Hassani, H., 'Education Spending: Secondary', *Centre for Environmental Studies Review*, Jan. 1980.
Hunt, A., *The Elderly at Home*, HMSO, 1978.
Hunt, J. and Heyes, L., *Housing the Disabled*, Torfaen Borough Council, 1980.
Hunt, J.S., *Education in Evolution*, Hart Davies, 1971.
Hyman, R., *Strikes*, Fontana, 1975.
Illich, I., *Deschooling Society*, Harper & Row, 1971.
Illich, I., *Medical Nemesis*, Calder & Boyars, 1975.
Institute of Economic Affairs, *Tax Evasion*, 1979.
Irvine, J., Miles, I. and Evans, J., *Demystifying Social Statistics*, Pluto Press, 1979.
Jencks, C., *Who Gets Ahead?*, Basic Books, 1979.
Jencks, C. et al., *Inequality: a Reassessment*, Basic Books, 1972.
Jencks, C. et al., *Inequality*, Penguin, 1975.
Jewkes, J. and S., *Value for Money in Medicine*, Blackwell, 1963.
Johnson, J.H. and Salt, J., 'Employment Transfer Policies in Great Britain', *Three Banks' Review*, no. 126, June 1980.
Johnson, R., 'Educational Policy and Social Control in Early Victorian England', *Past and Present*, 49, Nov. 1970.
Jones, I. (ed.), *Health Service Financing*, British Medical Association, 1970.
Jones, K., Brown, J. and Bradshaw, J., *Issues in Social Policy*, Routledge & Kegan Paul, 1978.
Jordan, B., *Freedom in the Welfare State*, Routledge & Kegan Paul, 1976.
Judge, K., 'Territorial Justice and Local Autonomy', *Policy and Politics*, vol. 3, *No. 4*, June 1975.
Karabel, J. and Halsey, A.H., *Power and Ideology in Education*, Oxford University Press, 1977.
Kay, J.A., Morris, C.N. and Warren, N.A., 'Tax, Benefits and Incentive to Seek Work', *Fiscal Studies*, vol. 1, *No. 4*, Nov. 1980.
Kelsall, R., Poole, A. and Kuhn, A., *The Sociology of an Elite*, Tavistock, 1972.
Kettle, M. and Lawsley, S., 'The New Poverty Line: the necessities that millions are having to go without', *Sunday Times*, 21 Aug. 1983.
Kiker, B.F., 'The Historical Roots of the Concept of Human Capital', *Journal of Political Economy*, vol. LXXIV, Oct. 1966.
Kincaid, J.C., *Poverty and Equality in Britain*, Penguin, 1973.
King, A., 'Overload: Problems of Governing in the 1970s', *Political Studies*, vol. XXIII, *Nos 2 and 3*, 1975.
King, A., *Why is Britain Becoming Harder to Govern?*, BBC, 1976.

Klein, R., 'The Case for Elitism: Public Opinion and Public Policy', *Political Quarterly*, vol. 45, *No. 4*, 1974.

Klein, R. et al., *Constraints and Choices*, Centre for Studies in Social Policy, 1976.

Klein, R., 'The Welfare State: a Self-Inflicted Crisis', *Political Quarterly*, vol. 51, *No. 1*, Jan.-March 1980.

Lambert, J., Blackaby, B. and Paris, C., *Neighbourhood Politics and Housing Opportunities*, C.E.S., 1975.

Landes, D.S., *The Unbound Prometheus*, Cambridge University Press, 1969.

Lansley, S., *Housing and Public Policy*, Croom Helm, 1979.

Larkey, D., Stolp, C. and Winer, M., 'Theorising About the Growth of Government', *Journal of Public Policy*, vol. 1, *No. 2*, May 1981.

Leeson, J. and Gray, J., *Women and Medicine*, Tavistock, 1978.

Le Grand, J., *The Strategy of Equality*, Allen & Unwin, 1982.

Litt, E., 'Civic Education, Community Norms and Political Indoctrination', *American Sociological Review*, vol. 28, *No. 1*, 1963.

Lipset, S.M., *Political Man*, Doubleday, 1960.

London Edinburgh Weekend Return Group, *In and Against the State*, Pluto, 1980.

Los, M., 'The Concept of Justice and Welfare Rights', *The Journal of Social Welfare Law*, Jan. 1982.

Mabey, C., 'Black British Literacy: A Study of Reading Attainment of London Black Children from 8 to 15 years', *Educational Research*, vol. 23, *No. 2*, Feb. 1981.

McCallum, D., 'The Development of British Regional Policy', in D. MacLennan and J.B. Parr, *Regional Policy*, Martin Robertson, 1979.

McCrone, G., *Regional Policy in Britain*, Allen & Unwin, 1969.

MacGregor, S., *The Politics of Poverty*, Longman, 1981.

Mackay, D. and Reid, G., 'Redundancy, Unemployment and Manpower Policy', *Economic Journal*, vol. 82, 1972.

Mackintosh, J.M., 'Has Social Democracy Failed in Britain?', *Political Quarterly*, vol. 49, *No. 3*, 1978.

McLean, M. and Jeffreys, M., 'Disability and Deprivation', in D. Wedderburn, *Poverty, Inequality and Class Structure*, Cambridge University Press, 1974.

Maki, D. and Spindler, Z.A., 'The Effect of Unemployment Compensation on the Rate of Unemployment in Great Britain', *Oxford Economic Papers*, 27, 1975.

Malenbaum, W., 'Health and Productivity in Poor Areas', in H.E. Klarman (ed.), *Empirical Studies in Health Economics*, Johns Hopkins Press, 1970.

Mann, M., 'The Social Cohesion of Liberal Democracy', *American Sociological Review*, vol. 35, no. 4, 1970.

Marshall, A., *Principles of Economics*, 1980.

Marshall, T.H., *Sociology at the Crossroads and Other Essays*, Heinemann, 1963.

Massialas, B.G., *Education and the Political System*, Addison Wesley, 1969.

Mathews, J., 'The Politics of Cancer', *Marxism Today*, May 1981.

Mathews, R. and Leather, P., 'Housing in England', *Roof*, May-June 1982.

Maynard, A. and Ludbrook, A., 'Budget Allocation in the National Health Service', *Journal of Social Policy*, vol. 9, *No. 3*, July 1980.

Meade, J.E., *The Structure and Reform of Direct Taxation*, Report of the Committee chaired by Professor J.E. Meade, Allen & Unwin, 1978.

Merelman, R.M. 'The Adolescence of Political Socialisation', *Sociology of Education*, vol. 45, *No. 1*, 1972.

Merelman, R.M., 'Social Stratification and Political Socialisation in Mature

Industrial Societies', *Comparative Education Review*, vol. 19, *No. 1*, 1975.

Middlemas, K., *Politics in Industrial Society*, Deutsch, 1979.

Midwinter, E., 'Education', in F. Williams (ed.), *Why the Poor Pay More*, Macmillan, 1977.

Miliband, R., *The State in Capitalist Society*, Quartet, 1973.

Miller, W.L., 'Education as a Source of Economic Growth', *Journal of Economic Issues*, Dec. 1967.

Mills, C. Wright, 'The Professional Ideology of Social Pathologists', *American Journal of Sociology*, vol. 49, *No. 2*, 1943.

Mishra, R., *Society and Social Policy*, Macmillan, 1977.

Mishra, R., *Society and Social Policy*, Macmillan (2nd edn), 1981.

Mittler, P., *People not Patients*, Methuen, 1979.

Moore, B. and Rhodes, J., 'Evaluating the Effects of British Regional Economic Policy', *The Economic Journal*, vol. 83, March 1973.

Moore, B., Rhodes, J. and Tyler, P., 'The Impact of Regional Policy in the 1970s', *Centre for Environmental Studies Review*, no. 1, July 1977.

Morgan, W. et al., 'Casual Attenders', *Hospital and Health Services Review*, vol. 70, 1974.

Moscovitch, A. and Drover, G., *Inequality: Essays on the Political Economy of Social Welfare*, University of Toronto Press, 1981.

Moylan, S. and Davies, B., 'The Disadvantages of the Unemployed', *Employment Gazette*, vol. 88, *No. 8*, Aug. 1980.

Moylan, S. and Davies, B., 'The Flexibility of the Unemployed', *Employment Gazette*, vol. 89, *No. 1*, Jan. 1981.

Mushkin, S.J., 'Health as Investment', in M.H. Cooper and A.J. Culyer (eds), *Health Economics*, Penguin, 1973.

Myrdal, G., 'The Relation Between Social Theory and Social Policy', *British Journal of Sociology*, vol. IV, Sept. 1953.

Navarro, V., *Medicine Under Capitalism*, Prodist/Croom Helm, 1976.

Navarro, V., *Class Struggle, the State and Medicine*, Martin Robertson, 1979.

Newman, K.J., 'International Comparison of Taxes and Social Security Contributions, 1971-8', *Economic Trends*, no. 326, Dec. 1980.

Nicholson, J.C., 'The Assessment of Poverty and the Information We Need', in DHSS, *Social Security Research*, HMSO, 1979.

Nickell, S.J., 'The Effects of Unemployment and Related Benefits on the Duration of Unemployment', *Economic Journal*, vol. 89, 1979.

Norman, A.J., *Right and Risk*, National Corporation for the Care of Old People, 1980.

Noyce, J., Snaith, A. and Trickey, A., 'Regional variations in the allocation of financial resources to the community health services', *The Lancet*, 30 March 1974.

O'Connor, J., *The Fiscal Crisis of the State*, St Martin's Press, 1973.

Offe, C., 'Advanced Capitalism and the Welfare State', *Politics and Society*, vol. 2, *No. 4*, 1972.

Offe, C., 'The Separation of Form and Content in Liberal Democratic Politics', *Studies in Political Economy*, 3, 1980.

Offe, C., *Competitive Party Democracy and the Welfare State*, Mimeo, 1981.

Offe, C., 'Some Contradictions of the Modern Welfare State', *Critical Social Policy*, vol. 2, *No. 2*, 1982.

O'Higgins, M., 'Tax Evasion and the Self-Employed: an Examination of the Evidence, II', *British Tax Review*, no. 6, 1981.

Ormandy, D., 'Housing Standards', *Roof*, Jan.-Feb. 1982.

Parker, S., 'Assisted Labour Migration', OPCS, 1975, quoted in J.H. Johnson and J. Salt, 'Employment Transfer Policies in Great Britain', *The Three Banks'*

Review, June 1980.

Parker, S.R. et al., *Effects of the Redundancy Payments Act*, OPCS, 1971.

Parkin, F., *Class Inequality and Political Order*, MacGibbon & Key, 1971.

Parsons, T. and Smelser, N.J., *Economy and Society*, Routledge & Kegan Paul, 1956.

Peaslee, A.L., 'Education's Role in Development', *Economic Development and Cultural Change*, vol. 17, *No. 1*, Oct. 1968.

P.E.P., 'Planning', *Medical Care for Children*, no. 222, 30 June 1944.

Piachaud, D., *The Cost of a Child: A Modern Minimum*, Child Poverty Action Group, 1979.

Pinker, R., *Social Theory and Social Policy*, Heinemann, 1971.

Piven, F. and Cloward, R.A., *Regulating the Poor*, Tavistock, 1972.

Plant, R., *Social and Moral Theory in Casework*, Routledge & Kegan Paul, 1970.

Popper, K., *The Logic of Scientific Discovery*, Hutchinson, 1959.

Pritchard, C. and Taylor, R., *Social Work: Reform or Revolution?*, Routledge & Kegan Paul, 1978.

Psacharopoulos, G., 'Family Background, Education and Achievement', *British Journal of Sociology*, vol. 28, *No. 3*, Sept. 1977.

Rawls, J., *A Theory of Justice*, Oxford University Press, 1972.

Rees, R.D. and Miall, R.H.C., 'The Effect of Regional Policy on Manufacturing Investment and Capital Stock Within the U.K. between 1959 and 1978', *Regional Studies*, vol. 15, *No. 6*, 1981.

Rein, M., *Social Science and Public Policy*, Penguin, 1976.

Rigby, P., Office of Population and Censuses and Surveys, *Hostels and Lodgings for Single People*, HMSO, 1976.

Ritchie, J., Jacoby, A. and Bone, M., *Access to Primary Health Care*, Office of Population and Censuses and Surveys, 1981.

Ritchie, J. and Wilson, P., *Social Security Claimants*, Office of Population and Censuses and Surveys, 1979.

Room, G., *The Sociology of Welfare*, Martin Robertson, 1979.

Rose, R., 'Ungovernability: Is there fire behind the smoke?', *Political Studies*, vol. XXVII, *No. 3*, 1979.

Rose, R. (ed.), *Challenge to Governance*, Sage, 1980.

Rose, R., 'What, If Anything, is Wrong with Big Government?', *Journal of Public Policy*, vol. 1, *No. 1*, 1981.

Rose, R. and Peters, G., *Can Governments Go Bankrupt?*, Macmillan, 1979.

Ross, A.M. and Hartman, P.T., *Changing Patterns of Industrial Conflict*, Wiley, 1960.

Ross, A.M. and Hartman, P.T., *Industrial Disputes: Essays in the Sociology of Industrial Relations*, Routledge & Kegan Paul, 1968.

Routh, G., *Occupation and Pay in Great Britain, 1906-1979*, Macmillan, 1979.

Rutter, M. et al., *Fifteen Thousand Hours*, Open Books, 1979.

Salt, J., 'Labour Migration, Housing and the Labour Market', in A. Evans and D. Eversley (eds), *The Inner City, Employment and Industry*, Heinemann, 1980.

Sawyer, M.C., 'The Effects of Unemployment Compensation on the Rate of Unemployment in Great Britain – A Comment', *Oxford Economic Papers*, 31, 1979.

Schultz, Th., 'Investment in Human Capital', *American Economic Review*, vol. 51, March 1961.

Senat, J., *Habermas and Marxism*, Sage, 1979.

Sharpe, R. and Green, A., *Education and Social Control*, Routledge & Kegan Paul, 1975.

Sharpe, S., *Just Like a Girl*, Penguin, 1976.

Bibliography

Shelter, *And I'll Blow Your House Down*, 1980.

Sheriff, T., *A De-industrialised Britain*, Fabian Publications, 1979.

Shipman, M.D., *Education and Modernisation*, Faber, 1971.

Shipman, M.D., *The Limitations of Social Research*, Longman, 1972.

Shonfield, I. and Shaw, S. (eds), *Social Indicators and Social Policy*, Heinemann, 1972.

Showler, B., *The Public Employment Service*, Longman, 1976.

Showler, B., 'Incentives, Social Security Payments and Unemployment', *Social and Economic Administration*, vol. 9, *No. 2*, summer 1978.

Simey, T.S., *Social Science and Social Purpose*, Constable, 1968.

Simon, B., *Studies in the History of Education*, Lawrence & Wishart, 1960.

Simpkin, M., *Trapped Within Welfare*, Macmillan, 1979.

Simpson, R., *Access to Primary Care*, Royal Commission on the National Health Service, Research paper no. 6, HMSO, 1979.

Skidelsky, R. (ed.), *The End of the Keynesian Era*, Macmillan, 1977.

Sleeman, J.F., *Resources for the Welfare State*, Longman, 1979.

Smith, A., *The Wealth of Nations*, Encyclopaedia Britannica edn, 1952.

Sorel, I., 'The Human Capital Revolution in Economic Development: its Current History and Status', *Comparative Education Review*, vol. 22, *No. 2*, June 1978.

Stonier, T., 'A Little Learning is a Lucrative Thing', *The Times Higher Education Supplement*, 1 May 1981.

Stuart Maclure, J. (ed.), *Educational Documents, England and Wales, 1816-1963*, Methuen, 1965.

Tapper, T. and Salter, B., *Education and the Political Order*, Macmillan, 1978.

Tarschys, D., 'The Growth of Public Expenditure: Nine Models of Explanation', *Scandinavian Political Studies*, vol. 10, 1975.

Taubman, P. and Wales, T., 'Higher Education, Mental Ability and Screening', *Journal of Political Economy*, vol. 81, *No. 1*, Jan. 1973.

Tawney, R.H., *Equality*, Allen & Unwin, 1964.

Taylor, J., 'The Behaviour of Unemployment and Unfilled Vacancies in Great Britain 1958-1971: An Alternative View', *Economic Journal*, 1972.

Taylor-Gooby, P., 'Mosaic to Kaleidoscope: the pattern of public opinion about legitimation issues in the welfare state', *Sociology*, May 1983, vol. 17, no. 2, pp. 165-84.

Thane, P., *Foundations of the Welfare State*, Longman, 1982.

Thieblot, A.J. (Jr) and Cowin, R.M., *Welfare and Strikes*, University of Pennsylvania, 1972.

Thirlwall, A.P., 'The U.K.'s Economic Problem: a Balance of Payments Constraint?', *National Westminster Bank Quarterly Review*, Feb. 1978.

Thirlwall, A.P., 'De-industrialisation in the United Kingdom', *Lloyds Bank Review*, no. 144, April 1982.

Timms, N. and Watson, D. (eds), *Philosophy in Social Work*, Routledge & Kegan Paul, 1978.

Titmuss, R.M., *The Gift Relationship*, Allen & Unwin, 1970.

Todd, J.E. and Walker, A.M., *Adult Dental Health, 1968-1978*, DPLS, 1980.

Topper, T. and Salter, B., *Education and the Political Order*, Macmillan, 1978.

Townsend, P., 'The Timid and the Bold', *New Society*, vol. 1, *No. 34*, May 1962.

Townsend, P., *Poverty in the United Kingdom*, Penguin, 1979.

Townsend, P. and Wedderburn, D., *The Aged in the Welfare State*, Bell, 1965.

Treasure, J., 'The Toll our Taxes Take', *The Times*, 12 Jan. 1968.

Usher, D., *The Economic Prerequisite to Democracy*, Blackwell, 1981.

Walker, A., 'Community Care and the Elderly in Great Britain: Theory and Practice', *International Journal of Health Services*, vol. 11, *No. 4*, 1981.

Walker, C. and Church, M., 'Poverty by Administrations: a Review of Supplementary Benefits, Nutrition and Scale Rates', *Journal of Human Nutrition*,
vol. 32, *No. 1*, 1978.

Walters, P.B., 'Educational Change and National Economic Development',
Harvard Educational Review, vol. 51, *No. 1*, Feb. 1981.

Walters, V., *Class, Inequality and Health Care*, Croom Helm, 1980.

Webb, A. and Falk, N., 'Planning the Social Services: The Local Authority Ten
Year Plans', *Policy and Politics*, vol. 3, *No. 2*, Dec. 1974.

Webster, B. and Stewart, J., 'The Area Analysis of Resources', *Policy and Politics*,
vol. 3, *No. 1*, Sept. 1974.

Weisbrod, B.A. et al., *Disease and Economic Development*, The University of
Wisconsin Press, 1973.

West, E.G., *Education and the Industrial Revolution*, Batsford, 1975.

West, R. and Lowe, C., 'Regional variations in need for and provision and use of
child health services in England and Wales', *British Medical Journal*, 9 Oct.
1976.

Whelan, E. and Speake, B., *Adult Training Centres in England and Wales*,
University of Manchester, 1977.

Whiteley, P., 'Public Opinion and the Demand for Social Welfare in Britain',
Journal of Social Policy, vol. 10, *No. 4*, 1981.

Wicks, M., *Old and Cold: Hypothermia and Social Policy*, Heinemann, 1978.

Wilensky, H.L., *The Welfare State and Equality*, University of California Press,
1975.

Williams, S., *Politics is for People*, Penguin, 1981.

Wolfe, A., *The Limits of Legitimacy*, Free Press, 1977.

Woolf, M., *The Housing Survey in England and Wales*, HMSO, 1964.

Wright, M. (ed.), *Public Spending Decisions*, Allen & Unwin, 1980.

Wright, N., *Progress in Education*, Croom Helm, 1977.

Zeigler, H. and Peak, W., 'The Political Functions of the Educational System',
Sociology of Education, vol. 43, *No. 1*, 1970.

Government publications/papers

Board of Education, *Educational Reconstruction*, Cmd 6458, HMSO, 1943.

Board of Inland Revenue, 120th Report, Cmnd 7092, HMSO, 1978.

Central Advisory Council for Education, *Early Leaving*, HMSO, 1954.

Central Housing Advisory Committee, Report, *Council Housing Purposes,
Procedures and Priorities*, HMSO, 1969.

Central Statistical Office, *Local Trends, Annual Reports*, HMSO.

Central Statistical Office, *Social Trends, Annual Reports*, HMSO.

Committee on Abuse of Social Security Benefits, Report, Cmnd 5228, HMSO,
1973.

Committee on the Economic and Financial Problems of the Provision for Old Age,
Report, Cmd 9333, HMSO, 1954.

Committee on Higher Education, Report, Cmnd 2154, HMSO, 1963.

Committee on Local Authority and Allied Personal Social Services, Report,
Cmnd 3703, HMSO, 1968.

Committee on Manpower Resources for Science and Technology, *The Brain
Drain*, Report of the Working Group on Migration, Cmnd 3417, HMSO, 1967.

Committee to Review the Functioning of Financial Institutions, Report and
Appendices, Cmnd 7937, HMSO.

Department of Education and Science, *Children and their Primary Schools*,
vol. 1, HMSO, 1967.

Department of Education and Science, *Statistics of Education, 1970, Vol. 1*, HMSO, 1971.

Department of Education and Science, *A Language for Life*, HMSO, 1975.

Department of Education and Science, *A Study of School Building*, HMSO, 1977.

Department of Education and Science, *Primary Education in England*, HMSO, 1978.

Department of Education and Science, *Aspects of Secondary Education in England*, HMSO, 1979.

Department of Education and Science, *Statistics of Education, 1979, Vol. 1*, HMSO, 1981.

Department of Employment, 'Characteristics of the Unemployed, Sample Survey, June 1973', *Department of Employment Gazette*, March 1974.

Department of Employment, *New Earnings Survey, 1976*, part A, Report and key results, HMSO, 1976.

Department of Employment, The Changed Relationship Between Unemployment and Vacancies, *Department of Employment Gazette*, Oct. 1976.

Department of Employment, Key Results of the New Earnings Survey, 1979, *Department of Employment Gazette*, Oct. 1979.

Department of Employment/DHSS, Report of the Joint Department, Rayner Scrutiny, *Payment of Benefits to Unemployed People*, HMSO, 1981.

Department of the Environment, *English Housing Conditions Survey, 1976*, HMSO, 1978.

Department of the Environment, *Housing Policy: A Consultative Document*, Cmd 6851, HMSO, 1977.

Department of the Environment, *Housing Policy*, Technical vol. II, HMSO, 1977.

Department of the Environment, *National Dwelling and Housing Survey*, HMSO, 1979.

Department of the Environment, 'Whose Featherbed?', *New Society*, 4 June 1981.

Department of Health and Social Security, *Health and Welfare: The Development of Community Care*, Cmnd 3022, HMSO, 1966.

Department of Health and Social Security, *Better Services for the Mentally Handicapped*, Cmnd 4683, HMSO, 1971.

Department of Health and Social Security, *Report of the Committee on One-Parent Families*, Cmnd 5629, HMSO, 1974.

Department of Health and Social Security, *Two-Parent Families Receiving FIS in 1972*, HMSO, 1975.

Department of Health and Social Security, *Priorities for Health and Personal Social Services in England*, HMSO, 1976.

Department of Health and Social Security, *Sharing Resources for Health in England*, Resource Allocation Working Party, HMSO, 1976.

Department of Health and Social Security, *The Way Forward*, HMSO, 1977.

Department of Health and Social Security, *Report of the Committee of Enquiry into Normansfield Hospital*, Cmnd 7357, HMSO, 1978.

Department of Health and Social Security, *Report of the Committee of Enquiry into the Pay and Related Conditions of the Professions Supplementary to Medicine*, HMSO, 1978.

Department of Health and Social Security, *Report of the Committee of Enquiry into Mental Handicap Nursing Care*, Cmnd 7468, HMSO, 1979.

Department of Health and Social Security, Residential Care for the Elderly in London, *Social Work Service*, HMSO, 1979.

Department of Health and Social Security, *Fatherless Families on FIS*, HMSO, 1979.

Department of Health and Social Security, *Income During Sickness: A New Strategy*, Cmnd 7864, HMSO, 1980.

Department of Health and Social Security, *Development Team for the Mentally Handicapped, Second Report 1978-79*, HMSO, 1980 (Jay Report).

Department of Health and Social Security, *Inequalities in Health*, Report of a Research Working Group (referred to as the Black Report), HMSO, 1980.

Department of Health and Social Security, *Primary Health Care in London*, Report of a Study Group, HMSO, 1981.

Department of Health and Social Security, *Report of a Study on Community Care*, HMSO, 1981.

Government's Expenditure Plans 1980-1, Cmnd 7746, HMSO, 1979.

House of Commons, *Second Report from the Social Services Committee, 1981-82, Vol. II*, House of Commons Paper 306-II, HMSO, 1982.

Minister of Reconstruction, *Social Insurance, Part I*, Cmd 6550, HMSO, 1944.

Minister of Reconstruction, *Employment Policy After the War*, Cmd 6527, HMSO, 1944.

Minister of Reconstruction, *Housing*, Cmd 6609, HMSO, 1945.

Ministry of Education, *Early Leaving*, HMSO, 1954.

Ministry of Education, *15-18*, HMSO, 1959.

Ministry of Education, *Half Our Future*, HMSO, 1963.

Ministry of Health, *A National Health Service*, Cmd 6502, HMSO, 1944.

Ministry of Health, *Report of the Committee of Enquiry into the Case of the National Health Service*, Cmd 9663, HMSO, 1956.

Ministry of Health, *A Hospital Plan for England and Wales*, Cmnd 1604, HMSO, 1962.

Ministry of Health, *Health and Welfare: the Development of Community Care*, Cmnd 1973, HMSO, 1963.

Ministry of Health, *Health and Welfare: the Development of Community Care*, Cmnd 3022, HMSO, 1966.

Ministry of Health, *Report of Hospital Inpatient Enquiry*, HMSO, 1967.

Ministry of Housing and Local Government, *The Housing Programme 1965-1970*, Cmnd 2838, HMSO, 1965.

Ministry of Labour, *Reports of Investigations into the Industrial Conditions in Certain Depressed Areas*, Cmnd 4728, HMSO, 1934.

Ministry of Social Security, *The Administration of the Wages Stop*, HMSO, 1967.

National Board for Prices and Incomes, *Hours of Work, Overtime and Shift Working*, Cmnd 4554, HMSO, 1970.

National Economic Development Council, *Conditions Favourable to Faster Growth*, HMSO, 1963.

Office of Population Censuses and Surveys, *General Household Survey*, HMSO, 1978.

Office of Population Censuses and Surveys, *General Household Survey, 1977*, HMSO, 1979.

Office of Population Censuses and Surveys, *General Household Survey, 1978*, HMSO, 1980.

Office of Population Censuses and Surveys, *Family Finances*, HMSO, 1981.

Royal Commission on the Constitution, 1969-73, Report, Cmnd 5460, HMSO, 1973.

Royal Commission on the Distribution of Income and Wealth, *Higher Incomes from Employment*, Report, no. 3, Cmnd 6383, HMSO, 1976.

Royal Commission on the Distribution of Income and Wealth, *Lower Incomes*, Report, no. 6, HMSO, 1978.

Royal Commission on the Distribution of Income and Wealth, Report no. 6, quoted in A.B. Atkinson and J.S. Flemming, 'Unemployment, Social Security and Incentives', *Midland Bank Review*, autumn 1978.

Royal Commission on the Distribution of the Industrial Population, Report, Cmd 6153, HMSO, 1940.

Royal Commission on the National Health Service, Report, Cmnd 7615, HMSO, 1979.

Royal Commission on the Poor Laws, Report, 1834.

Royal Commission on Population, Report, Cmd 7695, HMSO, 1949.

Royal Commission on the Taxation of Profits and Income, Second Report, Cmd 9105, HMSO, 1954.

Social Insurance and Allied Services, Cmd 6404, HMSO, 1942 (Beveridge Report).

Social Services Committee 1981-1982, vol. 11, Second Report, *House of Commons Paper*, 306-311, HMSO, 1982.

Supplementary Benefits Commission, *Annual Reports*, 1966-80, HMSO.

Index

Index